# History of Cookstown

by
Henry L. Glasgow (1866-1950)

Forewords by     Beatrice Miller
Ricky Glasgow

Introduction by     Graham Mawhinney

Moyola Books, 2008

ISBN 978-1-873345-29-0

This material first appeared in issues of the Mid-Ulster Mail,
22/3/1924 to 13/3/1926 inclusive.

Moyola Books
c/o Orr's Corner, Labby, Draperstown,
Co. Londonderry, N. Ireland, BT45 7BE

# Forewords

Don't you have to agree that in spite of modern media and modern ways, there is somewhere deep in most of us a strong feeling, a particular bond, for a certain locality? Its place names, its topography, its roads and buildings, its history, but most of all its people.

Henry Glasgow, one-time and long-time Editor of the Mid-Ulster Mail must have felt this sense strongly, as he embarked almost a century ago on the one-man task of producing a History of Cookstown, to be produced in weekly instalments in his newspaper. Problems, indeed. Where to begin? At the beginning, of course. So alone and single-handed, undaunted by distance and the discomfort of travel (and Dublin was a long way off), he carried out the necessary research, and his local history story began in the mists of myth and antiquity.

This publication, a reprint of part of Henry Glasgow's story, includes the mid-eighteenth century laying out and construction of the new town of Cookstown by that remarkable town planner without a university degree to his name, William Stewart. The town's progress is followed as, leaving larger and more prosperous neighbours like Moneymore and Stewartstown behind, Cookstown forged a new prosperity for itself through the exploitation of local water resources and the genius and resourcefulness of the entrepreneurs who saw the potential and seized the moment.

Other people are not forgotten, from the great and good of the town and surrounding area, to the men and women who oiled the machines, quarried the stone or lapped the linen. Named correspondents of the paper enter the story too, as week by week their informative comments on preceding articles are printed in full, serving to illuminate and elucidate, as well as adding the human touch.

But this reprint will not only interest the historian or industrial archaeologist. The diligent student of townland names and townland boundaries will find much to ponder on, and so will the casual turner of pages who finds the date of his church's opening, a familiar surname or a titbit of information about his street. Altogether, to old-time resident or "blow-in", this is a book to be treasured, even as it was a labour of love, and Graham is to be congratulated on opening up for our leisured perusal once more this mine of information. Talk about a sense of place. Henry certainly had it.

Beatrice Miller

When Graham Mawhinney asked me if I would have any objection if he produced a book from my grandfather Henry Glasgow's notes on the history of Cookstown, which appeared in the columns of the Mid-Ulster Mail almost a century ago, I said I would be delighted at the prospect. Henry Glasgow was the first editor, and co-founder with his brother John, of the paper in 1891.

On reading through the manuscript the extent of the hard work and long hours Graham has put into this project is evident and he should be highly commended for his efforts. Anyone interested in the history of Cookstown and its people cannot fail to appreciate this book.

I am sure that my late grandfather would also approve and appreciate the hard work Graham has put into this production and I wish him all the success he deserves with this venture.

Ricky Glasgow

*Henry L. Glasgow with his wife Maud and sons, John (left) and George (right) - 1920s*

# Introduction

In the last week of January 1949 the now-defunct Times Pictorial, a Dublin-based paper, featured the Mid-Ulster Mail on its front page under the headline "Octogenarian brothers run their own paper". The photo captions elaborated that the general manager, John Glasgow, was eighty-six while editor, Henry L. Glasgow, was eighty-two and that the paper, which was established in 1891, *is printed and published at Cookstown, Co. Tyrone.*

The Mid-Ulster Mail had been the brainchild of John and Henry who ran a family seed merchant business at William Street in the town centre. As they were also involved in the printing trade they decided in 1891 to launch a weekly newspaper. In addition to the newspaper they also did all kinds of commercial printing – books, leaflets, etc. They published local postcards – Glasgow's "Mid-Ulster Series" – and also, for a few years published local directories, like "The South Derry and District Almanac". During the early years "the Mid", as it became known, contained from four to eight pages and was distributed throughout East Tyrone and South Derry. The two brothers – as the late Maurice Corrigan, Henry's successor as editor, explained in the paper's 1991 centenary supplement – made the perfect business combination. *Henry (Harry as he was known was of a literary frame of mind and took on the job of Editor, a post he held for almost 60 years until ill health forced him to step down in 1949, then in his mid 80s. He died at Christmas the following year. Harry was a top class journalist and a fine editor, with a great wealth of knowledge which came to the fore in his work. His brother John, on the other hand, was not literary inclined but was an astute businessman and looked after the financial affairs, including advertising – then the perfect combination for the running of a successful newspaper.*
*Even though brothers, both of upright and honourable character, their personalities could hardly have been more different. Harry was a calm, reserved, even-tempered man, but John was considered to be an over-assertive, even rather aggressive type, and quick of temper. But one thing they had in common was the fact that both were strict teetotallers and had a strong abhorrence of alcohol and did not publish drink adverts. Harry, though, was a chain smoker.*

In the issue of the Mid-Ulster Mail dated 8 August 1919 Henry Glasgow wrote – *For a couple of years or more we have been collecting material for a History of Cookstown and the adjacent estates so far as they helped to build up the town ... ... ... ... .. Cookstown is, therefore, just 300 years old and we propose to celebrate the tercentenary by publishing a History of the town and surrounding district so far as it affected the growth of the town. We invite all readers who have any historical matter to lend it to us in order that the History may be worthy of the town.* Three months later, on 15 November 1919, the series began with an article on "The Castlestuart Tercentenary" and the story continued, on an almost weekly basis for many, many years. In many households these columns would have been cut out and kept and in house clearances these newspaper clippings are sometimes found inside books, in the pockets of old calendars or maybe still behind the mantelpiece clock. I still have some of these cuttings which were found among the possessions of local Draperstown antiquarian, Geordie Barnett, after his death in 1965. Barnett's correspondence with Glasgow sometimes appeared in the newspaper.

In 1988 I published a reprint of W. H. Maitland's "History of Magherafelt" which first appeared in 1916, being a compilation of earlier columns from the Mid-Ulster Mail. The original book was printed by Glasgow's "Mid-Ulster Printing Works" in Cookstown. So Henry Glasgow had encouraged Maitland by publishing his historical notes in the newspaper but had gone further and printed the final compilation as a book. There is no doubt that these two men had common interests and I suspect that, once Maitland's Magherafelt columns had finished, Glasgow had become inspired to undertake a similar project for Cookstown.

However, in 1988, I set out to market Maitland's book and I was well received in Sheehy's bookshop in Cookstown by the late Tom Sheehy (Senior). Tom looked at the book, his eyes lit up, and then he said "It's a pity there's not a book like that for Cookstown". I always remembered those words. Not many years later, while browsing in the Linen Hall Library, I discovered a scrapbook of cuttings from Henry Glasgow's columns and, even though it only reflected a few years' worth of his work, I was totally awe-struck with the mammoth task he had set himself. My admiration for the Cookstown newspaper editor continued to grow as I photocopied his newspaper articles from various library sources and started to read them. I resolved to make a typescript of them and, with the help of the typists in Magherafelt's Women's Group and, later, Mrs Ann Caulfield, the notes were honed into shape. For many years, over 700 pages have rested in a drawer at home but, at last, I have decided to take a selection – from the two years when he was dealing chiefly with 19th century Cookstown – and make the information available to a wider audience. There is much of interest in Glasgow's material on the more ancient history and, depending on how this offering is received, it may appear later.

It is stressed that this book is produced primarily to perpetuate the memory of Henry Little Glasgow's sterling work and that the historical content has not been subjected to the scrutiny of modern scholarship. I am also conscious that the final product could have been made more (to use the modern phrase) 'user friendly' by the addition of an index, a townland map and more colour illustrations, but costs would have been prohibitive. The book presents each episode (with the newspaper's date where it originally appeared), blemishes and all, in the hope that some valuable local history will be preserved and that future local historians will be enthused to dig even deeper.

The author's grandson, Ricky Glasgow, has kindly provided a foreword, on behalf of the family, and expressed his enthusiasm for the project. I thank him for his contribution. Beatrice Miller has given many inspirational lectures on the history of Cookstown, including a memorable one delivered to the Ballinascreen Historical Society in Draperstown in April 1994. I am greatly indebted to her for reading the complete script and composing a most appropriate foreword. The postcard illustrations are from the personal collections of Patrick Kelly and David Lennox, while the photographs of the author are courtesy of the Glasgow family. Sincere thanks are due to all of them.

*Henry L. Glasgow addresses an outing of Belfast Naturalists' Field Club – 1920s*

*Eighty-two year old Henry L. Glasgow still at work as newspaper editor – 1948*

# Contents

*Henry L. Glasgow (left) on a cruise to Palestine and the Holy Land – 1936*

# EARLY NINETEENTH CENTURY

# (22-3-1924)

The first quarter of the Nineteenth Century was not eventful to Cookstown. The town grew, but grew slowly. The boom in the linen trade was still in the future, for the power loom and the spinning jenny were in their infancy. About the end of that period, in the year 1824, the

Loy Street, Cookstown.

earliest directory that the writer knows about, giving the names of the general inhabitants of the town was published. Before reprinting these lists it will be convenient to mention some miscellaneous and unconnected events which occurred in that period.

First let us revert to the Killymoon family. Some readers may think that we have given too much prominence to this personal history, just as objections are made to the orthodox type of English history, that it is divided up into the reigns of successive sovereigns. The objection would be good if that were the case in economic history, but the political history of a country centres round the crown and, in exactly the same way, what may be called the political history of a town centres round the landlords of it, and, as it is that branch of the history of Cookstown that we are chiefly concerned with at present, the fortunes of the Stewarts of Killymoon are relevant to our purpose, as will be quickly seen.

Col. James Stewart, M.P., though opposed to the legislative union, was returned as member for Co. Tyrone, in the Parliament of 1802, his colleague being Sir J. Stewart, of Athenry, whose ancestor was also of Gortigal, and who got a baronecy for supporting the Union. The removal of the Parliament from Dublin to London , was a great change to the members, and was not without its effects. The social life of Dublin had been of a hectic character for a long time. Duelling was common, and one reads of the wildest escapades by men in Dublin society during the 18$^{th}$ century. London, too, had its faults, and just then the gravest social failing was the prevalence of gambling. Charles Fox, the opponent of Pitt, and the bugbear of George III, was an inveterate gambler, and so was the Prince of Wales, who was the centre of the gayest circles. Into them James Stewart was drawn. Though a man of 60 years of age when the Union took place, and though he was the patron of the strictest Presbyterians who lauded him to the skies, yet he was unable to stand aloof from the universal passion for the gambling table.

On one occasion it is said that he was playing with the Prince of Wales (afterwards George IV), and had a run of very bad luck. The stakes got higher and higher until Col. Stewart had no money left, but in the madness of the gambling fever he challenged his royal partner for the Killymoon estates. He lost, and left the table penniless and beggared, and Cookstown with the surroundings district became royal property. But next day the Prince met him and handed back the document which conveyed Killymoon to him, with the not too complimentary remark that he did not want his "dirty Irish cabin".

This incident has been coupled with Col. William Stewart in local tradition but we are assured that it was not that gentleman, who is remembered for his extravagant living, but his worthy father who was guilty of this wild gambling which, it will be noted, proved that the history of the town does depend very much on that of the owner. For had the Prince stuck to his winnings on that occasion, and took the Killymoon Castle and the estate, it would have made a material difference to Cookstown.

Col. Stewart was again returned for the Parliaments of 1806 and 1807, his colleague being his old friend, Thomas Knox, but, in 1822, the former disappeared from Parliament, Sir John Stewart, Bart., taking his place. Col Stewart was then 71 years of age, and was too old for attendance at Westminister, which entailed a long and tedious journey from Cookstown. Whether that was the reason for his retirement, or not, we have been unable to find, but that he was still a hale old man is evident from the fact that he lived till 1835, attaining the good old age of 94 years.

The representation of Co. Tyrone, however, did not long bar the Killymoon family, for at the next election, in 1818, Col. William Stewart was returned for the County, and sat till 1830, so that, with the exception of one Parliament, three generations of the Killymoon Stewarts sat for Co. Tyrone for 79 years. As already mentioned, he had been made a recipient of a presentation sword which is an heirloom in the family. The inscriptions reveal a difference:- that to James Stewart reads as follows:- "Cookstown Legion, presented to their Captain, Jams. Stewart, Esq., as a token of esteem", and the date on the blade is 1798. The blade is handsomely engraved with the royal arms, and monogram (G.R.) and trophies, while the handle represents a horse's head, and is of polished steel, the scabbard of dark blue steel, inlaid with trophies and with above inscriptions. The sword presented to Col. William Stewart, has a gilt scabbard inlaid with crimson leather, and an ivory handle, and on the scabbard is the inscription:- "The gift of the Cookstown Cavalry, to their second Captain, Wm. Stewart, Esq., as a token of esteem, August 1, 1804".

A very important event for Killymoon took place early in the century - the burning of the old castle. We have not been able to fix the date; the present castle is said to have been built in 1820, but that is a mistake, for as early as 1803 letters from Mrs. Stewart to her husband, Col. James Stewart, sent when in London, and which he preserved, refer to the building. Writing on 4 May 1803, she says:- "There came a mason from the County of Antrim, a very decent looking man. I told Bevan (the foreman) if he wished he might try him, and he is to begin work this day. This will now make 9 masons, and I hear he expects one clever one very soon from England, that is a stone mason". She adds that she thinks Col. Stewart was lucky to get rid of another foreman named Woodgate, "before worse mischief was done", and makes suggestions for altering the brickwork. In a subsequent letter, on 9th May, she writes:- "There are no

# History of Cookstown

new stones laid yet in the building, except some alterations in the foundation. The masons are getting a large quantity prepared before they begin to lay any". The masons, it is evident, were also stonecutters.

Turning now to Cookstown proper, as we have said it was growing, and new businesses were being started in the town. Two of them, dating from this period, are well known to all our town readers – Weir's and M'Collum's. The latter, which is more flourishing than ever, was founded by Adam M'Collum, a nephew of Adam Lynd, brewer and chandler, who lived in the block of houses between Harbison's and Allen's. The business was carried on there till the late Mr. M'Collum bought what had been the Primitive Methodist Chapel opposite Molesworth Street, which was converted into a fine shop and residence. This business will shortly attain its centenary in the town.

The other business, known recently and for a long time as Silas E. Weir and Co., is older, though it has now passed out of existence, and it attained its centenary over 20 years ago. The founder of it seems to have been Wm. Weir, whose people originally resided at Duncairne, Stewartstown. He came to Cookstown and started a Drapery business in what is known as the White House (next The Mid-Ulster Mail Office) in 1802. He was very successful, but died early, in 1824, at the age of 41 years. His only son was named Silas, and was then a boy of 18, who was destined for the bar, and was about to go to Edinburgh University, when his father met with a fatal accident. He was persuaded to take up the business, and when 21 years old he built the fine premises south of Burn Road where an extensive business was carried on in former years - probably one of the best known in Tyrone when Mr. Silas E. Weir was in charge. He had the advantage of a good connection; his uncle, who naturally looked after the young merchant, was married to Miss Collins, an influential family in Cookstown at the time; one of his sisters was the second wife of the Rev. T. Miller, another of Rev. A. Fleming - the two Presbyterian Ministers, both of whom had considerable families, mostly married locally, and marriage connections of this sort were (and to an extent still are) useful in business. But the great success Mr. Weir attained was chiefly due to his own ability – knowledge of what his customers needed and where to get the goods, coupled, necessarily, with straight-forward dealing. In later years Mr. Wm. Craig became a partner. He lived in what had been the Collins property, (now the Post Office) and the old–established cabinet making business of Mr. Cluff was acquired and removed to the same premises as the drapery. It need only be added that this property is now owned by Mr. W. MacSonald Porter, who devotes himself entirely to the furniture and undertaking business. With this exception no business now existing in the town was in existence at the time under review.

This period saw two of our Churches built. In 1804 a Secession Presbyterian Congregation was formed which called Rev. Mr. Miller, as Minister - a man who left his mark. The Church was built in 1806, as we know from the letter in Col. James Stewart's collection, asking that gentleman to select a pew in it. The writer was Thomas M'Geagh, father of the late Mr. John M'Geagh, and great-grandfather of Mr. J. D. Anderson, the present secretary of the congregation – an office thus held by four generations. In 1820 the present Parish Church was built, the Rev. William Maulever, M. A., being the Incumbent, the site being removed from the churchyard where the old Church still exists in ruins, to the Main Street. In the deed granting the land it is described as half an acre plantation measure, with 117 feet frontage, bounded on the west by the public road, east by James Stewart, Esq., north by John Humphries, and south by Wm. Webster. The petition asking that the site be changed on the ground that the old Church was over half a mile from Cookstown, and was too dilapidated for repair, was signed by the following landed proprietors:- W. Armagh; Castlestewart; James Stewart; Robert Lindsay; John Staples; James Lowry. The church wardens who signed were:- William Stewart and John M'Cormick; and the parishioners:- James Stewart, Robert Lindsay, Sam Wright, Sam Bates and John Young. What would strike one most in connection with the new Church is its size compared with the old one which was in building in 1622, showing that the town had increased, and was expected to grow more.

It has been stated that Colonel Wm. Stewart raised a battalion in Cookstown for the French war, and fought with them at Waterloo. We have been unable to verify this, much less get any particulars of the men, and the weight of evidence, such as it is, is against that.

Next week we will give the first directory of the town – the list of inhabitants in Pigott's Directory of 1824.

# ONE HUNDRED YEARS AGO

## (5-4-1924)

Pigott's Directory of Ireland for 1824 contains the first general list of the inhabitants of Cookstown, as well as a description of the town, and a note about the transit facilities.

The following is the full entry: -

## COOKSTOWN

A market, post and fair town in the County of Tyrone, is 81 miles north by west of Dublin, 4½ north west of Stewartstown, 3 south west of Moneymore, 8 north by west of Dungannon, 21 east north east of Omagh, and 34 west of Belfast. It consists of one street, near a mile length, through the greater part of which it is adorned on each side with a row of lofty trees. Adjoining the town is Killymoone, the beautiful castle and demesne of Lieut. Colonel Stewart, M.P. for the county, and proprietor of the place; on the opposite side, about half a mile distant, is Derry Loran Glebe, the residence of the present rector, the Rev. Wm Mauleverer. The Church is a neat stone Gothic edifice, with an elegant and lofty spire, finished in 1821. Near the glebe, part of the walls of the old church are still remaining. In the year 1761 a Presbyterian meeting house was erected here, and near to it, in 1802, one for Seceders. The Catholics and Methodists have also each a place of worship. The charitable institutions are a dispensary, under the superintendence of Surgeon Thos. Dickson, and two Sunday schools. A market is held on Saturday for linen cloth and provisions: the 7-8ths and 3-4ths linens are remarkable for their superior quality. A corn market is also held on Tuesday. There are fairs on the 8th and 16th of February, the 28th of March, the 8th of May, the 15th of June, the 7th of August, the 4th of September, the 10th of October, and the 6th of November. The population is near 1,500.

# GENTRY AND CLERGY

Caulfield, James, Esq.,Muff
Davison, Rev. John, Loy-hill.
Hamilton, Rev. Hugh, Loy-house.
Irvine, Mayor William.
Irvine, Rev. William John.
Lindsay, Robert, Esq., Loughry.
Lowry, James, Esq., Rockdale.
Lowry, Robert, Esq., Pomeroy.
McCook, Lieutenant Danl., Loy-hill.
Magill, Wm.,Esq. magistrate, Crieve.
Mauleverer, Rev. Jas., Derry Loran.
Mauleverer, Rev. Wm., rector, Derry Loran.
Millar, Rev. Thomas, Loy.
Molesworth, Rev. John, rector of Lissan, Muff.
Richardson, Wm. Stewart, Esq., Drum.
Spear, John, Esq., Desertcrete.
Staples, Thomas, Esq., Lissan.
Stewart, Lieut-Col. Wm., M.P. for the county, Killymoone-Castle.
Stiegletz, Henry, Gort Lowry.
Wilson, Miss, Loy-hill.
Wright, Samuel, Esq., magistrate, Loy-hill.

# MERCHANTS, TRADESMEN, ETC
## PHYSICIAN

Magill, William, M.D.

## SURGEONS

Dickson, Thomas, R.N. (to the Dispensary) Loy.
Hamilton, James.
Hutton, William.
Hutchinson, Hicks.
Young, John, R.N.

## ATTORNEYS

Adams, Hugh Y., and 28, George's Street South, Dublin.
Collins, Joshua.
Young, Alexander, and 28, George's Street South, Dublin.

## LINEN OFFICERS

Patteson, Benjamin, linen inspector
Patteson, Matthews, linen seal master.

## AGENT

McCormick, John.

## INNKEEPERS

Henry, Mary, King's Arms.
McAllister, John, Stewart's Arms,
    Gort Lowry.
Rodgers, Alexander, Grapes.

## SHOPKEEPERS, TRADERS, ETC.

Bell, John, grocer.
Black, John, grocer.
Brown, James, grocer, Gort Lowry.
Brown, James, corn miller, Killymoon mill.
Brown, Samuel, watch and clock maker.
Carrigan, Patrick, grocer.
Cluff, James, cabinet maker and upholsterer.
Collins, John, woollen draper and haberdasher.
Conlon, John, grocer.
Connor, Patrick, tallow chandler and soap boiler.
Crawford Arthur, woollen draper.
Duff, James, grocer.
Duncan, Isabella, milliner.
Duncan, Francis, tailor.
Ferguson, Charles, boot and shoe maker, Gort Lowry.
Ferguson, Peter, whitesmith, Loy.
Gibson, John, carpenter, Gort Lowry
Gilliam, William, grocer.
Gilmore, Robert, watch and clock maker.
Glasgow, Robert, baker.
Gourley, John, hardware dealer.
Haliday, William, cabinet maker and upholsterer.
Johnston, Benjamin, grocer and leather cutter.

Leslie, Wm, tailor.
Lynd, John, grocer and tallow chandler.
McCormick, John, grocer.
McCormick, John, toll collector.
McCully, Charles, saddler and harness maker.
McCully James, leather cutter.
McGeagh, John, grocer.
McGeagh, Robert, grocer.
McGeagh, Robert, woollen draper.
McKenzie, Henry, grocer.
McLernon, Michael, grocer, Loy.
Miller, James, baker.
Moore, James, grocer.
Morgan, Thomas, linen merchant.
Orr, Robert G., woollen draper.
Patteson, Edward, painter and glazier, Loy.
Patteson, Richard, painter and glazier, Loy.
Patteson, Wm., grocer and hardware dealer.
Potter, Peter, saddler and harness maker.
Richardson, Leander, letter-press printer and bookbinder.
Rodgers, Alexander, linen draper.
Rodgers, George, grocer.
Seller, Wm., carpenter, Loy.
Smyth, James, grocer.
Sterling, Mary Ann, haberdasher.
Taylor, Ann, earthenware dealer.
Thompson, Thos., linen buyer.
Weir, Silas E., woollen draper.

## PUBLICANS

Allen, Elizabeth, Gort Lowry.
Aston, William.
Ballintin, James, Loy.
Baxter, Samuel.
Black, John.
Charles, James.
Crookes, James.
Espy, Hugh.
Fox, Michael, Gort Lowry.
Glasgow, John.
Hagan, Hugh.
Hagan, Robert.
McCaldin, Isabella.

McGurk, James.
McGurk, Michael.
Mayne, Isaac, Gort Lowry.
Murphy, Edward.
Stewart, Patrick.
Trimble, Matthew.
Wilson, Thomas.

**POST OFFICE** – Post Master, Mr. Matthew Patteson. The Dublin Mail leaves at half-past twelve, and arrives at one in the day. The North Mail arrives at a quarter-past twelve at noon, and leaves at a quarter-past one. Letters for England go by the Dublin Mail, and those for Scotland through Belfast, to Donaghadee.

No Coaches pass through Cookstown. The Belfast Union Day Coach runs from Magherafelt distant seven miles, every Monday, Wednesday and Friday morning, at seven, (and returns on the following evening at eight). The Dublin Mail, also, from Dungannon, distant about eight miles, every day at four in the afternoon, and returns every morning at ten.

Goods are conveyed to any part of Ireland, by cars hired for the purpose.

Next week we will give some notes on above.


# NOTES ON RESIDENTS IN 1824

## (12 - 4 - 1924)

As promised last week we propose to give some notes on the persons whose names appear in the Directory of 1824 – the residents in Cookstown a hundred years ago. These notes will necessarily be incomplete, and if any reader can supplement them, or identify any of those who are not mentioned, the writer will be glad to have the information.

In the introduction reference is made to places of worship. As stated last week, the present parish church was then built and also the Secession Presbyterian Church. Of course, the old Presbyterian Church (now First Cookstown) dated back for a considerable period, being built on the present site about 1761. This was shortly after the street widening took place, and the manse is built to the new line of houses. We omitted reference to the Methodist Church, which, it appears, was in existence in

1824. The present church was built in 1858, but as early as 1805 there is a record of a Mission to build a new place of worship in Cookstown, the inference being that already there was one here. As John Wesley does not mention it in his Diary of his visit in 1783, it would be later than that time, and probably was only a room in an existing building.

The existence of a Catholic "place of worship" should also be noted. The Old Chapel, at Chapel Hill, was built in 1828, so that there must have been another at the earlier date. There is a tradition that Mr. Cooke, who then owned the Greenvale Bleach Works, gave the Catholics accommodation in a loft of his. That, however, will be dealt with later when we give the ecclesiastical history of the town.

The dispensary referred to under Surgeon Dickson was the predecessor of that founded under the Medical Charities Act. It had no connection with the Poor-Law, which dates from 1838.

The reputation of the linen market is recorded: these were the hand loom webs which were sold on the Oldtown, till superseded by the power loom factory products. Regulations as to width, etc., were enforced, and as will be seen that Matthew Patterson, the Post Master was the seal-master for the linen trade, which was strictly regulated.

The dates of the fairs are worthy of notice. This was the transition period between the original two-day fair every year and the present monthly fair. It will be seen there were then nine fairs, and that they were at very irregular intervals. Reference to a calendar will show this. Take, for example, the present year, and March 29 is Friday; 8th May will be Thursday; 15th June Sunday; 7th August Thursday; 4th September Thursday; 10th October Friday; 8th February will be Saturday and 16th February Sunday. We confess that we have been unable to find any system to explain these days, or the intervals, except that in December and January the winter weather may explain the gap. But why two in February with only eight days apart?

The population of the town is given as near 1,500, which may be taken as the outside figure. In 1881 it was 3,870, so that in about 57 years it had more than doubled.

Besides the neighbouring landowners, there were resident in the town a considerable number of persons who are classed in this old directory as "gentry". The first of these is James Caulfield, described as "of Muff." This is probably a mistake, unless he occupied the Rectory there as a tenant. At any rate, he resided at one time in Gortalowry House, the residence of the Misses MacKenzie and Miss Rowan. He was the son of James, 3rd Viscount Charlemont, whose son was the famous Earl Charlemont, the Commander-in-Chief of the Volunteers. Mr Caulfield probably came to reside in Cookstown in consequence of the intimate relations of his family with Colonel James Stewart, M.P., and it was in Gortalowry House that his son was born, who, on the Earl's male issue failing, became Viscount Charlemont, and inherited Drumcairne, and was, for a considerable time, comptroller of the Lord Lieutenant's Household.

Another of the "gentry" of 1824 was not only heir presumptive of a title, but actually belonged to the nobility, though he did not then use the title. This was Henry Stieglitz, who resided in what is now known as South End Cottage, the residence of Mr. Thomas Gibson, chairman of the Urban Council. He was a German baron who seems to have settled here after Waterloo, also, no doubt, through having made the acquaintance of Colonel Stewart. How long he had been living in Cookstown we do not know, but the fact that he was buried in Derryloran Old Church suggests that he had no landed interests elsewhere in the country. The Old Church was closed in 1821, and he died in 1824 and was buried at the extreme end of the chancel where the inscription, surmounted by his arms and the motto, "Spies mea in Dea", is prominent. From it we learn that three of his sons, who did not reside in Cookstown, were brought to Derryloran for interment - the eldest son Frederick Lewis, Baron Von Stieglitz, J.P. for Armagh and Down, who died at The Glen, Newry, in 1866; John, the 3$^{rd}$ son, who died in 1868, and Robert William, J.P. for Down and Kildare, the 5$^{th}$ son, who died at his residence Drumindony, Kilkeel, in 1876. The eldest son emigrated to Tasmania, where he made a considerable fortune, and, returning to Ireland, he claimed the title and married Miss Blacker of Portadown, where the Baroness Von Stieglitz is still favourably remembered.

Before proceeding further it would be well for readers to attempt to visualize Gortalowry as it then was, the place where two gentlemen, fathers of well known noblemen, had selected for their residence. We do not wish to detract from Cookstown as a residential town, for in several vital aspects it has no equal, in Co. Tyrone at any rate, but it is undeniable that the sites in question lost their attractiveness soon after this period. We do not know when Loy House was vacated by Mr. Caulfield, as the rentals seem to have been lost, but, when the estate was sold in 1852 to Mr. Thomas Adair, we do know that that gentleman spent a considerable sum on repairs to that House which seems to have been vacant. The reason for the change is obvious once the fact is grasped that it was not till 1833 that the mill was built at Greenvale, to be followed by the two factories. It was to these industries that Gortalowry owed its rapid increase of population; workers were attracted from the surrounding country, which was over-populated in the forties, and the whole character of that end of the town was changed. The houses, as is still evident from the best of them that remain, were of a very poor description, in keeping with the houses which sprang up at that time all over the country; the town houses were, indeed, superior, for none of them have the mud walls then so common. Gortalowry, in short, suffered the same transition which has taken place, and is still taking place, in every industrial centre where factory hands crowd together as near their work as possible. In Gortalowry there were no slums because the houses were built on the side of a very wide street with the open country behind, but the amenities of the place were changed completely from what existed in 1824.

# CORRECTIONS

We find that a fortnight ago we made a slip in reference to the marriage connections of Mr. Silas E. Weir. His sister was married to Rev. A. Fleming, but it was his aunt (sister of William Weir), who was the first wife of Rev. Thomas Miller.

A correspondent also points out that in connection with the ages of Colonel James Stewart, that the figures given are contradictory. That is so; it is another slip, and we are grateful for having it pointed out at once. According to Burke, Col. James Stewart was born in 1741. He was thus 60 at the Union, and he died in 1821. Amongst the family papers is a letter of condolence to his son, Col. Wm. Stewart, from King George IV.

Next Week – More note on the Old Inhabitants.

# INHABITANTS IN 1824

## (19 - 4 - 1924)

In the Directory of 1824, another of the gentry, then residing in Cookstown, was Major William Irvine. He lived on the top of Oldtown Hill, in the house now owned and occupied by Mr. S. A. Lewis, which had not any distinctive name to identify it, though it was one of the oldest, and most imposing, residences in the town. The deeds of the house go back as far as 1776, when William Stewart (who was responsible for the street widening) and his son Colonel James Stewart, M.P., gave a lease of the tenement, described as "on the top of the Hill" to David Richardson, of Oaklands, now Drum Manor. Even before that date the tenement was in the possession of Stephen Oliver and his sons, Andrew and James, and it will be remembered that, in our issue of 17th November last, we mentioned the lease of the brewery premises (between

Mr. Allen's & Mr. Harbinson's, in William Street) which were then leased to Adam Lynd, and had been in the possession of Stephen Oliver. Mr. Lewis's conveyance recites that in the same lease of 1776 was included two tenements at the bottom of the Hill on the east side of the street, 170 feet in front and extending back 21 perches, "except a convenient road along Loy Marsh to the back gardens", together with "land in New Buildings, bog, and a garden lying on the east side of the present gardens from the quarry to Loy Marsh". Undoubtedly this was the same property; Stephen Oliver was the brewer at the time before Lynd, and he lived in the house at the "top of the Hill". Moreover we get a glimpse of the state of the area now forming the market yard and north of it – it was marsh, with a path up to the gardens in the vicinity of the limestone quarry, before Molesworth Street or Union Street came into existence. The house in Oldtown had attached to it vacant ground where Mr. Mills' three houses stand. The property was leased by the Rodgers family, one of whom was married to George Shaw, a linen merchant, connected with the Greenvale factory; then it passed to Miss Gourley and the Blacks, and became mortgaged; William James Devlin got the equity from the Ulster Bank and built the three houses mentioned, and Messrs. George and Francis P. Gunning, got the principal house from the Belfast Bank, and made extensive improvements; in 1891 it was bought by the late Mr. W. H. Lewis, and finally by his brother, Mr. S. A. Lewis, the present owner.

Major Irvine occupied the house, as stated, in 1824, probably holding direct from Major W. S. Richardson, of Drum, in whom the interest of David Richardson vested. Major Irvine had been Captain of the 5<sup>th</sup> Dragoons, and is mentioned in Musgrave's *Rebellion in Ireland*, in connection with the defence of Ross, where a rather famous battle was fought on 5<sup>th</sup> June, 1798. The garrison consisted of 1,200 men of the Donegal, Clare and Meath Militia the 5<sup>th</sup> Dragoons, and Mid-Lothian Fusiliers, supported by the Dublin Regiment and some Artillery, and with 150 Yeomanry. The rebel general, Bagneal Harvey, advanced with 30,000 men, about a fourth of whom had muskets, and the rest pikes, and supported by four cannon. General Johnston refused to surrender, and the rebels (who were accompanied by a great number of priests carrying crucifixes, who had said Mass for the troops), advanced on the citadel. Captain Irvine was ordered to charge with detachment of the Dragoons and, when the rebels saw the cavalry approaching, they fled and took refuge behind ditches from which they fired at the troops, who had approached close and attempted to leap over. Three times did this take place, the Dragoons losing 24 men and horses, one officer & two N.C.O.s; Captain Irvine's horse was shot under him, falling on his leg, pinning him to the ground. The troops had retired and the rebels were approaching to kill him when "an artillery horse happened to pass by, and so near him that he laid hold of one of the traces and was dragged into the town, by which his life was saved". The rebels, it may be added, succeeded in forcing an entry into the town, but were finally repulsed, leaving 2,600 men dead. The loss of the Royal troops were Colonel Mountjoy, and another officer, 4 sergeants, 3 drummers, and 81 of the rank and file, with 54 horses killed. Captain Irvine became Major of the Tyrone Fusiliers, who took part in the battle of Arklow.

Rev. W. J. Irvine, also mentioned in the Directory, was a son of this gallant officer. According to Leslie's "Armagh Clergy", he was Curate of Ardtrea, and, in 1824, was appointed curate-in-charge of Lissan parish, the rector being the Rev. J. W. Staples, who built the present rectory in 1806, but was a pluralist, and resided then in Moville. It was noted last week that James Caulfield was given as living at Muff and we thought this an error, unless he resided in the rectory. Apparently he did, for the rector, it is stated, asked permission to set the rectory on the ground that his curate could look after the parish as well when living in Cookstown, but that arrangement was short-lived. Rev. Mr. Irvine subsequently went to live in Muff with his family. He also acted as curate-in-charge of Kildress for a time, the then rector being Rev. Richard Stewart, brother of the last Colonel Stewart. At a later period, Rev. Mr. Irvine was appointed rector of the parish of Killymoon, according to Leslie.

Major Irvine's eldest son was Lieut-Col. Charles Irvine, who served with the 96th regiment, and afterwards with the 38th Staffords, which he commanded. He retired in 1851, and later he came to Cookstown, buying Gortalowry House, where he resided with his wife and family, his eldest son (born in Nova Scotia, when the regiment was stationed there), being the popular sub-sheriff of Tyrone, Lieut-Col. Henry Irvine, C.B., D.L. The latter sold Gortalowry House in 1881, to Mr. John Thompson who had a succession of tenants in it, the chief being the late Mr. W.J. Venables, solicitor, and whose family recently sold the property to the present occupier, Mr Thomas M'Keown.

Several other names appear in the list of gentry then living in the town, whom we have been unable to place:- Lieut. Daniel M'Cook, Loy Hill; Samuel Wright, Esq., Magistrate, Loy Hill; and Miss Wilson, Loy Hill. Perhaps some reader can give us a clue to their identity. The reputation of Loy shows that, at this time, Loy and Gortalowry were really suburbs of Cookstown proper, or the residential part of the town.

(Next week – Notes on the surrounding gentry in 1824)

# NEIGHBOURING GENTRY IN 1824

## (26 - 4 - 1924)

Piggott's Directory of 1824 gives the names of gentry living, not in the town, but in the surrounding country. It might be objected that they do not properly come into a history of Cookstown, but the fact that the directory, a century ago, included them is sufficient reason for mentioning them here. Besides that, there is no doubt that the gentry in any neighbourhood do exert a very important influence on a market town in their midst, adding to its amenities, increasing its business and taking part in the local government, as well as taking the lead in social and charitable movements. As a matter of fact, the whole case against absentee landlordism, of which so much used to be heard, would fall to the ground if it were of no importance whether the gentry – to give the land-owning population a name falling into disuse – lived in the neighbourhood or not. Cookstown has been fortunate in having had such a resident gentry in the neighbourhood who were willing to give a lead in any public matter; at the same time, Cookstown has never been in the position of depending entirely on any great family, or being, in any sense, a pocket town, without initiation amongst the ordinary citizens. No doubt, during the "reign" of the Stewarts of Killymoon, up to the middle of the 19th century, that family took a foremost place, but merely as landlords; they encouraged improvements by giving perpetuity leases at low rents, and for religious or public purposes (as in the case of the Stores in the Market Yard) at nominal rents, but did not actually finance such improvements as was done, for example, in Moneymore and Magherafelt, where the Drapers and Salters Companies respectively were the owners of everything and the people depended absolutely on them. In Cookstown it was quite different; there was not so much spoon-feeding, and as a result there was more individual effort in all directions. In our view, Cookstown has been more fortunate than most towns, therefore, in the number and character of the neighbouring land-owning gentry.

William Stewart Richardson, Esq., Drum, was the representative, in 1824, of a family which has been closely associated with Cookstown from the first day Dr. Allan Cook got a lease of lands here, to the present day. The family cannot claim to be original undertakers, which in Ulster is much the same as "coming over with William the Conqueror" is to English families, or "in the Mayflower" is to some of the proudest of the New Englanders. But the Richardsons were very near that, for as early as 1619, when Sir Nicholas Pynnar visited the Plantation and reported on what progress had been made, he found that at Creighballe, as the estate was named. Alexander Richardson had succeeded Bernard Lindesay, the first patentee. The latter was brother of Robert Lindesay, of Tullyhog, both being court officials in Scotland, and the King had asked (so it is said) that Bernard return to Edinburgh, which possibly he was glad to do, for these early settlers found that the conditions in Ulster were rough compared with the civilisation of the Scottish capital and they were required to live on the estates. At that time, just over 300 years ago, Alex. Richardson had a timber house for his family, with a bawn of clay and stone, rough cast with lime, 90 feet square with four flankers – strong positions from which an attack could be repelled. The total strength of the little band of settlers was 39 men with arms. Altogether there were then 17 tenants, 11 of whom were cottagers, with a house and garden and common grazing for cattle. The others were lessees, or freeholders, one having a townland, two others having a couple of townlands jointly and three having two townlands each. From this small beginning arose the Drum estate, extending from the church lands of Kirktown, beside Cookstown, to the heights of Craigballyhacky, which alone preserves the original name, a hill 771 feet over sea level. The hard work of some dozen generations has converted what must have been a wild district into a place of neat houses and well-enclosed fields; the broad road, flanked with trees, leads to the entrance gate, and the enclosure of the demesne, in which a splendid Manor House was built, completed the transformation. If one could remove these human improvements of the plantation period it might be possible to realise what the district was like before that event.

The owner, in 1824, was the son of Capt. William Richardson, who married Isabella Brady, daughter and co-heiress of Patrick Brady, of Cloneroy Castle, Co. Cavan, and, in 1841, Major Richardson, as he then was, of the Life Guards, assumed the name and aims of his mother's family. Two years after the date of our directory he married Caroline La Viscount, daughter of the Hon. John La Viscount, of Antiqua. He died in 1864, leaving one daughter, who first married Major Hugh Massy, of the 85th regiment, when she assumed her father's name of Richardson. She married secondly the 5th Earl of Castlestewart, who was then Viscount Stuart, who assumed the name and arms of Richardson. However, as he left no sons, the name Richardson has died out, but his elder daughter, Lady Muriel Close, the present owner, who has come to reside at Drum, worthily carries out the traditional friendship of the family with Cookstown, and we feel complimented that her good husband, Major Maxwell Close, D.L., has selected Drum as his residence, in place of his family seat at Drumbanagher, where his eldest son lives.

# THE MOLESWORTHS

The following note regarding the Molesworth family, after whom Molesworth Street and Road are named, will be of interest.

Viscount Molesworth, M.P., of Breckonstown, Co. Dublin, to whom Dean Swift addressed one of his Drapier Letters, claiming him as a fellow-patriot, had been general under the Duke of Wellington, and saved the latter's life at the battle of Ramilles by lending him his own horse. Lord Molesworth was afterwards Commander-in-Chief in Ireland. He married, in 1743, a famous beauty, Mary Jenny Ussher, daughter of the Ven. Archdeacon Ussher, of Clonfect, and died in 1758 leaving a widow and young family. Five years afterwards, Lady Molesworth was burned to death in her house in Brook Street, London, in 1763. Horace Walpole, in his Letters, describes the scene, how Lady Molesworth, managed to get her three youngest daughters out of the burning house safely and fell back into the flames, in view of the horrified crowd, when attempting to save the two elder girls who also perished. One of the children who escaped with their lives fell on the paling, and, according to Walpole, her leg was so badly injured that it had to be amputated. She was adopted by the Earl and Countess of Blessington, and afterwards married the Rt. Hon. John Staples, P.C., and was the mother of Sir Thomas Staples, Bart., K.G., and of Rev. John Molesworth Staples, rector of Lissan and Moville and two other sons, as well as five daughters, one of whom became Mrs. Lenox-Conyngham, of Springhill, mother of the late Sir W.F. Lenox-Conyngham, K.C.B. Another daughter was married to the 1st Marquis of Ormonde, and three others to clergymen - Rt. Rev. R. Ponsonby, Bishop of Derry; Rev. H. Hamilton, rector of Innismacsaint, and Rev. R. Alexander, son of the Bishop of Meath. Of the other two daughters of Lady Molesworth who escaped, the elder, Hon. Elizabeth Molesworth married Col. James Stewart, M.P., of Killymoon, and the other, the Hon. Louisa Molesworth married, first, Lord Ponsonby and, secondly, the Earl Fitzwilliam.

Next Week – The Lindesays of Tullyhog.

# THE LINDESAYS OF TULLYHOG

## (10 - 5 - 1924)

"Robert Lindesay, Esq., Loughry", whose name appears in the Directory of 1824 amongst the gentry of Cookstown, was the father of Counsellor Lindesay, as he was familiarly called, who is still remembered by people who can hardly be called old. He lived till 1870, when he was succeeded by his son and namesake, Major Frederick Lindesay, and seven years later, by another son, Captain Joshua G. C. C. Lindesay, the last of the family to live in Loughry. During the latter's ownership the estate was sold under the Land Purchase Act, to the tenants, and on his death in 1893, the Manor House and demesne were sold by his cousin to the late Mr. J. W. Fleming, and subsequently purchased by the Department of Agriculture as a Dairy School. Extensive additions were made to the house to fit it as a residential school, where the daughters of farmers and others are taught not only dairying, but poultry farming and house-keeping in a practical way, under Miss Lang, and her staff of teachers employed by the Ministry of Agriculture. Thus, after three centuries, the people resume the occupation of the lands granted by James I in his scheme for the settlement of Ulster.

The family history is of interest from this point of view - the Lindesays, being the last descendants of the undertakers settled in the barony of Mountjoy who held the original estates, for the Earl of Castlestewart's estate is only a small portion of the land granted by King James to Lord Ochiltree, the chief undertaker in the barony, and the present estate is attached to the title only because it was purchased, not by descent, from the first patentee. Another thing which makes the Lindesay estate of interest is that, in 1824, and for a long time previously, it was the nearest of the undertakers' estates to Cookstown. Tullyhog is just over three miles from Dr. Cook's old town, the intervening land having been granted to native gentlemen, whose interests were bought up by the Stewarts of Killymoon. The Gortaville estate, which came up to Derryloran Glebe, was nearer, but it was broken up at a very early date, while the Orritor estate, which adjoins the Workhouse lands, and therefore was nearer still, was granted to a native gentlemen, not to a Scotch undertaker. In another way the Lindesay estate stands out prominent, for no other in Mountjoy barony, at least, was so well developed as a complete entity on the old feudal lines. It was a "small proportion", nominally 1,000 acres plantation measure, which equals 1,620 statute, and as the full measurement by the Ordnance Survey is only just over 2,000 acres, there were only about 400 acres for waste, water, woods and bog. Contrast this with, for example, the Orritor Estate where Brian Crossagh O'Neill got, in the townland of Killycurragh, an area of 773 acres counted as sixty.

The original undertaker was Robert Lindesay, Chief Harbinger to James VI of Scotland, and brother of Bernard Lindesay, who got the Drum estate with which he very soon parted. Robert died a few years after the Plantation and his tomb was afterwards discovered in the peculiar little circular graveyard of Donaghrisk. In 1619 Sir Nicholas Pynnar reports that he found Mrs. Lindesay, "late wife to Robert Lindesay", with her family, residing in a timber house inside a "good strong bawne of earth, with a quick-set hedge upon it and a ditch about it", at Tullyhog. The settlers of British birth or descent on the estate consisted of "twenty-two tenants, able to make 30 men with arms." Two of the tenants, however, had freeholds consisting of a couple of townlands each, seven others held the same extent of land on lease, and one had one townland; the remaining twelve were cottagers who held two townlands amongst them. This comprised the little band whose duty it was to civilise, according to English ideas, the district round the ancient capital of the O'Neills - to build stone houses, enclose fields, grow wheat, ploughing the land in the English manner instead of by tying the ploughs to horses' tails as the Irish did, and so on.

Tullyhog Fort was not on the estate; it formed part of the glebe lands, at all events in later years. The great Abbey of St. Peter and St. Paul at Armagh owned considerable land in the vicinity, though whether the fort was in it, or not, we cannot at the moment say. At any rate, when the Abbey was dissolved, prior to the Plantation and quite independent of it, the "Grange of Tullyhog" was forfeited to the Crown and subsequently was given to Sir Toby Caulfield in payment of his services, and as early as May 1612, less than a year after Robert Lindesay and his settlers appeared, Sir Toby got a grant for a market every Saturday, and three-day fairs twice a year, on the feast of All Saints and the next two days, and on the feast of St. Mark and the next two days. Sir Toby, therefore, had his eyes open to the possibilities of the new settlement; for some reason the patents were renewed in 1618, and in 1620, the latter being the year when Dr. Cook, Sir Thomas Staples and James Stewart, of Ballymenagh, appeared on the scene. There is no record how long these fairs continued; they were not simply marts for cattle, as at present, but places of amusement, as old people remember at Orritor, and there is a record that, about the beginning of the last century, young people used to resort to the Fort yearly for amusement. This has been supposed to be a relic of the games from which Tullyhog is believed to have got its name, the hill of the youths, but it is far more likely that these meetings for amusement were nothing more than a survival of the fair.

To return to the Lindesays, the eldest son was Robert, named after his father. He was 15 years old at his father's death. In 1630 he was granted denzation in Ireland and took out a fresh patent of the lands, then described as Manor Lindesay, paying a fine of £30. In 1639, he took out another patent. That was the time of Wentworth, the very active Viceroy of Charles I, who brought much gain to his master by detecting flaws in the titles of undertakers, or in the way they carried out their duties. The Irish Society's charter was forfeited in the same year, and a new patent given on a fine of £12,000 and it is probable that Robert Lindesay's patent was taken out under similar conditions. At all events there was a fine, and the Crown rent was raised to £14 1s 8d, against £5 6s 8d, the rent payable by his father under the Plantation Grant. At that date he had gone across the river to a new house he had built, with a large demesne, at Loughry, the date of which is 1632, and apart from the cost of other improvements by the tenants, the house would make him anxious to secure his title, if necessary, by paying a heavy fine. It was burned down, however, by the rebels in 1641. Those who noted our articles on that period well remember that the owner took part in the great trek of Protestants to Newtownstewart on the outbreak of the Rebellion, and that when he returned and found his place burned, and the women and children of the tenants all dispersed, he went to the army in Antrim and was responsible for the massacre of Templepatrick in revenge. He then crossed to England and joined the Royalist army, fighting at the battle of Worcester.

In view of the interesting story which Mr. James Mayne, in our correspondence column, recently told, a little digression here will be pardoned. It will be remembered that Mr. Mayne told how he heard, at Newcastle-on-Tyne, that when Charles I was delivered up by the Scottish army in which Earl Lindesay was a general, to the English, in consideration of a large sum of money, the men got only 4d each - or a groat, and they were so disgusted that they handed their payment to one of the an Lindesay, who came to Ireland and settled at Loughry. Now the surrender of the King to the English was in January 1647; the Earl Lindesay was a general of the Scottish army, which was lying at Newcastle, and had been co-operating with the Parliament of England, on condition that the latter paid the wages of the soldiers. Earl Lindesay, though fighting against the Royalists, objected to surrendering the King's person to the English, for which he was afterwards punished. Whether he was any relation to the Lindesay family of Tullyhog we do not know, but it cannot have been near, if any.

King Charles was brought to London and tried by the Parliament, in its capacity of a High Court, Cromwell first taking the precaution of excluding the Presbyterian members, as the Royalists and Catholics had been excluded. The King was convicted and executed and then followed Cromwell's campaign in Ireland, where he was opposed alike by the Royalist army and the forces of the Ulster Protestants, and it may be remarked, was helped in difficulties by Owen Roe O'Neill and his army. Cromwell returned to England to face the new situation created by Charles II, who was crowned at Scone, and, with a Scottish army, marched South. At Worcester, Cromwell and his army engaged the Royalists and inflicted a crushing defeat; the young King became a fugitive, and ultimately escaped to France. That was in 1651, and it was at this battle that Robert Lindesay, who built the first house at Loughry in 1632, and got a new patent of the estate in 1639, was an officer in the King's army.

Is there, therefore, any kernel of truth in the story which Mr. Mayne discovered at Newcastle? Earl Lindesay is out of it, and the inference which he naturally drew because he did not critically analyse it, that the coming of the Lindesays to Loughry followed the payment of £400,000 pay to the Scottish army in 1647, is obviously wrong. Robert Lindesay was a royalist who risked his life, as well as his property, for the King, and if Loughry means, the King's price, as suggested, the reason must be different from the Newcastle story. Robert Lindesay, it may be added, did not rebuild the Manor House till 1671, eleven years after the Restoration, and 30 years after it was burned by the rebels in 1641. The owner enjoyed his new home for three years only, dying in 1674.

The enclosure of the demesne at Loughry about 1632 has some topographical interest also. Before that time the road from Cookstown to Tullyhog crossed the river by the bridge at Greenvale, where anciently there had been a ford. The road then went round Derryloran Glebe to Strifehill, where there is still a public road. It comes out on the Dungannon road at Rockhead, but formerly ran on in a straight line through the demesne, the route being now marked by a hedge, along the side of the field. It seems to have emerged on the Stewartstown road at the Gatehouse - that is to say, this portion of the avenue was once the main road from Tullyhog. Moreover, we are assured that instead of the present, well-graded road from Tullywiggan bridge (The Prince of Wales Bridge it is named officially), the road ran up the hill into the glebe land straight for Tullyhog fort. Whether the diversion of the old road dates from the enclosure of the demesne we do not know, but the evidence is in favour of that theory.

Robert Lindesay was succeeded by one of his sons of the same name. Like his father, he experienced the horrors of war, having to take refuge in Derry, with his brother Alexander, of Cahoo, when James II, with his army of French and Irish, made it impossible for loyalists to live at home. Alexander lost his life in the siege, but Robert survived it for a short time, dying in 1691.

In the more settled conditions which obtained under William III, the next owner of Loughry, also a Robert Lindesay, became a member of Parliament, being returned for Co. Tyrone in the Parliament of 1727 in the room of the Hon. Richard Stewart on that gentleman's death. This was a stepping-stone to the bench, for, in 1733, he was appointed Judge of the Common Pleas. It was in his time that Dean Swift visited Loughry, and we have it on the authority of Sir Walter Scott, that Judge Lindesay was the "eminent lawyer" of Swift's works. Judge Lindesay was married to a sister of Chief Justice Singleton, and had one son, who, however, pre-deceased him, and he was succeeded by his brother John, who died in 1761.

We have now completed the family for John Lindesay's son, the next owner, was the Robert Lindesay who was living at Loughry in 1824. He, like his uncle, entered Parliament, sitting as member for Dundalk as far back as 1781. He was also deputy governor of Tyrone. He was father to Counsellor Lindesay, who, however, did not come into the estate till 1848, a nephew, son of his elder brother, engaging it for 16 years and dying without issue.

These were the times of Col. Wm. Stewart, when (as the late Mr. Alex. Molloy of the Gunning Arms Hotel used to relate) a dozen or more coaches, with four in hand, could be seen at Killymoon on occasion. It is to be feared that the last owner of Killymoon set a pace which neither he, nor some of the others, could keep up, and not merely their families, but the community generally, is the poorer thereby. One dose not need to probe into private matters to find evidence of extravagance in the Lindesay family. One instance, of a very public nature, will suffice. In 1859 the Counsellor was appointed High Sheriff of Tyrone. He got a great coach built, not unlike the royal coach used by His Majesty in State occasions in London, and this was dragged over the hills to Omagh to convey the judges to and from their lodgings. Even bailiffs, who now stand with silk hats ornamented with a blank cockade, and holding their white wands, were converted into a menacing force, armed with real battle axes! It was all pure obstenation – we had almost written vulgar obstination, for it was exactly the same thing which makes a servant girl spend three months wages on a dress for a ball "to take the shine" out of the girl next door. Counsellor Lindesay was determined to take the shine out of the preceding sheriffs and did so, at the expense of his family. In another way the family pride showed itself, for, long after Loughry was sold, the pew in Derryloran Church bore a brass label intimating to worshippers whose it was, as a warning, and even on the bench in the old Cookstown Courthouse, when the commission of the peace was limited to gentlemen of good birth, one chair had a similar brass plate, reserving it for a Lindesay. And so, as that great philosopher, Vere Forster, taught us to write long ago; "Pride goeth before a fall".

Next Week – The Lowrys of 1824.

## THE LOWRY FAMILIES

## (17 - 5 - 1924)

The names of two gentlemen appearing in the Directory of Cookstown in 1824 are "James Lowry, Esq., Rockdale", and "Robert Lowry, Esq., Pomeroy", who were full cousins. The former was the grand-father of the late Col. J. C. J. Lowry, V.L., and of Capt. E. L. B. Lowry, V.L., a Crimea veteran, who is still happily alive, though he has sold Rockdale and gone to reside in the South of England. The other gentleman was grandfather of Col. R. T. S. Lowry, D.L., the popular owner of Pomeroy.

In a directory of Cookstown at the present day it might be deemed presumptious to claim the owner of Pomeroy as one of the local gentry, for that place has made considerable progress as a market town under the fostering care of the Lowrys, and particularly of the present owner. However, a century ago the Dublin compiler classified him as one of the Cookstown gentry, and we willingly accept him. Cookstown is really the nearest Urban District to Pomeroy, and when the Poor Law Union was formed it was included in the area. Afterwards the building of the railway brought Pomeroy more into touch with Dungannon, but Mr. R. W. Lowry, as an ex-officio guardian, was brought to Cookstown as the centre of the Union, and, though Col. R. T. S. Lowry has not been on the board, still we imagine that his relations with Cookstown are closer than with Dungannon, and as President of the East Tyrone Unionist Association since the death of Mr. Gunning-Moore, D.L., he is always a welcome visitor to Cookstown.

Rockdale being considerably nearer Cookstown, only four miles distant against eight from Pomeroy, the successive owners have been much more closely connected with our town than their relatives in Pomeroy. This was especially the case with the late Col. J. C. J. Lowry, who took a leading part in the administrative work transacted by the Board of Guardians, as well as in religious movements. The fact that he was, till his death, President of the Y.M.C & L.A., in which he took a deep interest, is a testimony to the place he occupied in the life of our town.  He died as a result of an accident in his own house in 1897, falling from a ladder in the drawing-room where he was hanging a picture, and never recovering consciousness.  That evening he was to take the chair at a meeting in connection with the Methodist Church in Cookstown; the audience waited for him for about half-an-hour, when Mr. Venables, who organised the meeting, gave up hope and announced that as the Chairman had not arrived he would preside, adding, without any knowledge of the tragedy, that he never knew Col. Lowry to break an engagement before, and that something very serious must have prevented him from coming.  After the meeting concluded it was learned that only death itself had prevented the Colonel from fulfilling his appointment, and those who knew him best were not surprised, for nothing less could have done it.  He left two daughters, the elder of whom was married to Mr. T. MacGregor Greer, of Tullylagan, who went to live at Seapark on the death of his father; the younger is married to Col. W. A. Lenox-Conyngham, of Springhill, and both ladies, in their respective spheres, are leaders in religious, social and political movements which would have appealed to their late father.  He was succeeded by Captain E. L. B. Lowry, whose only son was killed in the South African war, and who, as stated, sold Rockdale a few years ago, and went to reside in England.  During his stay here he was proverbial for his generosity, and his interest in the district has not ceased with his removal.

The advent of these two families, at Pomeroy and Rockdale, as resident landowners, is very interesting, as showing how an aristocracy may be built up in a district.  This was due to the far-sightedness of the grandfather of the two residents in 1824, the Rev. James Lowry, M.A., rector of Desertcreat.  This clergyman was of the type known in English history as Empire-builders; men who believe in the future of their country and are determined that, so far as they can, their families shall enjoy that inheritance.  The family history in Ireland, according to Burke, dates from the early 17th century, when James Lowry emigrated from Scotland and settled at Ballinagory, Co. Tyrone, dying in 1668.  His son John Lowry, of Aghelis, near Caledon, was one of the besieged Protestants in Derry during the great siege, and appears to have died there, leaving his elder son Robert Lowry to succeed him.  This gentleman was married to Annie, daughter of Rev. John Sinclair of Hollyhill, near Strabane (second son of Sir James Sinclair, of Caithness) and the fourth son of this marriage was the rector of Desertcreat already mentioned, the Rev. James Lowry.

These several generations appear to have been adding to their estates in different parts of Tyrone: the village of Beragh, in the parish of Clogherney, belonged to them, and the old leases there, dating from about the middle of the eigthteenth century, describe it as "Lowrystown", but the name did not survive. The Rev. James Lowry (who married a daughter of William Richardson, M.P., of Rockdale, and sister of Viscountess Gosford), inherited considerable property in the upper end of Desertcreat parish, and built therein the two residences known as Pomeroy House and Rockdale, for his two sons, Robert and James. There is also a tradition that he built the huge rectory at Beragh, but that is not strictly correct, though he probably had an influence in it, for the Glebe House was erected in 1788, whilst his second son, Rev. John Lowry, B.A., was rector of Clogherney. There is little doubt, however, that it was Rev. Mr. Lowry who was responsible for ornamenting the Glebe at Ballymully by creating the rather extensive lakes or fish ponds there, and possibly it was he, also, who constructed the terraces on the side of Tullyhog Fort, in the rectory grounds, and planted an orchard.

According to the dates on the family vault in Desertcreat Churchyard, where generations of the descendants of this rector were brought for interment, he was born in the year 1711, but Lord Belmore in an article in the Ulster Archaeological Journal, says that the correct date is 1707, and gives as his authority the entry in his father's writing, in the family Bible. A few years difference will seem to our readers of no importance, but really is, for if the later date be correct, then, as Lord Belmore points out, he was ordained before he had reached canonical age. Whether he was only 21 years of age, or was 25, at all events in 1732 he became rector of Clogherney, which in that year had been constituted a separate parish from Termon Maguirke, the living being in the gift of his father, Robert Lowry. Thirteen years after he arranged with the Rev. Richard Dobbs, D.D., the rector of Desertcreat, to exchange and he held the latter parish till his death in 1786. His strenuous life may have inspired the lines on the family vault.

*Gentle reader, tell me, which is best.*
*The tiresome journey or the traveller's rest?*

His son, and grandson, succeeded Dr. Dobbs at Clogherney, and the latter was brought to Desertcreat vault for interment in 1852.

An elder brother of the famous rector of Desertcreat was Galbraith Lowry of Aghelis, who was member for Tyrone in the Parliament of 1761, the same Parliament as saw the first of the Stewarts of Killymoon returned. Like William Stewart, he sat in one Parliament only, being succeeded by his son Armar, who died in 1781, was elevated to the peerage with the title of Lord Belmore and, in 1797, was advanced to an earldom. Galbraith having married the daughter and co-heir of John Corry and assumed the name and arms of his wife's family, so that this branch became Lowry-Corry. The founder of the Corry family, according to Burke, was John Corry, a native of Scotland, who settled in Belfast in 1655; the next year he bought Castle Coole in Fermanagh, which, failing male issue, became the property of the great-grand-daughter who married Galbraith Lowry, and the home of the Earls of Belmore. It is thus that Corry became part of the legal surname of one branch of the family, and a popular baptismal name with the other branch.

The descendants of the Rev. James Lowry, of Desertcreat, were not confined to the families at Pomeroy and Rockdale. His second son, James, also entered the church, and after acting as curate to his father at Desertcreat for apparently a few months only, he was appointed rector of Clogherney in 1775, and, on resigning for a Waterford parish in 1794, his son again succeeded to Clogherney, which he held till his death in 1852. Lord Belmore had the patronage, but, in 1828, he sold it to Trinity College for £14,000, so as to provide for a succession of Fellows. The rector, who was of a rather independent type, resented this loss of the family parish, and, according to tradition, he said he would make the rectory so large that no Trinity College Fellow could afford to live in it. At any rate, he added immense wings to the building, which have since been pulled down. Lord Belmore, in an article in the Ulster Archaeological Journal, refers to his eccentricities, and possibly another story about him is true – that every year he visited Trinity College and strutted about the grounds to let the Provost and Fellows see that he was very much alive and that they need not soon expect to get a parish for one of their number, when he married and had to leave the College.

The fifth son of the former Desertcreat rector was William Lowry – the head of the Drumreagh Lowrys. His eldest son was General Robert W. Lowry, of Aghnablaney, Co. Fermanagh, and the latter's son, Robert Swinbourne Lowry, was married in 1892 to a sister of Mr. MacGregor Greer, lately of Tullylagan.

The different marriage connections of these families, important though they may have been to the individuals, are of no general interest, with one exception. The late Colonel J.C.J. Lowry, of Rockdale, married Elizabeth, daughter of Thomas Greer, of Tullylagan, a lady who was a widow, her first husband being the Rev. T. E. Bushe. The Bushes owned some estate in the district, but were non-resident; by this marriage connection, however, they were frequent visitors at Rockdale. The head of the family at present is Brigadier-General Bushe, late High Sheriff of Tyrone, who is living near Omagh, and is well known in Cookstown, but even better known is his sister, Miss Bushe, who is an enthusiastic social worker, and who exercised an immeasurable influence for good in the town some years ago, giving an impetus to religious and social work, particularly Total Abstinence amongst women, which must have far-reaching results.

# MANOR LINDESAY TOPOGRAPHY

In last week's article we referred to the bridge at Loughry on the way to Tullyhog as The Prince of Wales Bridge. It has been pointed out by a reader that this is the name given by the Ordnance Surveyors to what is popularly known as The Dark Bridge on the road to Grange. It is in the townland of Tullywiggan, but the O.S. name for the bridge we referred to is Tullywiggan Bridge.

Another reader, who is in a position to express an opinion which carries weight, writes that our statement that the old road from Cookstown to Dungannon, via Strifehill, went through the demesne and came out at the Gatehouse., is not correct. He points out that the O.S. map shows that the road crossed the river by a bridge near Loughry old mill and passed on, nearly in a straight line, a few perches from the front of Lime Park House, crossing the present road from Desertcreat to Tullyhog, at Mr. Leonard's house, on direct through Low Cross, coming out on the Donaghy road over half a mile from Tullyhog. This seems from the map to be correct, and from Loughry old bridge another road is indicated branching off to Ballymully, in a direct line for the Fort. Our correspondent adds that probably the demesne was originally much smaller, and that the Donaghrisk portion would be later than the Manor House, and the closing up of the old road later still, as the direct road to Cookstown could not have been made till the bridge was built at the Waterpower Factory. This Bridge, by the way, is named The King's Bridge by the O. Survey, and our correspondent suggests that the name Prince of Wales Bridge would fix the date for it between 1800 and 1820.

Next Week – Notes on other 1824 Gentry

# MORE GENTRY OF 1824

## (24-5-1924)

Two names appearing in Piggot's Directory of Cookstown in 1824 are "Thomas Staples, Esq., Lissan" and "Rev. John Molesworth Staples, rector of Lissan, Muff". These gentlemen were brothers, the latter being father of the late Sir N. A. Staples, Bart., who died 25 years ago, and grandfather of the present baronet and of Mr. Ponsonby Staples, of Lissan House.

As this family has been so closely connected with Cookstown since the early 17$^{th}$ century, when the first baronet actually owned the town for a time, we have had to refer to the members in past articles and a very slight reference only is now necessary. The interesting thing which the directory recalls is that, a century ago, the owner of Lissan was not a baronet, nor had several generations at Lissan before him enjoyed the title. The then baronet was Sir Robert Staples, who lived on his own estate in Queen's County, where he was an active officer during the Insurrection of 1798. He was unmarried and, on his death in 1832 (eight years after the date of our Directory), in the absence of nearer male relatives, the title came back to Lissan, and the owner became Sir Thomas Staples, the 9$^{th}$ baronet.

Sir Robert Staples, the youngest son of the first baronet, was left Lissan by his father, who died so long ago as 1653. Sir Robert succeeded to the title on his brother's death in 1673, represented Dungannon in William's Parliament of 1692, and Clogher in the next Parliament, and served as High Sheriff of Tyrone in 1703. These are early dates, but when, less than a century ago, the then baronet died it was through the fifth son of Sir Robert, and grandson of the first baronet Sir Thomas, that the title went to the Mr. Staples of 1824. The different generations are worth recording. This fifth son of Sir Robert was the Rev. Thomas Staples, rector of Derryloran, who married one of the two daughters of John Houston, of Castlestewart. Mr Houston had bought a considerable part of the old Castlestewart estate when it parted with the title after the death of the third baron, and his daughters inherited the estates round Stewartstown and to near Coalisland. One of these ladies married, as stated, the Rev. Thomas Staples, rector of Derryloran; the other married the Hon. and Rev. Charles Coulfield, rector of Donaghendry, and being co-heiresses their descendants - Viscount Charlemont and Sir J. M. Staples (or his representatives) will enjoy the mineral rights which are being developed by Sir Samuel Kelly.

Of this marriage of Rev. Thomas Staples, of Derryloran, the eldest son was the Rt. Hon. John Staples, who was a member of the Privy

Council, and was returned as M.P. for Antrim. He was twice married, his second wife being Henrietta, daughter of Viscount Molesworth – one of the three sisters who were saved from the fire, in which their mother perished, as mentioned a few weeks ago. By this alliance the Lissan estate was further enriched by valuable ground rents in the city of Dublin, as well as an estate at Swords, which still belongs to them. The two brothers, whose names appear in the directory, were the two eldest sons of this alliance, Thomas becoming the 9th baronet in 1832, and on his death without a son in 1865, he was succeeded by the eldest son of his brother, the rector of Lissan – Sir N. A. Staples. Another son was Major–General Thos. Staples, whose second son, Thomas also, is married to a sister of Mr. Thomas Greer, J.P., of Cratley.

Rev. J. M. Staples, rector of Lissan, was also prebendary of Moville, and, although the Directory of 1824 gives him as of Muff, yet it is evident that he was then living at Moville, and that the rectory was let to Mr. Caulfield. It was this clergyman who built the present rectory, a rather pretentious building out of the usual style, in 1807. There is a story that at that time he was thinking of matrimony and planned the new building with a view of attracting the intended bride, but when it was completed she married another suitor! However, he was consoled by marriage with a daughter of the Bishop of Meath, and had a family of ten. Like many other of the leading rectors of the time, he was a magistrate for the county, in his case for both Tyrone and Londonderry.

# THE MAGILLS

Another name appearing in the list of Cookstown gentry in the Directory of 1824 is "William Magill, Esq., magistrate, Crieve". This gentleman is well represented in our district, his great-grandson being Mr. S.R. Magill, manager of the Ulster Bank in Cookstown, while two grand-daughters are Mrs. Kennedy and Miss Magill of Mullentian. It is a remarkable thing that, in 1824, their father, Dr. William Magill, was practising in Cookstown, being the only physician mentioned in Piggot's Directory, though there were four surgeons. Dr. Magill lived on Loy Hill in his own house till he retired, and was succeeded by the late Dr. Henry Graves. His only son, the late Dr. C. L. Magill, resided afterwards at Curglasson. Another daughter of Dr. Wm. Magill was married to Mr. H. Wash Kinley, of Bloomhill, and died a few years ago leaving a considerable family. Still another daughter has made a fine reputation in London as an animal painter, her study of King Edward's dog being regarded as a masterpiece at the time.

To return to William Magill of 1824 directory; in his time marriage settlements appear to have been much more common than is now the case, and they had the great advantage to posterity, that being put on record they provided local historians with a good deal of information not otherwise available – and not now available owing to the destruction of the Four Courts. From this source we learn that Wm. Magill of Crieve, was married in 1787. As against his wife's dowry he brought into the settlement certain property, including a plot of ground 210 feet frontage in Cookstown, and extending back 21 perches, held under lease for lives renewable for ever, from William Stewart of Killymoon. In reciting this property, the Settlement states that the lessee had been James Magill, father of the bridegroom, and that the latter got it by agreement with his brothers, Robert and James. From these facts we get considerable information.

The date of this document will be noted - 1787, which is about 35 years or less, after William Stewart widened Cookstown street and gave leases for ever to enterprising persons who undertook to build the new town. Undoubtedly James Magill was one of these who settled in Cookstown, built a block of houses (to be followed later by another block) and had three sons to succeed him, one of whom was William Magill, described as a merchant in the marriage settlement of 1787, and as a magistrate in the directory of 1824. Of the other sons, one would be a half-brother of Mr. Magill, of Crieve, who settled in Dunmore. This family is extinct locally, Dunmore having been sold to Mr. James McGarvey, J.P., by the last owners, the Misses Magill, one of whom is married to Dr. Thos. Hogg, Belfast. Of the other we know little definite, but it may be noted that one of the two trustees to the settlement was Robert Magill, of Anahavil, who may have been brother to the bridegroom - a common arrangement. From the Report of the Drapers Company deputation in 1820 we learn that Robert Magill (spelled McGill in the report) was the tenant of Anahavil, where the company, on taking over the estate and building Moneymore, had erected a model scutch-mill, and that he had died in that year. His son, we learn, succeeded to the farm, and the deputation proposed that he should superintend the mill for one season and receive the earnings, and thought that after a year's experience he would become tenant of it. Of course he may not have been related, though a trustee, but another fact in favour of the theory is that, subsequently, the Crieve family bought Greenlodge and Drumgarrel, which is adjacent to Anahavil.

The marriage of William Magill, of Crieve, introduced a new name into the family, for the lady was Catherine, second daughter of Samuel Ranken, of Ballerena, in Limavady district. That gentleman's full name was the baptismal name given to three successive generations of his descendants. At his death certain property in Limavady and district came to his son-in-law at Crieve, and is still owned by the family; we believe that the war memorial recently unveiled in Limavady is on a site, part of which was given by Mr. Magill.

Dr. Magill, of Cookstown was the youngest son of Wm. Magill, who appears to have been the first of the family to own Crieve, where he built the present residence. He had two daughters who resided afterwards in Cookstown in the house on Oldtown Hill, which, on their death, was bought by the late Mr. Thomas Paul, and is now occupied by Mr. Lamont, M.R.C.V.S., and Mrs. Nobbs.

The elder son was named after his grandfather, Samuel Rankin Magill (the change of "e" for "i" should be noted by purists who sometimes get excited over very little). This gentleman resided at Greenlodge, presumably till his father's death, and occupied a very prominent position in Cookstown in the first half of the 19th century. He built a large number of houses in Coagh and Oldtown Streets to accommodate the increasing population, which property was kept intact till half-a-dozen years ago when the tenants were given an opportunity to become their own landlords. Mr. Magill was land agent for practically all the estates in the district, an enormous amount of money passing through his hands, and it was this fact that led to the opening of the first Joint Stock Bank in Cookstown. Mr. Magill went to the Belfast Bank and persuaded the directors to build the branch here, and he was, thereupon, appointed manager, with his son James as cashier. Prior to his time banking was transacted by some of the local merchants in an irregular sort of way, and the Belfast Bank was welcomed for its greater safety and convenience. Mr. Magill, however, fell out with that Bank and became local agent of the Ulster Bank, which was next in the field, and of which his grandson, and namesake, is the manager today. He died in 1862. He was appointed a magistrate for the two counties of Tyrone and Londonderry in 1835, when the Commission of the Peace was much more restricted than it has since become. He had four sons, two of whom died unmarried in recent years - Mr. Thomas S. Magill, A.B., J.P., who like his father, was a land agent, but on a much smaller scale, and Mr. S.R. Magill, who was for many years Poor Law Guardian for Lissan division of Cookstown Union. Both gentlemen are very favourably remembered in Cookstown; they were unmarried, and before the death of the latter he sold Crieve and went to reside in Mullintean with his cousin. A third son, James, who was the first cashier of the Belfast Bank and about whose promotion it is believed the rupture took place between the Bank and his father, died unmarried.

Another son was Robert Magill, who adopted the law as a profession and enjoyed a large practice, as will be understood from the fact that his father was agent for all the neighbouring estates and there was no other solicitor in Cookstown. For a time, also, he was assistant sheriff for Co. Tyrone, but found that it interfered too much with his profession. Unfortunately he died early, in 1872, leaving a family of seven small children who were bereaved of their mother a very short time afterwards. As stated already, one of them, the present Mr. S. R. Magill, is manager of the Ulster Bank: a brother occupies an important position in the Bank of France, in Paris, and another brother is in Australia, while the daughters of the family are living in England. There were two sisters—daughters of the first Mr. S. R. Magill. One of these married a Mr. Waggett, a landowner near Queenstown, where her family are residing, and the other married the Rev. Dr. Potter, nephew of Dr. Potter, of Gortalowry House, and protégé of Col. William Stewart, M.P., about whom we hope to have an article in an early issue, when we have exhausted this 1824 directory and get on to the next decade.

Next Week – Tirniskea and Springhill Families.

# MORE GENTRY OF 1824

## (31–5–1924)

In Piggott's Directory of Cookstown in 1824, the list of gentry is coupled with the clergy. The latter will be referred to later, when we take up the ecclesiastical history of the town, but before passing from the gentry we feel that we should supply two omissions from Piggott's list.

One of these is Mr. Baillie, of Tirniskea. This place is barely three miles from Cookstown, alongside the road to Pomeroy, and the only explanation we can think of for this omission by this directory-compiler a century ago, is that the owner of the place was Theodore Bailie, who, it will be remembered, was Lieut. of Cookstown Mounted Yeomanry, and therefore very closely connected with the town, in an honourable way, during the troublesome time when our country was threatened by enemies abroad and traitors at home. The house at Tirniskea is probably the oldest in our district, bearing the date 1632. It was, therefore, built at the same time as the first Manor House at Loughry, 2½ miles distant. Of the early history of this family we have not been able to ascertain any particulars. Captain Wm. Bailey (as the name was then officially spelled) was M.P. for Tyrone in the Parliament of 1798 only, with Colonel James Stewart, but he voted for the Union and was not re-elected. He was succeeded by his nephew Theodore. He was succeeded by Madame Baillie, who was resident at Tirniskea only occasionally. She is still remembered by even middle-aged people in Cookstown, as she was not content to drive into the town in a carriage and pair, but had a third horse in front. On her death she left the estate to her nephew, Thomas R. Gage, who assumed the additional surname of Bailie, prefixing it to his own name, which it will be noted, was not the usual method, the assumed-name, in every other case in our district at all events, coming last. Mr. Thos. Bailie - Gage was well known in Cookstown, though his official duties as solicitor to the Post Office, necessitated residence in Dublin so that he was able to make occasional visits only to Tirniskea. He sold the lands to the tenants under the Ashbourne Act, being, we believe, the first local landlord to do so, but retained the demesne and residence, which, however, were sold by his son, who is solicitor to the Great Northern Railway Co., and also has to live near Dublin.

# SPRINGHILL

The other omission from the list of gentry is that of the owner of Springhill, which is due, no doubt, to the fact that that family really belong to Moneymore. Springhill is only half-a-mile from Moneymore, though it may be mentioned that while the town and district to the north is on the Drapers' estate, Springhill, in the townland of Ballindrum, is on the old Salters' estate. At the same time the owners have always been closely identified with Cookstown, living only five miles distant; the late Sir William Fitzwilliam Lenox-Conyngham, K.C.B., D.L., as the owner of Coagh and magistrate for Co. Tyrone, for many years presided at the Presentment Sessions in Cookstown, which transacted the road business which forms the most important part of the duties entrusted to the Rural District Council by the L.G Act of 1898.

The founder of the family was Wm. Conyngham. He was a Scotch settler, a junior member of the family of the Earl of Glencairne in Ayrshire. His first connection with our district seems to have been in the year 1663, when he bought the six townlands of Coagh, Urbal, Drumconway (or Drumconvis as it is generally called), Mullagharony, Ballynargin and Ownaghmore. These townlands formed part of the original Castlestewart estate, which extended from Coagh to Coalisland, but were quickly dismembered. As early as 1630, Sir Andrew Stewart, the second baron, sold this bit of the property to Ann Boyse, who, with her son Nathaniel, sold to Wm. Conyngham in the year mentioned. Five years later, in 1668, Mr. Conyngham bought the townland of Ballindrum, in which the demesne is situated, and the present house, with its thick walls and old panelled rooms, may be taken as dating from that time, though it had been extended in after years. A few years later he bought the townland of Mullanahoe from the Earl of Suffolk, who married the only child of the third Lord Castlestewart, and dispersed the lands, the chief purchaser being John Houston. Church Lands around Ballydawley, between Springhill and Coagh, were leased from the Primate, and ultimately were acquired in fee. Wm. Conyngham, the elder, as he is described in some of the deeds, died in 1673. Of William Conyngham "the younger", son of the preceding owner, there are many mementos in Springhill. His portrait, by Lely, is one of the many family portraits on the walls; a gold watch is amongst the souvenirs, presented to him by the Salters Company in 1697, for his services as overseer of their woods; a number of his books, notably Presbyterian treatises, are treasured at Springhill. He seems to have been an outstanding figure of the time, and earned the title of The Good. This gentleman was married to Ann, daughter of Arthur Upton, M.P., in 1680. One sister married Sir Alexander Staples, Bart., of Faughanvale, second son of the first Sir Thomas Staples of Lissan, and her daughter Charity married John Walker, collector, of Dundalk, son of the famous Rev. George Walker, of Londonderry, and rector of Lissan, and in his will Mr. Conyngham bequeathed legacies to the children of his niece.

William Conyngham, the Good, played an important part in the siege of Derry, and many references to him, and to his father-in-law, Arthur Upton, will be found in MacKenzie's History. These two gentlemen, with Sir W. Franklin and Thomas Knox went to Dublin in December 1688 with copies of the warning letter which an anonymous friend had sent to Lord Mount Stewart, which made the Government take action. He got a commission in 1689, which is amongst the Springhill treasures, signed "William Henry Prince of Orange", as King William III then was, and when Lord Mountjoy came to Derry, Lieut.-Colonel Conyngham and Lieut. James Lennox were two of the eleven persons appointed to treat for terms.

William Conyngham, the Good, died in 1721, and left the property to his nephew, Colonel George Buttle, who assumed the name of Conyngham. The Buttles were landowners in County Antrim, near Glenarm, but the new owner of Springhill then about 30 years old, resided there for forty years. It was this gentleman who laid out Coagh, for which he got a charter in 1728 to hold a market every Friday, and four fairs in the year. His loyalty to the Protestant succession suggested the name for the fine street which he named Hanover Square. In connection with the corn mill he got into trouble, for, though it had existed from 1680, when it is set out in his uncle's marriage settlement, the sons-in-law of John Houston, the purchaser of the bulk of the Castlestewart estate succeeded in asserting their monopoly to the milling for the six townlands, and then the tenant of the mill had to be compensated for the loss of custom. He had also trouble with the Irish Society, which brought an action against him in 1731, for cutting trees they claimed. In 1745 the Jacobite rising took place, and the Irish Catholics were supposed to be waiting an opportunity for insurrection. Major Hamilton wrote to Col. Geo. Conyngham to have the arms at Springhill removed for fear of them falling into the hands of the rebels. As Deputy Governor of the county he got a letter in September 1745, to call up the Militia to be trained, and he supplied the names of gentlemen he recommended for commissioners. This gentleman, as will be gathered, was of the strong-minded type. His tenant, the miller, complained of his harshness, but he was no respector of persons, and was equally obdurate with the Lord Primate, who threatened that if Col. Conyngham further obstructed the collection of a cess to repair the end wall of Ardtrea Church, he would have it done directly and sue the Colonel for the amount. The same obstinate trait was displayed towards his only son, who was M.P. for Dundalk, and fought in the Seven Years War in Germany with distinction, but whose extravagance displeased his father. He disinherited him and left the estate to his daughter Ann, who married Clotworthy Lenox, and thereupon the family name became Lenox-Conyngham.

The Lenox family had important interests in Derry. The grand-father of the new owner of Springhill was James Lenox, who took an active part in the defence of Derry at the great siege, where he was associated with Wm. Conyngham, the younger. His portrait is one of the many at Springhill. He was an alderman of the city before the siege, but was afterwards deprived of his office, because he was a Presbyterian! It is when we come up against a concrete instance like this, of the working of the Test Act, that we begin to realise the fatuousness of the High Church party after the Revolution, who were willing to sacrifice the services of a gentlemen like Alderman James Lenox, of proved loyalty, good standing and honourable service, because he would not join the Established Church.

During the Volunteer movement Springhill was the centre of loyalist activity in the district. In the well of the stair-case there still hangs the old flag of the volunteers , with the name "Springhill Union" embroidered on each side, while underneath on the one side is the Harp and Crown, and, on the other, the royal arms, both designs being in an artistic border in which the shamrock is prominent, all worked by the then Mrs. Lenox-Conyngham, who was a skilful needlewoman. In May 1789, when the Corps was re-organised at a public meeting, and it was decided *to keep up the volunteering spirit as formerly and to appear in military array occasionally for the purpose of celebrating the annual return of memorable days, and also of co-operating, if necessary, with the magistracy, in the execution and support of the laws* it was unanimously agreed to offer the command to George Lenox-Conyngham of Springhill. His name also appears to a resolution ten years later. As follows:- *We, the inhabitants of Ballindrum and Ballydawley do associate and unite together as yeomen for the protection of our lives and properties, and the support of the laws and constitution of the King against all foreign invaders and internal insurgents,* and the rank and file have added, in another handwriting that they will *cheerfully sweare to protect the person and property of our worthy and well-beloved landlord George Lenox-Conyngham, Esq., against either foreign or domestic enemies, at the risk of our lives.*

There is, at Springhill, a copy of an important letter written by Mr. George Lenox-Conyngham, in 1799, to Sir Richard Musgrave, who had written asking for information regarding the Insurrection so far as Co. Derry was concerned. Mr. Lenox-Conyngham, in reply to definite queries, says that in 1793 the first insurgents appeared in the district. They were never called Defenders, but were distinguished by the name of Green Cockade. They paraded and exercised in the villages publicly till he reported the matter to the Government and General Whyte was directed to come to Springhill and an immediate stop was put to their public meetings. From that time more secret proceedings were adopted by persons styling themselves United Irishmen. They were composed of Presbyterians, Papists and some of the Established Church, and their object was to overturn the Government, both Church and State, and introduce a republic, on the very same plan as that of the French Republic. He was convinced that the Presbyterians and Baptists were jealous of each other from the first. When the rebellion broke out in Co. Antrim and Co. Derry few, or none, of the Papists appeared in arms. At Maghera about 300 men rose in arms but were soon discomfited and, of all the persons taken and tried, only one was a papist; they were all Presbyterians except one Church of England man. His opinion, based on what he heard and his own observation, was that the Presbyterians aimed at using the Paptists to get power, and that the latter were willing to be used in the belief that their greater numbers would give them absolute power and control in the end. Each designed to make tools of the other, but all the time their rooted antipathy existed.

The only son of this gentleman was William Lenox-Conyngham who married Charlotte Melosia, daughter of the Rt. Hon. John Staples. He served as High Sheriff of Tyrone in 1818, and of Londonderry in 1828, and was, of course, the owner of Springhill at the time of our Directory of 1824. His eldest son, of the same name, brings us down to modern times, being the late Sir William Fitzwilliam Lenox-Conyngham, K.C.B., who is still so favourably remembered in Cookstown, as well as in Moneymore. So long ago as 1859 he was High Sheriff of Co. Derry, and in 1868 of Co. Tyrone. He served with the 88th Regiment, and on retirement became Hon.-Commander of the Londonderry Militia, who, on one occasion, encamped at Moneymore for training. Sir William, as stated already, had been not only a Grand Juror, but took an active part in the more important road business at Presentment Sessions, and on Magherafelt Board of Guardians, and, on the passing of the L.G. Act, he was co-opted on Derry County Council, and as our file of 25 years ago shows, he looked after the interests of Moneymore district, which were endangered by the greater influence of the North Derry members.

Sir William married Miss Laura Arbuthnot, daughter of George Arbuthnot, of Elderslie, Surrey, and niece of Sir William Arbuthnot, Lord Provost of Edinburgh. Readers who happen to possess a copy of A. M. Sullivan's "New Ireland" will be interested to know that Lady Lenox-Conyngham was the sister of Eleanor Arbuthnot, whose abduction in 1854 at Holy Cross, Co. Tipperary, is described in that work at length. Laura and her younger sister were staying with a married sister, Mrs Gough, afterwards Lady Gough, whose husband was stationed in Ireland, and as Sullivan writes, "the fame of these fair young Saxons filled the county; they were young, handsome and accomplished and heiresses to considerable fortunes". One morning, when driving to church at Rathronan, a Mr. Carsden, of Barnane Castle, a rejected suitor of Eleanor, lay in wait with his men, and forcibly abducted her in spite of the efforts of her sister. However, he was arrested and sentenced to two years imprisonment. On serving his term, he renewed his attentions, and was bound to the peace, but cherished the idea that she secretly loved him, which was strengthened by the fact that she never married, though she had numerous suitors. For the full story we must refer readers to the Arbuthnot Abduction in "New Ireland".

Sir William had a large family, the eldest son being the present owner of Springhill, Lt.-Col. William Arbuthnot Lenox-Conyngham, who is a deputy lieutenant for the county and served as High Sheriff, and is married to the younger daughter of the late Col. J.C.J. Lowry, V.L., of Rockdale. He served in the Worcester regiment and had retired, but, on the outbreak of the Great War, he volunteered and saw a good deal of service in France. He represented Coagh on Tyrone Co. Council for a time and also Springhill division in Magherafelt District Council, and his popularity with all parties was shown by his election to the vice-chair, though there was a Nationalist majority. He regularly attends the local Petty Sessions and presides as senior magistrate, and is chairman of the Drapers Charity Trust. Two brothers fell in the war, Lt.-Col. John S.M. Lenox-Conyngham, of the Connaught Rangers, and Col. Herbert Maxwell Lenox-Conyngham, D.S.O., Veterinary Corps. The eldest daughter married Col. J.J. Clark, H.M.L., of Largantogher, still happily amongst us, whose eldest son, Commander Clark, D.S.O., after 23 years service in the Royal Navy, has settled down in our district, marrying the only surviving child of the late Col. Chichester, M.P., and Mrs. Chichester, M.P., of Moyola Park, and is the Area Commandant of the B Specials.

# THE 1824 DIRECTORY ENDED

## (14-6-1924)

We are afraid that, by this time, readers will have got tired of the biographical notes on the residents as given in Piggott's Directory of 1824 - just a century ago - and we propose to conclude our reference to it this week. The clergy, whose names appear with the gentry, will be mentioned again when we reach the ecclesiastical history of the town. Of the medical profession, besides Dr. Wm. Magill, who is described as a physician, there were four surgeons, one of whom, Surgeon Dickson, R. N., had charge of the Dispensary. He lived in the cottage at Tullagh. It is curious to reflect that while, in these days, those who specialise rather look down on the mere physician, a century ago relations were reversed, and we are reminded that going further back, surgery was hardly regarded as a learned profession. The barber's pole, with its red and white stripes, is a survival of the time when any man who could use a razor to remove a beard was also at liberty to use a lancet for any purpose which a client would allow. When Cookstown had one physician and five surgeons, a century ago, the two leading branches of the profession were about to level up. And it was about the same time that Stewartstown boasted of a "man mid-wife"; for obstetrics, the third branch of the profession, was still further behind.

In the law there were three Attorneys, as they then were willing to be named, of whom the only one leaving any permanent trace in the town was Joshua Collins. The name is extinct, but one of the female members of the family was mother of Thomas Morgan, a famous tea merchant, and of Rev. Dr. Morgan, of Fisherwick Presbyterian Church, Belfast. Another Miss Collins married John Weir, uncle of Silas E. Weir, of Cookstown, and their granddaughter was the wife of the late Mr. John W. Weir, of Cookstown. Joshua Collins had a son who went to practise law in Belfast, but died in 1851, at the age of 36. The obituary notice at the time says he succeeded his father, who was a leading solicitor in Tyrone.

The name Patteson, appears under "Linen Officers", Benjamin being linen inspector and Matthew being sealmaster. The latter was the postmaster in Cookstown and was succeeded by his daughter, the late Miss Patteson, the last of the name in the town, who will be remembered by those who can go back thirty years. Others of the name were in business, Richard being a grocer and hardware merchant, while Edward and another Richard were the painters and glaziers of the day, but whether related to the linen officers we do not know. The latter are represented by one of the leading merchants in Dundalk. The Pattesons had also, at the beginning of the century, the bleach-green and beetles at Greenvale.

The agent of the estate at this time was John McCormick and the same name appears as toll collector, but we think the latter was the nephew of the former. Hid father died when he was young and he was brought up by his uncle and, in due course, succeeded him as agent. He married Miss Aston, whose family had even earlier association with Cookstown. John McCormick, jun., was an outstanding figure in Cookstown, with which his descendants were long connected in a permanent way. He, himself, was a stalwart member of the Orange Order at a time when it was less popular than now, and an uncompromising Tory, just as his contemporary, the late William Glasgow, was an uncompromising Liberal, but it is remembered that these two gentlemen co-operated on one occasion when cholera ravaged the town and the dead bodies of the victims were left unburied by their terrified relatives. These two stalwarts, having no fear, volunteered for the unpleasant duty and coffined the bodies. Mr. McCormick was elected chairman of the earliest Town Commissioners, which office he held till his death. He also leased the markets from Col. Stewart, and, in this capacity, he was succeeded by his only son, Joseph, who lived to the early seventies and was succeeded by the late Mr. J. W. Fleming, his relative - so that Cookstown market, in its most palmy days, when it had few equals and no superiors, was under the control of the McCormicks. Mr. Jos. McCormick married a daughter of the Rev. Thomas Miller, who was a tower of strength to the town in his long generation, and, by this marriage, Mr. McCormick formed new relationships with influential families. His widow and daughters resided in The Cottage (originally known as Waterloo Cottage, having been built by a Waterloo veteran) and exercised a great influence for good in the Oldtown. The eldest daughter, since deceased, married Rev. J. W. Sharpe, of Moneymore, and the second daughter has also died, while the youngest, Miss McCormick, sold the Cottage a few years ago to reside in Belfast with her brother-in-law.

Three Inns are given in Cookstown a century ago, before the word hotel became fashionable. The King's Arms, owned by Mary Henry, was, we think, the present Commercial Hotel in Oldtown Street; the Stewarts Arms, owned by John McAllister, was not the hotel of that name which Mr. Mullan and his predecessor Mr. Patrick Molloy owned, now the Bank of Ireland, but was somewhere in Gortalowry, while the Grapes Inn, owned by Alex. Rodgers, was probably a public-house, with that sign, in the Oldtown also, but no one has been able to locate it for us so far.

In the list of "Shop-Keepers, Traders, etc.", there are some businesses which are still being carried on, but under different ownership. Our information about them is extremely meagre, because, while it is possible to trace the succession of land or houses by deeds, there is no record where one merchant takes over the business of another. Of the 51 names given, so far as we have been able to ascertain, not one business is now carried on by any descendant of the merchant of only a century ago. Judging by the names, too, the preponderance of Protestants was very great; only a few names are those of Roman Catholic families, and we are reminded by that fact that the influx of Catholics into the town was comparatively recent - a fact which is apt to be lost sight of when referring to the church accommodation of the period.

Two names coming together in the list of shopkeepers can be identified. The first is Peter Potter, saddler and harness maker, who, though a humble tradesman, the tenant of a house in either Oldtown or Coagh Street, is remembered long after most of his fellow townsmen are forgotten, and that through his piety. He was an enthusiastic Methodist, and, as a class leader, he did much for a young convert Willie Reilly, a native of Dublin then living in Cookstown, who, with Gideon Ouseley, became one of the most zealous missionaries of the Methodist movement in Ireland. When the great split came amongst the Methodists between those who wanted a separate church with its own ministry and communion, and those who adhered to the earliest, or primitive, system in which the Methodist Society was simply a preaching auxiliary of the Established Church, Potter adhered to the latter, and he was one of the two trustees who took the lease for the site on which the Primitive Methodist Chapel was built in Cookstown, to be opened by Rev. Adam Averall, the famous divine from Ballinderry. The other name is Leander Richardson, letterpress printer and book-binder, who was Cookstown's first printer, and the predecessor of Mr. Thomas McClelland. The rather peculiar baptismal name, Leander, is the second name of Mr. Murry L. Richardson, of Dungannon, who is either a grandson or grand-nephew of our Cookstown printer a century ago. Previously to coming to Cookstown, Richardson had worked at the craft in Magherafelt.

The publicans were thought worthy of a section by themselves in this old directory – they were 20 strong a century ago, when the population was only 1,500, but, of course, they relied largely on the big markets on Saturday. Of the score, we believe no representatives now exist in the town.

In connection with the Post Office, there is not much of interest in the directory except the fact that the Scotch letters travelled from Belfast via Donaghadee. The English mail went via Dublin, the Kingstown route being subsequent. The hours of the mails may be noted; the mail for Dublin left half-an-hour before the arrival of the letters from Dublin! For the north mail there was an hour to reply to the letters. No coaches passed through Cookstown, which lay between the coach services of Dungannon and Magherafelt. The coach passed through Dungannon for Dublin at 4pm., but the letters for it had to leave Cookstown at 12.30.

Leaving this century-old Directory behind (though we may have to refer to it again) we proceed with our sketch of the developments of the town. The Parish Church had been built in Gortalowry in 1821, and in 1824 the site was given for the old chapel, which was opened in 1826. The Methodists had a chapel somewhere in the town early in the century, as, in 1804, permission was given for a new "preaching house", as it was named, and this was held by the Wesleyans when the split came and the Primitive section built a chapel opposite Molesworth Street, now McCollum's shop. In 1835 the great split took place amongst the Presbyterians over the call of the late Rev. J. K. Leslie whose supporters left the old church, and after worshipping in the open air in the market yard, built the Third Presbyterian Church. These events are well known by those interested, and will be dealt with, in due course, in the ecclesiastical history of the town.

Next Week we intend to give an article on Dr. Potter, of Gortalowry House, built about 1832, and also refer to Drumcairne.

# DR. POTTER OF GORTALOWRY

## (21-6-1924)

Dr. Potter, who resided in Gortalowry almost a century ago, is remembered still as a practitioner who set a high value on his services. But, as will be seen below, when occasion arose, he acted up to the best traditions of the medical profession and did all he could for the poor, without fee or reward. The fact is that he was primarily the medical attendant of the Killymoon family. He was the close friend of Colonel

William Stewart, who appears to have brought him to Cookstown. Amongst the family papers still extant are the plans of Gortalowry House, just north of the new parish church, which Colonel Stewart was going to build for Dr. Potter, but from the lease it appears that Dr. Potter built it himself.

The lease, which is dated July 1832, was for lives renewable for ever, and it is interesting to note who were then selected as the most probable long livers. The "lives" were Andrew Stewart, son of the Hon. Andrew Stewart, of Lisdhu; Henry Theopholus Clements, son of Henry John Clements, of Ashfield, Cootehill and William Lenox-Conyngham, son of William Lenox-Conyngham, of Springhill. The latter was a popular life with those taking out leases, and he justified the choice for he lived long. At his death the owner took out a fee farm grant as entitled by law.

When referring to the Gortalowry House we may as well trace its subsequent history. Dr. Potter left it, by his will, to his niece Mrs. Alicia Burke, daughter of his sister Mrs. Anne Gibbons, who sold it in a few years to Major Charles Irvine, with whose family the house was long identified. He died in 1863, but it was not till 1881 that his son, Colonel Henry Irvine, C.B.,D.L., the Under-Sheriff for Tyrone, sold it to the late John Thomson. The purchase price then was £455; Mr. Thomson's family sold the property, which had, in the meantime, been let to the late Mr. Venables, on the latter's death to Mr. Thomas McKeown by private sale, at about three times the price paid forty years before; so much has the value of good house property gone up in Cookstown.

As mentioned, Dr. Potter was not only the medical attendant, but the intimate friend of Colonel Stewart. The latter was in rather poor health about 1830 and was advised to spend the winter in a warmer climate. Accordingly he went to Toulouse, which then held the place now occupied by the Riviera as a winter health resort, and he took Dr. Potter with him. Some letters from Colonel Stewart at this time reveal his political views. Reform was the burning question – that is the abolition of "pocket" and "rotten" boroughs and the extension of the franchise with a view to making the House of Commons more representative. The Irish constituencies had been reformed at the Union when the little boroughs of Augher, Clogher and Strabane were abolished, and Dungannon reduced to a single member, but in England a large number of the borough members were simply nominated by the local landlord, and seats were sold as commodities to such an extent that Pitt, when proposing to abolish them, proposed to pay the owners for their loss of revenue. Other reforms were demanded by the Chartists also, including such suffrage for men as we now have, but not, we think, votes for women. The movement had acquired a great impetus from Daniel O'Connell, who, in 1828, was elected as the member for Clare, though, as a Roman Catholic, he could not sit. But the ingenuity of his class and their ready application for agitation, made itself felt. The right of public meeting had been attained, and monster meetings in conjunction with the open voting, were an effective method of intimidating, or at least, of influencing electors, and the Irish method was quickly followed in England.

Colonel Stewart, writing to his mother, the Hon. Mrs. Stewart, had asked if she were a "Reformer", adding that he had always been one, "not for universal suffrage or annual Parliaments, but I am a friend to vote by ballot", and in a subsequent letter he expresses the opinion that "the Church requires a thorough reform as well as the Parliament". Mrs. Stewart apparently wrote that she was also for reforms, and Col. Stewart wrote as follows from Paris on 4th May 1832:-

*I was very glad to hear that you are a Reformer. You know I have always been one; I was afraid that King Dan being a Reformer would have frightened you. Were I less poor and stronger I would try my luck once more for Tyrone. I heard from Lord Caledon, who is a most gloomy anti-reformer, that Sir James Stronge does not offer himself.........*

Col. Stewart had represented County Tyrone in the Parliaments of 1818, 1820 and 1826, his colleague in the latter Parliament being Henry Corry. But in the Parliament of 1830, the latter was returned with Sir Hugh Stewart, Bart., of Ballygawley. The Alexander family, of which Lord Caledon was the head, were only beginning to make their influence felt, and a few years after had a bitter fight with the Hamiltons of Baronscourt, the election literature issued being particularly lurid and not at all creditable to either side.

To return to Dr. Potter:- In the same letter, of May 1831, Col. Stewart writes home to his mother:-

*You never saw a man so changed as P. (Dr. Potter); he appears well and in good spirits FOR HIM. What a misfortune to have such a temper. ..... I will, if you wish, go by Portpatrick and pay you a visit. It must be but a short one, as P. thinks it would be very imprudent of me to remain in Ireland after the end of August .... My cough has generally been better since my arrival here.*

That Dr. Potter was a good deal more than the family doctor is also seen from a letter from Mrs. Clements, sister of Col. Stewart, to her mother. She writes:-

*Poor little Mr. P. (Potter) is so anxious about you it makes me forgive him all his own fancies, particularly as he got provocation at times.*

*He (Dr. P.) has taken one of his very low fits for some days past - however it will go off soon, I am sure. I feel both to pity him and be provoked with him.*

In a further letter from Mrs. Clements to her mother, reference is made to her son Henry, who became Colonel Stewart's heir, the late Col. Henry Theopholis Stewart, of Ashfield Lodge. Mrs. Clements wrote:-

*Poor Potter looks most miserably ill himself – he is the most unhappy man I ever saw, but although he has said so many things of me that made me feel wretched, and that I thought excessively ill-natured, I shall never forget his care and attention to us all when we required it, and he has done so well for little Henry, who has now got quite stout after his influenza.....I feel frightened at the thought of losing P., but I shall be even more particular about all his directions when he is gone.*

These extracts from letters convey a good idea of the sort of a man Dr. Potter was – eccentric, gloomy and irritable, but loveable in spite of his faults because of his faithfulness. If anything were wanted to complete the picture it will be found in the following "song" which was written for the return of Col. Stewart and his medical adviser, after spending the winter of 1830-31 at Toulouse. The lines are entitled "A New Song in praise of Col. Stewart".

*Ye Bards of Erin, I pray excuse me,*
*These simple lines for to lay down;*
*It is concerning a worthy landlord,*
*That lives convenient unto Cookstown.*
*His worthy talents deserve great honour,*
*His principles being both firm and pure;*
*He is a friend and credit to his tenants round him,*
*And a benefactor to all the poor.*

*His absence long we are bemoaning,*
*Since he sailed unto a foreign clime:*
*But he is returned in strength and vigour,*
*With courage great and most sublime,*
*His grand arrival to his situation.*
*Great numbers daily were expecting soon,*
*Long length of days may he reign o'er Cookstown,*
*In that lovely seat called Killymoon.*

*It would delight you on a summer's evening,*
*To take a walk through these flow'ry vales,*
*Where the thrushes warbling with admiration,*
*The game abounding o'er hill and through dales;*
*For there is the woodcock and the golden pheasant,*
*The trout trepanning with free goodwill;*
*The lovely castle and the lofty temple,*

*Well situated near the purling rill.*

*Physician Potter, that worthy member,*
*Now I intend to extol his fame,*
*Who did accompany the noble Colonel,*
*As he crossed over the raging main;*
*But now he's returned in triumph and grandeur,*
*In peace and honour, and great renown;*
*Long may he live in the land of Erin,*
*In Killymoon, near to Cookstown.*

*When the dreadful cholera was in Erin raging,*
*Brave Doctor Potter did exert his skill*
*To save his town from its great outrages,*
*Which rich and poor did with terror fill*
*When awful death it did surround us,*
*With its dart appearing at each door*
*He would accept no charge for his worthy labours,*
*But gave it gratis to the poor.*

*I have ranged through Powerscourt, near to the Dargyle.*
*Captain Power, of Killyfane;*
*Mr. Lambert's, of pretty Bow-Park,*
*Townly Hall, and the Court of Slane,*
*To the great O'Grady, of the County Limerick,*
*Likewise, Squire Connelly's, of Kildare -*
*Of all these places I have been relating*
*With Killymoon they cannot compare*

*Now here I mean to make a conclusion*
*To these few lines I have penn'd down*
*Long live that noble, worthy landlord,*
*In peace and splendour near to Cookstown.*
*May his tenants long have him reigning over them,*
*Never to depart from his native shore,*
*But live content in the land of Erin,*
*In health and happiness for evermore*

Dr. Potter died on 12th July 1851, a few months after his patron Colonel Stewart, and at a time when Killymoon was being put up for auction and the estate was being parcelled up. He was unmarried, and, by a will dated 1848, left Gortalowry House to his niece. He had a nephew, Rev. Dr. Potter, however, through whom the Potter family are still connected with Cookstown, for when visiting his uncle here he became acquainted with Miss Magill, daughter of Mr. S. R. Magill, and the friendship eventuated in their marriage, one of their children being the Rev. Dr. Potter, Bishop of Cyprus.

Next Week – Drumcairne and other notes.

Drumcairne                                                    Stewartstown

# DRUMCAIRNE BUILT

## (28-6-1924)

The appearance of a countryside is greatly improved by the existence of gentlemen's "seats", as they used to be named - good class residences, castles or manor houses, in their demesnes, large or small. When occupied by a resident gentry the amenities of life are also influenced, nor are they without economic value to the community generally as they provide a class of employment and assist business in every direction. In this respect Cookstown has been rather fortunate in the past, and a complete history of the local country houses which are often taken for granted, but had a definite beginning, would be of much interest. One such fits into the chronology of our history, for it is a little less than a century since Drumcairne came into existence.

Drumcairne, which is one of the beauty spots beloved by picnickers who are privileged to go there, is situated 1½ miles from Stewartstown and 2 miles from Lough Neagh, a fine view of which is commanded from the demesne. It is the seat of Viscount Charlemont, V.L., the head of the house of Caulfield, but the lands never belonged to Sir Toby Caulfield, the founder of that family and its fortunes in the early seventeenth century. That fact, as well as the relationship of Viscount Charlemont to the Earls of Charlemont seems to have caused much confusion to writers in the Press, and is an excuse for a somewhat fuller notice than would otherwise be given.

We associate our older families in Ulster with the Plantation; Sir Toby Caulfield was, pre-Plantation, as his activities date to the reign of Queen Elizabeth. Though described as Master of Ordnance he was more a man of affairs than a soldier. Thus we find that about the year 1600 he is described as seneschal for the primate, and as such receiving the rents out of the Culdee's lands at Armagh, and when Hugh, Earl of Tyrone, fled from the country in 1608, Sir Toby was appointed by the Crown as receiver of the rents of that Earl, and his very detailed account of his stewardship gives us the best idea we have of the value of O'Neill's estate before the Plantation. For his services he received a grant of the lands of the Abbey of St. Peter and St. Paul, which included the Grange of Tullyhog; he received other grants of land of various sorts, including half of Beaghmore and Strawmacklemartin, and many other "tops of mountains". At the Plantation, as a servitor (not an undertaker) he was granted the lands of Ballydonnelly which became thenceforward known as Castle Caulfield, where he built a castle, now in ruins. Again, Sir Toby, who had commanded Charlemont Fort, received a grant of it in

1607, with 300 acres, where a town sprung up, which in time became a borough. True it was a "pocket borough", but it was through it that Henry Grattan entered Parliament, just as W. E. Gladstone owed his entry to Parliament to a patron who had a pocket borough as his disposal, for promising but uninfluential young politicians.

Sir Toby died unmarried in 1627, and was succeeded by his nephew, Sir William Caulfield in accordance with the terms of the patent creating the peerage. This nobleman left three sons who succeeded in turn; Toby, who was murdered in 1641 by Sir Phelim O'Neill, or his orders; Robert, who avenged that murder and died unmarried and William who was advanced in the peerage to the rank of Viscount, and was succeeded by his son William, the 2$^{nd}$ Viscount.

This Viscount Charlemont, the sixth peer within the seventeenth century, took up arms against James II, and was one of the Protestant gentlemen attained by the "Patriot Parliament of 1689". King William, however, made him Governor of Tyrone and Armagh, and of the Fort at Charlemont. Subsequently he served in the war in Spain. He had three sons, one of whom succeeded him while another entered the Church. The latter was ordained rector of Tartaraghan, and then went in 1727 to Ballyclog, which living he held with Ardboe. It was due to that accident, as we may fairly describe it, that Drumcairne is the residence of Viscount Charlemont.

The reason is this: James, the third Viscount, and the elder brother of the clergyman mentioned, was succeeded by his son, also James, who was promoted to an earldom, and was the Great Earl Charlemont, who was commander-in-chief of the Volunteers, and the patron of Henry Grattan. He died at the end of the 18$^{th}$ century, after the Union was carried in spite of his opposite, but before it became a fact. His son was the second Earl, and was succeeded by his grandson, who died without issue as recently as 1892, and on his death the earldom became extinct

But, through the rector of Ballyclog, son of the second Viscount, the latter title was preserved, though without the estates. That clergyman had, in the year following his settlement in Ballyclog, married Alice, one of the two daughters of John Houston, who had bought the remnant of the old Castlestewart estate. Stuart Hall and the lands around it, were not included, of course, because they had been bought by Colonel Robert Stewart, ancestor of the Earl of Castlestewart, from his elder brother, the second baron. But Stewartstown and all the lands as far as Coalisland (including the new coal fields) became the property of Mr. Houston. He is generally described as "John Houston of Castlestewart", because that was the early name of the town, the charter for the market being "Castlestewart", which name was subsequently changed to Stewartstown. Besides the lands, and the town with its market rights, Mr. Houston acquired the advowson of the parish, and, in 1742, on the death of the then rector Rev. Samuel Close (an ancestor of Major Close, of Drum Manor), Mr. Houston naturally presented his son-in-law, the Hon. and Rev. Charles Caulfield to the living, in exchange for Ballyclog. Mr. Houston had a son John, and it may have been he who was living in 1742, and gave the living to his brother-in-law. John Houston, Junr., died without issue, however, and the estate passed to his two sisters and co-heirs, wives of the rectors of Donaghendry and Derryloran (Mrs. Staples).

When Lord Ochiltree got the grant of the "large proportion" at the Plantation he built a fortified house beside the lake at Stewartstown. It was not an imposing place, for Sir Nicholas Pynnar reported in 1619 that "there is no more done now than was at the last survey; the castle is thatched and the Lord absent". It was burned by the rebels in 1641. Some time after Mr. Houston became the owner the "castle" was rebuilt, or rather a substantial residence was erected, some small remains of which are still visible, and this became the seat of this branch of the Caulfields, who resided on the estate inherited, not from the Charlemonts, but from the Houstons.

We have not yet Drumcairne, however, for the residence known as Castlestewart was in the townland of Castle Farm, as our Stewartstown readers know. It appears, however, that, about the end of the 18th century, the house was destroyed; there is a curious tradition that James Caulfield, having been appointed guardian to an infant relative in Co. Roscommon, which meant that he could not again reside at Stewartstown for 20 years, cleared the castle of its contents and blew it up! At any rate, in the Directory of 1824 we find James Caulfield, son of the above-mentioned, as tenant of Muff Rectory. He also occupied Mullintean and Loy House, and, in the latter, his son James Alfred was born, who when the Earl died in 1892, succeeded to the title of Viscount. The latter, as a small boy, actually laid the foundation stone of the new house which was erected on a site in the townland of Drumcairne, and that fact fixes the date of the house as between 1830 and 1835.

No one visiting Drumcairne to-day would imagine that less than 100 years ago the demesne was simply agricultural land. It might be centuries old, but when attention is called to it one does notice that the finest trees are quick-growing beech and fir, while oak are scarce. The lay-out of the terraced garden tells of the time when Italian landscape gardening was in the ascendant, and the "vista" of it through the avenue of trees is one of the favourite sights of visitors. The house, though comparatively modern, has been brought up to date by the present owner who succeeded, in 1913, on the death of his uncle without male issue. Thus is it that one of our created beauty spots, less than a century ago, is the seat of Viscount Charlemont, the bearer of a title created three centuries ago.

Next Week – The Building of the Stores

# THE MARKET YARD STORES

## (12–7–1924)

It has been said that the architecture of a country reflects the genius, or spirit, of its people, and the same is true, in a restricted degree, of a city or town. In what buildings in Cookstown are we to look for the spirit that created the town?

Ecclesiastically there is nothing very distinctive. Taking the Church buildings in chronological order, the premier place must be given to the First Presbyterian, the site of which would have been regarded as the most desirable in the new town in 1761, when the Presbyterians emerged from their sanctuary in Killymoon demesne and took up a position on the main street, at the corner of the new Fair Hill. The present building dates from 1846, and shows a dignified façade, not properly appreciated because of the surrounding trees, but of a type very common with Presbyterian Churches of that period. In order of time, the Second Presbyterian Church comes next, being completed in 1806, the plan being exactly similar to that of the church which Mrs. Stewart hurriedly erected just over a century before, when the Presbyterians were ousted from the old town commons. The Parish Church, with its neat spire, next appeared on the main street in 1821, but at the southern end, hugging, as it were, the road to Killymoon and holding out, by its situation, an invitation to the landed gentry of the country beyond rather than to the townspeople, but it also is of a common type. Of the old chapel, erected in 1828, it is enough to say that it represents the first permanent appearance of the Roman Catholic community after their long suppression, while the Church of the Holy Trinity, which succeeded it less than 35 years after, with its towering spire, added more recently, and its adjacent Convent, represents the splendid bloom of that early shoot under the favourable conditions of full toleration, but it has its equals in many another town. Of the Third Presbyterian Church, dating from 1837, it may be said to represent the struggle of democracy to assert its right to elect its pastor on the principle of the equality of man, irrespective of means, and it is a building which strove to give the largest possible accommodation at the least expense - again a common sort of church, while the Methodist Chapel follows a well-pronounced type. Thus, ecclesiastically the architecture of Cookstown is not distinctive.

Of the business buildings the same must be said. It is doubtful, indeed, whether for them progress can be claimed. Thus, of the four banks, the earliest, the Belfast Bank, is easily first in architectural design, standing aloof, moreover, within its own four walls, while the Ulster Bank spreads itself across all the site, and shares its gables with its neighbours. The Hibernian does the same, but gives the impression that it was being squeezed by those neighbours, while the Bank of Ireland has contented itself with putting a new stucco front on an old hotel. Of none of these can it be claimed that they embody any characteristic spirit of the town, unless a dwindling of ambition, which is in contrast with the Banks of some other towns.

Nor can any special significance be seen in the business premises; true, there are few towns which can show as level a lot of shops with dwellings overhead as Molesworth Street, but individually these have nothing distinctive nor are they any more imposing than, for example, the block built by the late Mr. Harbison three-quarters of a century ago, nor even of the block from Lennox's to Newell's, in William Street or from the Burn Road to Mowbray's, in James Street.

The domestic architecture, also, of the town, can hardly be described as striking. Coolnafranky and Glenavon are fine houses, but have their equals in other towns; the terraces, such as Cluff's, on Loy Hill, the detached and semi-detached houses, the better class artizans' dwellings are all of a common enough type, and, if visitors to the town speak slightingly of the very small houses of mill workers, we can only reply with the apology that they are the remnants of the distant past, such as are found in all industrial towns, for even they are not distinctive, and efforts to raise the standard have, in one block at least, only resulted in that abomination - back to back houses, for which there is no excuse in a street with the open country for a rere.

For two railway termini we might claim distinction, but that they are so common-place buildings; the Court House suits well its dual purpose of justice and amusement; our schools are unpretentious though those of Derryloran, having been built of brick, have earned the distinctive appelation of "red"; on the Fair Hill something unique might be made of the juxtaposition of the Orange Hall, the Academy and the Cinema, but that is an accident; for the Assembly-Rooms - built to accommodate a large Sabbath school - we might claim that it represents a spirit in the town, but it is hidden in the back-ground; as for the Workhouse, it is like all its fellows elsewhere, save that it is closed; so, too, is the Fever Hospital, and as regards the Gas Works - well, it is hardly reasonable to expect anything different from such concerns all over the world.

Where, then, if anywhere, shall we find a monument to the distinctive spirit which has made Cookstown? We suggest, in all seriousness, that it is to be found in that apparently common-place, but substantial, building known as the Stores which stands between the old and new market yards.

The popular idea about the stores is that they were built in the "Famine time", 1846-47, but, as a matter of fact, they date ten years earlier. No doubt the recurrent famines which have always characterised Ireland, and are happily almost a thing of the bad past, were responsible for the stores, for they were intended for grain, where one year's surplus could be used to meet the deficit of the next. No such storage accommodation existed in Cookstown at the time and the want was met in what we claim to be the characteristic Cookstown method, by the people providing it themselves. We have been far too apt to forget that Cookstown owes its importance, not to the patronage of a great family, nor to any Government help, direct or indirect, but to the self-reliance of its own citizens, and it is with much pleasure and pride that we recount for the present generation one out of many instances of the practical way in which that self-reliance was manifested by the generation who lived 80 or 90 years ago.

The Stores, as we have said, were built in 1836. So far as we have been able to ascertain there was no special reason for their erection at that time as regards scarcity of food, nor would it have been of much use to build stores when there was already a famine. The immediate reason for their erection was probably that that was the time when the Market Yard, or Shambles, as some persons still name it, was enclosed by Colonel Stewart, and the foundation was laid for what became one of the largest markets for agricultural produce in the North of Ireland. In the unfortunate absence of any record in estate books we cannot say definitely that the Market Yard dates from that year, but we do know that the site of the Stores, which bound the Yard, was described in the lease as bounded on the west by ground owned by Colonel Stewart - a pretty good proof that the Yard did not then exist, while if it was of much later date we would have some record of it. Then, in 1850, Col. Stewart leased the Market Yard, with the tolls, etc., under the Market Charter to John M'Cormick for £150 a year. The intervening period of the fourteen years from 1836 would be little enough to provide an estimate of the value of the Market Yard. Our theory, therefore, is that Col. Stewart, who had just bought out the Primate's interest in the Church lands of Cookstown, Killyman, Monrush, etc., for a sum of over £7,000, had decided, at the same time, to provide an enclosed market in a central position for the sale of certain produce, fitting it with the necessary weighbridges, beams, etc.

That, however, is only theory. We are on perfectly sure ground in regard to the origin and date of the stores, for, by a piece of good fortune, the original lease, dated 17th September 1836, has come into our possession. This lease, we may say, was executed by Colonel Stewart, whose signature was witnessed by "Samuel L. Potter"- his friend Dr. Potter, about whom we recently wrote, but it was not executed by the lessees for some reason, probably because there were a number of interlineations. For historical purposes that is immaterial because it expresses what was intended, and gives the names of the men who, at that period, joined together to provide the town with the much-needed accommodation for grain and similar products.

The lessees were the following, and given in this order:-
Wm. Stewart Richardson, Esq., of Oaklands.
Thomas Greer, junr., Esq., of Tullylagan.
John Weir, of Stewartstown, merchant
Robert Lind, Esq., Cookstown.
Robert M'Geagh, merchant, Cookstown
Robert Glasgow, merchant, Cookstown
Silas Ebenezer Weir, merchant, Cookstown.
James Moore, merchant, Cookstown
John M'Cormick, junr., merchant, Cookstown.
William Morgan, junr., merchant Cookstown
Samuel Rankin Magill, Esq., Loy.
William Magill, M.D., Esq., Loy.
Robert Hassard, Esq., Loy.
John Gibson, carpenter, Gortalowry.
Wallace Gibson, farmer, Gortalowry

The lease was for a plot of ground containing 117 feet in front and 29 feet from front to rere, bounded on the north by a garden in the possession of Joshua Collins, on the east, south and west by land in the possession of Col. Stewart. These measurements are those of the actual building. In addition the lessees got liberty of a road "opening from the new road leading past the new meeting house", 24 feet wide in front of the stores. The words quoted were added as an interlineation. Molesworth Street was then still a "new road", just as the Third Presbyterian Church, opened in 1835, was "the new meeting house". The road, 24 feet wide, can still be seen marked by a channel, and the entrance from the "new road" is also seen to be a gate opposite this right-of-way, but now rarely open, for the stores, of course, are open from the Market Yard.

It does not require one to be very observant to notice that the gable of the Stores is 8 feet back from the street line; it is very unfortunate that the street, now so congested on market days, was not up to that gable. The railway houses at the corner of Union Street also sit back, which gives the impression that it had been intended to widen the road, but the house at the main street corner (Messrs. Cosgrove's) limits the width at the important point.

To return to the lease; the rent of the site was to be £50 a year, but with the provision that, if the conditions of the lease are fulfilled, a sum of one shilling only will be received as rent. The chief condition is that the lessees shall not use the stores *for any other purpose but for stores for grain and other merchantege, nor will they use or occupy, or permit or suffer said premises to be used or occupied or employed for any other purpose or pretence whatsoever, nor will they permit, allow or suffer any gunpowder, flax tow, hemp, or any particularly inflammable substance to be stored or lodged in or about said premises.*

What arrangement was made by the lessees between themselves we do not know. The lease of the markets to John M'Cormick, dated 20th September 1850, from Col. Stewart just before his death, described the property as the Market Yard with the office, weighbridge, cranes and sheds there-unto belonging, together with the tolls and customs of the markets and fairs. The stores were not included, and the rental of the property prepared for the sale which took place after Colonel Stewart's death, makes this clear, for John M'Cormick is given as lessee of the market yard, markets, etc., at £150 a yard, while "the company who built the stores" are the lessees of the stores at 1s. a year for 99 years. The "company" was not, however, anything like a modern Joint Stock Company, being apparently a simple partnership, and with fifteen different persons it is obvious that it would be difficult to carry on, unless there was some far-seeing Deed of Partnership which provided for the death or removal of individual members. As the Stores were used in conjunction with the Market Yard, and to-day appear to be an important part of the markets, it is easy to understand that the lessee should acquire the interests of the others, using the building, of course, for its original purpose as required by the terms of the lease. When the transfer took place is unknown, but it was before 1858. Mr. Joseph M'Cormick got a lease of the Market Yard in October 1867 from the then owners, Messrs. Gunning and Moore, became the owner of the Stores, and on his death his widow, and not the new lessee, Mr. Fleming, was the owner. The subsequent history of the Stores is soon told; when the Great Northern Railway came to Cookstown, the old B.N.C. Railway Co., to protect their traffic, decided to run the line from the station yard to the Market Yard - a sensible and very convenient arrangement, but one which might not have been taken but for the competition. The Stores stood in the way, and to be able to run the line through the building the Railway Company purchased it from Mrs. M'Cormick in 1879. The Ground Rent of 1s. a year was subsequently purchased from the landlord, so that the London Midland and Scottish Railway Co. is now the owner in fee simple of the Stores which divide the two market yards, and had been erected through the public spirit of the men of two generations ago. The Stores, however, are still used for the original purpose, the change of ownership in no way affecting their use by merchants who need them for grain or grass-seed.

A word should be said about the building as such. It is a plain structure, four stories high, relieved only by dormers, which house the outside hoists, and in one part the hoist is inside. It is of solid masonry, with heavy beams, and we are assured that in no part has there ever been a crack. This may be regarded as not worth recording, but it is because the site on which it was erected was, at one time, a marsh, and, when it was built upon, the site must have been very soft. The foundations, no doubt, are wide, for the walls on the ground floor are 30 inches thick. Who the builder was we do not know, but the fact that one of the lessees was a carpenter, John Gibson, is a strong presumption that he had a good deal to do with it, and it remains a very substantial monument to those men, most of whom had no connection with the grain business, under Major Richardson-Brady, as he afterwards became, who, long before Co-operative Societies or limited liability companies were heard of, joined together and financed the erection of a building of such public utility. It is, in that way, that we venture to select the Stores as representing the self-relying spirit which has made Cookstown what it is - a spirit which we, of the present day, would do well to emulate.

In our next instalment (which will probably not appear till 26th July) we shall deal with some old maps which have just come to light, and which shed a great deal of light on the town as it was before, what we have called, the street-widening, but which really was town-planning of an altogether remarkable character.

# ADDENDUM

Since above had been put in type the writer has been enabled, through the courtesy of a friend, to see the Ordnance Map of 1833, and the first issued, and not now for sale. It shows the Market Place, as it is described, on the site of the present market yard. The next revision shows Molesworth Street for the first time, but with the boundary of the Market Yard on a line with the gable of the Stores. Subsequently the enclosing wall must have been built farther out, on a line with the front of

Mr. Cosgrove's house. The deeds of the latter, which have been placed at our disposal, do not recite anything earlier than 1847, when John O'Farrell got a lease of a tenement, or plot of ground, on which he was to build a substantial house within two years, but this was probably re-building an older house.

# MORE ABOUT TOWN PLANNING

## (26-7-1924)

We make no apology for reverting to the planning of the town, though it means going back to the middle of the 18th century, for, since we dealt with it last September and October, very important material has come to light, the existence of which was then unknown. This material takes the form of two old maps, with rentals or folios attached, which have been deposited, in the Record Office in Belfast. Regarding the Record Office, we may explain that with the blowing up and burning of the Four Courts in Dublin many valuable documents were destroyed, and the Northern Government decided to collect copies of as many as possible for reference. At the same time persons having original documents were invited to deposit them in the new Record Office: which is in charge of Dr. Chart and Mr. Heatley, two experienced officials from the old Record Office in Dublin. The first person to make a deposit of original documents was Mr. E. J. French, M.A., member of a well-known firm of solicitors in Dublin who had succeeded Messrs. C. & J. Gaussen, who were solicitors for the Killymoon estate at its sale in 1851. The result is that a map of Cookstown, dated 1726, has the honour of being officially designated "Original Document No. 1" in the new Record Office, while another map of Loy, Gortalowry, etc., is Document No. 3. We may just say, in passing, that any reader who has originals or copies of old wills, leases, or deeds of any description not required as proof of title to property owned by him, ought to forward them to Dr. Chart, of the Ministry of Finance, for deposit in the new Record Office.

Original Document No. 1 is described on its face as "Map of the land belonging to the Primacie of Armagh, held by William Stewart of Killymoon, Esq.", and it is signed by Arthur Atkinson and dated 1726. The scale is not given, but someone has subsequently written on it "about 60 or 65 perches to the inch". It is really five maps on one sheet, of five different estates leased by Mr. Stewart from the See of Armagh, as follows:-"The Sixteen towns of Cookstown in the parish of Derryloran:"

"The Thirteen towns of Ardtrea:" "The Nine towns in the parish of Ardboe:" "The Four in the parish of Carntael:" "The Four in the parish of Desertcreat", so that at that period the Stewarts held 46 townlands from the See of Armagh under leases, which were renewable, and in 1835 the Cookstown leases were converted into freeholds by the payment of a capital sum to the Primate. Attached to the map is a list of the tenants holding from Mr. Stewart, with the area of their holdings under the headings of arable land, moss, etc., moory land, scrub, and floe moss or bog. In addition to the Church lands, the townland of Tullagh, which was a freehold from the time of the Plantation when it was granted to a "native" gentlemen who sold to James Stewart, of Ballymenagh, is included.

The second map is evidently intended to supplement the former as it gives the rest of the freeholds which James Stewart had bought in 1632-34 and subsequently from the native proprietors – Loy, Gortalowry, Cullnafranky, Sullenboy, Maloon and also Tullagh. Attached to it is also a schedule of the tenants, with the area of the arable pasture and meadow of their holdings, the amount measured in for roads, and the size of the Loy, Maloon and Tullagh mosses, Cookstown moss and commons being given on the earlier map. This map is dated 1736, ten years after the former and was prepared by John Reed. Who that gentlemen was we do not know, but that he was connected with the estate in some capacity, probably as agent as well as surveyor, is shown by the following advertisment which appeared in the Belfast Newsletter of the autumn of 1759:-

## ADVT.

*That the house belonging to Mrs. Judith Avison, situate in Loy, adjoining to Cookstown, in the County of Tyrone (fronting the same street continued), containing 66 feet in front, two stories high and slated, with a good cellar, stable, cowhouse, garden, ten acres of good land convenient, and turf bog sufficient for the premises, are to be let to a solvent tenant from the first day of November next. Proposals will be received by the said Mrs. Judith Avison, or by Mr. John Reed at Killymoon.*

*N.B. – There is a good spring well convenient to said house, and turf cut for this year.*

A map of any estate as it was in 1736, showing the farms with the name of tenant, area, etc., must be interesting, but this map of the Stewart estate has a double interest which might not be appreciated by a stranger. For across it, running almost north and south, and obviously done after the map was completed, are six parallel straight lines as a schoolboy might draw with a ruler. The space between the inner four lines is almost exactly one-sixth of an inch; the outer lines are about half-an-inch from the next nearest. And lest there should be any doubt about their meaning, between the inner lines is the word "Street", and in one of the other spaces the other word "Gardings". In short, by a wonderful piece of good fortune, we have stumbled on the original plan of the new town of Cookstown, as designed by Mr. William Stewart some time between 1736 and 1750, and doubtless was carried out by John Reed.

We have said that the six lines run parallel, almost north and south. On the west side, however, the line which marked the back of the intended gardens stops at Loy Hill and two parallel lines are drawn there at right angles to a little circle which is Tullagh Fort, and thence, at a wide angle two other lines run to the river and across it to the next estate, which was then known as Manor Annesley, a huge house appearing on the north side with the name Mr. Henderson. That this design, evidently the original, was actually followed is shown by the fact that the road laid out to Tullagh is wider at the end next the proposed main street until it reaches the boundary of Loy and Tullagh mosses, and is the present Fair Hill, which everyone knows narrows just before it gets to the Sports Field. North of the Fair Hill no line bounding the proposed gardens is shown on the west side, and this reminds us of the terms of some of the leases in William and Oldtown Street - so many feet of frontage, and "extending back to the bog". In subsequent leases the extent is defined, the boundary being in a line with the gardens in Loy and Gortalowry, though the actual gardens are longer, the surplus being held as a yearly tenancy with the object of providing for a new street. Finally, as regards the south end of the town, beyond the Drum Road and the road to Killymoon only the two inner lines are shown: that is the wide roadway, but not the frontage of the houses nor gardens.

Next Week we shall give more details gleaned from these remarkable maps.

# THE 1726-36 MAPS (Continued)

## (2-8-1924)

Last week we described the finding of two old maps of Cookstown and vicinity, dated 1726 and 1736, and how, on the latter, the outline of the new town of Cookstown was drawn. The first question which must have occurred to anyone who was able to visualise our description was - where was Cookstown before that time? We confess that what the maps show amazed us. We wrote, last September and October, of the street widening, and our conception of the town before that event was that it was a place, perhaps like Stewartstown (without the Square), a long narrow and, more or less, straight line of houses on each side of the roadway. But the maps prove conclusively that it was nothing of the sort.

The map of 1726 shows a little square plot on the west side of the roadway somewhere about Oldtown Hill. The only physical feature by which its location can be determined is the Burn, which was the boundary between the townlands of Cookstown and Loy, and this would fix the location of the plot about the top of the hill but it might be on either the north or south slope. In the schedule attached this plot, No.12, is described as "William McClellan's tenements", and the area is 1 rood 10 perches. This is, of course, Irish measure, and equal to half an acre statute. It is shown as square in shape, which would give a frontage of 49 or 50 yards. How many houses were on this little plot we cannot say, as they are given together as "tenements" with Wm. McClellan the tenant. This half-acre plot is in the corner of a farm (shown as one field though probably divided), and on the farm a house is drawn. The tenant was "James Alleine", and the area of the farm was 31a. 1r. 22p., with 2 acres of moss, or about 54 acres statute.

On the opposite side of the roadway was another farm of 30a. 6p. (about 49 acres statute) with a house sitting away back belonging to Robert Rutherford. The lane between the artisans' houses and Mr. Joseph Allen's new houses might have been the old farm lane to this house. At the southern corner of the farm, and just opposite Wm. M'Clellan's tenements, was Rutherford's garden, measuring 1a. 3r. 24p., and to the north of it another plot of ground, of about the same size, i.e., 1a. 3r. 6p., which gives a frontage about 350 feet. This plot appears on the schedule as "John M'Clellan's tenements". Now the astonishing thing is this :- In 1736, a century after Dr. Allen Cook had leased the land and got a charter for a market and fair, which were both flourishing, the only houses in what is now the Urban District of Cookstown, except one house on the Drum Road, were these two little tenements. All the rest was agricultural land or bog. What we called the street-widening was simply the lay-out of an entirely new town. The houses were not set back because there were no houses; the street was not widened for it did not exist.

It is really difficult to appreciate this fact, and till we do it is impossible to appreciate what Mr. William Stewart undertook in the middle of the 18$^{th}$ century. Instead of being a long row of houses like Stewartstown, as we imagined, Cookstown, in 1726, simply consisted of two blocks of houses, the entire area of which was just under 3½ statute acres. The place which is nearest it, in this district, is the Rock, though it is flattering old Cookstown to make the comparison, for the houses were undoubtedly poor and it is doubtful if there were so many. Yet if we take the Rock as a comparison we will begin to appreciate the vision of Wm. Stewart. What would be thought if the local landowner should take down a map of the Rock and proceed to lay out on it a town with the main street over a mile long, straight across the fields and over two bogs? A street with 120 feet distance between the proposed houses, and gardens behind and to each building plot would be attached a portion of land as town parks. We fear that doubts would be expressed as to his sanity, yet that is what Mr. Wm. Stewart did, and the event proved that he was quite sane. Cookstown, as a town, does not owe anything, except its name, to Dr. Allen Cooke, who founded it, nor to his successor, Mr. James Stewart, of Ballymenagh, who purchased Cooke's lease, nor to his son, Mr. William Stewart, the first of the Stewarts of Killymoon, but to the latter's grandson it does owe all that characterises it from towns which simply grew in a formless and aimless manner.

Next to the insignificance of the "town" up to 1736, the most striking fact shown in the maps is the extent of bog. We are reminded that John Wesley, in one of his earlier itineraries about 1773, described it as a long street running through a bog. Had he visited it thirty years earlier he would have been wrong, for the street did not exist at all, though the bogs did. To get to the town of that time he would, on crossing the river at Derryloran, have climbed the hill to where the road branches out. Taking the left he would have gone by Chapel Hill, the Cemetery and straight on behind the Workhouse to Morgan's Hill and thence to the Oldtown – all names well known to our town readers, but which were then unknown. On the other hand, had Wesley been coming from Derry, as he did later, and wanted to call at Killymoon he would have taken a road over Oldtown Hill, which cut across from about Steenson's gateway to the Royal Hotel, but has now completely disappeared. The continuation of this main road is still in existence, being the laneway past the Lime Kilns and on over the Midland Railway to the present Coagh Road. On the south side of the Coagh Road it has disappeared, like other bits of lanes which were closed when the new

Coagh Road was made, but beyond Mr. Kidd's farm another length of the old road remains and comes out on the Ardtrea road. Its route can still be traced by hedges in spite of the interference by the G.N. Railway line till it reaches Killymoon Demesne. Finally, we may mention that from Killymoon a road ran direct to Greenvale (as it is now named), joining with the main road already mentioned.

These were the main roads to and from Cookstown before 1736; they are now lanes or back-roads where they exist at all, being replaced by the main street. The reason for what must appear so circuitous routes was simply that they avoided the bogs. These bogs are well shown in the two maps. Starting with Wm. M'Clennon's tenement, on the west side of Oldtown Hill, what is called Cookstown common moss, lies to the west and south to the burn which divides it from Loy and Tullagh mosses. The bridge on the Burn Road is the point where the three townlands met in the moss which not only came over the line of James Street and the Market Yard on the one side of Loy Hill, but continued right across to the Sports Field on the other side, and across it by the Fever Hospital in Sullenboy, crossing the line of the street again where Derryloran Schools now are. The new main street of the town, planned by Mr. Stewart, ran right over three hills and through two bogs, with a width of 120 feet from house to house. Along it building sites, apparently 105 feet as a general rule, were leased in perpetuity to persons to build houses, the lease including gardens running back 21 perches, and with grazing or arable lands somewhere convenient, for it should be noted that what we now call townparks were, in 1736, simply agricultural land occupied by farmers.

The next point of interest is the names of these farmers across whose lands the town was laid out, or who lived adjacent. Two names have already been given – James Alleine, who had 33½ acres on the west of the Oldtown, and Robert Rutherford, who had 32 acres on the other side, both having houses in the middle of their farms - not in the "town". On the south side of Oldtown Hill, from the moss to Tullagh, was all one farm of 70 Irish acres (say 114 statute acres), all arable, for the moss on it was the common moss of Cookstown. Loy moss, which lay south of the Burn Road, was 12¼ acres in extent, and south of it on the rising ground, was the farm of David Acheson, 33½ acres Irish, while Samuel Fleming held the rest of Loy, almost the same area, which takes us out to New Buildings. The tenants there or in Tullygare, Cranfield, Drumern or Drumgarrel are not given, presumably because their lands were not required for the proposed town, but in Clare we find Widow Brisbane with 40 acres of arable land and 6½ acres mossy land and bog, and another tenant named Thompson with 36a. 3r. of arable land. In Coolnahavil were also two tenants, John Nixon with 22½ acres, and John Black with 16¼ acres, and in Ardcumber, due south of Nixon, was a farmer named Adams with 33 acres of arable land. The rest of Ardcumber measured then 56 acres good land with 13 acres scrub next the river. In the townland of Gortalowry, close to Killymoon on the border of Coolnafranky and just outside the demesne and therefore convenient to the Presbyterian Church, the Rev. Mr. M'Cleaor, the minister, occupied 12 acres of land; between him and the road, Mr. Wm. Leadley had the same area. The latter, however, lived in a house north of what is now Drum Road, and occupied the land to the south, as far as the river and the boundary of Coolnahavil, this farm being 30 acres in area. Two adjoining farmers were John Moore, with 9½ a. and Wm. Black, 34½ acres, both along the main road, which was measured into them, 22 and 36 perches respectively.

The rest of Gortalowry, all the land from the river around the bridge, now Greenvale Mill and Factory and all up along the river presently owned by Mr. Adair, was in the occupation of two men - John Harkley in the north and from the fort south by Hugh Goorley, Esq., whose acreage was 27½ acres Irish. That the latter should have got the description of "Esq." from the map-maker in 1737, though he had considerably less land than Wm. Leadley who got "Mr." to his name, or than many of the others, leads one to believe that he was in a better social position and may have been engaged in bleaching at Greenvale before the Faulkners, Pattesons, or Cook, who are the earliest persons we know positively were in the linen business there up to the 19th century.

Another name appears, not on the schedule of tenants, but on the map itself by way of a note. This is Mr. Oliver. His land appears between Leadleys and Killymoon, the house being also on the north of the Drum Road and in the line of the gardens. It is the only house, other than the two tenements, in the Oldtown, which was in what became the Urban District. Across the field were drawn only two lines, marking the new roadway, but not lines of houses, and the note on the map reads, "In the space marked 151 in Mr. Oliver's field, at 120 feet broad, down from the road to ye (illegible) there is 1a. 1r. 31p. B 2a. 2r. 0p." B refers to the plot of land or field to the end of the road. The meaning of the map in relation to Mr. Oliver is doubtful; possibly Mr. Wm. Stewart was undecided whether to take 2¼ acres statute in the middle of his field to make a wide roadway which would lead nowhere because the bridge at the Waterpower Co., nor the road to it, had not been then built. Mr. Oliver was possibly not an ordinary tenant farmer for, in 1790, a Mrs. Oliver was associated with the Viscountess Lifford and the Hon. Mrs. Stewart in starting Derryloran Sabbath School, which was a flourishing institution. In August of that year there were 100 children at the school learning to read and write in addition to getting "instruction on the principles of religion and morality" under the direction of "those very amiable and benevolent characters" – the three ladies mentioned, with the support of subscription from the gentry of Cookstown and the parish. In 1795 no less than 493 children had passed through the Sunday School, and there were then on the roll 230, "but the number of subscriptions being very limited, and the funds barely sufficient to defray the expense of books and teachers", money for prizes was being raised by means of a ball to be held at Henry's Inn on Tuesday 29th December – Admission, gentlemen 3s 3d; ladies 2s 8½d. An Oliver was also connected with the early brewery, and four persons of that name, Stephen Oliver, deceased, and his sons William, Andrew and James Oliver, are referred to in the lease dated 1776 to David Richardson, of the premises now owned by Mr. S. A. Lewis on Oldtown Hill, with two houses on the east side 170 feet in front (the property north of Harbisons), 10 acres of land in New Buildings, 5½ acres in Monrush and 3 roods of turf bog.

To return to our maps – only three other farmers are mentioned. In Maloon, John Maxwell had 43 acres and John Hagan, to the north, had 8 acres odd, while apparently the rest was in the occupation of Hugh Rinkin.

Ballymenagh was probably still occupied by the Stewarts. At that date there were 90 acres arable ground, 9 acres mossy, besides 4 acres of bog and no less than 29½ acres of scrub. To-day it is one of the best farms in the district, not because of its natural fertility, but chiefly through the industry of successive generations, and the same may be said to be the case with most of the other land around Cookstown.

In giving Mr. Wm. Stewart credit for taking a long view of planning for the future we feel also bound to say that he pushed his ideas of straight roads too far. We feel sure that the good folk of Aughlish, Gortnaglough and Mackney will agree with that view when we mention that, before the town was laid out, there was a branch from the road past the cemetery, which joined it at what is now Farley's farm, and ran along the south side of Tullagh hill towards Orritor. Our town planners, however, decided on a Fair Hill on a road at right angles to the top of Loy Hill, and carried it on up the top of Tullagh hill, where it got the bend which connected it to the Orritor Road and the former road, still traceable, was abandoned. As every boy knows, who ever went to bathe in Tullagh, it is a bad climb up the hill and a steep drop down at right angles, both of which could be avoided and were avoided by the road of 1736, and it is worse for farmers from Aughlish direction who have to cart their produce into Cookstown. The discovery had been made that a straight line is the nearest way between two points, and this discovery was being applied to roads, but Mr. Stewart or his technical adviser John Reed, pushed it to an extreme in this instance at least.

One other reference might be made to the map. On it is shown the Commons of old Cookstown, at the extreme north of the townland bounded by Monrush, Coolreaghs and Killymam. The area of the Commons and street is given as 4a. 0r. 13p., or about 6½ acres statute, and, as the townland boundary would not have changed owing to Coolreaghs being on a different estate, we know pretty well where these Commons were – at the corner of the new Lissan Road and probably on both sides of it.

Next Week – The Ordnance Survey.

Oldtown, Cookstown.

# THE ORDNANCE SURVEY

# (9 – 8 –1924)

So accustomed have we become to reliance on the Ordnance Survey that it is difficult to understand how people got on without having such an authoritative and reliable source of information. Yet the first Ordnance Maps of this district were published so recently as ninety years ago; before that time the only maps available were estate maps, or the productions of private surveyors which were far from reliable, and, at best, gave only parts of the country. The Government, however, undertook a complete survey of Ireland, and, in 1833, this was carried out in our district by Captain Wright and Lieut. Bailey, of the Royal Engineers, with a staff of "sappers". Not being either a private, or a commercial, undertaking, the work was done in a thorough manner, regardless of cost, and, while it must have appeared to many economists of the day to be a great waste of energy and money, no one now disputes the value of the undertaking. The scale was six inches to the mile; the survey has been revised at intervals since then; in 1909 a map, showing every field and its area, was issued on the scale of 15 inches to the mile, while the town plan of Cookstown is on the scale of 60 inches. Smaller scale maps have been also issued - one inch, half inch and quarter-inch to the mile, but one and all are based on the original survey of 1833, when the field work was preceded by a very exact trigonometrical survey. The best talent available was employed in it; Mr. Drummond, afterwards the famous Under-Secretary for Ireland, was one of the engineers, and be invented the oxy-hydrogen limelight, so much used in "magic" lanterns, to get the signals from Fair Head in Antrim to Slieve Snaght in Co. Donegal, but the survey as a whole, will ever be associated with the name of Larcom, who was the officer in charge.

The earliest map, published in 1834, is not now obtainable, but by the kindness of a friend we have been able to study a tracing of it which gives us some physical features of Cookstown and immediate district at that period. Last week we described the roads which were shown on the estate map of 1726-36 starting at Derryloran Bridge, and then keeping round by Chapel Hill and the Cemetery, behind the Workhouse and over Morgan's Hill to the Oldtown, on the west side of the town and the other road on the east side which cut across from Oldtown Hill at an angle to the old road by the Lime Kilns and thence southward to Killymoon. When our attention had been thus directed to it we see, at a glance, the same roads in the 1833 map, down the centre of which, like a back bone, lies the wide street of Cookstown laid out by Mr. Wm. Stewart. A bit of the road then abandoned, which was to the south of Tullagh Fort, was still to be seen, and the rest of the old road is complete; on the west, the portion to Coagh Street had been built over in 1833, but the remainder was also complete, running due south from the boundary of New Buildings to where it joined the lower Killymoon avenue, close to the castle. This lower avenue seems to have been the main road to Killymoon, as the present avenue was not even fenced, being simply shown as a road through the demesne.

The King's Bridge, as the bridge over the river at the Waterpower Factory is named, was built before 1833, and, of course, the road cut through Linen Hill connecting the town with it, and the extension to the "Finger Boards", and the Demesne was then walled in, though the work must have been done not long before. The walling of the demesne was due, it is stated, to some bullocks having been stolen from Killymoon - an expensive way of preventing such larceny, for in spite of the low rate of wages in the 19$^{th}$ century, it cost a fortune. It was carried out by Colonel Wm. Stewart; we have not been able to fix the date, but it must have been very soon before the Ordnance Survey. There is a story about old Mr. Greer of Tullylagan, or New Hambors as he named the place, who belonged to the Society of Friends. Riding into the town he passed the masons at work, and Col. Stewart overseeing them. The latter remarked to Mr. Greer, "You see I am building myself in", to which the shrewd Quaker replied, "Friend, take care that thou does not build thyself out" – which gives an idea of what his neighbours thought of Col. Stewart's expensive undertaking.

Perhaps the most important difference in the map of 1833 and the present day conditions, is that, at that time, Molesworth Street and Road did not exist. The "Market Place" is there, but no roadway except the front street. The way to Coagh then was by the present Coagh Street and old Coagh Road; when Molesworth Street was opened, which was done before 1836 (as the lease to the Stores proves), it was taken alongside the Market Yard and round by an easy gradient to the great cross-roads from Cookstown to Ardtrea, now known as Fountain's Road. At the same time, a short bit of road connected with the old road from the Lime Kilns which had already a bit of road on the east side. This was continued in a fairly good gradient through New Buildings, skirting Tullyagre and in to Cranfield, whence it ran direct to Littlebridge, the junction of this road and the Old Coagh Road being subsequent to the 1854 survey.

One of the striking things about the 1833 map is the number of quarries then open. Everyone passing along Coagh Street is acquainted with the sunken yard of what used to be the "Greyhound Hotel", and one has only to look across the street to see the houses built on the solid limestone. Obviously the yard referred to (known to the last generation as the ball alley) had been created by quarrying out the limestone. The O.S. map of 1833 shows that, and also that at that period there was actually a lime kiln in the middle of the quarry, which adjoined the back of the gardens. Another lime kiln in its own quarry (three are shown) was further along the old road, north of the railway where the quarries are being still worked. Again, in New Buildings, extensive limestone quarries are shown. The short bit of road mentioned above was obviously made to get at them and ran up north into them and back at right angles. Further on, in Tullygare was still another quarry, with a lime kiln in it.

In the townland of Clare, north of the Ardtrea road, and alongside what was the old road from New Buildings to Killymoon, was another kiln in its own quarry, represented today by a hollow in the field, while south of the Ardtrea road and to the west of the G.N. Railway line was still another limestone quarry, making six quarries, with four kilns, on or near the road between the Oldtown and Killymoon.

Again we find a limestone quarry at the angle of the "Sweep Road", as it is called – the south west corner where the broad road from Derryloran to Killymoon intersected the continuation of the main street. Anyone today would recognise this field as the remains of a quarry, but few would guess that limestone had been quarried there, for 100 yards to the north are the great freestone quarries worked so extensively 50 years ago, while 300 yards to the south are also freestone quarries worked less than a dozen years ago.

This does not exhaust the list of quarries. Close to the road past Chapel Hill and just across the way from the New Cemetery was another limestone quarry worked in 1833, and 220 yards off, to the west of the circular road was a freestone quarry. Finally, in Killymam, there was an old freestone quarry in 1833, which must be the quarry about one mile north-west of the Workhouse, stated in the Geological Survey to have provided the stones for Killymoon Castle. Subsequently, near the Workhouse, was opened another freestone quarry on the Orritor Road, now devoted to dumping mud from the streets of Cookstown, where the stone was got which built most of the houses in Molesworth Street.

This extraordinary number of quarries, shown on the O.S. map of 1833, has led one observer to remark that quarrying was the industry which made Cookstown. That, however, is hardly the case. No doubt the freestone from the large Gortalowry quarry was worked very extensively, and the stone was taken to Belfast for good public buildings, while the newer quarry at the Linen Hall provided stone which was said to be equal to Portland stone, and both gave a good deal of employment. The limestone quarries also gave employment to men to raise stone for burning and selling as quick-lime, and we still have this industry with us, providing employment for a score or so of men, year after year. But the multiplicity of quarries in 1833 was due, we think, chiefly to the demand for building stone for new houses in the town – the town created the quarries rather than the quarries the town. When it is remembered that all the houses in the town, built as they were of stone and lime, were erected from about 1750, the demand for ma'erial must have been very considerable, and, of course, created a fresh demand for the houses for the masons and carpenters.

Before leaving this map of 1833, reference should be made to one other feature on it – a nursery laid out behind (to the east) of the Gortalowry quarry. The main street was planted with trees along both sides, and on every hill, or fort, was a ring of scotch firs as can still be seen, and there is no doubt that Colonel Stewart started the nursery with the object of providing young trees for use on his own estate outside the demesne.

The Ordnance Surveyors did not confine themselves to map making, but collected information of other sorts, and next week we hope to give an article based on the Name Book of Derryloran Parish.

# THE MARKET IN 1819

## (16 – 8 – 1924)

Though we know of the Ordnance Survey of 1833 chiefly in connection with maps, the reason for its appointment was to revise the valuation of lands and other hereditaments. Prior to that date, money for public purposes, chiefly for road-making, was assessed (hence the word "cess") on land according to the area, without regard to the quality. The unfairness of this was realised when the rates began to rise, and, in 1825, a Boundary Survey was set up, and the first thing to be done was to have an accurate survey of the whole country. The townland was taken as the unit; it is not clear how individual residents divided the cess between them, but, in view of the previous practice, it is probable that it was in proportion to the acreage held by each. That is to say, each townland was valued according to the productiveness of the land and the scale of prices, and an amount was assessed on it, and then each occupier in that townland had to contribute according to the size of his farm. Subsequently, in 1838, the Poor Relief Act was passed and the townland valuation was abolished for the present system of valuing each man's tenement separately. Griffith's valuation came later, in 1852.

The present writer was fortunate enough to get access, before the upheaval in Dublin, to the Name Book prepared by the surveyors for Derryloran Parish. These books give a certain amount of information regarding the different townlands, to be used, apparently, for valuation purposes.  Under the heading of Cookstown townland we read:- *Town parks; very good land, highly cultivated; plenty of limestone; £2 to £3 per acre.*

Cookstown in 1833 is described as follows by the Ordnance Surveyors:

*Is a market and post town, composed of three parts which go by the several denominations of Cookstown, Loy and Gortalowry, together forming a street 1¼ miles in length, standing very nearly N and S; ornamented through Loy and Gortalowry with a row of fine trees on each side.  The inhabitants may be estimated at about 5,000.*

*The proprietor of the town is Colonel Stewart, of Killymoon.  The Church, finished in 1821, and build after a design by Mr. Nash, the celebrated architect, is a very pretty Gothic building, with a handsome façade.  It is large enough to accommodate the numbers which attend. There is also a Presbyterian and a Seceding Meeting House as well as a Roman Catholic Church a little way from the town, and two Methodist Churches.*

*A fair is held on the first Saturday of every month for the sale of horses, cows, pigs and sheep.  It is considered a good fair for cows and pigs, but not at all good for horses or sheep.  A weekly market is held every Saturday for the sale of linen, yarn, pork, butter, potatoes, meal, and other produce.  The average number of slaughtered pigs sold at each market for six months is about 100; carts of potatoes from 40 to 50; sacks of meal about 30; crocks of butter about 100.  The town is tolerably well supplied with butcher's meat, but not very well with fish, vegetables, or milk.  A corn market is held every Tuesday, from 180 to 100 sacks of oats are sold during the season.  The fairs and markets are Custom free, except for sales from standings in the street, which pay 1d each.  Charge of Craneage, 2d for each pig or crock of butter; meal 1d per cwt.*

Such is the Ordnance Survey's description of Cookstown in 1833, a few years before the Stores were built.  The pork market was only in the cold weather, six months in the year; the butter was sold in crocks, and there was a regular weekly sale of oatmeal.  The latter, of course, has disappeared.

The absence of mention of eggs will be noticed, for at present the egg trade is the most flourishing in the Saturday market, the stores gradually encroaching on the butter sheds.  In 1833 eggs were not reckoned as of much value.  Indeed, we were assured by the late Mr. Thomas Wallis, the station master of the N.C. Railway, that in his early days it was regarded as undignified for a farmer's wife to sell eggs, and he recounted how he used to watch women coming in with baskets hidden under their long cloaks, which they handed over surreptitiously to dealers. Other days – other manners; today the egg shippers are the aristocrats of the market, and the egg the only branch of agriculture boasting of an inspector all to itself.

As explained above, the name books give a report on the soil of each townland. They also give the names of each, and until this date there was no official spelling. The practice was for the surveyor to consult the local rector (who was a sort of parochial official as well as a clergyman), the landlord or any others who might be expected to know the correct spelling. The surveyors were generally Englishmen and did not profess a knowledge of Gaelic, but the Government retained the services of a number of Irish scholars to advise. This district was fortunate in being in charge of Dr. O'Donovan, who visited the locality, and when there was doubt regarding a townland name he got the people to pronounce it for him, and in that way he got as near as possible to the correct word. He went over the Name Books and wrote in the Gaelic spelling, with the meaning of the name. This was done before the mapping took place, apparently, as the name book for Derryloran is dated 1819. That his etymology is correct in every case would be too much to expect for, as Dr. Joyce points out in his work on Irish Names of Places, the words became corrupted. Loy is a good example; O'Donovan found nothing else but the one syllable, but, from the deeds, we know that it is a contraction of a much longer word with several aliases. Another apt illustration of how names get corrupted is Coolnafranky. Had the surveyors consulted the original grant to Mary Neill, or referred to the baronial map of 1609, it would have been seen that the name there was Coolnafrangen, and O'Donovan would have seen that instead of the "corner of the rate", the meaning of the townland name would be "corner of the bilberry" or blaeberry, as the Scotch call it.

Next week we shall give the full list of townland names in Derryloran parish, with O'Donovan's meaning for each, and also the average yield of wheat, oats, potatoes and flax, which was the basis of the townland valuation.

## TOWNLAND NAMES AND PRODUCTIVENESS

## (23 – 8 –1924)

Last week we explained that the Ordnance Surveyors reported, in the Name Books, on each townland. Where there was doubt regarding the name they collected all the varieties which they found, and these were considered by the Surveyor-General and the official name settled, with the English spelling. This may seem a small thing, but when one remembers that there are sounds in Gaelic which are not represented by English letters, it is obvious that, even where there was doubt regarding the name, they collected all the varieties which they found, and these were considered by the Surveyor-General and the official name settled, with the English spelling. This may seem a small thing, but when one remembers that there are sounds in Gaelic which are not represented by English letters, it is obvious that even where there was a well-established Gaelic pronunciation, the official spelling was a problem. One well known case is that of the big townland of Broughderg. If any reader cares to make the experiment, let him ask an English or Scottish commercial traveller to pronounce that name as he sees it, and also ask any person resident in the upper part of Lissan or Kildress parish what the name really is, and he will be struck by the difference. The Surveyors had a difficult task in representing the breathing sound of Gaelic in letters which were meant to convey Latin sounds only. Nor is that the only difficulty they had; on the contrary, there were many instances in which the Director General had to decide which of two current names was correct. A striking example is that of a townland below Coagh – Drumconvis. That is the only name one hears nowadays, and it was the name used by the map makers in 1609. But the Surveyors found that Drumconaway was also used, and the Director unfortunately adopted it; and it is today the official name. We do not know why he selected this alias – possibly he was misled by some local person in authority, who impressed the Surveyors with his knowledge; it often happens that the man who is most emphatic in such matters is wrong.

Appended is the list of townlands in Derryloran parish, with the meaning of the names as given by Dr. O'Donovan, and also a general description of the soil, and definite figures giving the average yield of the principal crops – wheat in hundred-weights per acre: oats in bushels per acre: potatoes in bushels per acre, and flax in stones to the peck.

**Derryloran** - Loran's Oak Wood. *Authority Rev. Wm. Mauleverer, rector. Part in the barony of Loughinsholin, Co. Derry, and part in the Dungannon barony, County Tyrone. Area 12,100 acres, greater part of which is highly cultivated. Abounds in limestone which is much used for manure. Soil light, easily cultivated, produces good general crops. There are many freestone quarries employed in building. Rivers – Loughrey and Kildress rivers are joined in Killymoon Demesne and take the name of Ardtrea river. They are not navigable. Plenty of trout; a few salmon are taken near Kildress bridge. The only manufacture is linen.*

**Annahavil** – Marsh of the Orchard. *There is a large flax mill in this townland; it belongs to the Drapers' Company.*

**Ardcumber** – Hill of the confluence

**Ardvarnish** – (No meaning given) *Property of Mr. Colquhoun. Average rent 15s per Irish acre, 12 cwt. wheat, 50 bus. oats, 290 bus. potatoes, 3 stone flax to the peck. Bog purchased in the neighbourhood at the rate of £4 per annum.*

**Aughlish** – (No meaning given). *Property of the Earl of Castlestewart. Average rent £1 per acre. Contains large piece of uncultivated land on the top of Aughlish hill. It is tolerable grazing, capable of producing very good crops, and will soon be all under cultivation. Soil cold and stiff loam, 18 cwt. wheat; 50 bus. oats, 3½ st. flax.*

**Ballyforlea** - Town of the Grey Man. *Property of the Drapers Company, rent £1 per Irish acre. All under cultivation. Bog is obtained in Ballyloughan; as much may be got for 9s. as will be sufficient for the general run of houses; 20cwt. wheat, 70 bus. oats, 600 bus. potatoes, 3 st. flax.*

**Ballygroogan** – Groogan's town. *Cold clay land, contains considerable quantity of bog and uncultivated ground. The property of Theodore Bailie, Tirnaskea; 14 cwt. wheat, 45 bus. oats, 310 bus. potatoes, 3½ st. flax.*

**Ballynasollus** – Town of the lights. *Property of Earl of Castlestewart. Light and gravelly soil, only small portion under cultivation, 12s. to 16s. per acre, 30 bus. oats, 180 bus. potatoes. Bog given free.*

**Ballyloughan** – Town of the small lough. *One third part uncultivated. Rent of arable land £1; 19 cwt. wheat, 75 bus. oats, 220 bus. potatoes, 3½ st. flax.*

**Ballymenagh** – Middle town. *Property of Col. Stewart. £1 per acre. Good land, all under cultivation except two small pieces of bog. Soil red till. There is a tradition that a royal family of the name of Mallon had the seat of their government at Ballymena. There are people of the name of Mallon at Kirktown.*

**Ballyreagh** – Grey-town. *Property of Col. Stewart. Rent 22s per acre, 12cwt. wheat, 45 bus. Oats, 240 bus. potatoes, 3 st. flax. The inhabitants purchase turf by the load, brought from the mountains.*

**Ballysudden** – Sodan's town.. *Property of J. Lindesay. Good land, nearly all under cultivation; rent 14s to 40s per acre. Bog purchased in Strews at the rate of £3 per acre. Limestone quarry.*

**Claggan** – A rocky hill. *Property of Col. Stewart. All under cultivation; soil light and sandy. Rent 16s 6d to 25s. per acre, 40 bus. oats, 150 bus. potatoes, no wheat sown. Lime used as manure, brought* *from Cookstown at 10d per barrel. Fuel from Drumgarrell bog free of rent. No quarries or gravel pits; roads repaired with river gravel.*

**Clare** – A table or plain. *Property of Col. Stewart. Rent 35s per Irish acre. Nearly all under cultivation. Abundance of limestone; 20 cwt. wheat, 50 bus. oats, 310 bus. potatoes, 4st. flax. Bog free.*

**Cloghog** – Stoney land. *Drapers Company's property. Nearly all under cultivation; contains several freestone quarries. Rent 20s per acre, 12 cwt. wheat, 50 bus. Oats, 190 bus. potatoes, 3½ st. flax. Part of this townland taken into Killymoon demesne, and is planted.*

**Cluntydoon** – Lawns of the fort. *Property of the Earl of Castlestewart. Not more than half under cultivation. Great quantity of mountain bog and bad land. Rent 14s per acre; 35 bus. oats, 180 bus. potatoes. Bog free. Lime obtained at Gortreagh, 7½d per bushel.*

**Coolkeeghan** – Keeghan's corner or angle. *Property of Jas. Lowry, of Rockdale. Very good land, all under cultivation. No bog, rent 28s per acre; 14 cwt. wheat, 55 bus. oats, 290 bus. potatoes, 3½st flax. Bog £3 per acre.*

**Coolnafranky** – Corner or angle of the rate. *Property of Col. Stewart. Let to inhabitants of Cookstown at £3 per acre for town parks. Very good land, all under cultivation.*

**Coolnahavil** – Corner or angle of the orchard. *Very small townland, the property of Col. Stewart, the greater part of it in his own hands. It is chiefly pasture and plantation; part is in the demesne.*

**Coolreaghs** – Grey backs. *The property of Sir Thos. Staples. Nearly all under cultivation; a considerable part of the bog on the Lissan Road is not yet reclaimed; 18 cwt. wheat, 50 bus. oats, 250 bus. potatoes; bog free at Fegarron.*

**Craigs** – Rocks. *Property of Earl Castlestewart. Rent 10s to 18s per acre, bog free; 45 bus. oats, 220 bus. potatoes. Land too light for wheat. Not more that half under cultivation, rest bog and rocky ground. There is rather a singular rock forming a head line which is a conspicuous object in the country. It is probable that the name of Craigs was derived from it. Cornmill.*

**Cranfield** – Wood of the wild garlic. *Property of Col. Stewart. Rent 30s; bog free from Drumgarrell; 15 cwt. wheat, 65 bus. oats, 280 bus. potatoes, 4 st. flax.*

**Derrycrummy** – Oak wood of the hunched back. *Drapers' Company's property; good land. Nearly all under cultivation; small quantity bog. Rent 30s; 11 cwt. wheat, 50 bus. oats, 200 bus. potatoes, 3 st. flax. Bog 9s per holding.*

**Derryloran.** *Property of Colonel Stewart. Rent 21s; 17 cwt. wheat, 60 bus. oats, 250 bus. potatoes, 3½ st. flax. No bog; bought at £4 per acre.*

**Doorless** – Strong fort. *Property of John Lindesy of Loughry. Rent not yet known, being under lease, 20 cwt. wheat, 60 bus. oats, 300 bus. potatoes, bog free. There is a curious old fort, of an oval shape, with parapet on top. The exterior of it is now entirely covered with thick wood. The interior is converted into a garden.*

**Drumcraw** – Ridge of the cattle folds. *Property of Col. Stewart. Land pretty good but small quantity almost exhausted bog. Rent 25s; 12 cwt. wheat, 50 bus. oats, 280 bus. potatoes, 3½st. flax.*

**Drumgarrell** – Correll's ridge. *Property of Col. Stewart. Good land, considerable part white bog, rent 25s. 13 cwt. wheat, 50 bus. oats, 270 bus. potatoes, 3½ st. flax. Mr. Magill has a bleach green here but it has not been in use for the last five or six years since the linen trade has been on the decline.*

**Drumard** – High ridge, or long hill. *Property of Earl Castlestewart almost all under cultivation, except a large piece of exhausted bog on Kildress road; rent 16s per acre; 18 cwt. wheat, 60 bus. oats, 210 bus. potatoes, 3½ st. flax. Bog free.*

**Drumearn** – Ridge of the alders. *Property of Col. Stewart. Rent 15s to 20s per acre; strong, cold land, considerable quantity of mountainy bog and rocky uncultivated ground, particularly on the west side of the townland. Very little wheat grown; 45 bus. oats, 250 bus. potatoes, lime obtained from Gortreagh at 7½d per bushel.*

**Drummond** – A ridge. *A very small townland; the great part of it has been taken into the demesne. Rent 21s per acre.*

**Drumrot** – Red ridge. *Property of the Drapers' Co. A very small townland, all under cultivation, rent 20s per acre, 20 cwt. wheat, 70 bus. oats, 200 bus. potatoes.*

**Dunman** – Fort of the points. *Drapers' Co. property, all under cultivation. Rent 25s; 10 cwt. wheat, 55 bus. oats, 200 bus. potatoes, 2½ st. flax. Bog 9s per lot.*

**Feegarron** – Geran's wood. *Property of Sir Thomas Staples; rent 14s per acre. Mountainous townland, the greater part of which is yet uncultivated. Contains a great deal of rocky land which can never be of much value. Soil gravelly and poor. No wheat, 35 bus. oats, 250 bus. potatoes. Bog 5s per rood for cutting and drying.*

**Galla Nagh** – White marsh. *Property of John Lindesay of Loughry. Very good land, all under cultivation; contains excellent limestone; no bog. Rent 28s per acre; 18 cwt. wheat, 50 bus. oats, 300 bus potatoes, 3½ st. flax.*

(To be continued)

# NOTE

Quarries – In regard to the numerous quarries noted close to Cookstown by the Ordnance Surveyors it has been suggested that besides providing building stone and lime for burning, they were used for road repairs. This is true; until quite recently limestone was used on the smaller roads.

# DERRYLORAN TOWLANDS
## (continued)

## (30 – 8 – 1924)

**Glebe (Derryloran***). Good land, excellent house is situated on the glebe; grounds very ornamental with plantation. Rev. Dr. Bardin is the present incumbent. Ruins of old church on the glebe; burial ground still used.*

**Gortalowry** – O'Lavery's field. *Property of Col. Stewart. Rent £2 to £3, part town of Cookstown. The parish church is situated here. There is excellent freestone and limestone quarries. There is no bog. There is a bleach green near Derryloran bridge. R.C. Chapel and flax mill here.*

**Gortin** – Small garden. *Property of Earl of Castlestewart; soil, light clay and sand. All under cultivation; bog obtained from the neighbouring townland on the estate. Here is a very large fort of oval shape, comprised of a small parapet without ditch. Rent 10s per Irish acre; 14 cwt. wheat, 35 bus. oats, 200 bus. potatoes. Plenty of freestone.*

**Gortreagh** – Grey field. *Property of Earl Castlestewart. Pretty good land, all under cultivation. Soil partly sand and partly stiff clay; 14 cwt. wheat, 40 bus. oats, 250 bus. potatoes. No bog; tenants get from Drumearn. If they require more they buy it in Killycurragh at 5s per rood.*

**Kilcronagh** – Wailing wood. *Colonel Stewart's property. 14cwt wheat, 35 bus. oats, 340 bus. potatoes, 4½ st. flax. No bog; turf from the mountain.*

**Killycurragh** – Wood of the Moor. *Earl Castlestewart's property. Rent 14s per acre. A mountainy townland, the greater part of which is yet uncultivated. Soil light and gravelly. 35 bus. Oats, 180 bus. Potatoes, land too poor for wheat. Lime obtained at Gortreagh; bog free.*

**Killybearn** – Wood of the gap. *There is a large piece of bog at the North East corner. A great deal of it very wet. Property of Mrs. Downing; rent 26s. 14 cwt. wheat, 60 bus. oats, 200 bus. potatoes, 3½ st. flax; bog rent £3 per acre.*

**Killyman** – Wood of the women (Killyman - Custom, Rev. Mr. Mauleverer, and old map of 1778; Killymam, Rev. John Mauleverer; Robert Hassard; M'Crea's and Knox's map). *Property of Col. Stewart. Here is a very perfect fort, with high parapet and deep ditch. Old freestone quarry. Rent 20s to 25s per acre. 18 cwt. wheat, 60 bus. oats, 200 bus. potatoes. Bog free from Drumgarrell, but owing to the distance and bad roads it is less expensive to produce it in Tubberlain at 1s 4d per perch.*

**Killymoon** – Mugania's Wood. *A beautiful demesne, the property of Col. Stewart. The house was built by Mr. Nash, the celebrated architect. It is reported to have cost about £50,000. There is a large garden and vast quantity of ornamental plantation. Loughry and Kildress rivers unite in the demesne.*

**Knockaconny** – Hill of the fire-wood. *Property of Col. Stewart. Good land, all under cultivation, average rent 15s per Irish acre, 18 cwt. wheat, 40 bus. oats, 300 bus. potatoes, 4 st. flax. Bog purchased at £3 per acre.*

**Loughry** - Abounding in rushes. *Property of John Lindesay; rent 26s per acre; very good land, contains plenty of limestone. The property and residence of John Lindesay. The house is old and not distinguished by any particular style of architecture. There is a large and productive garden. The grounds contain a good deal of ornamental plantation. A cornmill is within the demesne. There are some old standing stones called a Giant's Grave. The stones are very large and have been brought to the spot for some purpose or other.*

**Loy** – a hill. *Property of Colonel Stewart. Very good land, £2 to £3 per acre. Part of Cookstown is situated in it.*

**Maloon** – Plain of the lambs. *Colonel Stewart's property. Good land, all under cultivation with the exception of a very small piece of nearly exhausted bog at the back of Cookstown. It produces very good crops. Rent 30s to 36s per Irish acre.*

**Monrush** – Bog of the point or wood. *Property of Col. Stewart. Very good land, all under cultivation, with some parts sandy; 20s to 55s per acre, 20 cwt. wheat, 60 bus. oats, 200 to 300 bus. potatoes. Rent high owing to being so near Cookstown.*

**Moveagh** – Bog of the birch. *Property of Theodore Bailie. Wet, stiff land with considerable pieces of bog and rough ground. 24s per acre, 14 cwt. wheat, 40 bus. oats, 320 bus. potatoes, 3st. flax.*

**New Buildings** – Property of Colonel Stewart. *Nearly all under cultivation; 30s per acre. Good land with plenty of limestone, which is carried from the quarries to many parts of the surrounding country for agricultural purposes. 19 cwt. wheat, 75 bus. oats, 200 bus. potatoes, 4st. flax. Bog free at Drumgarrell.*

**Rockhead** – Property of John Lindesay. *Very good land, all under cultivation; rent 28s; 22 cwt. wheat, 45 bus. oats, 250 bus. potatoes, 4st. flax. Bog at Donaghy at rate of £4.*

**Sullenbuoy** – Yellow place of sallows (salicetum fascum). *Property of Col. Stewart. Stiff clay all under cultivation. On a height there is one of the forts common to this part of the country. Land is let to the inhabitants of Cookstown at £2 to £3 per acre: 18 cwt. wheat, 65 bus. oats. 290 bus. potatoes, 4 st. flax. No bog.*

**Scotchtown** – Property of Colonel Stewart. *Very small townland, all under cultivation. A good part of this townland has been taken into the demesne. It probably derives its name from a Presbyterian meeting-house erected here, the ruins of which are still standing within the demesne. Let in small lots to the inhabitants of Cookstown.*

**Strifehill** – Property of C. Colquhoun. *Rent 20s per acre. All under cultivation, 13 cwt. wheat, 50 bus. oats, 290 bus. potatoes, 4 st. flax.*

**Tamlaghmore** – Great burial place. *Property of the Drapers' Company. Good land, nearly all under cultivation. 13 cwt. wheat, 55 bus. oats, 200 bus. potatoes, 3st. flax. Bog purchased 5s to 7s sufficient for one fire.*

**Terressan** – Hessan's land or district. *Property of the Drapers' Co.: good land, nearly all under cultivation. Rent 20s; 12 cwt. wheat, 50 bus. oats, 190 bus. potatoes, 3 ½ st. flax. Bog rent 9s.*

**Tubberlane** - Broad well. *Property of Col. Stewart. Rather cold land, nearly all under cultivation. Contains two pieces of nearly cut-out bog. Light sandy soil. 15 cwt. wheat, 45 bus. oats, 230 bus. potatoes. Manured with dung or soiled with bog mixed with lime from Gortreagh quarries, given by the landlord at a reduced price, 7 ½d per barrel. Some of the tenants got bog free from adjoining townland of Tullycoll.*

**Tullagh** – A hill. *Col. Stewart's property. Good land, all under cultivation; rent 18s to 65s; 18cwt. wheat, 65 bus. oats, 300 bus. potatoes, 4 st. flax.*

**Tullybuoy** – Yellow hill. *Drapers Co. estate. Good land all under cultivation. There is no bog; rent 20s to 30s per acre. 20 cwt. wheat, 70 bus. oats, 250 bus. potatoes, 4st. flax. Fuel obtained from Ballyloughan bog, which is divided into lots supposed to be sufficient for the general run of houses and let at 9s per lot.*

**Tullycoll** – Cahill's hill. *Earl of Castlestewart's property. Rent 17s to 24s per acre, bog free. Rather cold stiff land; contains a quantity of bog and uncultivated ground; 16 cwt. wheat, 45 bus. oats, 250 bus. potatoes. Lime obtained from Gortreagh at 7 ½d per barrel.*

**Tullygare** – *Property of Col. Stewart. Rent 26s per acre, 15 cwt. wheat, 65 bus. oats, 240 bus. potatoes, 4 st. flax. Bog free from Drumgarrell.*

**Tullywiggan** – "Tullagh" a hill; "wiggan" uncertain. *Property of C. Colquhoun. Rent from head landlord at 20s, and let to under-tenants at 32s per acre; 16 cwt. wheat, 50 bus. oats, 260 bus. potatoes, 3st. flax.*

The above is the complete list of the townlands in Derryloran parish as given in the Name Book. As showing how the official names were fixed the following memo, sent from headquarters to the Surveyor, returned and filed, will be of interest and explains itself.

"M'Geagh's well, Sheet 29. In Derryloran parish, townland Coolreaghs. M 'Geagh's well – this correct? Larcom, 19th Jan., '34. To Bailey, L.R.E."

"Yes. That is the name it goes by. C.B."

"Adopted. J.S.S. 21st June, 1834." Thus it was that M 'Geagh's well, from being a local name, became immortalised on the Ordnance Survey maps. In the case of Oona Bridge on the Caledon Road, the query was sent down whether it should not be Una, and Dr. O'Donovan, after referring to an entry in the Four Masters for the year 1576, when O'Donnell made a trespass on the territory advises that "Oona" is the best spelling, and Larcom adopted it.

In the list of townlands above it will be seen that the average produce of wheat (where given), oats, potatoes, and flax varies, and readers in the neighbourhood will be able to form their own opinions as to how far correct these figures are. Obviously they cannot be taken in an absolute sense, for the yield varies greatly from one year to another; the question is whether they are relatively correct. We have no definite information as to the way these figures were converted into the valuation, but we know generally that land which grew wheat well was more highly valued than light land which did not, and, if the figures given above are arranged in order of productiveness of wheat and oats, it will be found, we think, that the average valuation of the arable land in each townland follows the same order. We invite suggestions from readers who have opinions on the matter, and also on the etymology of the names as given by O'Donovan.

Next Week – Rental of 1786

# RENTAL OF 1785 TO 1788.

## (6–9–1924)

A few weeks ago we turned back in the chronological order of our history to describe the town as shown in the recently discovered maps of 1726 and 1736. It was the most important discovery made in connection with the history of the town, though our description did not fully convey all that it meant, but we hope to have a map, based on these old maps, drawn to the common 6 in. scale, which we can publish, and which will set out graphically what the town was like before it was planned.

Since those articles appeared another discovery has been made, second only in importance to the map. This is a rental of the Stewart estates in 1776, 1777 and 1778, with arrears due November, 1775. At that time Mr. William Stewart owned no less than 97 townlands. Most of these were Church lands which were leased at a fairly substantial rent - at all events a much larger rent than the Crown rents reserved on freeholds, but still the gross rental, totally in 1787 no less than £5034 19s, must have meant a very handsome net income.

No distinction is made between leaseholders and tenancies at will; the holdings are all numbered in consecutive order, and where there has been a change of tenancy the number is repeated – that is the holdings, not the tenants, are numbered. The estates are different from what they were in 1726, when, it will be remembered, the Primary or Church lands consisted of 16 towns of Cookstown in Derryloran, 13 in Ardtrea, 9 in Ardboe, 4 in Carnteal, and 4 in Desertcreat. In 1776 the Ardtrea leases had disappeared - possibly the same family provision as was the case when the Slaghtfredin property was settled on a younger son, but, as stated, the total townlands amounted to 97. First are 4 in Carnteel (Aughnacloy); then there are 17 lying between Carnteel and Dungannon; next come 6, starting with Moree; then 8 more in the same neighbourhood, the largest being Ballymena (Newmillls); next are 4 by themselves – Ross, Tullaghmore, Lurgy and Sherrygroom, and 3 more forming part of the old Gortarill estate - Knockaconny, Ballyreagh & Colcrunagh (to give it the estate office spelling in 1788); Mackany is also by itself, let to one tenant, Dickson Coningham, Esq., whose daughter, Mrs. Maughan, has a mural tablet to her memory in Derryloran Parish Church.

A miscellaneous lot of townlands follows – Coolnafranky, Maloon and Drummond, all freeholds beside Cookstown. Then we have Clagan B. Donnelly, which is quite different from Claggan beside Cookstown or Clagan in Lissan, being as the name indicates, the Claggan of the old territory of Ballydonnelly or Castlecaulfield. It and the adjacent townland of Mulnagore were let to Mr. Hamilton at £44 & £84 respectively. With them there were Crossdermott, Gortindarragh, Crosscavanagh, Clonovaddy, Knockavaddy, Moneygar, Drummond and Sessiah - 10 townlands in the same district.

The 13 towns of Ardtrea follow, and their names need not be given here, and then 4 more from Sandholes direction, Gortachar and three Anaghs. Next we return to Ballymenagh and the Cookstown estate, 17 townlands in all, not arranged on any intelligible principle seeing that Scotstown and Monrush are together, while Tullagh, a freehold, follows Cranfield, which was church land.

That the rental is concerned with Mr Stewart's income alone, is shown by the omission of the Demesne lands, but the inclusion of the mill, and the Customs. The latter were the market fees, or perhaps the amount at which they were leased by John Moore, the tenant in the rent roll. The amount £27 6s is a great contrast to the value of the markets today, but we take it that it meant tolls only, possibly on linen webs or yarn, and perhaps on cattle to the fair.

But while the market has become much more valuable, the mill has not. In 1786, however, it was worth to Mr. Stewart no less than £120 a year, more than the rental of several townlands in the country. The miller was D. Galloway, and, in accordance with the practice of the time, every tenant on the estate had to have his grain ground with him. In the lease of the premises owned by Mr. J. D. Anderson, for example, John Henry, the innkeeper, who held with the houses land in Killymam, was required to *grind all the corn and grain which shall grow on such premises, and also all such malt and other grain as he shall make use of in distilling or brewing therein, at the mill of Killymoon and pay the customary toll therefor, and he shall pay 10s for each barrel ground elsewhere.*

This was the usual terms in a lease or letting of land – that the tenant shall patronise the estate mill. It has been denounced as "grinding the faces of the poor", but there is another side of it. It ensured the provision of a mill, in charge of a good miller, and his charges were limited. These restrictions on competition were swept away in the wave of individualism, which accompanied the industrial revolution, but we see them creeping in. In the co-operative creameries the new rules provided exactly the same thing, and Socialism simply means that the State shall occupy the position which, in the 18th century, the landlord occupied in many ways.

In connection with the mill we are fortunate in being able to copy the miller's list, found also amongst the Stewart papers. It is undated, but as the miller was David Gallaway, who was being succeeded by John Alexander, it was after 1788, but during the lifetime of Mr. William

Stewart, who died in 1797, so that the list was made out less than 10 years after the rental. The mill, however, was not for the whole of the estates mentioned above, but only for 32 townlands, the furthest away being Tullaghmore, Lurgy, Ross and Sherrygrim. It is described as "A list of succor of Killymoon Mill, being a copy taken from the list that David Gallaway had" and then follow the names of the townlands. Of the first five we are told that "These 4 towns pays the 18th grain", and the next 11 freeholds pay the same. Of the church lands we read: - "All pays ye 18th grain for oats, ye 16th for hard grain and ye 20th for mault". Succor is the Scotch name for mill dues, and payment was generally in kind. That this was so in Killymoon is evident from the note of "Articles on the mill given to John Alexander, etc., 3 pecks, 12 aiks, good and bad", the aiks being stores for the meal. Another note is that "William and James Stewart, Esquires, to have their grain ground free", and finally we read that "Distillerys and Bruerys to pay for grinding their malt 1s 1d per bole, and no more".

Next week we shall give the rental – the names of the tenants and the rent paid for each holding whether held by lease or from year to year.

# RENT ROLL IN 1786-88

## (13–9–1924)

Below we give first half of the Rental of the Stewart estates as described last week. Carrantale, with which it commences, is a long way from Cookstown and hardly enters into our history, but we give the rent roll complete, as it is such a unique document.

| CARRANTALE | | £ | s | d |
|---|---|---|---|---|
| 1 | Andrew M 'Williams | 24 | 11 | 4 |
| 2 | James M 'Williams | 34 | 15 | 2 |
| 3 | James Fleming | 22 | 5 | 0 |
| 4 | John Caldwell | 18 | 8 | 6 |
| 5 | Robert M 'Williams | 13 | 13 | 11 |
| 6 | Wm. & Jas. M 'Williams | 13 | 14 | 0 |

LISKINDUFF.

| | | | | |
|---|---|---|---|---|
| 7 | W. Erskin & J. Keenan | 27 | 6 | 0 |
| 8 | Mrs. Mary Lawson | 43 | 1 | 0 |

SHANALURG.

| | | | | |
|---|---|---|---|---|
| 9 | James Creighton | 6 | 6 | 0 |
| 10 | J. Creighton & W. Moffett | 5 | 4 | 4 |
| 11 | J. M 'Neese and A. Moffett | 10 | 3 | 0 |

ANAGHBEG.

| | | | | |
|---|---|---|---|---|
| 12 | Roger Anketell | 42 | 0 | 0 |

| | | | | |
|---|---|---|---|---|
| | Total | £261 | 8 | 3 |

AGHAKINDUFF.

| | | | | |
|---|---|---|---|---|
| 13 | Mr. John Moore | 26 | 0 | 0 |

COOLHILL.

| | | | | |
|---|---|---|---|---|
| 14 | Widow Bell | 17 | 13 | 8 |
| 15 | John Sloan & John Atwell | 8 | 8 | 0 |
| 16 | Widow Steenson | 6 | 12 | 4 |
| 17 | Henry Elison | 6 | 6 | 0 |

MULNATOMACK.

| | | | | |
|---|---|---|---|---|
| 18 | John Hethernton, etc | 12 | 2 | 6 |

CASTLETOWN.

| | | | | |
|---|---|---|---|---|
| 19 | Thomas Moore, etc | 29 | 8 | 0 |

CRANISCLOGH.

| | | | | |
|---|---|---|---|---|
| 20 | Wm. David & John Irwin | 29 | 8 | 0 |

CLANTOFOLLOW.

| | | | | |
|---|---|---|---|---|
| 21 | Robert Wilson | 9 | 9 | 0 |
| 22 | William Wilson | 9 | 11 | 0 |

DERNABORY.

| | | | | |
|---|---|---|---|---|
| 23 | James Knox | 15 | 7 | 6 |
| 24 | J. Reed and J. Fleming | 15 | 0 | 0 |

ESKERAGH.

| | | | | |
|---|---|---|---|---|
| 25 | James M 'Farland, etc | 6 | 0 | 0 |
| 26 | John Hardy | 6 | 6 | 0 |
| 27 | Archibald Reed | 6 | 6 | 0 |
| 27 | Thomas Kelly | 16 | 10 | 9 |
| 28 | John Givins and Saml. Maxwell | 8 | 13 | 3 |
| 29 | John Young and W. Williamson | 10 | 7 | 8 |

| | | | | |
|---|---|---|---|---|
| 30 | John Fleming | 6 | 6 | 0 |

EDENTALONE

| | | | | |
|---|---|---|---|---|
| 31 | Hugh Donaldson, etc. | 7 | 7 | 0 |
| 32 | J. M 'Williams & D. Barnet | 7 | 7 | 0 |
| 33 | John Steenson | 7 | 7 | 0 |
| 34 | John Davison | 14 | 8 | 9 |

KNOCKNARNY.

| | | | | |
|---|---|---|---|---|
| 35 | John Steenson, etc. | 16 | 5 | 8 |
| 36 | John Thompson and Jas. Fleming, etc. | 16 | 4 | 4 |
| 37 | James Brown | 11 | 18 | 10 |
| 38 | John Burton | 11 | 16 | 0 |
| 39 | James Fleming | 13 | 9 | 4 |

LISFERTY.

| | | | | |
|---|---|---|---|---|
| 40 | Thomas M 'Williams | 12 | 17 | 3 |
| 41 | Robert Carson | 5 | 16 | 6 |
| 42 | Widow Carson, now Andrew Job | 4 | 8 | 3 |
| 43 | Robert Little | 5 | 0 | 0 |
| 44 | John Fleming and Joseph Reed | 13 | 2 | 6 |

LEANY.

| | | | | |
|---|---|---|---|---|
| 45 | William Miller | 15 | 17 | 6 |

MULLYRUDON.

| | | | | |
|---|---|---|---|---|
| 46 | John Reed | 33 | 12 | 0 |
| 47 | John Agnew and James Cousens | 4 | 0 | 0 |
| 48 | William Wilson, etc. | 11 | 0 | 0 |

MULNAHUNCHAN.

| | | | | |
|---|---|---|---|---|
| 49 | James Kyle | 10 | 10 | 0 |
| 50 | Charles Beatty | 5 | 5 | 0 |
| 51 | William Carson | 5 | 5 | 0 |
| 52 | Robert Glover | 8 | 16 | 6 |
| 53 | John Babby | 8 | 16 | 6 |
| 54 | John Thompson, etc. | 8 | 16 | 6 |

MULLYCARR.

| | | | | |
|---|---|---|---|---|
| 55 | Owen Develin | 17 | 14 | 10 |
| 56 | Richard Lee | 6 | 6 | 0 |
| 57 | John and Jas. Dickson | 6 | 6 | 0 |
| 58 | Wm. And Alex. Beatty | 5 | 5 | 0 |
| 59 | James and Wm. M 'Mullan | 14 | 14 | 0 |
| 60 | Widow Dickson | 9 | 5 | 1 |
| 61 | Robert Dickson | 7 | 10 | 8 |

| | | | | |
|---|---|---|---|---|
| 62 | Wm. John & Hugh Dickson | 6 | 6 | 0 |

**MULLANEESE.**

| | | | | |
|---|---|---|---|---|
| 63 | Mr. Thomas Moore | 9 | 9 | 0 |
| 64 | James Fleming | 11 | 13 | 0 |
| 65 | William Wilson | 3 | 19 | 3 |
| 66 | James Swan | 16 | 7 | 6 |
| 67 | John Hethernton | 6 | 15 | 0 |
| 68 | James Swan | 7 | 15 | 6 |
| 69 | Wm. Rainey and John | | | |
| | Hethernton, etc. | 11 | 16 | 7 |

**RESKATERRIFF.**

| | | | | |
|---|---|---|---|---|
| 70 | Ben. Smyth, etc. | 23 | 14 | 0 |
| 71 | John Johnston | 3 | 3 | 0 |
| 72 | Adam Reed | 6 | 6 | 0 |
| 73 | Samuel Jordan, etc. | 6 | 6 | 0 |
| 74 | Daniel and Wm. White | 11 | 17 | 6 |

**MOREE.**

| | | | | |
|---|---|---|---|---|
| 75 | Alexander Irwin | 46 | 4 | 0 |
| 76 | Charles M 'Guigan, etc. | 21 | 0 | 0 |

**GORTAVALE.**

| | | | | |
|---|---|---|---|---|
| 77 | Widow Willson | 8 | 8 | 0 |
| 78 | Edward Campbell | 9 | 15 | 10 |
| 79 | John Stewart, Esq., | | | |
| | Domk. Loy | 11 | 0 | 6 |
| 80 | Domk. Loy | 12 | 12 | 0 |
| 81 | Patrick Toner | 4 | 4 | 3 |

**ALLEN.**

| | | | | |
|---|---|---|---|---|
| 82 | Robert Sooter | 12 | 12 | 0 |
| 83 | James, John and Thomas | | | |
| | Miller | 10 | 10 | 0 |
| 84 | Robert Williams | 11 | 11 | 0 |
| 85 | Arthur Williams, succon | 4 | 4 | 0 |

**ANAGH.**

| | | | | |
|---|---|---|---|---|
| 86 | Charles O'Neall, etc. | 9 | 13 | 9 |
| 87 | Widow Coy | 6 | 7 | 0 |

**CORLONAN.**

| | | | | |
|---|---|---|---|---|
| 88 | David Fleming | 22 | 1 | 0 |

**DRUMBALLYHUL.**

| | | | | |
|---|---|---|---|---|
| 89 | Gilbert Kennedy | 6 | 0 | 5 |
| 90 | Charles Richardson, Esqr. | 16 | 9 | 9 |
| 91 | Widow Seaton | 10 | 0 | 9 |
| 92 | William Howard | 2 | 0 | 2 |

MOYNAGH.

| | | | | |
|---|---|---|---|---|
| 93 | Rev. George Simpson | 13 | 13 | 0 |

KILMORE.

| | | | | |
|---|---|---|---|---|
| 94 | John Shaw | 50 | 5 | 4 |
| 95 | John and Isaac M 'Gowan | 14 | 3 | 0 |
| 96 | Archibald M 'Gowan | 7 | 19 | 1 |
| 97 | Alexander Hoyns | 5 | 18 | 4 |
| 98 | Archibald Moyle | 7 | 15 | 5 |
| 99 | Bryan Kelly | 6 | 2 | 9 |
| 100 | Patrick and Terence Kelly | 15 | 1 | 9 |
| 101 | James M 'Minn | 23 | 3 | 5 |

GORTNAGOLA.

| | | | | |
|---|---|---|---|---|
| 102 | John Somerville, etc. | 19 | 2 | 2 |
| 103 | Patrick and Daniel Kelly | 3 | 9 | 0 |
| 104 | Charles M 'Ghee | 3 | 9 | 0 |
| 105 | Francis and Chas. M 'Ghee | 4 | 8 | 2 |
| 106 | John Shaw | 3 | 18 | 8 |
| 107 | Peter and John Woods | 3 | 5 | 0 |
| 108 | John Woods | 5 | 18 | 3 |

CLANBURRISK.

| | | | | |
|---|---|---|---|---|
| 109 | Patk. Hughes, Hy. Hoynes | 14 | 12 | 2 |
| 110 | Dominick Donally | 5 | 9 | 8 |
| 111 | Terence, Patk. & H. Kelly | 6 | 16 | 1 |
| 112 | Archibald Gilkinson | 19 | 9 | 6 |
| 113 | Hy., Jas. and Patk. Hoyns | 7 | 18 | 6 |

KILNASLEE.

| | | | | |
|---|---|---|---|---|
| 114 | Robert McMinx | 7 | 9 | 8 |
| 115 | John McMin | 17 | 14 | 4 |
| 116 | William Steenson | 12 | 12 | 0 |

CANGO

| | | | | |
|---|---|---|---|---|
| 117 | John Sinclar | 25 | 18 | 2 |
| 118 | Wm. McClelland | 17 | 9 | 8 |
| 119 | John Farlow | 17 | 19 | 4 |
| 120 | Thos. McKane and Jas. Hamilton | 18 | 6 | 9 |
| 121 | Wm. McKeldon | 6 | 11 | 6 |
| 122 | James Hamilton | 4 | 16 | 0 |
| 123 | Thomas McKane | 6 | 6 | 0 |
| 124 | William Jackson | 2 | 7 | 3 |

GORTNAGLUSH

| | | | | |
|---|---|---|---|---|
| 125 | Revd. Wm. Kenady | 34 | 4 | 4 |
| 126 | John Irwin | 18 | 9 | 7 |

# RENT ROLL FOR 1786-88
## (Continued)

## (20 – 9 – 1924)

| BALLYMENA | | £ | s | d |
|---|---|---|---|---|
| 127 | James Harkness | 17 | 17 | 0 |
| 128 | John Otterson | 7 | 7 | 8 |
| 129 | John McCoard | 6 | 19 | 2 |
| 130 | Wm. Bell & Alex. McArdell | 4 | 7 | 11 |
| 131 | William Bell | 4 | 8 | 9 |
| 132 | William Wray | 15 | 0 | 2 |
| 133 | Thomas Smyth | 5 | 16 | 8 |
| 134 | John & Wm. Eagleson | 7 | 10 | 0 |
| 135 | Phil Neall | 5 | 15 | 6 |
| 136 | Andw. McNally,T. McKane | 2 | 12 | 6 |
| 137 | James Howard | 7 | 3 | 4 |
| 138 | Phil Murphy | 7 | 17 | 9 |
| 139 | James McCoard | 4 | 19 | 10 |
| 140 | Arthur Murphy | 9 | 4 | 3 |
| 140 | James McCoard | 6 | 2 | 10 |
| 141 | Patrick Hurson | 4 | 18 | 8 |
| ROSS | | | | |
| 142 | John Leard | 15 | 15 | 0 |
| 143 | John Leard | 9 | 11 | 4 |
| 144 | John Boyd | 9 | 11 | 0 |
| LURGAY | | | | |
| 145 | Robert Henry | 6 | 16 | 6 |
| 146 | James Hill | 5 | 7 | 0 |

| | | | | |
|---|---|---|---|---|
| 147 | Hugh and Wm. Robson | 8 | 8 | 0 |
| 148 | John McTyre | 5 | 5 | 0 |
| TULLAGHMORE | | | | |
| 149 | James Hening | 6 | 19 | 8 |
| 150 | James McQuawan | 20 | 10 | 6 |
| 151 | Wm. Mitchell | 6 | 13 | 4 |
| 152 | John Sloan | 6 | 13 | 4 |
| SHERRYGRIM | | | | |
| 153 | John McTyre | 9 | 9 | 0 |
| 153 | Widow McTyre | 25 | 14 | 6 |
| 153 | John McTyre | 32 | 3 | 2 |
| 154 | Andrew McGladragin | 9 | 4 | 9 |
| 155 | Paul M'Gahan | 11 | 8 | 4 |
| 156 | Widow Creighton & Jas. Creighton | 16 | 6 | 10 |
| 157 | Robert Creighton, now Jas. Ceighton | 15 | 11 | 0 |
| 158 | Francis Shaw | 9 | 12 | 1 |
| 159 | Archibald Weir, now Francis Shaw | 8 | 9 | 0 |
| 160 | James Hutcheson | 5 | 7 | 6 |
| 161 | Francis Shaw, now Jas. McKee | 10 | 5 | 9 |
| KONCKACONEY | | | | |
| 162 | Wm. Fleming | 18 | 7 | 6 |
| BALLYREAGH | | | | |
| 163 | Joseph Lynd | 11 | 15 | 9 |
| 164 | Hugh & R. McCormick | 11 | 15 | 9 |
| 165 | Henry McNally | 4 | 2 | 6 |
| COLCRUNAGH | | | | |
| 166 | John Swan | 9 | 19 | 6 |
| 167 | John Sinclair | 9 | 19 | 6 |
| MACKANY | | | | |
| 168 | Dixon Cunningham, Esq. | 30 | 0 | 0 |
| KILLYMOON MILL | | | | |
| 169 | D. Gallaway | 120 | 0 | 0 |
| COLNAFRANKY | | | | |
| 170 | Miss McClave | 6 | 12 | 0 |
| 171 | Rev. Mr. Murray | 10 | 4 | 0 |
| MALOON | | | | |
| 172 | Robert Rutherford & Andrew Rutherford | 4 | 19 | 3 |

| 173 | James Hagan | 8 | 10 | 7 |
|---|---|---|---|---|
| 174 | John Rankin | 8 | 8 | 0 |
| 175 | Alexander Rankin | 8 | 8 | 0 |
| 176 | Robert Park | 4 | 19 | 9 |
| 177 | Robert Galway | 1 | 18 | 2 |
| 178 | Alexander Rogers | 5 | 7 | 9 |
| 179 | Robert Hutcheson | 3 | 3 | 0 |
| DRUMOND | | | | |
| 180 | Paul Mean | 2 | 2 | 8 |
| 181 | Widow Mean | 2 | 2 | 8 |
| 182 | Thomas Mullen | 2 | 2 | 8 |
| 183 | Widow Ned Mullen | 2 | 2 | 8 |
| CLAGAN B. DONELLY | | | | |
| 184 | Mr Hamilton | 44 | 0 | 0 |
| MULNAGORE | | | | |
| 185 | Mr Hamilton | 84 | 0 | 0 |
| CROSSOERNED | | | | |
| 186 | Samuel Farr | 27 | 11 | 1 |
| 187 | William Hood | 27 | 11 | 1 |
| 188 | Michael Quin | 7 | 11 | 7 |
| GORTENDARAGH | | | | |
| 189 | Mr Williams | 9 | 4 | 6 |
| CROSSCAVANAGH | | | | |
| 190 | Mr Hamilton | 16 | 6 | 8 |
| CLONOVADDY | | | | |
| 191 | Mr Jones | 21 | 0 | 0 |
| KONCKAVADY MONYGAR | | | | |
| 192 | Mr Bailie | 16 | 0 | 0 |
| DRUMOND AND SESSAGH | | | | |
| 193 | John Sooter | 31 | 3 | 9 |
| ENESKILLIN | | | | |
| 194 | John & Jas. McCoard | 12 | 0 | 10 |
| 195 | Robt. and Wm. Ferguson | 12 | 12 | 3 |
| 196 | Andw. and John Dunn and Adam Irwin | 16 | 1 | 1 |
| 197 | James Dunn | 8 | 4 | 4 |
| 198 | Robt. Ferguson, Robt. Wiley and Widow Baxter | 23 | 4 | 0 |
| 199 | James Baxter | 14 | 13 | 0 |
| 200 | James Baxter | 8 | 11 | 1 |
| 201 | Samuel McReynolds | 7 | 13 | 11 |

EDERNAGH

| | | | | |
|---|---|---|---|---|
| 202 | Wm. Gibson and Mill | 63 | 0 | 0 |
| 203 | James Cowan, etc. | 32 | 2 | 6 |
| 204 | Patk. and John Ferguson | 24 | 18 | 0 |

BALNAHONE

| | | | | |
|---|---|---|---|---|
| 205 | James Hogg | 16 | 13 | 5 |
| 206 | J. Cook and R. Johnston | 35 | 16 | 6 |

LISNAHALL

| | | | | |
|---|---|---|---|---|
| 207 | John Seaton, etc. | 53 | 17 | 3 |

DERRYGONAGAN

| | | | | |
|---|---|---|---|---|
| 208 | Oliver Porter | 26 | 0 | 9 |
| 209 | Samuel Purvis | 30 | 13 | 3 |
| 210 | John Wilcoks | 21 | 1 | 0 |

CLAGGAN

| | | | | |
|---|---|---|---|---|
| 211 | Adam Irwin | 33 | 19 | 6 |
| 212 | Oliver Trimble, etc. | 17 | 0 | 0 |

LISCASEY

| | | | | |
|---|---|---|---|---|
| 213 | James Trimble | 14 | 0 | 10 |
| 214 | Joseph Trimble | 14 | 0 | 10 |
| 215 | Wm. Gibson | 14 | 0 | 10 |
| 216 | J. Johnston & S. Crawford | 13 | 4 | 6 |

LISBOY

| | | | | |
|---|---|---|---|---|
| 217 | William Miller | 11 | 2 | 3 |
| 218 | M. Burns, etc. | 16 | 16 | 0 |
| 219 | Robert Winning | 25 | 6 | 10 |
| 220 | Widow Winning | 16 | 16 | 0 |
| 221 | Jas. & Wm. Patterson | 12 | 14 | 10 |

TULLYORCHAN

| | | | | |
|---|---|---|---|---|
| 222 | Robert Mitchell, etc. | 21 | 14 | 8 |
| 223 | Thomas Grier | 20 | 6 | 10 |

TULLYVEAGH

| | | | | |
|---|---|---|---|---|
| 224 | Thos. & Adram Ferguson | 10 | 10 | 0 |
| 225 | Fergus Ferguson and Wm. Hamilton | 16 | 10 | 3 |
| 226 | Alex and Wm. Ferguson | 12 | 4 | 2 |
| 227 | John Machonchy | 9 | 19 | 0 |
| 228 | James Lindsay & Patk. Ferguson | 12 | 12 | 0 |
| 229 | Wm. Ferguson | 12 | 4 | 0 |
| 230 | John Purvis & Thos. Art | 23 | 7 | 0 |

TULLYRAW

| 231 | Widow Kinibrough | 9 | 18 | 0 |
| 232 | Christopher Lease | 18 | 12 | 9 |

TULLYWEARY

| 233 | James Trimble | 27 | 16 | 6 |
| 234 | Mr. Willcocks | 9 | 18 | 5 |

TIVENA

| 235 | John Sinclair | 70 | 9 | 2 |

GORTACHAR

| 236 | Noher Doories, etc. | 45 | 5 | 10 |
| 237 | Henry Hamilton | 20 | 17 | 8 |
| 238 | Patk. McCamill, etc. | 8 | 13 | 3 |
| 239 | Wm. Brown & O. Purvis | 18 | 10 | 2 |
| 240 | John Madden | 15 | 4 | 6 |

ANAGHANANUM

| 241 | Thomas Johnston | 28 | 16 | 11 |
| 242 | Thomas Johnston | 12 | 19 | 6 |
| 243 | John McCullagh | 17 | 17 | 0 |
| 244 | John Forrest | 16 | 1 | 3 |
| 245 | Wm. & John Forrest | 16 | 15 | 0 |

ANAGHTEAGUE

| 246 | Nathaniel Marshall | 21 | 5 | 1 |
| 247 | Mrs. Ash | 17 | 19 | 1 |

ANAGHMORE

| 248 | Robert Seaton | 25 | 0 | 0 |
| 249 | Widow Moffett | 13 | 17 | 2 |
| 250 | Widow Moffett | 6 | 8 | 8 |
| 251 | Samuel Glassey | 3 | 8 | 3 |
| 252 | Andrew Ferguson | 6 | 1 | 9 |

BALLYNENAGH

| 253 | Alex Crooks, etc. | 34 | 3 | 0 |
| 254 | Edward Devlin | 5 | 16 | 0 |
| 255 | Charles Richardson, Esq. | 48 | 17 | 3 |

KIRKTOWN

| 256 | Hon. & Rev. Dr. Hewitt | 4 | 6 | 6 |
| 257 | Hugh & Neall McWray | 22 | 1 | 0 |
| 258 | Ferd. Mellon | 6 | 16 | 6 |
| 259 | Hon. & Rev. Dr. Hewitt | 16 | 7 | 6 |
| 260 | Jas. McCrorey | 10 | 4 | 0 |
| 261 | Neall Canavan | 6 | 2 | 0 |
| 262 | James McCrorey, etc. | 21 | 5 | 8 |
| 263 | Hugh Heselton | 1 | 6 | 1 |

| | | | | |
|---|---|---|---|---|
| 264 | Fred Mellon | 6 | 0 | 9 |
| NEWBUILDINGS | | | | |
| 264 | Mr. Brisbain | 5 | 0 | 0 |
| 265 | Dr. Collins | 8 | 15 | 10 |
| CLARE | | | | |
| 266 | Charles Quinn | 5 | 18 | 11 |
| 267 | Denis Cavanagh | 3 | 11 | 8 |
| 268 | Widow Boyd | 8 | 4 | 10 |
| 269 | Widow Boyd | 3 | 2 | 0 |
| 270 | John Moore | 6 | 4 | 0 |
| 271 | Richard Brisbain | 11 | 5 | 9 |
| 272 | Peter Mullen | 6 | 12 | 7 |
| 273 | Wm. Minguis | 9 | 14 | 3 |
| 273 | Richard Brisbain | 3 | 3 | 0 |
| 273 | John Purvis | 3 | 2 | 6 |
| 274 | Widow Hamilton | 2 | 2 | 7 |
| 275 | Hugh Faulkner | 5 | 11 | 3 |
| 275 | Richard Brisbane | 8 | 5 | 7 |
| 276 | Matthew Newbanks | 4 | 15 | 6 |
| 277 | John Cooke | 9 | 16 | 4 |
| SCOTSTOWN | | | | |
| 278 | Widow Thos. Nickson | 1 | 11 | 6 |
| MONRUSH | | | | |
| 279 | Henry Dunn, Jos Adams | 8 | 7 | 1 |
| 280 | John Rogers | 8 | 3 | 9 |
| 281 | William Cluff | 10 | 11 | 1 |
| 281 | Charles Richardson, Esq. | 9 | 17 | 11 |
| 281 | Alex Rogers | 9 | 17 | 4 |
| 282 | Robert Gallaway | 9 | 11 | 0 |
| 283 | James Allen | 12 | 15 | 1 |
| TULLYGARE | | | | |
| 284 | Thomas McClelland | 8 | 9 | 7 |
| 285 | Wm. Cluff | 2 | 19 | 3 |
| 285 | John Taylor | 4 | 8 | 3 |
| 286 | Mary Carson | 0 | 11 | 4 ½ |
| CLAGON-HILL | | | | |
| 287 | Thos. McClelland | 9 | 17 | 7 |
| 287 | Robert Hutcheson | 9 | 17 | 7 |
| 288 | John Miller | 6 | 5 | 9 |
| 289 | John Brown | 11 | 10 | 5 |
| 290 | Robert Millar | 8 | 7 | 6 |
| 291 | Samuel Knipe | 4 | 17 | 8 |

| | | | | |
|---|---|---|---|---|
| 292 | Wm. Mosgrove | 4 | 17 | 8 |
| 293 | George Mosgrove | 9 | 2 | 2 |
| KILLYMAM | | | | |
| 294 | Robert Allen | 1 | 16 | 9 |
| 295 | David Ferson, etc | 36 | 2 | 4 |
| 296 | John McQuin | 17 | 10 | 0 |
| DRUMCRAW | | | | |
| 297 | Widow Jas. Brisbain | 10 | 4 | 6 |
| 298 | Joseph Ferguson | 11 | 17 | 3 |
| 299 | James Espy | 17 | 0 | 2 |
| 300 | James Gay | 6 | 14 | 4 |
| 301 | Thomas McConkay | 24 | 5 | 7 |
| DRUMGARROL | | | | |
| 302 | Mr. Wm. Magill | 14 | 3 | 6 |
| 303 | Samuel Anderson | 21 | 0 | 0 |
| 304 | David Little | 10 | 4 | 0 |
| 305 | Widow Blair | 9 | 5 | 5 |
| 306 | Richard Blair | 9 | 9 | 0 |
| CRANDFIELD | | | | |
| 307 | John Carson | 5 | 1 | 4 |
| 308 | Henry Anderson | 3 | 0 | 6 |
| 309 | John Anderson | 8 | 15 | 1 |
| 310 | Wm. Davison | 9 | 17 | 4 |
| TULLAGH | | | | |
| 311 | John Black | 11 | 6 | 10 |
| 312 | John Collins | -- | -- | -- |
| 313 | Robert Gallaway | 3 | 11 | 7 |
| 313 | Edward Pattison | 2 | 18 | 3 |
| 313 | Henry McNulla | 4 | 7 | 8 |
| ARDCUMBER | | | | |
| 314 | Neall Mullen | 8 | 16 | 0 |
| 315 | Phil Mullen | 8 | 16 | 0 |

(To be continued)

# RENT ROLL FOR 1786-88
## (Continued)

## (27-9-1924)

**COOKSTOWN**

| | | £ | s | d |
|---|---|---|---|---|
| 316 | Robert Rogers, etc. | 10 | 17 | 4 |
| 317 | James Allen | 5 | 13 | 0 |
| 318 | James Vandell | 22 | 1 | 0 |
| 318 | Michael Clarke | 17 | 8 | 4 |
| 319 | Thomas McClelland | 1 | 0 | 0 |
| 320 | William McClelland | 1 | 15 | 8 |
| 321 | James Oliver | -- | -- | -- |
| 322 | William Faulkner | 3 | 18 | 7 |
| 323 | William Henry | 2 | 13 | 9 |
| 324 | David Richardson, Esq. | 9 | 2 | 0 |
| 325 | James McCormick | 10 | 14 | 10 ½ |
| 326 | Mrs. Kenady | 7 | 5 | 7 |
| 327 | Mr William Cluff | 7 | 5 | 9 |
| 327 | Mr William Magill | 7 | 5 | 7 |
| 328 | Mr William Cluff | 7 | 19 | 4 |
| 328 | Mr Alex Rogers | 7 | 19 | 4 |
| 329 | Mr Edward Patterson | 6 | 18 | 1 |
| 330 | James Aston | 7 | 13 | 1 |
| 331 | Robert Rutherford | 6 | 14 | 11 |
| 332 | William Henry | 7 | 7 | 3 |
| 333 | Mr Edward Patterson | 6 | 10 | 5 |
| 334 | William Allen | 3 | 5 | 7 |
| 335 | Robert Allen | 3 | 5 | 7 |
| 336 | Mr. William Cluff | 1 | 2 | 9 |
| 337 | Francis Tewguard | 12 | 15 | 0 |
| 338 | Robert Hutcheson | 6 | 19 | 8 |
| 338 | James Aston | 16 | 5 | 0 |
| 339 | James Marshall | 3 | 8 | 10 |
| 340 | William Devlin | 5 | 8 | 4 |
| 341 | Robert Hutcheson | 1 | 1 | 3 |
| 342 | William Lynd | 4 | 12 | 11 |
| 343 | Jas Hanna now John Young | 6 | 6 | 3 |
| 344 | Mr William Magill | 12 | 7 | 6 |
| 345 | Wat Taylor | 6 | 11 | 3 |

| 346 | James Sterett | 9 | 7 | 2 |
|---|---|---|---|---|
| 347 | Francis Henry | 3 | 7 | 3 |
| 348 | Daniel Young | 3 | 7 | 3 |
| 349 | Dr. Fleming | 3 | 19 | 11 |
| 350 | John McGaughey | 4 | 9 | 4 |
| 351 | Robert Galway | 3 | 10 | 10 |
| 352 | Mr. William Cluff | 3 | 0 | 5 |
| 352 | Dr. Fleming | 4 | 3 | 0 |
| 353 | Do. | 3 | 3 | 0 |
| 354 | John Moore, for the Customs | 27 | 6 | 0 |

LOY

| 355 | Dr. Collins | 6 | 9 | 9 |
|---|---|---|---|---|
| 356 | Widow Lessly | 2 | 6 | 9 |
| 357 | Richard Blare | 2 | 7 | 0 |
| 358 | William Kelly | 2 | 4 | 8 |
| 359 | David McKinley | 9 | 16 | 11 |
| 360 | Daniel McClane | 0 | 14 | 5 |
| 361 | Dr. Collins | 4 | 12 | 5 |
| 362 | Adam Beatty | 2 | 7 | 2 |
| 363 | Chas. McClean now Jas.Collins | 4 | 15 | 7 |
| 364 | Samuel Bryson | 3 | 6 | 2 |
| 365 | Ned Patteson | 2 | 10 | 0 |
| 366 | Widow Burnett | 3 | 3 | 0 |
| 367 | John Charles | 2 | 16 | 0 |
| 368 | William Burns | 2 | 7 | 0 |
| 369 | John Collens | 2 | 4 | 11 |
| 370 | Robert McClelland now Wm. McClelland | 4 | 10 | 0 |
| 371 | Robert Henery | 0 | 13 | 2 |
| 372 | William McClelland | 1 | 7 | 0 |
| 372 | James McClelland | -- | -- | -- |
| 373 | Jas. Collens now John Collens | 3 | 5 | 8 |
| 374 | George Robinson | 3 | 19 | 9 |
| 375 | John Maguigan | 3 | 7 | 3 |
| 376 | John Collins | 4 | 8 | 6 |
| 377 | Robert Galway | 2 | 5 | 11 |
| 378 | John Collins | 4 | 0 | 7 |
| 379 | John McGaughey | 6 | 15 | 9 |
| 380 | Mary Blair | 2 | 2 | 6 |
| 381 | Jas. Rogers and Widow Dun | 2 | 4 | 8 |
| 382 | Robert Glasgow | 4 | 10 | 0 |

| 383 | Mrs. Cunningham | 5 | 10 | 8 |
|---|---|---|---|---|
| 384 | John Cooke | 33 | 0 | 7 |
| 385 | Richard Hall | 1 | 11 | 6 |
| 386 | John Kenady | 0 | 14 | 5 |
| 387 | William Kenady | 0 | 13 | 2 |
| 388 | John Hatchell now John Young | 0 | 13 | 2 |
| 389 | John Moncrieff | 1 | 6 | 0 |
| 390 | Fergs. Atcheson | 5 | 13 | 5 |
| 391 | John Young | 2 | 16 | 10 |
| 392 | James Dooras | 2 | 4 | 5 |
| 393 | Wm McCrea now John Collins | 2 | 3 | 7 |
| 394 | Alex. Johnston | 2 | 9 | 1 |
| 395 | John Collins | 2 | 1 | 10 |
| 396 | Richard Carr | 6 | 15 | 8 |
| 397 | George Rollins | 0 | 11 | 3 |
| 398 | Robert McKee | 0 | 13 | 2 |
| 399 | John Collins | 4 | 10 | 6 |

GORTALOWRY

| 400 | Owen Mooney | 4 | 18 | 1 |
|---|---|---|---|---|
| 401 | Wm. Park | 1 | 10 | 7 |
| 402 | Andrew Park | 0 | 8 | 10 |
| 403 | Wm. Clarke | 6 | 6 | 7 |
| 404 | Hugh Faulkner for Blair's Ter. | 1 | 6 | 3 |
| 405 | Matthew Newbanks | 0 | 13 | 2 |
| 406 | James Sands | 0 | 14 | 5 |
| 407 | John McCoard | 2 | 2 | 0 |
| 408 | Ben McCord | 0 | 13 | 2 |
| 409 | Edward Patterson & Edward Lackey | 11 | 4 | 9 |
| 410 | James Mellon | 3 | 11 | 7 |
| 411 | John Campbell | 3 | 13 | 4 |
| 412 | John Tamany | 4 | 16 | 6 |
|  | Henry McCoart | 3 | 19 | 3 |
| 413 | John Camaron, Ned Patterson | 1 | 14 | 7 |
| 414 | James Sanderson | 2 | 7 | 6 |
| 415 | Ben Thompson | 2 | 4 | 7 |
| 416 | Isabella Wiere | 2 | 10 | 0 |
| 417 | Ben Thompson | 4 | 4 | 1 |
| 418 | Wm. Davison | 3 | 16 | 11 |
| 419 | John Anderson | 2 | 5 | 11 |
| 420 | Henry Anderson | 2 | 14 | 4 |

| | | | | |
|---|---|---|---|---|
| 421 | Charles Anderson | 5 | 7 | 10 |
| 422 | Arthur McCoart, now Wm. McCaskey | 0 | 13 | 2 |
| 423 | John Purvis | 0 | 13 | 2 |
| 424 | Widow Burnside | 0 | 13 | 2 |
| 425 | William Nichson | 0 | 15 | 6 |
| 426 | William Bell | 1 | 4 | 5 |
| 427 | Alex. Johnston | 1 | 15 | 7 |
| 428 | William Clark | 4 | 8 | 2 |
| 428 | | | | |
| 429 | George Gibb | 1 | 7 | 3 |
| 430 | Roger McLoughlin | 1 | 17 | 0 |
| 431 | Daniel McLoughlin | 0 | 13 | 2 |
| 432 | William Anderson | 0 | 13 | 2 |
| 433 | Daniel Brady, now Robert McLoughlin | 0 | 16 | 0 |
| 434 | Robert McClelland, now Thomas Hutchinson | 0 | 16 | 6 |
| 435 | Andrew Moore, now Ben Thompson | 3 | 1 | 6 |
| 436 | Michael Doorus | 2 | 4 | 8 |
| 437 | John Mulhennon | 2 | 5 | 3 |
| 438 | John Moore | 2 | 8 | 7 |
| 439 | Widow Gourley | 0 | 14 | 5 |
| 440 | Henry Nickson | 2 | 4 | 11 |
| 441 | Andrew Sanderson | 3 | 14 | 6 |
| 442 | John Moore | 3 | 1 | 4 |
| 443 | Widow Thos. Nickson | 0 | 13 | 11 |
| 444 | John Moore | 1 | 8 | 10 |
| 445 | David Ferguson | 0 | 14 | 5 |
| 446 | Hugh McCormick | 0 | 17 | 10 |
| 447 | do. | 2 | 4 | 8 |
| 448 | James Doorus | 0 | 17 | 0 |
| 449 | Mr. James Cooke | 13 | 17 | 9 |
| 450 | Mr. Patterson | 6 | 2 | 10 |
| 451 | Mr. John Cooke | 6 | 15 | 0 |
| 452 | Widow Burnside, Henry McCoard | 5 | 16 | 5 |
| 453 | David Ferguson | 3 | 15 | 8 |
| 454 | David Bell | 6 | 3 | 11 |
| 455 | Samuel Faulkner, Esq. William Glassey (£4 yearly) | 3 | 12 | 10 |

# NOTES ON THE RENTAL

# (4-10-1924)

In the last three weeks we have given the full rental of Mr. William Stewart's estate in 1786 to 1788, though scattered over Tyrone, being numbered consecutively. For the purpose of a History of Cookstown the most important are those numbered 316 to 455 in the townlands of Cookstown, Loy and Gortalowry, as these include all the leaseholders – the men who, when the town was laid out in 1750, or thereabouts, took leases of sites in the town and built the first houses thereon. No distinction is made in the rental, however, between these leaseholders (who generally appear to have got leases renewable for ever) and the holders of the town parks created out of the original farms. In some cases, however, where the tenant in 1786 was not the tenant in 1788, the rent was raised and there would be fields taken for the season; in other cases the rent remained constant, and probably these were leaseholders.

It will be seen that three degrees of social rank are recognised; there is, for example, plain John Moore, David Ferguson or James Doorus, to take three at random from the bottom of the Gortalowry list; then we have Mr. John Cooke, Mr. James Cooke, and Mr. Patterson, which was the rent office spelling of the name Patteson, these three being connected with the linen industry as bleachers and finishers; and we have "Samuel Faulkner, Esq." who was also in the linen business, but presumably on a larger scale.

At the other end of the town, in the townland of Cookstown, we find the same social distinctions - Robert Rogers, James Allen, and Thomas M'Clelland, followed by Mr. Edward Patterson, Mr. William Cluff, and Mr. William Magill, and David Richardson, Esq. The latter was of Oaklands; Mr. Wm. Magill was of Crieve as well as Cookstown, and Mr. Wm. Cluff was one of the Kildress family. The latter is particularly interesting because while he was tenant of Nos. 327, 328 and 352, in the year 1786, he ceased to be tenant next year, and as a matter of fact the tombstone in Kildress graveyard shows that he died in 1787, aged 56 years. That was only 35 years or so after the original planning of the town, and we were inclined to assume that Mr. Cluff was, therefore, one of the men who took part in the great adventure of building a new town, as a mile long continuation of the old town – the hamlet of 1736. But the deeds lent us by Mr. J. D. Anderson, mentioned some months ago, show that that is unlikely. In 1788 Mr. James Richardson, of Bloomhill, who was acting executor for Mr. Wm. Cluff's will, conveyed certain premises 105 feet frontage, known as "John Henry's tenements", with 2½ acres of land in the townland of Cookstown, and 2½ more in Killymam to Alex. Rogers, inn-keeper, which premises had been owned by Mr. Wm. Cluff.

These premises were what old people talk of Frank Harbison's "Head Inns" of a century ago; older people mention the Rogers – the same family who owned the Grapes Inn on the north of Oldtown Hill – the house with the date stone; the rental gives us a peep earlier for it shows that in 1788 the tenancy of No. 328, the rent being £7 19s 4d, was changed from Mr. Wm. Cluff to Alex. Rogers (see last week's issue). When Mr. Cluff became the owner of "John Henry's tenements" is not known, but the agreement for the lease, still extant, is between Mr. Wm. Stewart and John Henry direct; he was to build two good houses of lime and stone, each 50 feet at least of frontage and 16 feet high in the side wall, with oak or fir timber; if roofed with slates or shingles a reduction of 10s to be made in the rent. These premises were afterwards divided, and, of course, have been rebuilt, and include Mr. Anderson's property in Oldtown Street, and the Commercial Hotel about to be re-opened by Mr. M'Gucken.

## MR. WM. CLUFF

Mr. Wm. Cluff was the eldest son of Richard Cluff, who died in 1751, and was apparently the first of the family to own Kildress, which was originally leased from the See of Armagh, because in the Hearth Money Rolls the name is absent. His will, which was admitted to probate in the Perogative Court in 1753 was executed in October 1749, and was witnessed by John Coningham, Frederick Coningham and James Early, the first mentioned being, no doubt, the curate of Kildress at the time, while the executors named were David Richardson, Esq., of Drum, and Mr. Walter Hynd, near Cavan. By the will it appeared that Richard Cluff left Kildress and Magheragless townlands to William and failing him to the next son Alexander; William also was to get leaseholds in Tullycoll and in Stewartstown and all other leases except the property at Dawson's Bridge (Castledawson) which was left to Alexander. William was also to get "all bills, bonds and debts of what nature or kind soever", and also all stock, etc., subject to a life interest to his wife in the farm and legacies to his daughters.

Mr. Wm. Cluff was born in 1731, so that he was only 20 years of age when his father died, and it was just then that Cookstown was laid out by Mr. Stewart of Killymoon. Mr. Cluff seems to have come into the town to reside, where the Commercial Hotel now is. He occupied a rather good position, being not only a magistrate, but a grand juror for County Tyrone. As mentioned, he died in 1787, and it will be seen that Mr. Wm.

Magill got one holding, Mr. Alex. Rogers another – while a Dr. Fleming got a third. The latter was probably a bit of town park, for whereas Mr. Cluff's rent was £3 0s 5d, Dr. Fleming was paying £4 3s 0d for the same holding, thus proving that it could not have been held under lease. Mr. Wm. Cluff, we may add, died without issue, and the property went to his brother Alexander who had six sons, one of whom appears in the directory of 1824, and was the founder of the well-known cabinet making business in Cookstown.

# THE STEWARTSTOWN VOLUNTEERS

Since the publications of the articles dealing with the Volunteers, Yeomanry and political agitation which culminated in the rising of 1798, more original manuscripts have come to light, and it will be convenient to give these here. It is unnecessary to enter into any long explanation of them; they simply supplement what has been already published.

The first is an invitation to Mr. James Stewart, in 1779, to become Lieut-Col. of the Stewartstown Volunteers. It is as follows:-

*Sir, - The Stewartstown Volunteers having unanimously made choice of you to be their Lt.-Col. it is with great pleasure that I comply with their order in transmitting the information, and I am also enjoined to impress in the most respectful manner their earnest request that you would not decline doing them the honour to accept of the command.*

*Signed by order of the Company.*

*ROBERT RAINEY. Sergt.*

*Stewartstown, Dec. 5, 1779.*

The next is from Col. Caulfield to the Killymoon Battalion of Volunteers, which, it should be noted, was stationed at Stewartstown in 1784.

*To the Gentlemen of the Killymoon Battalion stationed at Stewartstown.*

*Lieutenant-Colonel Caulfield's most respectful compliments and regards to the officers and gentlemen of the Killymoon Battalion. He is most heartily sensible to, and highly grateful for, the honour they so kindly conferred upon him of choosing him their Lt.- Col., and shall ever look upon this mark of their esteem as the most honourable circumstance of his life. He laments that his being obliged to leave the country, and the probability of but little residence in it for some time to come disables him from paying that attention to his duty which is due to the battalion, and in justice to them begs permission with the truest sense of the honour of being their Lt.-Col. to resign it into their hands. At the same time he begs*

*leave to assure them he will be ever happy to join them in any capacity as a volunteer, whenever the necessity of his country requires it.*
    *Drumrea, Thursday, 1ˢᵗ July 1784.*

# REFORM MOVEMENT OF 1793

Next follows an important letter from Dr. Reynolds, who was almost the only Cookstown man to be prominently identified with the rising of 1798. We have not been able to find out much about him; he was not a tenant in 1786, but in 1793 he seems to have taken a leading part in the political agitation of the time. As already explained, Mr. James Stewart was in sympathy with the Reform movement, but when it assumed a disloyal attitude he cut himself away from it. In 1793 it was apparently no more than an ordinary political movement, and Dr. Reynolds was associated with such leading men in Cookstown as Hugh Faulkner, James Cooke, Wm. Park, Joseph Lynd, and others, who met at Derryloran Parish Church. The vote of thanks to Rev. John Glendy, of Maghera, is interesting in view of the fact that that clergyman, after influencing some of his congregation, and making Maghera a hot-bed of disloyalty, was allowed to leave the country instead of being prosecuted.

The correspondence is as follows:-

*At a numerous meeting of the friends of liberty and good order, inhabitants of Cookstown and the adjacent county, on the 1ˢᵗ January, 1793, the following resolutions were unanimously entered into, James Reynolds, M.D., in the chair;-*
    *1ˢᵗ – Resolved – that at this momentous crisis, when the public mind is so much disquieted, we deem it incumbent on every man who wishes well to the interests of his country to peace, liberty and good order, to step forth and publicly avow his sentiments.*
    *2 – Resolved – that we are truly loyal, that we wish to support the prerogatives of the Crown with the same zeal that we will defend the rights of the people.*
    *3 – Resolved - that we believe a Government vested in the hands of the King, Lords, and Commons, the Commons being an equal representation of all the people, is that best adapted to the preservation of the peace and happiness of this country, and that we would support such a Government with all our abilities.*
    *4 – Resolved - that the present inadequate representation of the people is the source from which all their many intolerable grievances have originated.*

*5 – Resolved - that we hold sacred the rights of private judgement, and are convinced the peace and prosperity of Ireland require the speedy abolition of all civil and political distinctions on account of religious opinions, and by a Radical, complete Reform in the Commons House of Parliament.*

*6 – Resolved – that we will strenuously co-operate with all our countrymen in directing our exertions with united and unremitting energy to this point only – thinking that, these accomplished, all abuses will soon be redressed.*

*7 – Resolved – that we view the seditious promoters of anarchy as enemies to the interests of their country, as well as all those who would involve it in the horrors and miseries - unavoidable attendants on a revolution.*

*8 – Resolved - that those will alone be accountable for these calamities who seem determined to persevere in their system of corruption, and who, adding insult to injury, contumaciously persist in opposing every attempt towards Reform, thereby exciting discontent and commotion.*

*9 – Resolved - that we highly approve of the plans proposed by the "Friends of the Constitution, Liberty and Peace", and by the inhabitants of Belfast, Derry, etc., etc., of holding parochial meetings for the purpose of collecting the sense of the whole nation on the necessity of a Parliamentary Reform, and that, with diffidence, we recommend it to our neighbouring parishes, to hold such meetings as early as possible, and we hereby appoint our chairman, Mr. Hu. Faulkner, Mr. James Cook, Mr. Wm. Park, and Mr. John Holbert, Mr. Andrew Reynolds, and Mr. Jos. Lynd a committee, having full powers to correspond with all societies, friends to a Parliamentary Reform, and all our fellow subjects in our names and in concert with them to pursue measures deemed expedient for the general welfare of the people, to procure county meetings and provincial conventions, and to call the inhabitants of this parish together for discussing public questions and appointing delegates to county meetings and provincial conventions.*

*10 – Resolved – that the Derryloran parochial meeting shall be held at the church on the 8$^{th}$ inst., and that a volunteer company shall then and there enroll their names.*

*11 – Resolved – that we thus publicly offer our sincere thanks to the Rev. John Glendy, Presbyterian pastor of Maghera, for his dignified, manly, disinterested conduct, demonstrated in different forms, with a design of establishing the rights of man. In him, by a conscientious regard to duty, we view "An honest man the noblest work of God".*

*12 – Resolved - that our warmest thanks are justly due to all Irish Volunteers, to all the friends of Reform and particularly to our representative, James Stewart, Esq., and that a committee be now appointed to draw up an address to him expressive of our gratitude.*

*Doctor Reynolds having left the chair, and Doctor Caldwell being called to it -*

*Resolved that the thanks of this meeting be, and are hereby, given to our worthy chairman for his very liberal, impartial and proper conduct on the occasion.*

# THE ADDRESS

The address was as follows:-

*Sir, -- At a time when venality and corruption have pervaded every department of the State, at a time when the honours of the Peerage are sold to raise funds for the purpose of bribing the representatives of the people, we, a numerous body of men, uninfluenced by faction, unconnected with party, assembled here today, feel ourselves happy in having an opportunity of testifying our unanimous approbation of your virtuous and upright conduct in Parliament, and of your strenuous, alas! ineffectual exertions in favour of a much wanted Reform in the Commons House thereof. Accept, sir, the well earned tribute of our honest thanks; in paying you this respect we do honour to ourselves.*

*Local circumstances have no share in inducing us to offer these expressions of our gratitude. We are not parasites; we are men – men who view you as one of the virtuous few. You possess the confidence of the people, a greater honour than Kings can bestow, which we are sure never will be forfeited by any fault of yours. Go on, then, in that same, virtuous line which hitherto so conspicuously marked you. We doubt not you will endeavour to that darling object of the people, a Parliamentary Reform.*

*The time is awful, the occasion important and arduous, but nothing can be difficult to a firm, united people, determined to recover their rights.*

*We have the honour to be, with respect, esteem and gratitude, sir, your obedient servants.*

*Signed by order.*

   *JAS. REYNOLDS, Chairman.*

*To James Stewart, Esq., one of the representatives in Parliament for the County of Tyrone.*

Next Week – More light on '98.

# THE YEOMANRY

# (18-10-1924)

The following letter, marked "Private" was sent by Mr. Thomas Knox to Mr. Stewart, of Killymoon, dated 6th September 1796. Mr. Knox was apparently at Dublin waiting the arrival of Mr. Pilhom, the Chief Secretary of the time, from England. The letter is of topical interest in view of recent events in Ulster, and the formation of the Special Constabulary. Mr. Knox wrote:-

*Dear Stewart – The times are becoming so extremely critical that we ought not to lose a moment in taking measures for our internal defence. The Duke of Portland's letter to Ld. Camden has caused the greatest alarm at the Castle, and there is every reason to suppose, from the preparations making in France, that a visit may be made us from thence, and very shortly.*

*Depots are forming at Hillsborough and Omagh, and several regiments coming from England. Government will encourage gentlemen to raise corps of cavalry, but as to infantry, our mode of defence, they have come to no decision, waiting, I believe, for the arrival of Pelham, who is expected in a day or two. I believe you will concur with Lord Charlemont and me in our representation to Lord Camden that cavalry cannot be had in our district and that on infantry alone, and they exclusively Protestant, must we rely. I submitted to the Ld. Lieutenant the following plan, on which I should be glad to have your opinion.*

*That certain gentlemen in Tyrone and Armagh be empowered to raise companies consisting of 100 men each. Subalterns to be supplied from the unattached or half-pay lists – Privates to get a jacket, trousers, pair of shoes and hat, musket and cartouch box, and when called out either for drill or actual service, to be paid a shilling per day. Companies not to be moved out of the two counties. Six companies to be considered as a regiment, and field officers, taken from the above-mentioned lists appointed to superintend them, and in case it should be necessary to bring them together, to command them. Field officers to be magistrates. Persons not qualified by law to carry arms, inadmissible. Military pension for associator maimed or wounded in actual service – the whole to be under the command of Col. Commandant Lord Charlemont. I have the pleasure to tell you that when the mode of arming the country shall be finally decided upon, Lord Charlemont will take a most forward part in person, and I think we in Armagh and Tyrone cannot do better than marshal ourselves under him in a measure of this kind. The value of his name, exclusive of his local influence, would be inestimable. He waits, as I do, for Pelham's arrival, and then will set out for the North. Much benefit, in my opinion, would be derived from resorting to the unattached or half-pay list for field officers, and particularly subalterns, the appointment of whom would occasion, as in the volunteer time, much jealousy, and that description of gentleman would serve the cause more effectually by falling into the ranks – besides they would be less efficient than military men.*

*There is another plan which I believe would be more palatable to Government who startle at the idea of putting arms into the hands of Protestants exclusively, many of whom must be of Orange persuasion – that gentlemen should be commissioned to embody such of their neighbours as they can trust who have arms of their own, corps so raised to be clothed and paid agreeable to the first-dated plan.*

*That Government have had information that an invasion is probable cannot be questioned, otherwise why all this bustle? Why a depot at Omagh? And should the event take place, and the troops consequently withdraw from the interior, in what situation should we find ourselves? Vigorous measures must surely be taken by us, and quickly. I wish you were in town that we might agree on a plan to be submitted to Pelham, for without our joint representation I am convinced nothing will be done. If you should shrink from a troublesome journey, which is natural enough, pray write me a letter such as I can show, with your ideas on the subject of arming the country, tho' recollecting that you had thoughts of going to Dublin when I last saw you, I shall hope to see you instead of a letter. – I am, dear Stewart, very faithfully yours,*

*THOS. KNOX.*

*Dublin, Sept. 6. 1796.*

## MORE ABOUT 1798

A fortnight ago we gave the text of resolutions passed at a meeting in Cookstown in 1793, Dr. Reynolds presiding, when a long series of resolutions regarding Parliamentary Reform were passed and an address of thanks to Mr. James Stewart, M.P., was ordered to be presented. That Reform movement, with its professions of loyalty to the Crown, quickly developed, under the influence of Wolfe Tone and others, into undisguised republicanism and at each move it shed some of its supporters. Col. Stewart was one of those to soon disassociate himself from the movement when its disloyal tendency was revealed, and when the outbreak of 1798 took place, Dr. Reynolds was on the one side and the owner of Killymoon was on the other.

To his influence, and to the existence of the Killymoon Yeomanry, we attributed the absence of any open overt acts by the rebels around Cookstown. But there was another cause, for it now transpires that a company of regular troops were stationed here under the command of Colonel Leslie, who apparently was quartered in Killymoon Castle. In May 1798, the public thanks of the townspeople were accorded to Colonel Leslie and his men at a meeting at which Mr. James Stewart, M.P., presided. The following is the text of his covering letter to Col. Leslie, and of the resolution:-

*Dear Sir, - I have the honour of enclosing to you a copy of resolutions which were unanimously agreed to this day at a very numerous meeting in Cookstown, where all ranks of people appeared sensible of the meritorious and honourable conduct of the detachment you commanded, and anxious to express in the most respectful manner their gratitude to you. I am happy at being employed to communicate to you sentiments in which I heartily coincide, and in every opportunity of declaring the high esteem with which I have the honour to be, dear sir, your faithful and obedient humble servant,*

*JAMES STEWART*

Killymoon,
May 12, 1798.

## COPY OF RESOLUTIONS

*At a meeting of the principal inhabitants of Cookstown and its vicinity, held at Cookstown, on Saturday, May 12, 1798, James Stewart, Esq., in the chair, the following resolutions were unanimously agreed to: -*

*Resolved unanimously – That the grateful acknowledgements of this meeting are justly due to the Hon. Lt.-Colonel Leslie in particular, and to the officers, non-commissioned officers and privates of the Loyal Tay Fencibles, lately quartered in Cookstown under his command.*

*The strict attention to discipline and the orderly and exemplary conduct of the whole detachment during more than a year and half that they were quartered here, entitle them to our warmest approbation and thanks. We lament their departure and shall always remember with gratitude the security which the peaceable inhabitants of this town and neighbourhood enjoyed during the time the Loyal Tay Fencibles were stationed with us.*

*Resolved unanimously – That we are indebted to Lt. Col. Leslie, not only for his conduct as commanding officer but likewise for the moderation, firmness and effect with which he acted as a civil magistrate.*

*Resolved – That our chairman be requested to communicate these resolutions to the Hon. Lt.–Colonel Leslie.*
   *Signed by order of the meeting*

*JAMES STEWART, Chairman*

Next Week – Mr. Stewart and the Parliament of 1812.

# COL. JAMES STEWART AS M.P. FOR TYRONE

# (25-10-1924)

Col. James Stewart entered the Irish Parliament in 1769, as one of the members for Co. Tyrone in succession to his father, who had only sat for one Parliament. He continued to represent the county without a break till the Union, against which he voted, his colleague in the last Parliament, being Somerset Lowry Corry. In the United Parliament James Stewart was again returned, with John Stewart of Athenry, a distant kinsman, both being descended from a Scottish immigrant, who settled in Gortigal under the first Lord Castlestewart. In 1806 James Stewart was again returned with Thomas Knox, of Dungannon, and in 1807 these two gentlemen were re-elected.

But, in the Parliament of 1812, Thos. Knox was returned with Sir John Stewart, Bart., of Ballygawley, and the veteran owner of Killymoon disappears from the political arena, but in the next Parliament of 1818, his son, Colonel William Stewart, took the place of Knox. We are naturally interested to know why Mr. James Stewart dropped out -- was he defeated or did he not stand? Some papers recently discovered show that neither is an accurate statement of what occurred. He published an address as follows: -

## ELECTION ADDRESS

*To the gentlemen, clergy and freeholders of the County of Tyrone.*
   *Gentlemen, - With gratitude for the favours repeatedly conferred on me by the County of Tyrone, and for the generous confidence long reposed in me, I once more offer myself to your notice, and request the favour of your votes and interest, to replace me in the distinguished situation of a representative of this county in the next Parliament.*

*My conduct during forty-four years that I have served in that capacity is now before you, and at the approaching election you will pass judgement upon it.*

*To your decision I shall bow with deference – having the honour to be, gentlemen, your obliged and faithful humble servant.*

*JAMES    STEWART*

*Killymoon, Oct 3, 1812.*

Some light is thrown on his position by the report of meetings at Ballymagrane, which took place 10 and 12 days later. The document is as follows: -

## COUNTY OF TYRONE

*At a meeting of the Independent Electors of the Manor of Ballymagrane, convened by public notice at the Meeting House of Crilly in said Manor, the 13th and 15th days of October, 1812, for the purpose of taking into consideration the part they should take on the approaching General Election for said County.*

*The address of James Stewart, Esq., one of their late representatives being read –*

*Resolved unanimously – That our most grateful thanks be returned to him for his long, faithful and honourable services as one of our representatives in Parliament, and that we sensibly feel his kindness in offering a continuance of them.*

Resolved – That we will to the utmost of our power and at our own expense support the said James Stewart on the approaching Election, and trust that the honour and independence of this great county will not be tarnished with the removal of such their faithful representative for such a series of years.

*Resolved – That Robert Pettigrew, of Crilly, be requested to forward these our resolutions to James Stewart, Esq., and that the same be published three times in the Belfast and Strabane Newsletters.*

*The opposition to Mr. Stewart was evidently too strong, and at the hustings he withdrew. His speech in doing so was printed, and we copy it below: -*

## VALEDICTORY ADDRESS

The following is the substance of the address to the freeholders, delivered by Mr. Stewart, of Killymoon, on the Hustings at Omagh, on the opening of the Court on Tuesday, the 20th day of October, 1812.

*Mr. Sheriff and Gentlemen Freeholders.*

*In consequence of the support uniformly afforded to me by some highly respectable and independent interests in this county, I considered it to be my duty to make the best possible preparation to give effect to their kind intentions at the present Election - such preparation has been made, but on examination and enquiry, it appears that the junction formed by my opponents, has given them so great an advantage over me that I have determined (after consultation with some experienced friends, and by their advice) to decline a contest, which might disturb the peace and harmony of the county, without a probability of terminating to the advantage of my cause – I therefore take my leave of you for the present, DISAPPOINTED, I confess, but not DISMAYED; for I find consolation in reflecting, that during forty-four years passed in the service of this* county, my endeavours have been uniformly exerted (according to the *best of my judgement) for the good of my country, and that the sacred trust, which you are now about to transfer to other hands has never been sullied in mine.*

*Gentlemen, allow me at parting to offer by sincere thanks to the freeholders at large of this county for past favours and to declare my warm and everlasting gratitude to those friends who have generously stood forward in my support on this occasion.*

## A FREEHOLDER'S PANEGYRIC

His withdrawal drew out the following letter which seems to have been sent to some newspaper, but we quote from a reprint. It is headed "Tyrone Election", with the quotation, "Falia fando, quis temperet a lacbrimis", and is signed "A Tyrone Freeholder". He gives an insight into the character of the opposition to Mr. Stewart. He writes: -

*The mind impressed with sorrow, in utterance alone finds consolation, and lightens the burden in proportion as it imparts its distress amongst its sympathising friends. Under such impulse and feelings, may I resort to the medium of your liberal paper to partake of that relief.*

*In this degraded county, amidst an awful and solemn silence, in presence of a self-condemned assembly on one side, and of generous but dejected hearts on the other, have we witnessed, at the Hustings (in language, causing every string of the heart to vibrate), our venerable Senator take leave of that people, whose faithful servant he hath been for a period of forty-four years! Let us pause; of forty-four, did I say, and devoted to the service of his country? Yes: and in what manner; let us take a retrospect.*

*We view him in the proud period of our Volunteer Army – the now forgotten glory of Ireland – the colleague and chosen friend of the illustrious Charlemont, and of all those illustrious characters who acted in unison, to rescue our Country from her then degraded state. We since have beheld him opposing the transfer of our country, with its noblemen, gentlemen, and wealth, to be dissipated in another land. We have beheld him in every period opposing corruption in all its forms – zealously watching and exerting himself to relieve the lower orders of the community from such burdens, as would bear heavy on their necessitous state. And here, what has he effected? – more, much more, than is thought of, or appreciated. He has been the means of relieving not only this county, which has discarded him with ingratitude, but nearly the whole population of Ulster, from being taxed for the bountiful gift of the benevolent Creator – that light which cheers the cottage of the peasant – that light, which enables the tenant of the griping landlord to bring his manufacture cheaper to market, the advantage of which may be traced into the pocket of the landlord himself. He has been actively instrumental in relieving the oppressed tenant from the exorbitant discount exacted in many places in lieu of gold; and also in providing that the duty on his receipt shall be paid from the more ample revenue of his landlord.*

*If the feelings of this ungrateful County are too obdurate to be moved, let me at least interest, in our behalf, those of our more generous neighbours.*

*Hitherto we have viewed Mr. Stewart only as a public character, in which situation, without place or pension, one shilling of public money has never found its way into his pocket, or that of any of his friends, during a period of forty-four years.*

*On turning to his private character, I find a great hazard of offending his pre-eminent modesty and delicacy of feeling; but I must encounter and risk it to present to the world that character, which this duped County has rejected from her confidence and service. And here we find him as a Husband, Father, Master and Landlord, affectionate, tender, kind, moderate. His example in the face of the country, chaste, virtuous, moral. I spare to make comparisons – I am willing to allow our now youthful Senator, or his more aged Colleague, any merit you please. – We want no foil – we have neither occasion nor inclination for invidious comparison, or adventitious aid. We stand proud on our own eminence – from the summit of its elevation, lesser objects diminish to a point.*

*Such is the man this great independent County has discarded. Let me judge hereafter insult our feelings from the Bench, by a repetition of such bombast and nonsense.*

*Oh, my friends and brother freeholders! Must we submit to mighty Lords and their arrangements? Must we submit to have our dearest rights transferred by bonds and articles of junction, and wrested from the purest hands that ever held the sacred trust, to gratify ambition and resentment? Rather let us say, that each of us, having preserved from our now-expiring embers, a hallowed spark, shall treasure in his bosom the sacred fire (in due time), to fan into a flame the freedom of our county, and wipe off the stain of base ingratitude.*

### A TYRONE FREEHOLDER

We may round up this article with a reference to the death of Mr. James Stewart, which took place in 1821. The notice in the English newspapers was in the following terms:-

*Died on Thursday night, the 18th of January, 1821, in the 79th year of his age, of a Bilious fever, James Stewart, Esq., at his seat Killymoon, County of Tyrone. This respected gentleman was descended from an ancient family and represented the County of Tyrone forty four years, during which time he acted like a Constitutional Whig, a True Patriot, an Enlightened Country Gentleman and a sincere friend to his King and Country. He enjoyed to his last hour the friendship and regard of his Sovereign, to whom he was personally and warmly attached, he closed without a struggle or a sigh his honourable career, lamented by his family, regretted by his tenants and the poor and mourned by all those who had the happiness of his acquaintance.*

*With manner courteous and with temper mild.*
*In sense a man, simplicity a child.*
*Beloved by all who circled round his board.*
*By foes revered and by his friends adored.*
*Stewart long lived his country's boast and pride,*
*And tho' adorned by years, untimely died.*

### ROYAL REGRET

Finally we give a copy of the Earl of Blessington's letter to William Stewart, Esq., enclosing a letter written by the King's orders, Jan. 24, 1821

*St. James' Terrace.*
*Jan. 25, 1821.*

*My dearest Stewart,*

*I have great pleasure in sending you the enclosed which shows that His Majesty retains his feelings of private friendship and estimation of rare worth*
*Return it to me when read,*
*Yours ever truly,*

*B.*

*Carleton House.*
*Jan. 24, 1821.*

*My dear Lord,*

*I have not failed to acquaint the King with the melancholy intelligence conveyed in your Lordship's letter of yesterday. His Majesty has lost in the demise of Mr. Stewart a long tried loyal subject and faithfully attached friend, and under such sentiments I need not add the regret and distress which this event has occasioned.*
*His Majesty is sensible of your Lordship's attention.*
*I have the honour to be, etc., etc.,*
*B. BLOOMFIELD.*
*To the Earl of Blessington.*

Next week – Colonel William Stewart's Illness and Death.

# MORE PASSING NOTES

## (15 – 11 – 1924)

Three weeks ago we announced that the next instalment would deal with the illness and death of Col. William Stewart, introducing the sale of the estate which opens up a new period. Pressure on our space prevented the publication of the article till now, and in the meantime some additional notes on the earlier period have turned up, which we propose to clear off first. Thus we gave an address from the people of Cookstown to Colonel Leslie, who was in command of the troops here during the 1798 troubles, and which was sent through Col. James Stewart, M.P. The following reply was received, and is preserved in the Stewart papers of the period:-

*Carrickfergus,*
*17<sup>th</sup> May, 1798*

Dear Sir,

Your letter of the 12<sup>th</sup> inst., I had the pleasure of receiving this morning, accompanied by the resolutions of a meeting held at Cookstown, on that day.

These resolutions, so highly favourable and flattering, have been received by every one of us with true gratitude, and the strongest sentiments of regard and esteem for the very respectable meeting which has done us so much honour.

We look back with regret to a quarter which was rendered so pleasant to us by the unbounded kindness and attention which we experienced there, and in its neighbourhood, and we are unable to express the grateful sense we have of this additional proof of them.

We can only offer our best and most unfeigned thanks, and request you will have the goodness to present these to the meeting, together with our most sincere wishes that peace and happiness may ever accompany each individual composing it.

We are proud, my dear Sir, to receive these resolutions, from your hand and the very handsome manner in which they have been communicated, we are truly thankful to you for - But we cannot omit this opportunity of displaying the sentiments of gratitude we feel for the unremitting attention, politeness and kindness with which we have been constantly favoured by you and your family, and which we shall ever highly prize the remembrance of. Permit me to add one word for myself.

To have my conduct approved of by a meeting of gentlemen whom I so much regard and respect, will always be considered by me as the highest honour, and afford me the most complete gratification.

The uncommon and distinguishing marks of favour which I have so universally received, call for my warmest acknowledgements and they shall always be present to my memory with pleasure that I have experienced them and with regret that they are past.

In the name of the officers and men composing the detachment of the Loyal Tay Fencibles, lately quartered in Cookstown.

I have the honour to be, dear Sir, with true regards, your much obliged and obedient servant,

*DAVID LESLIE*
*Lieut.-Colonel L.T.F.*

J. Stewart, Esqr.,
  Killymoon.

# BIOGRAPHICAL NOTES ON THE STEWARTS

Mr. M. S. Patterson, of Bangor, who is so well and favourably known to many readers around Cookstown, writes:-

*In the Mail of 25ᵗʰ October it is stated that John Stewart of Athenry, was a distant kinsman of James Stewart of Killymoon, both being descended from a Scottish immigrant who settled in Gortigal.*

*Sir Bernard Burke says;-*

*"Capt. Andrew Stewart accompanied Lord Ochiltree from Scotland, settled at Gortigal about the year 1627." He was ancestor of the Stewarts of Ballygawley. ("His younger brother James, of Ballymenagh, Co.Tyrone, was ancestor of the Stewarts of Killymoon.")*

*In the Castlestewart Tercentenary, published in Mid-Ulster Mail, 15ᵗʰ November, 1919, you say another son of Lord Ochiltree, (and brother of the second Lord Ochiltree, who afterwards became the first Baron Castlestewart) "was Robert of West Braes, who, Burke says, was probably the ancestor of James Stewart of Killymoon and of the Stewarts of Ballygawley."*

*The family names were different. The Ballygawley family were John and Hugh alternately – the Killymoons were Wm. and James alternately, indicating that although having a common ancestor, they were not very closely related. It is surprising how the Killymoons descended from the younger brother, acquired so much property, and were able to build such a castle and wall in their demesne within a comparatively short time.*

*Mr. Oswald Dallas writes in last week's "John O'London's Weekly" that "tradition certainly makes Mary Queen of Scots RED-HEADED, as indeed all the Stewarts were." Probably this accounts for BLACK ANDREW, who may have been the exception that proves the rule.*

## NOTES ON TOWNLAND NAMES

Mr. H. Alfred Moore Munn, Clerk of the Crown and Peace for Co. Londonderry, who has devoted much time on an investigation into the meaning of the place names in his county, and has a monograph on the subject in the press, writes suggesting alternatives to the derivations given in the O.S. Name Books by Dr. O'Donovan for the following:- Tullygare, Tulaig-geare, "The short hill". Tyressen, Tireasa, "The land of the water falls", or Tirthe-eissean, "The land of the young grouse"; Tullycoll, Tulaig-coll, "The hill of the hazel"; Tullywiggan, Tulaig beagan, "The little hill". For the parish name Derryloran, Mr. Munn prefers Hogan's derivation meaning "The oakwood of the lepers".

## LOY

Mr. M. S. Patterson also writes:- *"The old name of Loy was Ballincloughy, bally (Irish baile) meaning a town or townland. The bally is found in many townland names all over Ireland, and in many cases has been dropped, as is evident from the names found in old records. Ballyincloughy would mean the townland of the lough, which at some period had occupied the valley from the weaving factory, by the Workhouse gate, on both sides of the Burn Road, across what is now the main street, and down to Newbuildings. On sinking anywhere in this valley one comes to peat, which filled up the old lough, as most of the townland bogs in Ireland do occupy the sites of what were once shallow lakes or marshes. Dropping the bally and the article we have the name Loughy, which by an easy transition became Loy.*

*The depth of the peat was considerable, as is evident from the height of the Orritor road above the fields on either side. It would not require a high dam at the first railway bridge to convert this low ground into a lough at the present day. On the old Estate Map of 1736, this is marked as turf bog, and the old leases included plots of this bog in connection with the building sites".*

Next Week – Description of Killymoon Castle in 1841.

# KILLYMOON CASTLE

# (22 – 11 – 1924)

Up till the building of the Great Northern Railway some forty years ago Killymoon Castle was secluded from the public view, but now (or until the woods were cut down recently), it was the central feature in one of the most picturesque views to be seen by travellers. It is not, by any means, a large residence, even for an Irish landowner, and at one of the sales by the late owner the Dublin auctioneers expressly described it as a "small castle" - of course, to emphasis the fact that it was suitable for the residence of a man of moderate means. At the same time, it is not only commodious but an imposing pile, the appearance from a distance being greatly enhanced by the towers from which it derives the description of "castle". At the near view the most imposing part of it is the porch, built of massive blocks of freestone. This stone has been described as Portland, but even the most extravagant architect would hesitate to specify stone from there to be brought so far inland in the North of Ireland, especially when good stone is to be found on the estate. As a matter of fact, as the geological surveyors reported not long after its erection, the castle was built from stone raised in a quarry in Killymam, beside the Oldtown, and old men not long dead remembered (or perhaps heard from their parents) that these blocks of stone were hauled from the quarry by teams of bullocks – a fact which would be sure to remain in the mind of the people

The architect was Mr. Nash who was responsible for building most of Regent Street, London and the date was some time about the beginning of the last century. The year 1820 has been mentioned, but it was probably earlier, as it was built before the present parish church was completed in 1821. The reason for its erection is popularly supposed to be that the previous residence was burned down, but it is peculiar that no reference to such a fire is to be found in any of the personal papers of the Stewarts, and the only public reference we have found to any fire is in the article reproduced below from *The Irish Penny Journal* of 10th April 1841. This article is not correct, as Killymoon was not bought from the Earl of Tyrone, but from Shane roe O'Neill, who was a son of Shane the Proud, the mortal enemy of the Earl, but an historical error of that nature, regarding a sale made over 200 years before, is quite different from a statement regarding a fire only 20 years or so previously. The cost, it will be seen, is put at £80,000. What authority there is for this we cannot say; it was a vast sum to spend on a house in those days when labourers were getting under a shilling a day, and skilled artizans in proportion. Lewis, in his *Topographical Dictionary*, published in 1837, says that it was built of "pure Saxon style", but he is not at all a reliable authority. The writer of the article in the *Penny Journal* four years afterwards who signs himself as "P", and contributed a series of articles on leading Irish residences, expresses a different opinion. The article is illustrated with a wood engraving, and is as follows:-

## KILLYMOON, COUNTY OF TYRONE

### *The Residence of Lieutenant Colonel W. Stewart*

*The subject which we have chosen as an embellishment to our present number, is a view of one of the most aristocratic residences in the province of Ulster, or, as we might perhaps say, in all Ireland. It is, therefore, deserving of a place in our topographical illustrations from its own importance; but we confess that it is not on that account only that we have thus selected it for illustration, and that, even if its attraction had been less, it would still have paramount claims on our notice, as the residence, when delicate health permits, of one of the best of landlords, and most estimable and accomplished gentlemen in his native province. Such, at least, is the impression made on our mind from all that we have ever heard of Colonel Stewart's private character; and it is only, therefore, in harmony with what might be expected of such a proprietor, that the enjoyment of the beauty and magnificence which nature and art have conjointly contributed to create at Killymoon should not be restricted to himself or friends, but be freely extended without solicitation to all ranks of the community, whom indeed he may justly and proudly class under the same denomination.*

*Killymoon House, or Castle, as it is popularly called, is situated in the immediate vicinity of Cookstown, and on the north bank of the Ballinderry or Kildress river, a beautiful stream which winds through the demesne. It was erected for the father of the present proprietor by the celebrated English architect, Mr. Nash, and the cost, it is said, no less a sum than £80,000.*

*Like that of most architectural compositions of Mr. Nash, the general effect of Killymoon is at once imposing and picturesque. Its form is that of a parallelogram; the north and east sides, which are the principal architectural fronts; and contain the chief apartments, being but little broken in their surfaces, and forming two sides of the square; while the remaining sides, which contain the offices, are of an irregular ground-plan, and are much hidden by trees. The east, or principal front, which is that represented in our wood-cut, has a large circular tower nearly at its centre, and is terminated at its northern angle by an octagon tower of inferior height, but otherwise equal dimensions; and the north front, extending from the octagon tower above mentioned, has a square tower at its west extremity, with which is connected, in a nearly continuous line, a structure in the style of a Gothic chapel, having stained glass windows, and buttresses intervening, and a belfry at its western termination; this portion of the building, however, is used as a library, and is the only part remaining of the original mansion which existed on the estate when the ancestor of Colonel Stewart purchased it from the Earl of Tyrone, and which was subsequently destroyed by an accidental fire. The north or entrance front is adorned with a porch leading into a small vestibule, and thence into the hall, which is of great size, and is terminated by a stone staircase having two return flights leading to a corridor which communicates with the bed chambers. This hall also communicates by doors with the several portions of the building below, those on the west side leading to the servants' rooms, and those on the east to the state apartments, which consist of a breakfast parlour, dining-room, ante-room, and drawing-room, all of which are of noble proportions, and their woodwork of polished oak.*

*It will be seen from the preceding description that the general character of this building is that of a castle: and, we may add, that the details of its architecture are for the most part those popularly but erroneously called Saxon. But, like most modern structures of this kind, it has but little accurate resemblance to an ancient military fortress, and its architectural details present that capricious medley of styles of various ages, ecclesiastical, domestic and military, so commonly found in modern buildings of this description. Such an incongruous amalgamation of styles, however, in an architectural composition is, it must be confessed, not very consistent with refined taste, and cannot be too strongly reprobated; but it has existed for a considerable time, and will unfortunately continue, till architects become skilful antiquaries as well as tasteful artists, and their employers acquire such an accurate judgement and knowledge of art as will enable them to form a correct opinion of the capabilities of those they employ, and not take their estimate of them, as now, from fashion or popular reputation.*

*The demesne attached to this noble residence ranks second to none in Tyrone in extent, the beauty of many of its features, and the fineness of its timber. The Kildress river, which passes through it, is crossed about the centre of the demesne by a picturesque bridge of five arches: and from this point the most favourable views of the surrounding scenery are to be had. Looking northwards, the sloping banks of the river, at the opposite side of an extensive meadow, are thickly planted with larch, fir, beech and ash, from the midst of which, an aged oak is here and there seen to rise above its younger and less aspiring companions: and looking westward, the turrets of the castle overtop the deep measures of foliage which cluster round it on every side. In like manner, to the east, the river winds its way through a tract of rich meadow land, the banks of which are fringed with sallows and thorn trees; and to the south, the grounds slope gently up from the river, and present detached groups of elms and oaks of the most luxuriant character. The views in this demesne are indeed such as might naturally be expected in conjunction with a mansion of such magnificence, and will, as we are persuaded, not create a feeling of disappointment in the minds of any, whether artist or pleasure tourist, who may be led by our remarks to visit them.*

## LOY

Sir – In your issue of 15th inst. your printer has given the old name of Loy as Ballinacloughy, instead of Ballinaloughy, or as it was sometimes written, Ballineloughy. The former would mean the townland of the stone or stones; the latter the townland of the lough or loughs. The marshy land where Capt. Fountain's road leaves the main street was probably at one time a small lough. This is not the only instance of a similar alteration of a townland name in the district. The old name of the townland of Craigs, near Orritor, was Ballinacreggy, and, no doubt, many other names were shortened in a like manner.

M.S. PATTERSON

Bangor, 15th Nov, 1924

Next Week – The illness and death of Colonel Stewart.

# DEATH OF COLONEL WILLIAM STEWART

## (29-11-1924)

For many years before his death in 1850, Colonel Wm. Stewart was in delicate health. Reference to that was made in the article published last week from the *Irish Penny Journal* of 1841; it will also be remembered by readers that, in 1830, he had to spend the winter in France with his medical adviser, friend Dr. Potter, and his return was celebrated in verse. Even earlier, in the year 1825, Col. Stewart had so serious an illness that it was feared he would not recover. He did, however, and the result was that the leading men in Cookstown decided to present an address of congratulation. After allowing for the exaggeration of complimentary addresses it will be felt from the following that the people had a deep and real attachment to the owner of Killymoon. The address and reply are as follows:-

*Congratulatory Address of the inhabitants of Cookstown to William Stewart of Killymoon, Esq., M.P.*

*Sir, - With no ordinary feelings of grateful pleasure we, the inhabitants of Cookstown, have lately heard the joyful intelligence of your progressive recovery from a severe, dangerous, and long protracted indisposition. Few occurrences, if any, have ever excited the same interest among us as your illness. To have had the indulgent resident landlord – the upright magistrate – the independent representative and the patron and liberal supporter of every charitable and benevolent institution, taken away from us in the midst of his days, would have been felt by all as a calamity of no common occurrence.*

*Conceive then, Sir, what our feelings are, on hearing of your being considered out of danger; and still more on hearing of that pious feeling which suggested that public expression of gratitude to the Almighty in the house of prayer. Gladly do our hearts respond to the intimation. Fondly and fervently shall we supplicate the Giver of all Good, who has brought low and who has raised up, that you may be speedily confirmed in restored health - that you may be more abundantly endowed with every excellence and virtue which could make you happy and useful and that you may be long spared to be an ornament to society and a friend to your country. Anxiously will we long for continued intelligence assuring us of your re-established health and well being ; and fondly will we look forward to the period when we shall once more see you in the midst of us.*

*Be pleased, therefore, Sir, to receive this inadequate expression of our congratulations. We remain, sir, with much respect, your sincere well-wishers and grateful tenants.*

*(Signed by Order)*

*ALEXANDER RODGERS*
*Chairman*

*Cookstown, 27ᵗʰ Aug, 1825.*


In answer to which has been received the following pleasing reply:-

*Gloucester*
*12ᵗʰ Sep. 1825*

*Gentlemen, - I return you my most grateful thanks for your affectionate and very flattering Address, and I feel totally inadequate to express my obligations in words sufficiently strong. To be so regarded by our friends and neighbours, with whom I have been so intimately acquainted for such a number of years, is most gratifying; and I trust that when I have the happiness to return and live amongst you, that I shall continue to enjoy your esteem and good opinion.*

*Believe me, gentlemen, with the greatest sincerity. Your faithful and obliged humble servant.*

*WM. STEWART*

*To Mr. Alexander Rodgers and the other inhabitants of Cookstown.*

---

Politically he was just as popular, though it will be re-called that his father lost the seat in Parliament through the antagonism of the "great lords" and the son proclaimed himself (in a letter to his mother in 1830) as a "Reformer". What was thought of him in the county generally will be gathered from the following invitation to stand again in 1830, which we give in full, with Col. Stewart's reply.

### INVITATION AND REPLY

*At a meeting of some of the leading citizens in the County Tyrone, held on the 9th January, 1830, John C. Moutray, in the chair.*

### RESOLUTIONS

*I – That a premature canvass for this County having been commenced, our chairman be requested to write to Col. Stewart, to ascertain whether he has any intention of resigning his seat for this County, it being our intention to support him as long as he wishes to represent us, and continues to maintain those principles upon which he was returned.*

*II – That Col. Stewart be requested to inform us through our chairman, whether he will, in the event of a dissolution of Parliament, again offer himself to the notice of his constituents, and in the event of his declining so to do, he will make the first communication of such to him.*

*III – That Sir Hugh Stewart be requested to offer himself in case of a vacancy, or of our finding it necessary to call upon him in support of our principles.*

*IV – That our thanks be communicated to Mr. Corry, for his uniform conduct in Parliament, and our confidence that the same harmony which has always existed between his family interest and ours will continue.*

*V – That the Chairman, if he sees any occasion, will call us together – and will accept our thanks for his dignified conduct in the chair, etc.*

## COL. STEWART'S REPLY

16 February, 1830

*My Dear Sir,*
*Yesterday I had the pleasure to receive your letter of 26th ult. enclosing a copy of resolution which had been agreed to at a meeting held at Dungannon on the 9th January last. To you and the other gentlemen who agreed to them, I return my most grateful thanks for the kind offer of support made to me , and I feel highly flattered by this mark of confidence. It gives me sincere gratification to find that my parliamentary conduct has met with approbation, and trust I shall be so fortunate as to merit a continuance of it. Understanding this, my friends will pardon the irregularity of my attendance. It is not my attention to resign my seat during the present Parliament, but in the event of a dissolution, I feel that the state of my health will not authorise me to offer myself again to my constituents, being incapable of that attendance which the fulfilments of my duties as their representative requires.*

*I remain Dear Sir,*
*Wm. Stewart.*

The decade which followed saw important changes in Cookstown. For one thing it saw the arrival of Mr. Thomas Adair from Broughshane to start the first spinning mill, followed by factories, which made Cookstown an industrial town and entirely altered the character of Gortalowry, from that of a select residential quarter to a closely populated district of poor houses. The same period saw the creation of Molesworth Street (which did not exist when the Ordnance Survey was made in 1833) and the existence of that street or road decided the terminus of the railway years after; it was almost certainly in the same ten years that the present market yard was set apart for that purpose and enclosed; these two developments tending to draw business from the Oldtown direction, but to keep the business centre on the north side of Loy Hill.

Apart from these physical changes, however, there was a very important legal change made in the middle of that decade. As readers know the Stewarts held the portion of the town north of the Burn as lessees from the See of Armagh, while Loy and all the rest of the land south of the Burn was freehold land bought from native proprietors. The townlands of Ballymenagh, Tullygare, Cranfield, Drumcra, Drumgarrell, etc., were likewise leased from the See, being Church lands. These leases had to be renewed from time to time, and a fine (apparently equal to a year's rent) paid at each renewal. At first the lessee had no interest after the lease expired, more than at present in an English building lease, but apparently, as time went on, the want of security of tenure was recognised as a hindrance to improvements. It is, indeed, remarkable that many of the houses built after the town was planned were so substantial considering uncertainty of the tenure. Perhaps, however, by 1750, there was some guarantee that the leases would be renewed, though in the form used by the Stewarts, to these tenants there is a covenant to renew the sub-lease only if the superior lease is renewed. It is remarkable that no legal historian, so far as we can ascertain, has ever taken the trouble to trace the evolution of these See Leases, but so it is. However, in the reign of William IV, when the Reform Act was passed, slavery was abolished in the British Empire, Poor Law overhauled and municipalities put on an improved footing, these See Leases were tackled, and in 1833 or 34 an Act was passed by which the leases of the temporalities of the Church of Ireland might be converted into freeholders. The principle of the Act was that the lessee had the option of redeeming the yearly rent by the payment of a lump sum, the sub-lessee being protected by being given the same right to redeem his rent. If the latter was not in a position to do so the chief tenant (the landlord) could advance the money and charge 6 per cent. interest. Colonel Stewart was one of the first to take advantage of this Act, for on 6$^{th}$ June, 1835, he paid to Lord George Beresford, as Archbishop of Armagh, the sum of £7,365 4s 8d, and so secured the freehold of the townlands held under lease. How much of that amount he paid personally we do not know because, as explained above, his tenants had the right to redeem their rents, and any reader who holds a lease of that part of the town dating before 1835 will find therein how much his predecessor paid as part of the £7,365. The whole rent was not redeemed, as £365 remained as a charge. The effect of this transaction, however, was that Colonel Stewart no longer held any part of Cookstown under a lease, but held the whole town as freehold, and his tenants became owners in perpetuity under the new leases.

Colonel Stewart must have been a comparatively wealthy man when his mother died and left to him all the property in Dublin that she had inherited from her father, Viscount Molesworth. But he led an expensive life. The late Mr. Alexander Molloy, of the Gunning Arms Hotel, used to describe, with enthusiasm, the scenes at Killymoon when he was butler there - how he could count twelve (or was it twenty) four-in-hands at once round the Castle. These were great days, but there is generally another side to such ostentation, and it is to be feared that more than one family was financially crippled in trying to keep up the pace set by the owner of Killymoon. He, himself, might have kept it up till the end, but for an unfortunate transaction; he went security for a friend to the extent of £50,000, and had to pay that amount. When that took place or who the principal was, is not known, but there is no doubt of the fact. Even the loss of that sum, large as it is, need not have crippled Colonel Stewart had he been living within his income and had the moral courage to cut down his expenditure to his new conditions, but that was not the case, and, by 1850, when a man of seventy, all the accumulations of five generations from wealthy marriages, had disappeared simultaneously with his own life. He lodged a petition with the Encumbered Estates Court to realise the estates, and it is said that he prayed that he might not live to see Killymoon go into the hands of a stranger. The date fixed by the Court for the auction of the Killymoon Estate was 17th January, 1851, but Col. Stewart's wish was granted, for he passed away a few weeks before, and was interred in the family vault in Derryloran Old Churchyard with his forefathers.

Next Week – The Sale of the Estate.

## SALE OF THE KILLYMOON ESTATE

## (6 – 12 –1924)

The Killymoon estate, which was about to be sold at the death of Colonel Stewart, must not be confounded with what is now named the Cookstown estate, much less with Killymoon Castle and demesne. These were but fragments of the whole property. The latter, indeed, was only one of twelve lots, and it may be remembered that when Dr. Macaura first put it up to auction he divided it again into twelve lots; in the time of Colonel Stewart that would have been regarded as the merest peddling. As it was, there was a good deal of criticism about the estate being sold in lots instead of as a whole, which would have meant that some wealthy family would have been resident here. Fortunately the business end of the town was purchased by a family which, for seventy years, became resident and probably did as much to advance the town as any nobleman resident in Killymoon would have done. But that is anticipating.

The estate which Col. Stewart sought to sell through the Incumbered Estate Court consisted of thirty-one townlands, containing 4,768 acres, and *containing the beautiful house and demesne of Killymoon,* to quote from the short advertisement which appeared in April 1851. It adds:- *It is situated in the County of Tyrone, nearly in the centre of Ulster. The town of Cookstown stands on the estate. The house, or castle, of Killymoon was designed and executed by the late Mr. Nash at a large expense, about forty years ago. It is in good order and contains every accommodation and embellishment which the late well known taste of the architect could produce. Upon the demesne there is a profusion of beautiful and valuable timber of the finest growth, valued some years ago at £23,359, 17s 1d. It is watered by two rivers which unite under the windows of the house. The grounds are nearly surrounded by a high demesne wall, which secures privacy. The woods are well stocked with pheasants and other game. Numerous flocks of wild fowl frequent the rivers upon which are two falls of 15 feet, each admirably adopted to drive spinning machinery for bleachmills in that fine flax-growing country.*

*The gardens and pleasure grounds are very extensive, and in good order, with a range of 150 feet of graperies and peach houses in full bearing. The neighbourhood is peaceable and the inhabitants are orderly and industrious. The timber on the land adjoining Killymoon and Cookstown, exclusive of that in the demesne, has been valued at £3,562 14s.*

*Cookstown is a flourishing town with a population of 3,000, having two weekly markets and a monthly fair. The parish church and five other places of worship are in the town. It is on the mail coach road from Dublin to Coleraine, nine miles from Dungannon, three from Moneymore, eight from Magherafelt and forty from Belfast, to which there is an easy mode of access on the one side by the Ulster, and, on the other, by the Belfast and Ballymena railways.*

Large as the property was in extent it will be remembered that 65 years before, in the time of Mr. Wm. Stewart, the rental (which we published some weeks ago) showed that he owned 95 acres in Co. Tyrone. The shrinkage would be chiefly accounted for by See leases falling and not renewed, though some of them may have been assigned to younger members of the family as was done before the time of Colonel Stewart's grandfather ,when his brother Patrick got what is now known as the Slaghtfredin estate. The emphasis on the value of the castle and demesne, and especially of the timber will be noted, while nothing is said of the prospects of annually increasing revenue from the town, even in 1851 when it had attained considerable importance.

The estate was offered for sale in 12 lots, and it will be convenient to give these at this place so that reference to each can be made by number. They were as follows:-

LOT NO 1. – The Mansion House and Demesne of Killymoon, consisting of the townland of Killymoon, and portions of the lands of Drummond and Scotchtown, held in fee simple; part of the lands of

Ardcumber, and the lands of Ardvarnish, held in perpetuity; the entire containing 584a. 3r. 5p., statute measure, subject to the yearly rent of £14 7s 6 ½d, and the tithe rent charge £22 18s 11d.

LOT No 2 – The lands of Colnahavil, held in perpetuity, and a part of the town and lands of Drummond, held in fee simple, containing 57a. 2r. 9p., statute measure, subject to the yearly rent of £9 6s 4d, and producing a nett annual income of £55 8s 2d.

LOT No 3 – The lands of Gorticar, Annaghanaman, Annaghteague, and Annaghmore, held in perpetuity, containing 645a. 1r. 13p., statute measure, subject to the yearly rent of £72 1s 2d, and producing a nett annual income of £346 9s ½d.

LOT No 4 – The lands of Knockaconny, Colcrunagh, and Ballyreagh, held in fee simple, containing 582a. Or. 29p., statute measure, subject to the yearly quit rent of £11 1s 6d and producing a nett annual income of £339 13s 9d.

LOT No 5 – The lands of Kirktown or Derryloran, held in perpetuity, containing 174a. 0r. 38p., statute measure, subject to the yearly rent of £23 7s 7d, and producing a nett annual income of £109 2s 7d.

LOT No 6 – The lands of Gortalowry, Sullenboy, and a part of the lands of Scotchtown, held in fee simple, and also the lands of Clare, and part of the lands of Ardcumber, held in perpetuity, containing 544a. 3r. 25p., statute measure, subject to the yearly rent of £22 5s 4d and producing a nett annual income of £835 11s 0d.

LOT No 7 – The town of Tullagh, held in perpetuity, containing 156a. 1r. 39p., statute measure, subject to the yearly rent of £24 6s 0d, and producing a nett annual income of £123 7s 4 ½d.

LOT No 8 – The lands of Maloon, held in fee simple, containing 161a. 3r. 36p., statute measure, and producing a nett annual income of £180 0s 0 ½ d.

LOT No 9 - The Lands of Loy, held in fee simple, and also the lands of Cookstown, Killymam, Clagon, Monrush, Ballymenagh, Tullygare, Newbuildings and Cranfield, held in perpetuity, containing 1327a. 3r. 28p., statute measure, subject to the yearly rent of £174 18s 8d, and producing a nett annual income of £1,498 12s 0d.

LOT No 10 – The lands of Colnafranky, held in fee simple, containing 87a. 3r. 16p., statute measure, and producing a nett annual income of £124 9s 9d.

LOT No 11 – The lands of Drumcraw held in perpetuity containing 158a. 0r. 32p., statute measure, subject to the yearly rent of £18 7s 5d, and producing a nett annual income of £84 3s 3 ½ d.

LOT No 12 – The lands of Drumgarrell held in perpetuity, containing 286a. 3r. 30p., statute measure, subject to the yearly rent of £17 7s 2d, and producing a nett annual income of £78 19s 8d.

The solicitors (attorneys they were called in 1851) having carriage of the sale were Messrs. Charles and John Samuel Gaussen of 17 Gardiner's Place, Dublin, members of the Ballyronan family and the rental was signed by Henry Carey, assistant secretary to the Commissioners, and dated 24<sup>th</sup> August, 1850.

## SALE OF THE ESTATE (Continued)

## (13-12-1924)

The Rental was printed, with maps of each lot specially prepared by order of the Commissioners, and lithographed on different scales. The maps showed the boundaries; the rental set out the names of all the tenants and how they held, and is a valuable list of the residents at that date. It is necessary to make this clear because, from stories as to the subsequent dealings, one would imagine that no particulars were available to purchasers as to area or anything else, whereas every perch was accounted for in the maps and the rental set out exactly who was in possession and by what title. To take an example at random; in Loy the first tenant was John Weir, who paid 3s 11d rent charge on 1a. 0r. 7p., the yearly rent being £10 12s 3d. He held under lease dated 1<sup>st</sup> September 1814 made by James Stewart for three lives renewable for ever, and in the "observations" column we are told that "Part of the town of Cookstown stands on this townland. A nominal fine on renewal, a ground rent", and there is reference to general observations on ground rents. The next three tenants are again John Weir for 1a. 3r. 18p., rent £2 19s 2d; Rev. Thomas Miller for 7a. 3r. 8p., rent £10 11s 4d, and Thomas Blair for 2a. 3r. 18p., rent £4 12s, each holding from year to year, and the holdings described as "Town Parks". Then there was David M'Clelland, 2r. 1p., rent £1 6s 0d, described as "Town Parks and building ground", and then came Rev. Thomas Miller again for 3r. 38p., held at 1s a year, under lease made 13<sup>th</sup> October 1835, to "John M'Cormick and others, trustees of the Seceding Meeting House", for three lives renewable for ever, and the "lives in being" then were "Henry Clements, W. Lenox-Conyngham, junr., and John Staples, junr."; and the observation colum gives the gist of the lease. Some of the leases were then quite recent. Three which come together may be mentioned as the terms were different. John O'Farrell got a lease on 1<sup>st</sup> January 1847, for 30 perches of land, the lease being for 99 years with a provision that at the end of the time the lease shall be renewed at a rent to be determined by arbitration. Patrick Molloy got a similar lease on 27th January 1849, and Andrew Campbell three days later. These three premises are now those occupied by Mr. Cosgrove, the Bank of Ireland, and Mr. Mackle respectively. Across the burn, in Cookstown townland, John Harbison got a lease on identical terms to O'Farrell's and on the same day, 72 feet frontage to William Street by 400 feet deep, with the cottages thereon, also the old house or kiln adjoining, 25½ feet frontage to the lane by 19½ feet deep, reserving to W. A. Collins a right of way 8½ feet wide. This lane is "Brewery Lane" of course. The witnesses to the memorial were Kinley Tener, of Moree, and John Rickard. The former was agent for the estate, and it may be that it is to him that these 99 year leases, renewable on terms to be arbitrated, were due.

The same minute details are given regarding not only every part of the town but of all the agricultural portion of the estate. The names of the tenants are set out, and, in the case of farmers who had not town parks, we learn that they held from " year to year ending 1st November in each year". Coolnafranky was all town parks - a fact of which the late Dr. Mullin was ignorant when he wrote his autobiography and described Mr. Jas. Gunning as taking the land from farmers. The persons who held fields in that townland were James Cluff, John Mulloney, John A. Smith, James Ballentine, Peter Graham, James Kidd, George Rutherford, and Robert Hamilton. Colonel Stewart had three lots in his own hands, measuring about 23 acres, of which 8a. 3r. 4p. was described as "Loy Hill" valued at £15 a year and was, no doubt, the top of the hill where Mr. Gunning built the house he named Loymount. Incidentally, we are told that "The Horse Fair of the town of Cookstown is held on this townland". The horse fair never seemed to be of any importance, but apparently the back avenue was at the time used to try the wind of the horses.

In Gortalowry the first tenant is Charles Mooney, who held 1a. 24p., from year to year at a rent of £6 10 8d. In the observation column it is explained that there is a good dwelling house erected on the land, and that the rent in that, and all other cases where the term "ground rent" is used, "is only chargeable for the ground, exclusive of the improvements". This is quite an interesting feature of these holdings. If held under lease it would be a normal state of affairs, but the tenants had built houses on land held from year to year, having no security beyond the landlord's sense of justice. That state of affairs, we believe, exists to the present day in parts of Gortalowry and Loy, and it is fortunate for the tenants that the property did not fall into the hands of owners who were prepared to insist on their legal rights and might have raised the rents to the full value of the houses. Chas. Mooney appears as tenant of six lots in Gortalowry: Thomas Campbell, Widow Donnelly, Robert Acheson, John M'Loughlin,

Daniel Owens, George Murphy, John Warnock, Wallace Gibson also appear as tenants of small lots of land, ranging from 36 perches to 2r. 36p., and being merely the sites of houses with gardens attached, all held from year to year. Dr Potter's name appears next, so that we imagine that these are the houses starting at Fountain's Road on the east side of the street towards the parish church, as the doctor lived in Gortalowry House. His ground rent, we may say, for 2r. 23p. was only 5s, against £4, or so, if at the same rate as the rest.

Outside the town proper, in Gortalowry townland, one of the tenants was Rowley Miller, who held 16a. 3r. 5p., under lease for two lives at a rent of £12 16s 4d. Of the lives his son was the only one then existing, and we learn that he was 69 years of age. This lot was the hill owned by Mr. Adair opposite the cemetery. Mr. Millar also had 5a. 1r. 4p., at a rent of £6 5s 10d from year to year, and in the town he had 1a. 2r. 10p., held for three lives, renewable for ever, at a rent of £7 9s 6d, with a renewal fine of £2 2s payable on the fall of each life. The lease was given in 1812 to James Cooke, and the lives then in being were those of Mary Ann Cooke and Elizabeth Cooke. This property now belongs to Mr. E. J. Malone, solicitor; James Cooke was the owner of the bleach green at Greenvale at the time and lived in what is now Mr. Malone's house.

These old leases were not without restrictions. On the same page in the rental we find two holdings, the tenant being Thomas Adair. The first was for 5a. 3r. 23p., held under lease dated 1833 for three lives – John, Hugh and Sarah Wallace, all in being at 1850 with a renewal fine of £2 on the fall of each life. This was the bleach green, and there was a covenant against converting it into a flour, or corn, mill without leave – an indication that, in 1833, there was no certainty that the linen trade, or at least the spinning end, might not be abandoned for the then profitable business of grinding wheat or oats. The second holding of Mr. Adair was 31a. 2r. 36p., held on a short lease of 41 years from November 1841. It formed part of the bleach green and there was covenant by the lessee "to pay a penal rent of £5 per annum for every house that may be built in addition to the two dwelling houses on this holding". Mr. Adair had also 17a. 20p., held under a lease of 1800 to James Cooke for their lives renewable for ever at a rent of £33 4s 8d. "This lease contains a covenant by the lessee not to consume more than half part of the water flowing from the river Derryloran for the use of the mill erected on this holding". The restricted use of the water forced Mr. Adair to buy the land on the other side of the river in Kirktown, or Derryloran, as the townland was sometimes called.

The Corn miller was John Vance, who held under lease of 1834 at a rent of £100. The acreage he had was 13a. 29p., of which 6a.

2r. 13p. was in Ardcumber, and we are informed in the observation column that "Colonel Stewart undertook, in writing, that if he, or his heirs, should decline, on the expiration of the lease, to grant a renewal, that the lessee should be allowed a fair remuneration for all permanent holdings he should erect on the premises, provided the same was made as therein stipulated for, and that the amount should not in any case exceed £500".

Three miscellaneous notes may be added in connection with Gortalowry. The Free Stone quarry was then in the possession of the proprietor, but had been let for £10 a year; Loy House was also in the possession of Col. Stewart, and is described as "a valuable dwelling-house and offices usually set for £60 per annum"; John K. Tener, treasurer of the Dispensary, and Miss Richardson appear as tenants of the last lot, the former paying £14 11s 4d and the latter £12 19s 2d for the house which must have been situated somewhere in Gortalowry.

(To be continued)

# THE RENTAL OF 1850

## (20 – 12 – 1924)

As the extracts from the printed Rental for the sale, dated July 1850, have created more interest than we expected, we propose to give some more particulars. Mention has already been made to John Weir, Rev. Thomas Miller, Thomas Blair, and David M'Clelland, whose names are at the top of the rental. There is then a list of tenants of holdings described as "Ground rent", held from year to year - that is, of houses and gardens belonging to the occupier but on ground belonging to the landlord. Presumably they are in order as they existed along the street, though this is not expressly stated. At any rate, between the Second Presbyterain Church and the Infant School (now the Foresters' Hall) the tenants were: John Allen, Thomas Blair, James Ballentine (a leaseholder); George Johnston, John M'Elhatton, Joseph Acheson, David M'Clelland, jr.; Widow M'Elhennon, Rev. W. M'Conville (leaseholder); John Charles, Jas. Glassy, John Charles, Fergus Hughes, Peter Ferguson, Peter Graham, John M'Clelland, and Aaron Thompson. The lease to Rev. Wm. M'Conville, falling about half-way, is doubtless part of the site of the Catholic Church, which materially altered the appearance of the street. Out of all the above we believe that Peter Graham is the only owner now represented.

On page 2 of the Rental we find as tenants paying a "ground rent", John Ramsey and Robert Hamilton. Then comes Wm. Morgan, junr., £5

4s 7d (lease); the Old Methodist Chapel, in names of John Gourley and others, rent 11d; John Collins, junr.; Andrew Campbell, John O'Farrell and Patrick Molloy, all leases of 1847-49 renewable, as explained last week. Edward Quin, John Kane, Jane Lamon, Thomas Blair, and Rev. J. K. Leslie, the latter paying £9 14s for 4a. 23 perches. Dr. Graves had two leaseholds, £12 (lease to Hugh Hagan in 1832), and £1 10s (lease to Wm. Magill in 1846); Matthew S. Glasgow had two holdings with ground rents of £9 and £4; Jas. Cluff had a lease made in 1837 to Daniel M'Cooke for 3 lives, rent £18 12s 5d; William Morgan, senr., had a lease to himself in 1833, rent £12 12s. The largest rent payable for any holding by any private individual in Loy was £19 3s, which was the amount paid by Wm. Morgan, junr., for 10a. 3r. 15p., described as "a garden".

It would be tedious to give details of all the holdings; the names of the tenants who paid ground rents must suffice. They were David Kennedy, George Owens, John M'Callin, Robert Hamilton, junr.; John Ramsey, junr.; Samuel Ramsey, Joseph Johnston, Eliza Smith, Thomas Blair, Mary Longford, Charles Mooney, John Dooras, Silas E. Weir, James Cunningham, Alexander Harvey, Robert Moran, James Sweeny, Widow Tullan, John Molloney, John Mooney, Cornelius M'Elhone, James Mullan. So utterly has the personel of the town changed in 75 years that it is hardly possible to identify the street where these persons owned houses, but the name Robert Moran will help to fix part of it.

The larger houses were generally secured by leases, which follow, commencing with Thomas Ferguson (lease to Wm. Sellor). Then we have the "Old Meeting House" (First Presbyterian Church), with a town park held by Rev. H. B. Wilson; John Stewart, a ground rent, from year to year. Then follow Silas E. Weir (lease to self); Dr. Hamilton (lease to Jas. Hamilton); John Gourley (lease to self); Thomas M'Allister (lease to James Moore); Mrs. Dr. Young (lease to Matthew Trimble); John Bell (lease to self); John M'Cormick and Andrew Dickson (lease to Robert Gilmore); Henry O'Farrell (lease to self); New Methodist Chapel (lease to Peter Potter and Edward Addy, 1826); Samuel Brown (lease to self); Dr. Charles (lease to Edward Patterson); John Vance (lease to self); John Molloy (lease to self); Michael M'Guigan (lease to Henry O'Farrell). The peculiarity of all the leaseholds in the last paragraph, covering practically the whole of the west of James Street, is that, except the Methodist Chapel (Mr. M'Collum's), every lease is dated 7th or 8th August, 1827. There were probably some older houses, not rebuilt, but from that date there must have been a great building scheme, commencing at the Burn Road.

Amongst the miscellaneous items in the rental will be noted a lease of 1836 to Matthew Patterson and others for the "New Meeting House" (Third Presbyterian Church); while Rev. J. K. Leslie had an agreement for a lease for his manse. The rent was 1s a year, to be raised to £20 if it ceased to be the minister's residence, and £50 if used for anything but a private residence. Then "the Company who built the Stores" appear as tenants under lease to W. S. Richardson and others, 1838, at 1s a year, to be raised to £50 if the covenants are not observed. The Paymaster was the tenant of the Police Barracks at £24, and for the Petty Sessions room, offices, etc., paid £26, these being the old Courthouse and Imperial Hotel premises. The lessee of the "tolls and customs of the town of Cookstown" was John M'Cormick, who paid £150 a year therefor, and had also a lease of 1a. 16p. for 150 years. Finally, four tenants, Henry O'Farrell, Silas E. Weir, Dr. Hamilton and William Morgan, junr., held "valuable town parks, worth four times the present rents", by lease for 18 years from November 1839. The four times seems moderate enough as O'Farrell had 1½ acres at 15s; S. E. Weir for 1a. 2r. 33p., paid 18s 8d, while Wm. Morgan 3a. 29p. for 8s 4d - the rate thus being 10s an acre. We had almost overlooked a school in Loy, 1r. 32p., at 1s a year (tenant being "F. Miller".)

Next Week  - Tenants in Cookstown, Killymam, Clagan and Monrush.

*Cookstown, from Loy Hill.*

## THE RENTAL OF 1850 (Continued)

## (27 – 12 – 1924)

The townland of Cookstown follows that of Loy in the rental of 1850, as printed for the purpose of the sale. It will be remembered that Cookstown was Church land, leased from the See of Armagh up till 1835, when Col. Wm. Stewart bought out the superior interest by the payment of £7,365 4s 8d, portion of which was contributed by the under-tenants who then became owners in perpetuity subject to a small rent. The entire Church lands were left subject to a rent of £356 odd payable by Col. Stewart or his successors, and the proportion of this on Lot 9 was £174 8s 9d.

Instead of taking the names of the tenants seriatim it will be more interesting to take them by groups, according to the tenure. First place must be given to those who held "for ever", these being leaseholders who had converted their status into freeholders by joining in the payment of the £7,365 to the See of Armagh. In addition to the rent to Col. Stewart they became liable to a small rent charge. Thus we have, first on the list, William Charles, whose lease was dated 1840 and held 9a 3r 25p, including 5a 0r 32p in Clagan at a rent of £4 7s 5d, together with 15s rent charge. Next was Major Wm. S. Richardson-Brady, who held 19a 2r 13p, including 16a 19p in Newbuildings, and 4a 8p of bog in Drumgarrell at £7 rent under the lease of 1840, and £1 6s 8d rent charge. The other persons holding for ever in Cookstown townland were the Misses Rogers (lease of 1840 to Mary Rutherford and others), Miss Magill (lease of 1844 to Mary Magill), Samuel R. Magill (lease to self in 1841), Joseph Rogers (lease to self in 1840), William Charles and Robert M'Geagh, (lease to Wm. Patterson, 1840), William Aston (lease to self in 1845), William M. Collins (lease to self in 1845), Thos. Dawson (lease to self in 1845), George Aston (lease to self in 1845), John Black (lease to self in 1845, and a second lease to Alex M'Cooke in 1840), Andrew R. M'Cooke (lease to self 1840), Thomas Black (lease to self 1847), William Glasgow (lease to self 1840), Robert Glasgow (lease to self 1842), Lieut. Robert Lynd (two leases to self 1840), Doctor Charles (lease to self 1842), John Taylor (lease to self 1842), John Gourley (lease to self 1842), John Vance (two leases to self 1842), Joseph Rogers (lease to George Rogers 1840), David W. Henry (two leases to self 1843), James M'Entire (lease to John Lind 1843), R. Harkness and John Gourley (lease to Daniel J. Young 1841), Mrs. Agnew (lease to Elizabeth Agnew and others 1841), Archibald Nesbitt (lease to self in 1841).

These names are those of the owners of the house property on both sides of the main street and in Orritor and Coagh Streets at 1850. The dates of the leases do not convey much; many of them went back to the building of the town about 1750, as the present holders can see, but as explained, these leases had to be renewed from time to time, as the Stewarts renewed their lease from the See. Though placed under the heading of Cookstown, in the majority of cases the holding included, as in the two instances given above, substantial areas of land in other townlands - New Buildings, Killymam, Monrush, Ballymenagh and Drumgarrel bog, and this is doubtless the reason why these townlands were included in the one lot with Cookstown and Loy. By granting the leases of town sites, together with land in the vicinity in other townlands it was practically impossible to separate the latter.

In addition to those whose tenure was simply "for ever", we find others almost as good. Thus John M'Cormick had 9a 3r 16p at a rent of £14 15s, held under a lease of 1$^{st}$ May, 1850 - three months before the rental was prepared - for 60 years. Widow Wm. Allen held 8a 2r 18p, including 3a 3r 32p in Killymam, at a rent of £3 2s 10d for seven years, renewable toties quoties - that is, as often as the superior lease was renewed, the agreement for the lease dating back to 1772, but never executed. There was a fine of £3 2s 10d payable on each renewal. This was one of the cases where the tenant did not contribute to the £7,365, but she was entitled to a conveyance in perpetuity on paying her share, £38 5s 5d to the purchaser of the estate. Wm. Morgan, junr., had exactly the same area at the same rent, renewable every seven years with the same fine, and was entitled to a perpetuity grant on payment of the same amount. The rent charge, however, was only 9s 10d, while Mrs Allen was liable to 11s 10d. The similarity of the areas, etc., leads one to think that the lot originally agreed to be leased had been equally divided and this is corroborated by the fact that Wm. Morgan's lot was held under a lease of 1834 to Rev. Robert Allen. This whole property was the block immediately north of the Burn, now owned by Mr. Porter and Mr. Alexander. Another leaseholder was Jos. Smith, who held under lease for three lives or 31 years from 1831, at a rent of £1 12s 9d for 1r 5p. It was evidently a corner lot as there was a covenant to pay 4s a foot for frontage of any additional house. Widow Devlin was another leaseholder who had not contributed, but was entitled to a conveyance in perpetuity on payment of £9 2s 2d. Her rent was only 14s for 2r 1p and the lease, dated from 1807, given to William Devlin for seven years "toties quoties". George and James Young as representatives of James Dunbar were in the same position. They had 18a 1r 2p in Monrush, and 30 perches in Cookstown at a rent of £7 1s 3d, and were entitled to perpetuity grant on payment of £58 6s. The renewal fine in above cases was one year's rent, but D. W. Henry had a lot of 1a 5p at a rent of £3 12s 0d, under lease to self of 1843, and the fine was only 1s.

Another group held "valuable town parks worth four times the present rent", to quote from the observation column of the rental, as in the case of some tenants in Loy, mentioned last week. The rent was at the same low rate, about 10s per acre, and in every case there was an agreement for a lease for 18 years from November 1839. The tenants were Robert M'Geagh, William Charles, Samuel R. Magill, Miss Rogers, John M'Cormack, Miss Magill, Joseph Rogers, Dr. Charles, Robert M'Geagh, Lieut. Lynd, Wm. Morgan, jun., William M. Collins, John Black, William Glasgow, Robert Glasgow, Widow Wm. Allen, and Joseph Smith. What we read into this is that at the November gale day of 1839 these tenants had, for some reason, asked for and got security of tenure for 18 years. The holdings ranged from 29 perches, in the case of Robert M'Geagh, to 2a 2p in the case of Joseph Smith. The whole area of 23 lots was only 16a 1r 32p, and the total rent secured under these leases only £14 11s 6d.

Where, it will be asked, were these "townparks" worth four times the rent which they were yielding at the time of the sale in 1850? The rental is silent on the point but the sequence of the names gives a clue. Wm. Morgan, junr., had 12 perches at a rent of 6d; Widow Allen had 10 perches at a rent of 6d; Robert Glasgow and Wm. Glasgow had 9 perches at the same rent; John Black had 1a. 2r. 7p. at a rent of 15s 5d. Not one of these tenants is now represented by a descendant in the town; indeed, of the whole of these tenants who got leases for 18 years, the only one whose property is still owned by a descendant is Samuel R. Magill, and most of this was recently sold to the occupants. But we know that Morgan's property was immediately north of the Burn; next came Widow Allen's, now owned by Mr. Alexander; then came Robert Glasgow's, still owned by a descendant, but leased to Mr. Anderson; next was William Glasgow's, now divided and owned partly by the proprietors of The Mid-Ulster Mail and by Mr. Little; then came a big block, now owned by Mr. Joseph Devlin (1 house); Mr. F. P. Devlin (2 houses); Mr. Newell, and others. The leases to these properties, when converted to freeholds in 1855 or afterwards, set out that they are so many feet of frontage, varying with each lot, but all extending back for 400 feet. The original leases, granted by Wm. Stewart when the town was built, described the lots as "going back to the bog", and the "valuable town parks worth four times the present rent" are simply the small bits at the bottoms of the gardens between the leased areas and the fields. The areas, 9, 10, 12 perches and so on, correspond with the widths of the frontage, and, as if to make the proof more complete, the present rents are four times what they were when the estate was sold - at any rate the six penny rents are now two shillings. This throws light on the four "valuable town parks" in Loy, mentioned last week, leased by Wm. Morgan, jun., Dr. Hamilton, Silas E. Weir and Henry O'Farrell, which were undoubtedly the lower parts of the gardens to the houses on the west side of James Street. These properties were leased in 1827 for lives renewable for ever; in 1835 the lands north of the Burn became freehold, and Colonel Stewart retained this strip for the purpose, it is understood, of a street at some future period to run parallel with the main street, and in 1839 he agreed with the owners of the respective properties to give a lease for eighteen years at a nominal rent of 10s per acre of these small lots of the gardens

There were in this townland a few ground rents payable out of premises held from year to year, as was common in Gortalowry. That these rents were for sites only is evident from the fact that the first tenant was John Marshall, who had 1r 13p at a rent of 1s - and no security of tenure. Other such tenants were Mrs. M'Cully, Wm. Rutherford, Mrs. Rutherford, Miss Magill, Thomas H. Miller and John Moffat. The last name of this group is William Oliver, probably one of the family who were here in 1750, who had a ground rent and town park, a total area of 20a 16p, of which 1a 19p were in Monrush, at a rent of £18 2s 4d.

Finally there were the holders of town parks, pure and simple. In the townland of Cookstown there was not much land which could be so described as it is hemmed in by Tullagh and Maloon a short distance down the Burn Road, by Coolreaghs and Monrush in the Oldtown direction, and by Tullygare and New Buildings on the east. Dr. Charles, however, had 16 acres at a rent of £28 10s 6d; Robert M'Geagh, William Charles, Robert Glasgow, John Vandal, James Allen, James M'Caffrey, Mrs. M'Dowall, Joseph Rogers, James M'Entire, Robt. Harkness, Wm. Collins, Archibald Nesbitt, Widow James Allen, Wm. Charles, Joseph Smith, Widow Moffatt, and John Loughran, all held lots, the last being only 21 perches at a rent of 4s 6d while the largest was Widow Allen's 11a 2r 8p, at a rent of £17 11s 10d.

The limestone quarry was in this lot. The area was 3r 31p, and it was "in possession of owner, valued at £10 a year for building ground, it being in the centre of the flax market". This quarry was undoubtedly the one shown on the O.S. map of 1833 to the west of what is now Union Street - the yard of the Greyhound Hotel and stores owned by Mr. Laurence Higgins. It was leased for a good deal more than £10 a year; as regards building ground, it may be noted that the frontage to Union Street has just been completed by the erection of three houses by the present owner Mr. Wright.

We must keep the rental of the agricultural land on this lot till next week.

# SOME TENANTS IN 1850

# (3 – 1 – 1925)

As part of lot 9 at the sale in 1850, there were sold, along with the Loy and Cookstown parts of the town, seven townlands which adjoined the latter and were let to agricultural tenants.   Some of these were classified as townparks and in all seven townlands were some townparks which were held in perpetuity with town sites.  The townlands in question were Killymam, Claggan, Monrush, Ballymenagh, Tullygare, New Buildings and Cranfield, and the names of the tenants three-quarters of a century ago will be of interest.

KILLYMAM – In the observation column we are told that this townland "adjoins the town of Cookstown and is adapted for town parks," but with the exception of the first tenant, Wm. Morgan, junr., who had a field of 2a 3r 5p at a rent of £1 13s 11d, none of the tenants appear to be residents of the town, which we take to be the essence of a townpark - land held, by persons in the town for accommodation.  The largest farm was held by William Rankin, 19a 3r 4p, at a rent of £15 3s 6d; but William Conwell ran him close on area, having 19a 1r 33p, at a rent of £15 8s 2d.  Two other tenants, Thomas Faulkner and Daniel M'Guckin, had each 17 acres odd at rents of £8 12s 2d and £8 7s 6d. Patk. M'Guckin had 14 acres at £9 4s 4d; William Faulkner had about 13½ acres at £8 18s; John Gilchrist had nearly 11½ acres at £7 14s, and James Robinson had 8 acres at £6 9s 10d.  Of all these the Faulkners are, we think, the only survivors after three-quarters of a century.  The total area of these holdings, it will be seen, with 2 acres for roads, was 126 acres, while in the valuation of 1837 the area is given as 156a 3r 31 perches.   This difference would be the extent held under leases with houses in the town. In Griffith's Valuation of 1859, the names of Wm. Paul, Joseph Rogers and Samuel "M'Gill" appear as lessees who had sub-let land in Killymam.

CLAGON – The spelling is that of the rental, and every holding is described as a "townpark of Cookstown".  Whatever may have been the case in 1850 we know that subsequently some of these holdings became ordinary farms.  But on referring to the valuation list of 1837 we find that in neither Killymam, nor in Claggan, were there any houses valued, but in Griffith's Valuation are shown 11 houses in Killymam valued at from 25s to 10s a year, while in Claggan were 18 houses, ranging in value from £2 5s to 5s a year.  As to the tenants, James Brown had 17a 23p at £13 3s 8d, which was the most valuable lot; Wm. Brown, junr., had 17a 8p at

£10 12s 2d; John Musgrave had 17½ acres at £10 18s 4d; Widow Knipe had about 15½ acres at £10 11s 6d; John Faulkner had just over 11 acres at £6 16s. The other holdings were smaller, the tenants being Robert Brown, James Lynd, Wm. Lynd, William Faulkner, Wm. Brown, Samuel Miller, Robert M'Connell, and Robert Dunseith. Several of these holdings are still held by descendants of the tenants in 1850, and no doubt the smaller holdings have been absorbed by the larger. They all held as yearly tenancies except James Lynd, who had 8a 16p under lease for ever at a rent of £3 16s 2d, with 8s Rent Charge. When this rent is compared with the others we see how much land had increased in value.

MONRUSH – All the holdings in this townland were described as town parks, and we imagine the description was correct, as it is to-day, part of the townland being inside the town boundary and forming part of the street. In 1850 the largest holding was that of Silas E.Weir, who had 15½ acres at a rent of £27; Robert M'Geagh had just over 8 acres at £13 11s 8d; the Misses Rogers had 7½ acres at £12; John Harbison had under 7½ acres at £11 7s 10d. The other tenants, who had smaller lots were Thomas M'Allister, Dr. Charles, James Allen, Wm. Rutherford, Wm. Morgan, jun., Robert Miller, John M'Cullagh, Thos. Miller (Listler), Mrs. M'Cully, Jos. Smith, Widow Rutherford, Thomas Black, James Vandal and Thomas Black. The rents of Monrush were substantially higher than of Claggan, reaching £2 2s for one acre held by John M'Cullagh, while James Allen paid £8 for less than 5 acres. Mr. Weir paid exactly 30s per acre, which may be regarded as the normal rent. In 1837 the valuation of the whole townland was £200 for 160 acres.

BALLYMENAGH – This townland is farther from Cookstown, averaging about a mile distant and only two of the holdings on it were described as town parks. These were held by Andrew Wilson, who paid £10 3s 4d for 7¾ acres, and George Rutherford, who paid £7 8s 4d for 8a 1r 8p. The principal tenant in the townland was Chas. Quin, who held three separate lots. The largest was 45½ acres at a rent of £48; the other two measured 36½ acres and the rent was £39 13s 6d. This is the farm now owned by Mr. Alexander Cameron, J.P., and was the seat of James Stewart, who bought the lease in 1620, before Killymoon demesne was in existence. The ruins of the old "castle" are still standing, but in 1837 the housing must have been very poor as the total valuation of houses in the townland was only £4 15s. By 1859 this total had risen to £7 10s yearly valuation, of which the entire buildings on Charles Quin's farm amounted to £2 10s. Other tenants in 1850 were Wm. Cooke, James Bell, William Crooks, Samuel Crooks, George Johnston, Jas. Crooks, and John Bane, most of whom are still represented.

TULLYGARE – This townland adjoins Ballymenagh, and we are told that "it is adapted for town parks". It is small, only six holdings being in it in 1850, apart from those held under lease with town houses. There were really only three farmers in it; John Anderson, who had almost 15 acres at a rent of £10 13s 4d; Thomas Harvey who had 13½ acres at £14 9s and Jas. Johnston who had 5a 2r 29p at £6 8s. In addition Wm. Morgan, junr., who seems to have had a hunger for land, held 3½ acres in Tullgare at £5 8s; Wm. M'Conney had 1r 33p at 22s a year, and Archibald Nesbitt had 1r 8p at 6s 10d a year - the latter two being merely small gardens.

NEW BUILDINGS – This townland, also described as adapted for town parks, was also small, and the first name on the rental is again William Morgan, jun., who had 8a at £6 2s 2d. The largest holding was that of James Kidd, who had almost 17 acres at £15 5s; John Kidd had 11 acres at £12 12s 4d; Henry M'Kenzie had nearly 7 acres at £9 11s 4d; John Johnston had 10½ acres at £12; Thos. Walker had 3½ acres at 16s 2d; Wm. Shaw and Francis Shaw paid £3 each for under 3 acres. These names will be recognised as those of the present residents, showing how little agricultural land changes its ownership compared with town properties. Why this townland got the name "New Buildings" is still a puzzle; it certainly had more buildings than Monrush or Claggan, but nothing to make a name of, judging by the fact that in the valuation roll of 1837 the total amount put on the houses was only £3 9s and in 1859 was only £10, of which £3 10s was on the buildings of James Kidd.

CRANFIELD – This is the last townland of this lot. Only one holding is described as a townpark, 1r 19p held by Archibald Nesbitt at 1s a year. The chief tenant was Thomas Beatty, who had over 26 acres at a rent of £18 16s: John Anderson had nearly 18 acres at £15 13s 6d; Wm. Davidson had 12½ acres at £10, and John Vincent had 11½ acres at £10 4s 8d. Smaller tenants were Elizabeth Thompson and James Davidson, while Thomas Walker had 3r 2p, at £1 1s 8d, and Patrick Reid had 37 perches at 4s 10d. The only other tenant was Jas. Anderson, who had 5a 2r 39p, at £1 3s 3d a year, and about it we are informed that "This is worth £40 a year, but at present let to an old man as a gratuity".

The total rent of Lot 9 was £1,728 9s 10d out of which the proportion of head rent payable to the See of Armagh was £174 18s 8d, and the rent charge paid by the landlord was £54 19s 2d, making a net rental of £1,498 12s 0d. The timber on this lot was valued at £815 12s 10d.

Next week we shall give similar information from the rental regarding Maloon, Tullagh, and other townlands on the estate.

# TULLAGH AND MALOON IN 1850

# (17 – 1 – 1925)

Last week we gave the names of the tenants of the agricultural holdings and townparks in Lot 9 sold in 1850 and taken from the rental then published. Though not of very general interest, still it will be admitted that these names are of historical value, and being in the rental gives them a more definite connection with the town than if in a mere directory. At all events we know the tenants of 1850 are of great interest to their successors in 1925, and, at the risk of exhausting the patience of those who do not live in these townlands, we are continuing the information this week.

TULLAGH – Unlike Lot 9, which included, with the town sites in Loy and Cookstown, no less than seven adjacent townlands, giving a net income of £1,498 12s, the townland of Tullagh comprised an entire lot (No. 7), with a net income of only £123 7s 4½d. This was also Church lands, held from the See of Armagh and leased by the Stewarts, but converted into perpetuity by Col. Wm. Stewart in 1835, subject to a rent of £24 6s. We associate it with the hill of that name, and quite properly, for the townland is named after it, being in fact the anglicised form of the Gaelic word for a hill. The youth of the town name the river at the foot of the steep declivity as the Tullagh river (Kildress river is the official name till it gets to Killymoon when it becomes the Ballinderry), perhaps because the only way they can get out to the popular bathing place is up one side of the hill and down at right angles, the old road of 1736 being closed, when the straight roads were introduced by Mr. Wm. Stewart as part of the plan of the town. Many people, therefore, are unaware that they reach Tullagh townland when walking along the Burn Road towards the Workhouse gate, the little stream being the boundary. Hence it is that the thirty ex-servicemen's houses, built on part of the Workhouse farm, and known as Mount Royal, are officially described as in Tullagh. To farmers who attend Cookstown Fair we may say that the Fair Hill is in Loy, but they will have noticed that the road narrows at the Sports field, and at that point Tullagh begins, Mr. Stewart having taken the townland boundary as leaving sufficient space for the fair green, which he substituted for the commons at the far end of Oldtown. Though so near the town, it is worth noting that the Rental does not claim that the lands of Tullagh were townparks: it only says that "several of the holdings are used as townparks". Only two of these were leased in 1850, the Poor Law Commissioners were the lessees of 17a. 2r. 6p. at a rent of £35 3s- about £2 per acre. This is the holding on which the ex-servicemen's houses are built. This was an addition to the Workhouse farm, and the lease was executed on 28th April 1849, when Col. Stewart was in the last year of his life. The lease was for 60 years, from November 1848, and apparently the Commissioners were doubtful of the propriety of taking this extra land for they had a surrender clause by which they could have given it up on six months' notice, on payment of half-a-year's rent as a fine.

Visitors to Mount Royal will certainly notice that before they reach the houses from the county road they pass a fine hay barn, the property of Mr. M'Mahon. The small plot of land, about 24 perches, which seems to be a farmyard without farm or residence, was not included in the lease and on it a little thatched cottage existed till recent years, when it was removed – it was burned down in fact. The Guardians failed to secure it though the house and little garden were evidently part of their field. In 1850 the rental shows that the tenant was Nicholas Lambe, who paid a rent of half-a-crown per annum for it, and today that tenant is remembered only by the fact that the ascent up to Mount Royal is known as Lambe's Hill. It was typical of many little thatched cottages and gardens which were scattered over the country when there was a much denser agricultural population than now exists, the disappearance of which is causing the demand for labourers cottages built by the ratepayers. And it is, we think, a testimony to the consideration of Col. Stewart that when he leased the land to the Poor Law Commissioners he did not exercise his right and throw in poor Lambe's little holding for which he got only half-a-crown a year.

The only other leased land was held by Doctor Thomas Dickson. This was the cottage or house now owned by Mr. Farley, which had been leased by Col. Stewart to Dr. Dickson in 1843 for the life of William S. Dickson – probably a healthy young son, likely to live long – or for 31 years, whichever was the longer. The area was 18a. 1r. 37p. and the rent £16 10s, so that he held at less than half the rent which the Poor Law Commissioners were willing to pay. Dr. Dickson resided on the holding, though whether he built the house we do not know.

The rest of the townland was held from year to year. Some of this was undoubtedly accommodation land. Matthew S. Glasgow, who lived on Loy Hill opposite the Fair Green, had 8 acres at £7 a year; Charles Mooney had two holdings - probably just two fields - amounting to 9½ acres at £19 19s; John Mooney had just over 3 acres at £2 19s 6d; Dr. Hamilton had 7 acres at £10 - undoubtedly accommodation land or town parks. On the other hand John Sally had 6a. 1r. 10p, at £6 a year, and his representatives are still there; John Reid had 10a. 1r. 8p. at £7 7s, and it is not long since the last of the Reids left Tullagh. Other tenants were Neal M'Cartney, who had nearly 11 acres at a rent of £5 13s 6d, showing that the rents were not screwed up as the value of the land increased; Thomas M'Loughlin had 9½ acres at £11 16s 7d; George Davidson had the same area at £6 10s 4d - probably an earlier "take" when land was cheaper. John Reid had a second holding of 5 acres odd at £4 4s. Other tenants mentioned in the rental are Joseph Black, Thomas Blair, John Molloy, Amelia Roberts, and John Glenn, while Thomas Adair had a small plot of 2r 10p, no doubt adjacent to the river, at a rent of 5s.

The plantations in Tullagh measured 22 perches and the timber was valued at £13 6s. The total rental was £154 3s 9d, out of which the landlord paid £6 10s 4½d Rent Charge, and £24 6s Head Rent to the See of Armagh.

MALOON – This townland, which adjoins Cookstown and Tullagh, was also put up for sale in one lot as none of the land was held with house property in the town under a common lease. Maloon was one of the townlands granted by James I. to a native gentleman who sold to James Stewart, of Ballymenagh, or perhaps his son William, about 1630. It was, therefore, freehold, subject only to a Crown rent, or Rent Charge as it was called, of £7 15s.

The Workhouse is situated on this land. The original site was only 6a. 1r. 6p., leased at a rent of £18 1s 7½d by the Poor Law Commissioners, but in 1845 they got 1a. 2r. 17p. more at a rent of £4 12s 4d, so that, while Col. Stewart and his agents were tender enough when dealing with poor, like Nicholas Lambe, they did not hesitate to extort a big rent when dealing with public officials. The lease of the Workhouse also contained a covenant (which is still operative for anything we know to the contrary) that if the lessees wish to sell, they must give the lessor the option of buying at a price to be fixed by arbitration. These leases, we should say were for 999 years.

Half a dozen tenants had agreements for a lease, which gave them as good a title and saved some legal expenses. John M'Cormick had an agreement for a lease for 60 years of his holding of 13 acres, at a rent of £19 6s. Mr. M'Cormick was virtually the agent of the estate, but it cannot be said that, though the agreement was the made only in May 1850, when he probably knew the estate was going to be sold (the rental is dated August) he made a good bargain for himself, the rent being 30s a year. Four other lots were also subject to agreements for leases for 18 years from 1839 – the same period and from the same date as the "valuable townparks" mentioned in the case of Cookstown townland, and which we identified as the strip at the foot of the gardens. The lessees were Samuel R. Magill, 1a. 3r. 17p. at 18s; Wm. Morgan, jun., had just over 2 acres at £1 1s 9d; Joseph Rogers 3r. 17p. at 8s 6d, and Lt. Lynd 1a. 1r. 27p. at 12s. These rents, it will be seen, are round 10s per acre, and when compared with Mr. M'Cormick's 30s per acre, the value of the land in the vicinity of the town had trebled from 1839 to 1850.

Maloon extends northwards towards Milburn Factory, and many readers who go along that road – the original road to Cookstown from Derryloran - will have seen a little stream which they have learned rises out at Balance's well. Therefore, when we find that the second tenant in the rental is Jas. Balance, who had 13a. 1r. 10p. at a rent of £11 13s 6d, we have little doubt as to where his holding lay. He, like Nicholas Lambe, though leaving no issue locally to perpetuate his name, is immortalised in the nomenclature of the countryside. Other tenants were William Faulkner, Samuel M'Kenny (as it is spelled), John Patrick, Wm. Miller, John Gourlay, Wm. Rankin, Robert Rankin, John M'Gucken, Wm. Rutherford, and Nathaniel Rankin. Most, if not all these, were farmers, of whom the Rankins are the best known, living as they recently did in a comfortable house alongside the Orritor Road. John Black was the largest farmer in the townland, having two holdings with an aggregate acreage of 33 acres at a rent of £34 8s 8d. Then there was David M'Clelland, who had 7½ acres at £8. Finally Dr. Hamiton appears as tenant of 2r. 26p. - a garden with possibly a cottier house on it – at a rent of 10s yearly.

The quarry was, at this time, rented by Thomas Blair at £5 a year, This, we take it, is the old quarry close to the Workhouse grounds, presently in the occupation of the Urban Council as a dumping ground, but out of which the freestone came to build the houses in Molesworth Street, then unbuilt. Whether Blair was a contractor or not we cannot say at the moment; perhaps some reader can enlighten us.

Next Week: Drumcraw and Drumgarrell

# DRUMCRAW AND DRUMGARRELL

## (24 – 1 – 1925)

These two townlands, which adjoin and lie along the Coagh road from Cranfield to Co. Derry mearing, were sold as two separate lots. They were also Church lands, but had been bought by Col. Wm. Stewart, who held in perpetuity, the former subject to a rent of £18 7s 5d and the latter to a rent of £17 7s 2d. They were let as agricultural holdings, and the net income from Drumcraw was £84 3s 3½d, and of Drumgarrell £78 19s 8d. The latter contained a large quantity of bog, which accounts for its size, having an area of 286 acres, while Drumcraw has 158 acres.

Special historic interest attaches to Drumcraw, with which Drumgarrell is closely associated. The late Mr. Gunning-Moore on one occasion told the present writer that he owned "Tullagh temple", but what, or where, it was he had no idea. At the time we were unable to enlighten him, but subsequent examination of the map of 1609 disclosed that it was then the name of a "bally" or townland on which a roofless church was shown. It adjoins on the map, which is a rude production, the townlands of Ballymenagh, Lismoney, on the one side, and Tirassan and Crangbett (Cranfield) on the other, while between it and the river are Tullocarrabim, Dromsey and Tollaghdromgerrill. These three latter, with Tullagh-temple, seem to correspond to the present townlands of Drumcraw and Drumgarrell. In the title deeds of the Killymoon Estate, lodged in the Four Courts, which the writer was privileged to study by special permission, the leases to the Stewarts of the lands owned by the See of Armagh, dating back to the 17th century, recited the names of the townlands, always beginning with Tullagh-temple, which was, of course, the reason why Mr. Moore had noticed the name in his conveyance from the Incumbered Estate Court, though possibly the conveyancer did not know what or where it was any more than he did.

There can be no doubt of the identity of the place with Drumcraw; the ruined church shown on the map proves that, for Drumcraw was originally the name of a parish quite distinct form Derryloran. The union of the parishes took place in 1449, by order of Primate Mey, Archbishop of Armagh, who will be remembered by students of Irish History as being the cleric who, for a time, acted as Lord Deputy when the Earl of Ormond was Lord Lieutenant, and who subsequently refused to attend the Irish Parliament as a Lord spiritual because the Archbishop of Dublin used force to prevent him having a cross carried before him in the streets of Dublin, so keen was the antagonism of the two dioceses for priority. That, however, is another story. Before Mey was elected to the bench of bishops at all, the rector and vicar of Derryloran had their eyes on Drumcraw or Drumgaa as it was sometimes called, and, in 1440, when the parish was vacant, they petitioned to have it annexed to Derryloran and made one parish, the ground of the application being, not the convenience of the people, but that their livings were so small that they could not maintain the usual hospitalities or discharge the episcopal duties. They represented that the two churches were only a mile apart, and the revenue of Drumcraw did not, by common estimation, exceed one mark sterling per annum (thirteen shillings and fourpence) which they proposed should be divided between them - the rector and the vicar getting half each. The rector of Derryloran at this time was Owen O'Connollan and his vicar was William O'Connollan, a family who seemed to have supplied Derryloran with many clergymen. The mile distance must have caused a wrench on their consciences, and the parishioners who had to walk from Drumcraw, via the road, now largely disappeared, via Killymoon to the old Church at Derryloran, had a long trail.

It is now impossible to say how much of the present parish of Derryloran belonged originally to the parish of Drumcraw. It may be taken for certain that all the townlands across the border, which are in the civil parish of Derryloran - Annahavil, Ballyloughan, Tullyhog, Ballyforlea, Dunman, Derrycrummy, and Drumrott, which lie beyond Drumcraw, were annexed at that time. Few, if any, of the inhabitants of these townlands belong to the present parish of Derryloran, but are in either Lissan or Desertlyn, and no doubt many of them are puzzled why they should be described in official and legal documents as in Derryloran. Well, they have to thank the Rector in 1440, Rev. Owen O'Connollan, and his vicar, Rev. Wm. O'Connollan. But for them they would have had a parish of their own, with, no doubt, the people of Cranfield, Clare, and perhaps of Corcreagh, or the north end of Cookstown, for it is to be assumed that the church of Drumcraw was more or less central in the parish.

The old Church at Drumcraw was stated by the late Rev. Dr. Carter, in his Bazaar Handbook of 1891, to be on the hill beyond the school, on Mr. Espy's farm, and Dr. Carter adds that the "remains of it existed till a few years ago", but had then disappeared as had the churchyard, though "interments were made in it within living memory". The existence of any ruins of the Church, after being closed 400 years, is very doubtful, but there was a field altar there in penal times, and long afterwards it was regarded as consecrated ground by the Roman Catholics of Cookstown. The name only remains, but by a curious accident the old parish name has become the name of the townland, displacing Tullagh Temple – the hill of the Church.

At the time of the sale, in 1850, there were ten tenants in the townland, the largest farm being 37½ acres held by Bernard M'Kenna at a rent of £30.  John and James Espy held 31 acres at £18 15s 8d; John Greer had 15½ acres at £9 10s; James Mullan had 14½ acres at £9 7s; Andrew Boon had 13½ acres at £8 5s 6d; James Espy had 12½ acres at £9 13s; Widow Mullan had 11½ acres at £10 9s 8d, while Widow Espy, Robert Conn and Benjamin Gourley held from 3 to 6 acres each.  Most of these tenants are still represented in the townland.  The timber was valued at £90, showing that there was much more than at present.  In 1837 the valuation of the townland was £85 14s 10d on land and £4 4s on buildings, so that the rent was 25 per cent more than the valuation.  In Griffith's Valuation of 1859 the amount on the land was £102 15s while the annual value of the houses was £10 15s, of which £3 was on that of Esther Espy, while Charles M'Kernan's came next at £1 15s, and the others were all 15s or 10s - small thatched cottages.

Drumgarroll, as it is spelled in the rental, was larger.  In the observation column it is stated that "attached to the townland there is a valuable Turf Bog, about 30 acres thereof are held by tenants of Cookstown under perpetuity leases.  The remainder has been given to other tenants in Cookstown as easements to their holdings, but they have no legal claim to it, and it is worth £50 a year".  Readers will note that, at that time, Cookstown and Loy bogs having been cut out, inhabitants of the town got a bit of bog for turf in Drumgarrell.  As we remarked before, the leasing in perpetuity was a grave error because the tenants cut it as long as they got anything and left it in the condition in which it now exists - a useless swamp – whereas, if the turbary had been properly controlled by the land agent it would have been valuable meadow land.  No less than 94 acres were either held under perpetuity leases or given to tenants as easements and remains a monument, on the roadside to Coagh, to the misdirected generosity of indulgent landowners - probably will remain till some Ministry of Labour takes it, and similar places, in charge and provides test work for applicants for the dole.

There were nine tenants in Drumgarrell, all of whom held from year to year except Samuel R. Magill, who held 83½ acres under a perpetuity lease made in 1841, at a rent of £29 3s 8d, and £2 18s 6d Rent Charge.  In Griffith's Valuation of 1859 Mr. Magill appears as the owner in fee.  The house, known as Greenlodge, was valued at £5 10s, which was considerably more than most farm houses, and the bleach mill and offices at £13.   The next largest tenant in the rental was Samuel Anderson, who had 40 acres at £26 14s 8d, the dwelling-house being valued in 1859 at £2; Thomas Blair held 24½ acres at £19, and Wm. Gourlay held 11½ acres at £8 7s 10d, these houses having a valuation of £1 per annum.   The other tenants were William M'Elhenny 7 acres,

Patrick M'Elkenny 6 acres, James Little 5½ acres, and Andrew Room, who had 2r 12p – a garden and presumably a cottage on it, rent 7s 6d. The timber in Drumgarrell was valued at £43 9s.

Next week we propose to touch on Coolnahavil and Scotchtown, and adjacent townlands in the south end of the town, parts of which were held as town parks.

## LETTER TO THE EDITOR

## Dr Dickson of Tullagh

*Sir, - In the instalment of the History of Cookstown, published last week, you mention a small farm in Tullagh, held under a lease by Dr. Thomas Dickson, and say you do not know whether he built the house on same. Dr. Dickson was at one time a well-known man in the district. His father had been the Presbyterian minister of Sandholes, and must have been a man of considerable energy, as it was in his time, about 1795, the meeting house was built, which, with some additions, is still standing. Dr. Tom, as he was known, was for a good many years a surgeon in the Navy, and, in the early years of the nineteenth century, saw some stirring times during the war with France. Retiring with a pension he settled on a farm in Killygarvin , about 4½ miles from Cookstown, where he had a large practice as a medical man. He was a fine type of man, and was considered to have great medical skill.*

*When the Cookstown Workhouse was built he was appointed the first dispensary medical officer of the Cookstown district, and for some time walked regularly to and from Cookstown - a long walk for an elderly man. An old farmer, whose house he passed on the way, told me that, as long as Dr. Dickson walked regularly to Cookstown, he did not require a barometer. If the doctor carried a walking stick a fine day might be expected, but if he carried an umbrella, the farmer felt certain there would be rain. Finding the long walks too trying the doctor acquired the small farm in Tullagh to which you refer; he himself designed the peculiar cottage which is still standing, and which he got built. It was said he selected the site because he could lie in bed, with his window open, and listen to the water falling over the weir below.*

*In his later years the doctor was said to have become somewhat eccentric, and on one occasion, at a meeting of the Board, a guardian said he had been asked to make a complaint that the doctor did not keep a proper supply of medicines. This was too much for the guardian for the*

*Sandholes division, afterwards for many years a well-known figure at the Board, known for his dry humour, expressed with great deliberation. He at once rose and said:- "Augh! What are you talkin' about! He could do more with a stone of salts than the most of the doctors with all the medicines you could give them". The old doctor passed away soon after, and the late Dr. Graves was appointed to succeed him.- Yours, etc.*

*ANTIQUARY.*

## COOLNAHAVIL ETC.
## IN 1850

## (7-2-1925)

Coolnahavil (the orchard of the corner) is a little townland adjoining Killymoon Demesne, and lying between it and Gortalowry. The total area is only 42 acres, showing that most of the original townland had been merged in the Demesne, for a ballyboe (or townland) was 60 acres Irish of arable land, which a team of oxen was supposed to be able to plough in a year, hence the name. In 1850 some 26 acres was in the possession of Col. Stewart as an addition to the demesne, but outside the wall, and the rental put down was £39, as it "would let for this rent". This, it will be seen, was at the rate of 30s per acre, which may be taken as the letting value of good land in conacre, at that time, near the town. That the rent was not uniform is indicated by the fact that two tenants had accommodation land at very different rates; Andrew Saunderson had over 7½ acres at £8 11s 4d, while Wallace Gibson paid £2 16s 8d for 1a 2r 19p. The only other tenant in the rental was James Johnston, who had almost 4½ acres at £7 4s 6d. These tenants had disappeared in 1859, as Griffith's Valuation shows that Godfrey O. Lyle was then the occupier.

Drummond was joined with Coolnahavil to make one lot at the sale, although it lay on the other side of the demesne. Only 15 acres of the original ballyboe remained, the rest having been absorbed by the demesne. The wall followed the county road at this point, and these 15 acres were a fragment which lay on the other side of the road, adjoining Doorless and Ardvarnish. The present size of the townland was, therefore, determined by the road makers when the old straight roads were made about the middle of the 18th century. Of this small area about 2 acres were the county road; the balance was held by three different tenants - Arthur Mayne, Hugh Mullan and Charles Mullan, the latter having merely 6 acres and the other between 3 and 4 acres. Their holdings were probably a sub-division as the rents were £2 16s 1d each, and the area about equal. The timber on the whole Lot was valued at £74 10s. Drummond, it may be mentioned, was held in fee by Col. Stewart, his ancestor having bought out a native freeholder who got the townland at the Plantation. Coolnahavil had been Church land, the lease of which was converted into perpetuity in 1835, subject to a head rent of £9 6s 4d. The net income out of this Lot was £55 8s 2d and we are told, as an inducement to investors, that "the neighbourhood is very peaceable and the lands are occupied by an industrious tenantry".

Ardcumber was sold in Lot 6, with Gortalowry. It also was a fragment of the old ballyboe, containing only 31 acres, of which 6 were roads, and about half an acre plantation. This was also Church lands, or lands held by the herenagh from the bishop at a low rent, with a responsibility for maintaining the local Church. The first lease we have met in which it appeared is dated 13th July 1362, when Nilo, Archbishop of Armagh, with the consent of the Dean and Chapter of Armagh, let to Benedict Oculean, Canon of Armagh Cathedral, "the lands of his archbishopric at Tullyhog, Dalinlega, Balconnleery and Ardcumo", at £5 3s 4d yearly rent. In the rental of the Deanery of Tullyhog in 1428 we find that Ardcombye paid 3s 4d half-yearly – the rent being half a mark. This does not convey much to us now, the value of money being so different from what it was 500 years ago, but the relative importance of Ardcumber can be guessed from the fact that, at the same time, the Derryloran herenagh paid 2 marks yearly – only four times as much. Arboe (spelled in the rental Ardboo) which has a very large tract of Church lands, held at one time by the Killymoon Stewarts, and Artrea, where are also extensive Church lands, paid also 2 marks, while Tamlaght, Ballyclog and Drumglass paid only one mark. Lissan, which had attached a very large extent of country - the whole of the Staples estate - paid one mark yearly rent, while Kildress, which had a very extensive amount of herenagh lands, as readers in that parish are aware, was rented for half a mark, the same as Ardcumber. These comparisons will give us an idea of the importance of the latter in former times, shrunk as it had become in 1850 to 31 acres. It also shows that though now portion of Derryloran parish, Ardcumber, like Drumcraw, was originally an independent parish which had been absorbed. One is tempted to point out how history repeats itself, for in the Church of Ireland as well as in the Presbyterian Church, the same process of uniting parishes and congregations is now going on, the weaker being joined and ultimately absorbed by the stronger, but we imagine (though we have no proof) that in the 15th century there was less consideration for the minority that now exists.

Scotchtown was another small townland which was included in Lot 6 with Gortalowry. It also lies between Gortalowry and Killymoon, south of Fountain's Road and in 1850 had only 24 ½ acres. This land was all let as townparks, and at that time the tenants were Thomas Wilson, James Johnston, John Harris and Wallace Gibson, the latter having over 12 acres, or half the townland. The name is, of course, modern and it has been suggested that it got it because the Presbyterian minister lived there before the church and manse were built in the town. It is very probably the part of the ballyboe of Tirnegan, which adjoined Coolnafranky as shown on the map of 1609, these two being given at the Plantation to Mary Neill, daughter of Sir Cormick, who married William Stewart, and whose son Robert sold to James Stewart of Ballymenagh in 1632. At any rate it was held in fee simple by Col. Stewart, free of rent.

Clare was also included in Lot 6. It contained just 144 acres, and, being mostly arable, the present townland no doubt corresponds with the old ballyboe. It lies east of Coolnafranky and Loy, and quite close to the present town boundary: the main sewer, when it leaves the Great Northern Railway yard, is the boundary, so that a good deal of the G.N Railway sidings are in it. In 1850 the principal tenant was John Cooke, who was, we believe, a member of the family who had owned the mill at Greeenvale half a century earlier. He held under an agreement for a lease dating back to 1769. It was Church lands also and the lease was (or was to be) for seven years, renewable as often as the Stewarts renewed the chief lease from the See of Armagh. As already stated this Colonel Stewart had bought out, as we now say, by paying £7, 365, to which sum many of the sub-tenants contributed their quota, but the Cookes, who were in low water financially, had failed to do so. This did not affect their right to a grant in perpetuity as we read in the observation column. "Tenant entitled to conveyance in perpetuity upon paying £74 7s 6d, being his proportion of purchase of the fee". The rent, we should say, was £9 14s 6d, with a fine of the same amount every seven years on renewal of the lease, and the purchaser of Col. Stewart's interest was entitled to that sum. It should be explained that when a sub-tenant failed to pay his share of the £7,365, Col. Stewart had to pay and was entitled to interest, at, we think, 6 per cent. on the money. The rent was, as already stated, £9 14s 6d, for which Cooke held almost 30 acres (29a 3r 6p) which gives an idea of the low letting value of land adjacent to Cookstown in 1769.

The rest of the townland was held from year to year, as ordinary holdings. John Crooks had 22 acres at £13 12s 2d – probably a fairly old letting for the Stewarts did not raise the rents, so far as we have observed, on existing tenants, as the value of land increased. Widow D. Mullan had 17 acres at £14 13s, and Hugh Mullan had 11 acres at £9 9s. The other holdings were small, from 41 perches to 7½ acres, the tenants being Widow John McElroy, John McElroy, Margaret Cregan, Daniel Owens, John Stewart, and Charles Ferguson, in order of size of holdings. The rents on these little farms rose to as high as 30s per acre.

The timber on Lot 6 – Gortlalowry, Sullenboy, Clare, Ardcumber and Scotchtown – was valued at £1,824 10s 6d. The Tithe rent charge payable by the landlord was £29 13s 8d, and the head rent payable to the See of Armagh was £22 5s 4d, a total outgoing of £51 19s, leaving the rental at £835 11s 0d for 545 acres.

# ERRATA

Mr Alfred Moore Munn points out that in the article on the townlands of Co Londonderry, which we thought would be in the extinct parish of Drumcraw, we were mistaken in stating that these now belonged to Lissan and Desertlyn. None of them are in the latter parish. He gives us the following list: - Anahavil is "partly" in Arboe and partly in Derryloran; Ballyloughan, Dunman, Derrycrummy and Tyressan are entirely in Derryloran, while Lismoney is in Lissan.

Another reader has drawn attention to a misprint in the same article, the name Tullyhog appearing as one of the townlands which were probably in Drumcraw parish. This was a printer's error for Tullyboy (the yellow hill), which is part of the civil parish of Derryloran. Tullyhog is in the parish of Desertcreat on the south side of Derryloran and could never have been part of Drumcraw.

Another correspondent writes that it is erroneous to say that Drumcraw was part of the estate of Mr. Gunning-Moore. That is so. The article did not expressly say that it was, but that was conveyed by the reference to Mr. Gunning-Moore, who said that "Tullagh Temple" belonged to him. It is an illustration of the curious fact that conveyances repeat names which have become meaningless. Tullagh Temple was the first name in the old See leases and, with others which had disappeared, it was repeated in deeds, on the principle that it is safer to include anything extraneous than to omit something which may prove important. The actual purchasers of the various lots will be given shortly.

Next week we shall give similar information from the rental regarding Lot 4 – Ballyreagh, Colcrunagh and Knockaconny.

# BALLYREAGH, COLCRUNAGH
# AND KNOCKACONNY IN 1850

## (14-2-1925)

These three townlands were included in one lot in the rental for the sale in 1850. Though none of the land was so near as to be used as townparks, yet we feel justified in referring to them. Ballyreagh comes up to Derryloran Glebe, and is, therefore, quite close to the town, and it is due to that proximity that it was in the Killymoon Estate at all. The reason for this is interesting from several points of view and goes back almost to the Plantation. The first Protestant rector of the parish was Rev. Wm. Darragh, and was married to a sister of Mr. Stewart of Ballymenagh. Incidentally he held also the livings of Arboe and Clonoe, and was chaplain to Lord Caulfield, and was murdered in the insurrection of 1641. He seems to have been one of the old type of clergymen who were fond of farming: at all events he was not satisfied with the Glebe at Derryloran, but rented Ballyreagh, Colcrunagh and Knockaconny, which were portion of the precinct or manor of Gortaville, granted to a David Kennedy, but speedily broken up.

Like a wise man, the Rev. Mr. Darragh got a lease in perpetuity, though it meant saddling himself and his heirs for ever with the rent charge. But what was the result? On his death his interest passed to the Stewarts, who were merely tenants. Kennedy, the landlord, sold his interest and it passed through various hands, being ultimately bought as an investment by Rev. J. Lowry of Desertcreat through whom it descended to the Rockdale family. But in 1850, when the rental amounted to £350, the owner in fee got only £11 1s 6d, while Colonel Stewart, the tenant in perpetuity, got £339. These figures are illuminating as showing the great increase in the cash value of land following the Plantation. The real value did not increase so much because money had fallen in purchasing price. Thus, in the years preceding the Plantation, a tenant who had to pay £11 rent had the option, which he generally exercised, of driving fourteen or fifteen cows to his landlord, or if they had their calves with them, eleven would be accepted for the rent. We see, however, in this case, as we saw when considering the perpetuity rent for the Orritor Estate which Hans Baillie agreed to pay to Lord Annesley, that the value of land rose so enormously as to make the interest of the owner in fee absolutely insignificant.

Turning now to the rental, we find that there were 237 acres in Ballyreagh, held by a dozen of tenants, the largest farm being 35 acres, held by John and Andrew Ferguson at £22 13s 6d rent. This, and most of the other farms, were held under leases - in this case for three lives or 31 years from 1797. In 1850 the lives in being were Andrew Ferguson and the Earl of Ranfurly. We think that we are correct in saying that there was a disagreement of opinion amongst the tenants here and elsewhere, as to the advisability of accepting leases, which bound them to a certain rent, but though 31 years, or even three lives, was a very different proposition to perpetuity, still it must be agreed that they were better off than those who held from year to year. In addition to the rent mentioned the tenant was liable for a rent-charge of £1 3s 8d.

There was another farm larger than this, having 39 acres, held under lease to Adam Lynd, made in 1797, and the only remaining life was the Earl of Ranfurley, but in 1850 it was subdivided between Thomas Wilson and "Duffy and Boyle". The rent was £22 19s 7d, with £1 7s 1d rent charge. The highest rent was £24 5s 10d paid by John Lynd, the representative of William Lynd, who had got the lease from Col. Wm. Stewart in 1837 for three lives and, though only 13 years had passed, the Earl of Ranfurly was the only life then in being. The rent was not substantially higher than in the older leases because, as we noticed already, Col. Stewart did not practise rack renting. Three other leases existed in the townland, all made in 1803 for one life or 21 years. The tenants who got the leases in that year were Thomas McCormick (almost 29 acres at £18 5s 10d rent), Hugh McCormick, Jr. (almost 20 acres at £16 9s 7d rent), and Rosanna McCormick (almost 11 acres at £8 11s 10d rent). The "lives" were all in being in 1850 (Hugh McCormick, David Hamilton and Thomas Lindsay respectively). The tenants in 1850 were John McCormick, Hugh McCormick and George Fleming for the three holdings.

The rest of the holdings were from year to year. James Harris had 14 acres at £11 16s 8d rent; Widiw McGahan had almost 6 acres at £5 8s 2d rent; John Kane had 5 ½ acres at £5 0s 5d rent: Hugh McCormick had just over 6 acres at £6 17s 4d rent, while John Kane had a larger holding of 31 ½ acres at £19 1s 10d rent.

Colcrunagh (or Kilconagh as it is officially written) lies adjacent to Ballyreagh along the road to Sandholes which travellers will notice had been straightened like the rest of the principal roads on the Stewart estate. It contained 184 statute acres, so that there was less waste land originally, and presumably what was arable was better, though it does not always follow owing to the difference in the type of tenants. In this townland, again, leases were common, several dating from 1797. The largest farm was held by James Fleming. The lease had been given in 1837 to John Moorhead, £20 3s for under 24 acres of land. It is peculiar in two respects. One was that there was to be an additional rent of £5 for every house built in addition to the dwelling-house – a "penal rent" it is called in the Observation, and the name is apt. One can understand such a clause in a lease of land which was likely to become building ground, and it is far more preferable than leaving ground vacant and unprofitable, but it is very peculiar to find a provision of that sort in a purely agricultural district. Perhaps there was some reason, not apparent to the writer, but we are inclined to attribute it to a fad of whoever was agent of the estate in 1837. The other peculiarity of the lease was a provision that in case John Moorhead, one of the "lives" should be absent from the United Kingdom when it expired, or any time afterwards should be absent for two years, the lease was to terminate. Though this seems to limit the movements of the tenant it is not unreasonable, being, in effect, a way of assuming the death of the person named in the lease. We would not be surprised if, previous to this, some case had arisen where a man had emigrated and the lessee had held that the lease was good till proof of death.

James Fleming had another farm of 12 ½ acres at a rent of £21 1s. He held under a lease of 1837 for his own life or 31 years and the same conditions regarding penal rent of £5 for each house, and the termination of the lease if the lessee was out of the Kingdom. In both cases there were also covenants against underletting. A third farm was held by James Fleming (we assume there was only one man of the name), 15 ½ acres: rent £10 17s 2d, from year to year.

John Lynd held 13 acres at £7 13s under a lease of 1837 for 31 years, and there was the same provision of a penal rent of £5 for each additional house built, and covenant against underletting. Patrick Graham had 22 acres at £10 13s under an older lease, 1797, to Edward Donaghy for 3 lives or 31 years. Of the "lives" the only one remaining in 1850 was "William Cunningham". Another farm was held by William and Anne McGuffin, who together had 19 acres at £8 14s 6d. The lease of 1797 was made to Hugh McGuffin for 3 lives or 31 years, and the Earl of Ranfurly was the only "life" then in being. Andrew Ferguson had almost 14 acres at a rent of £7 12s 8d. This was also leasehold, the lease being given to Patrick McElhenen in 1797 for 31 years or 3 lives. One of these lives was Edward McElhenen – probably a son, who had been a healthy looking lad in 1797 – and another was David Richardson, both living in 1850. The latter's name appears in a lease given to Patrick McGivern for 15 acres at £7 8s 11d rent, also in 1797.

The only other leaseholder in the townland was Thomas Wilson, who had a farm of 13½ acres at £7 9s 1d rent, and 12s 6d tithe rent charge, under lease of 1832 to Patrick Mayne, senr. The lease was for 21 years of one life - Robert Hassard. In this, and all the leases of the same period (1832 and 1837) four gale days were given in the year – 1$^{st}$ February, 1$^{st}$ May, 1$^{st}$ August and 1$^{st}$ November. This, like the penal rent for extra houses and the other provisions, looks very like new ideas imported by some new agent. Two other tenants were Wm. Gamble who had 20½ acres at £10 17s 2d and John Moore who held not quite two acres at £2 12s 8d, both from year to year.

Knockaconny was in the same lot with Ballyreagh and Colcrunagh. It has an area of 160 acres and in 1850 was held by two tenants only. Josias Fleming had 90 acres at a rent of £47 4s 6d under lease to himself, for 31 years from 1797 or three lives, of which there were then in being – John Fleming and the Earl of Ranfurly. The other tenant was William Fleming who held over 69 acres at a rent of £36 17s 4d, the lessee being himself. All three lives, selected 53 years before, were then in being – George Fleming, Wm. Hamilton and the Earl of Ranfurly. The tithe rent charge payable by the leaseholders was £3 6s 10d and £2 14s 8d respectively.

In 1859 Griffith's Valuation showed that there were then three owners in fee. Instead of the 90 acre farm there was one of 60 acres, occupied by David Fleming, and another of 30 acres occupied by Thomas Fleming. The other farm of 69 acres had also been divided, William Fleming appearing as owning 38 acres odd, and George Fleming 31 acres. The houses were of a superior class to the ordinary tenant farmer's dwelling, two of them being valued at £4, and one at £2 10s per annum. This may appear quite modest, but farm houses were valued very low – in Ballyreagh the highest was £1 15s per year. The total valuation of the buildings in Knockaconny was £14 5s and the land £100. In 1837 the valuation of the houses was £12 15s and of the land £84 3s 11d.

Next week we shall conclude this analysis of the rental by giving particulars of Lot 3 - Gorticar and the Annaghs.


## DRUMCRAW and DRUMGARRELL

Since the article on these townlands appeared, in consequence of some discrepancies we have stumbled on an interesting fact. These two townlands lie along the Coagh road, the boundary between them being the little cross road below Mrs Espy's house. To the right of the road, going from Cookstown, is a considerable bit of cut-out bog, as far as the county mearing of Killybearn. The area is about 20 acres. Reference to the Ordnance Map will show that this is the townland of Drumcraw, but to our surprise we find that in the map prepared for the Commissioners for the sale of Incumbered Estates, it is in Drumgarrell. There were other mistakes made in the map, a well known example being that the Gate Lodge to Killymoon was shown in Coolnahavil so that the owners of the Castle and demesne had to lease the gate house! But an error of 20 acres is something different, and makes the shape of Drumcraw so different that it could hardly be overlooked. Presumably the map for the sale was prepared from estate maps, which makes an error more unlikely still. This raised the question whether the Ordnance Survey map is correct. To question it is, to many people, next to questioning the accuracy of the Bible, but, as a matter of fact, it is the Ordnance Map, and not the estate map, which has been altered. This is obvious from a comparison of areas. The area of Drumcraw, as given in the rental, is 158a. Or. 32p., but the area given in Griffiths' Valuation of 1859 is 181a. Or. 9p. The area, however, given in the valuation of 1837, signed by Richard Griffith, Commissioner, Hugh Stewart, Robert W. Lowry and S. Galbraith, members of the Committee of Revision, is 159a. Or. 25p., or practically the same as in the rental, proving that it is the official area that has altered. We do not suggest that the Ordnance Surveyors were guilty of an error. It was not unusual to alter a townland boundary, when the lands were on the same estate, but this seems to be a record change.

# GORTICAR AND THE ANNAGHS

## (21-2-1925)

We have now reached the last group of townlands in the Killymoon estate, as set out in the rental of 1850. They made up Lot 3, and were Gorticar, Annaghteague, Annaghmore, and Annaghananam. They lie further from Cookstown than Knockaconny, and are in the parish of Desertcreat. Next to Gorticar, further to the south-west, lies the first of the Rockdale estate, then owned by Mr. James Lowry, and to the south are the lands of Mr. Thos. Greer, and Desertcreat.

These four townlands, forming Lot 3 were Church lands, originally leased from the See of Armagh, which lease Col. Stewart had converted into perpetuity by purchase, but still subject to a rent to the See of £72 1s 2d, as well as a tithe rent charge of £20 16s 6½d. The gross rental was £439 6s 9d, leaving a rental of £346 9d 0½d, as none of the tithe rent charge was paid direct by the tenants, as was the case in Knockaconny and other leased lands.

Gorticar, which means the fields of rocky land, had an area of 226 acres, showing that at the Plantation considerably more than half of it was regarded as waste. It was let to 14 tenants, the largest farm being 33½ acres held by Henry Hamilton at £25 10s 8d. Samuel Geddis had almost 32 acres at £20 a year; Henry Mooney had abut 22½ acres at £8 15s 8d; James Dooras (as the name appears in the rental) had over 20 acres at £11 13s 9d; Widow Dooras held 19½ acres at £12 17s 6d; John Dooras had about 17½ acres at £9 12s 6d; Henry Mooney had about 17 acres at £10 11s 6d; Robert Watt had just under 16 acres at £9 13s 3d; Margaret M'Crory held 13 acres at £5 14s 10d, and the others were all under 10 acres - Daniel M'Donald, Patrick Dillon, Patrick Campbell, Widow Gillian and John Gillian, while 4½ acres were county roads which, unlike farm roads, were not measured into the adjacent farms.

Annaghteague has an area of 117 acres only, which would be little more than the regulation size of a balliboe – 60 acres Irish of arable land. It also abounds with limestone. The prefix "Annagh" to this, and the other two townlands, shows that it had been originally in the nature of a marsh – flat land subject to flooding, but with the limestone subsoil, capable of improvement. There were only four holdings in it. John Hagan held 39½ acres at £26 2s yearly; George Fleming had just over 30 acres at £25 5s rent; Robert Hawshaw had 25½ acres at £20 19s, and Widow Blaney had 16½ acres at £10 15s 5d. The roads totalled 3a. 1r. 8p., and there was a limestone quarry, then in the possession of Col. Stewart, valued at £10 a year. At 1859 John Hagan had got Hawshaw's farm, and the total area in Griffith's Valuation was then given at 68½ acres, while James Mason had succeeded Widow Blaney. George Fleming's house was then valued at £4 10s a year, which was unusually high, and John Hagan's at £2 15s, which was also much over the average. In the Valuation of 1837 the houses in Annaghteague were valued at £6 1s and were the only houses in the four townlands to be valued at all.

Annaghananam - a name whose derivation baffles us and is possibly a corruption – had an area in the Rental of 163 acres, held by 11 tenants. The largest holding was Robert Henderson's 25 acres at £20 4s 8d rent; John Johnston had 23 acres at £18 3s 8d; Robert M'Allister held 19½ acres at £14 9s 2d; Thomas Johnston had almost 17 acres at £14 5s 4d; Robert M'Allister had 19½ acres at £14 9s 2d; Betty M'Cord had nearly 15 acres at £11 4s; Joseph M'Culloch held almost 14 acres at £13 3s 2d; Samuel Sloan held 13½ acres at £10 11s 8d, and the smaller farms were held by John Blair, John Brisban and Widow Mullan. There was also 6 acres of cut-out bog, in the possession of Col. Stewart, which was said to be worth £2 2s for grazing, but if reclaimed would be worth 12s an acre. Whether reclaimed or not we do not know, but it would have been hardly worth reclaiming six acres for an increased value of 30s a year. The roads in this townland amounted to 1a. 1r. 23p.

The last townland was Annaghmore, which obviously means the great marsh or bog, but which also abounded in limestone. The total area was 139 acres, held by no less than 16 tenants in 1850. The largest farm was 18 acres held by Robert Seaton at £14 7s rent; George Moffatt had about 13 acres at £7 4s 10d, and the rest were all under 10 acres – Thomas Fleming, Widow Mayne, George Meabin, Wm. Greer, Andrew Warnock, George Moffatt, Daniel M'Donald (2 farms totalling 13 acres); Wm. Fleming, Robert Henry, Wm. Calder, Wm. Henry, Patrick Keenan, and Wm. Grier. There was also over 10 acres cut-out bog, valued at £3 10s for grazing , and worth £6 when reclaimed – 50s a year extra as interest on the cost of reclaiming 10 acres.

By 1859 there had been considerable changes in the personel of the tenants in this townland. George Hagan appears in Griffith's Valuation as the occupier of 24 acres, valued with house at £20; the next largest farmer was Samuel Mayne, valuation £10 5s; then Wm. Henry, 15¼ acres, £9 10s; Robert Henry, almost 10 acres, £10 15s valuation; Alexander M'Donnell had two farms, 19½ acres, valuation £8. The Valuation Roll also shows that there were half-a-dozen cottiers in houses valued at 10s or 15s a year, without land. The valuation of the land had gone up from 1837 by only £2 11s 5d, while Annaghteague land, on re-valuation in 1859, was increased £11 15s 1d, and Annaghananam £17.

Note on Kilcronagh. – A valued correspondent points out that Kilcronagh does not touch the Sandholes road, but lies along a narrow road from it which intersects the townland and joins the Pomeroy road. He also suggests that the object of the penal rent in case an additional house was built was to prevent sub-letting and to keep away poor people who were sometimes permitted to put up wretched cabins and who afterwards became chargeable to the rates. This explanation seems to the writer to be sound; the number of very small farms in Annaghmore, for example, where 14 out of 16 tenants had under 10 acres of land to live on, would doubtless suggest to a new agent the desirability of preventing sub-division. The agent about the time when the leases were granted, 1832, was Mr. Hassard, father of the late Mr. R. Hassard, J. P., of Desertcreat, and it is doubtless to him that this precaution, the introduction of four gale days in the year and other changes, were due.

Next week we shall proceed to describe how the sale of the estate proceeded.

# SALE INTERRUPTED BY DEATH

## (28 – 2 – 1925)

The Rental of the Killymoon estate, which we have been analysing, shows that it was to be put up in 12 lots for sale by public auction on Friday, 17th January 1851, by order of the Commissioners for sale of Incumbered Estates in Ireland at their Court, 14 Henrietta Street, Dublin. This Court was established a short time before, in 1849, to provide machinery by which landowners might realise their estates, and the necessity for it is shown in a Return made in May 1851. Up till 31st March 1851, no less than 1676 estates had been dealt with, half of which had been in the hands of receivers, and in 147 cases the owners had actually taken the benefit of the Insolvent Debtors Act. The gross rentals of these estates was £1,036,976, and the incumbrancers on this land totalled the huge sum of £17,971,321, secured on 227,329 acres of land, or one sixty-fifth of the arable land of Ireland.

These figures give some idea of the position in which many of the old landlords found themselves – some from their own fault and some because of circumstances over which they had no control. The boom in land values, which had begun a century before and was not affected one way or the other by the Legislative Union of 1801, had been brought to a stop – so sudden a stop that a large number disappeared. The court put up their estates and a new class of landlord took place, who, in the North at any rate, had made money in the linen trade. Many persons attribute the unpopularity of landlordism to this class, who, taking advantage of their powers, raised rents so much that, thirty years after, the Land Act of 1881 was needed to come between them and the tenantry, and fix fair rents and create virtually dual ownership. Whether this judgement is fair we have not the means of ascertaining, but we are inclined to believe that the rents were raised on the estates of the old, as well as of the new, landlords alike, and it is certain that when the Land Courts began to operate, some of the rents were reduced below the level of 1850. It was, indeed, a grievance with more than one local landowner that he had bought an estate with a rental, which he said was guaranteed by the State, and when the State, through the Land Courts, reduced the rent below that amount, he should be compensated. The rental, of course, was not guaranteed by the Incumbered Estates Court, but merely set out for the information of the purchasers who took the risk, though when they bought no risk was apparent. That, however, is a digression.

The petition of Colonel Wm. Stewart to the Court set out, as a reason for his embarrassment, that he had lost £50,000 which he had secured for a friend. No particulars of this transaction are known – who was the friend nor when the default took place. In itself that loss, great as it was to a gentleman who, in 1830, represented himself as a "poor man", would not have meant complete insolvency, for the Killymoon estate realised between £80,000 and £90,000, so that, if he had been living within his income, he would have had quite a decent amount left, ample for the needs of a single man of 70 years of age. But from the traditions of Killymoon in his time we know that he lived on an expensive scale. Generous and open-handed, he had, apart from this particular loss, got into financial difficulties, and it must be recorded for his credit that, in spite of that, he did not treat his tenants harshly, or press them unduly for rent in the bad times; the amount of arrears due him is ample proof of this.

It is said that, though he lodged the petition for the sale of the estate, he prayed that he might not live to see Killymoon pass into the hands of a stranger. From what we knew of the Castle and demesne at that time, one cannot help sympathising with that wish. It must have been dire necessity which forced him to contemplate the sale and take the necessary steps, and if he did express the wish that he might not live to see its consummation then the wish was granted, for, in December 1850, a month before the sale was due, he passed away, to be followed, in July, by his faithful medical adviser and friend, Dr. Potter.

The funeral of Colonel Stewart was long spoken of by old people as an outstanding event in their recollection. Unfortunately the Press was, even 75 years ago, not at all alert, and we have failed to find any reports such as would now be given of it, and the merest reference to his death. But we know that that death was regarded by the community as a calamity, intensified, no doubt, by the knowledge, which everyone then had, that the estate was about to be broken up, and by fears as to the future. Colonel Stewart was not without his faults, but they were purely domestic; to the people he was all that a good landlord should be, and more. Every movement for the betterment of the town and district found in him a patron, and if his means did not allow him to shoulder the cost of extensive improvement or bear the sole expense of social and philantrophic schemes in the way, for example, that the Drapers Company did in Moneymore and the Salters Company did in Magherafelt, the people gained in self-reliance thereby. Cookstown never was spoon-fed, and the fact that the townfolk had to rely largely on themselves developed the qualities which raised it, in a short century, from the position of a mere hamlet to being the principal town in the district.  In his position as landowner, Colonel Stewart afforded facilities to others to engage in industrial and business enterprises, though he remained outside them personally, and in consequence his death was no check to the growing prosperity of the town.  But the people felt that it was a personal loss, for while his mother, the Hon. Mrs. Stewart, had ruled as the mistress of Killymoon, more or less autocratically, her favourite son was essentially democratic – a man of the people identifying himself with their aspirations and interesting himself in their well-being.

The death of Colonel Stewart stopped the sale of Killymoon estate, as he had been the petitioner.  He left one brother, the Rev. Richard Stewart, of Kildress, who lived till 1869, and one sister Mary Eleanor, who died unmarried in 1866.  Another sister, Louisa, had married Colonel H. Clements, of Ashfield, Co. Cavan, but both she and her husband had predeceased Col. Stewart, leaving a son, Colonel Henry Theophelus Clements, now deceased, whose family are next-of-kin of Col. Stewart.

Next Week we shall tell how the sale proceeded.

ANNAGHANANAM. – Mr. Alfred Moore Munn, Clerk of the Crown and Peace, Londonderry, who is an authority on townland names, writes that the derivation of above is "The Marsh of the Soul".  Dr. Joyce, in his "Irish Names of Places", says that the names containing the word "anam" - Gaelic for soul, puzzled him.  He says that some believe that places with such names were bequeathed to some church or monastery for the health of the soul of the donor or a relative, while others assert that the names originated in ghosts, but it was all conjecture.

# COLONEL STEWART'S WILL

## (7 – 3 – 1925)

Nothing connected with the history of Cookstown has given the writer more trouble than the comparatively recent sale of the Killymoon Estate which took place when the late Mr. Gunning Moore, D.L. was a boy of ten. The sale of a town like Cookstown, or a mansion and demesne like Killymoon would, in these days when the Press is wide awake, have been deemed worthy of a column or two in the newspapers. But, in 1851, the Press was really in its infancy, though the Belfast Newsletter was then long established, and the Northern Whig was in its vigorous youth. The files of these papers show that sales of land in the Incumbered Estates Court were advertised in almost every issue, but only a small paragraph was ever devoted to the results - less than we give to the sale of a little farm. And, so far as the sale of Col. Stewart's estate is concerned, which was to have taken place on 17$^{th}$ January 1857, the Belfast and Dublin papers were absolutely silent.

We now know that the sale was interrupted by the death of Colonel Stewart but the first clue to this was a second advertisement which appeared on 19$^{th}$ April 1857. It began as follows:-

*In the matter of the estate of William Stewart, owner and petitioner, continued in the names of Mary Eleanor Stewart and Henry Theophilus Clements, executors and devisees of the last will and testament of William Stewart* and went on to describe the property - 31 townlands containing 4,768 acres, with the beautiful house and demesne of Killymoon, adding, incidentally, that the town of Cookstown stands upon the estate. It adds:- *The house or castle of Killymoon was designed and executed by the late Mr. Nash at a large expense about forty years ago. It was in good order and contains every accommodation and embellishment which the well-known taste of the architect could produce. Upon the demesne is profusion of beautiful and valuable timber, of the finest growth, valued some years ago at £23,359 17s 1d. It is watered by two rivers in which there is excellent trout fishing; both streams unite under the windows of the house. The grounds are nearly surrounded by a high demesne wall which screens its privacy. The woods are well stocked* and it intimates that the sale would take place in Belfast on 8$^{th}$ August 1851.

This advertisement was the first intimation that Col. Stewart had left a will, and that his brother, Rev. Richard Stewart of Kildress, who survived him, was not the heir as would have been the case had the property been entailed. Again the difference in the facilities for historical material in our days and even 75 years ago, was illustrated. It is now the easiest thing in the world to get a copy of a will in the District Probate Office, but the Registry at Armagh did not then exist. Wills were proved in Dublin, and before the writer realised that Col. Stewart had made a will which dealt with the property, the Four Courts, with all its documents had disappeared. The family knew nothing of it and search everywhere was unavailing. But, by one of those coincidences which do occur in real life, when he had almost abandoned hope of finding the document, a certified copy was presented to the Northern Record Office by a Dublin solicitor, Mr. French, who had found it amongst a lot of papers in his office. Needless to say, when the receipt of the document was acknowledged in the Press we lost no time in perusing it and making a copy. It reads as follows:-

*I, William Stewart, of Killymoon, in the County Tyrone, do make this my last will and testament in manner following, hereby revoking all former will or wills made by me. Subject to my just debts I leave and devise all and singular my estates in the County Tyrone and in the County and City of Dublin, and also my interest in the following leases, viz., of a part of the land of Clohogue, in the County of Londonderry, of Ardvarnish, in the County of Tyrone, and also of Coolkeehan in the County of Tyrone, to my sister Mary Eleanor Stewart for the duration of her natural life, and at her death to my nephew Henry Theophilus Clements, of Ashfield, in the County of Cavan, and to his heirs and assigns for ever. I leave to my sister Mary Eleanor Stewart the use of my books, plate, pictures and household furniture for her life and at her death I devise them to my nephew Henry Theophilus Clements, his heirs and assigns for ever; my horses, carriage, cattle and farming stock of every description whatsoever, together with all rent and arrears of rent which may be due to me at my death I devise to my sister Mary Eleanor Stewart, whom I leave my residuary legatee. I hereby appoint my sister Mary Eleanor Stewart and my nephew Henry Theophilus Clements executors of this my last will and testament. In witness whereof I have hereunder set my hand and fixed my seal this 12th day of June, 1845, - WILLIAM STEWART.*

The witnesses to the will were Robt. Hassard and W. Ballentine, the former being then the estate agent.

By this will it will be seen that Col. Stewart made his nephew heir to all his property (except certain chattels), subject to a life interest to his sister, who lived until 1866. The absence of any reference to his brother, the rector of Kildress, is significant, but will not surprise any who remember, or have heard of that clergyman. He had a rich living, Kildress being one of the best parishes in the district before the Disestablishment of the Church, but he was, to say the least, eccentric, and apparently extravagant, for we have the authority of the Rev. J.B. Leslie, M.A., author of "Armagh clergy and parishes" in saying that during his incumbency the parish was sequestrated several times – that is to say, the revenue was seized by creditors. The date of the will should also be noted – 1845, or five and a half years before Col. Stewart's death, and the fact that he then still owned the Molesworth property in Dublin and vicinity, which he had received from his mother. What became of it we have not learned, as it does not really affect our History, but it is obvious from the text of the will that, in 1845, the loss of the £50,000, which Col. Stewart had sustained, had not taken place. The will, we should add, bore a stamp of £100, which would, at that time, have covered a very considerable estate, but £99 10s of that sum was returned. The will was duly admitted to probate, and Miss Stewart, as tenant for life, executed at least one document – a conveyance dated 31st May 1852, to Rowley Millar of land in Gortalowry, which he held under lease, and which was then converted into fee, and now the property of Mr Adair, the house attached being the property of Mr. E. J. Malone, and originally the residence of James Cooke.

But for the unfortunate circumstances which embarrassed Col. Stewart, his nephew would have succeeded to the Killymoon estate and have been the owner of Cookstown, with a fine revenue from the Molesworth property in Dublin. Some reference to that gentlemen will, therefore, be of interest to our readers and form a fitting conclusion to the present article. The Clements, unlike the Stewarts, were English Puritans, the founder of the family, Daniel Clements, coming to Ireland with Cromwell's army in 1646. He settled at Rathkenny, Co. Cavan, and on his death in 1680 he was succeeded by his son Robert, who leased the Manor of Ashfield, where the family still reside, from Thomas Ashe in 1714. According to Burke this gentleman occupied the important position in the Irish Government of deputy Vice-Treasurer. He was succeeded by his son, the Rt. Hon. Theophilus Clements, who was M.P. for Cavan. Another son was John Clements, who got Rathkenny and a third, Henry, was killed at the battle of Fontenoy. The youngest son was the Rt. Hon. Nathanial Clements, M. P., who was deputy Vice-Treasurer in the Irish Government in the early part of the 18th century, and was married to Hannah, daughter of the Very Rev. William Gore, Dean of Down, by whom he had a large family.

Their eldest son was Lt. Col. Robert Clements, who was created first Earl of Leitrim, and the second son died without issue. It is in the third son that we are interested, the Rt. Hon. Henry Theophilus Clements, P.C., Lt. Col. of the 69th Regiment, who sat in the Irish Parliament for Cavan and Leitrim. He was, therefore, a fellow member with Mr. James Stewart, - "Old Killymoon", as he was called - and the friendship was cemented by the marriage of the former's son, Col. Henry John Clements, M.P., with Mr. Stewart's eldest daughter Louise, which took place about the year 1811. It was their son, Col. Henry John Clements, M.P., who was born in 1820, who was Col. William Stewart's nephew, to whom he left his estates by the will of 1845, and who, but for the unfortunate circumstances already mentioned, would probably have come to Cookstown to live, in Killymoon Castle, as the resident landlord of Cookstown. He died in 1904, and his widow, the daughter of the Rev. Canon Markham, still survives, with her family of two sons - Mr. Henry John Beresford Clements, D.L., of Killadoon, County Kildare, Major Marcus Louis Stewart Clements, of the King's Royal Rifles, of Ashfield, Co. Cavan, and two daughters. While we have no reason to regret the turn of events which made Mr. Gunning–Moore, D.L., a resident landlord of the business end of Cookstown, it is certain that Killymoon would have been a very different place had the intentions of Col. Stewart, embodied in his will of 1845, been carried out.

Next Week – How the sale proceeded.

## TWO COL. STEWART STORIES.

As illustrating Col. Stewart's love of Killymoon we are informed that on one occasion the land steward wanted a beam for the mill. The colonel went out to pick a tree to be cut down, but one after another was rejected because it would spoil the view, and at last the man was despatched to Coalisland to buy the timber, as none could be spared in Killymoon!! As regards his relations with the townspeople, so much did he wish to be regarded as a friend rather than a superior, that when he went into a shop to do business he would take off his hat just as if in a drawing-room.

# PROGRESS OF THE SALE

## (14 – 3 – 1925)

The second date fixed for the sale of the Killymoon estate was 8th August 1851. Search in the files of the Belfast papers revealed a further advertisement, in the Newsletter of 6th Aug., announcing that *the sale of the unsold portion of the estates, advertised to take place on 8th August, will be postponed till 28th October, before Mr. George Hyndman, in Castle Place, Belfast.* The word "unsold" indicates, for the first time, that some of the property had been sold prior to the advertised auction, so we read with interest the list of the property still offered as follows:- *House and demesne, the lands of Coolnafranky, Coolnahavil, part of Scotchtown, part of Gortalowry, Ballyreagh, Kilconaghan, Anaghmore, Anaghteague, Drumcraw, Drumgarrell, part of Kirktown, and part of Annaghananam.* The advertisement proceeds to say that the timber was valued, some years before, at £23,359 17s 1d; the woods were *well stocked with pheasants and other game; flocks of wild fowl frequent the rivers upon which are two falls of 15 feet, each admirably adapted to drive spinning machinery or bleach mills in that fine flax-growing country. The gardens and grounds are very extensive and in good order, with a range of 150 feet of graperies and peach houses in full bearing. The neighbourhood is peaceable and the inhabitants orderly and industrious. The timber on the land adjoining Killymoon and Cookstown (exclusive of that in the demesne) has been valued at £3,562 14s. Cookstown is a flourishing town with a population of 3,000, having two weekly markets and a monthly fair. The parish church and five other places of worship are in the town. It is on the mail-coach road from Dublin to Coleraine, 9 miles from Dungannon, 3 from Moneymore, 8 from Magherafelt, and 40 from Belfast, to each of which there is easy mode of access on one side by the Ulster and on the other by the Belfast and Ballymena Railways.*

The advt. concludes as follows:- *John K. Tener, Esquire, Moree, Dungannon, agent of the estate, and the solicitors having carriage of sale, are authorised to receive proposals in writing for the purchase of the whole or any portion of the estate yet to be sold, by private contract, and to submit same to the Commissioners for their consideration up to 20$^{th}$ September next, after which date a notice will be published setting out the lots in which the lands, or such parts as shall remain undisposed of, will be offered for sale by public auction on the 24$^{th}$ October next, as mentioned in the commencement of the advertisement. Charles and John Samuel Gaussen.* We have only to add, in this connection, that this notice did not appear, but there was an advertisement of the sale of the furniture, etc., to be held on 14$^{th}$ October and following days by G. C. Hyndman, in which we are not interested.

Readers who have followed this sale closely will have noticed that Lot 9 - Cookstown, Loy, Killymam, Clagan, Monrush, Ballymenagh, Tullygare, New Buildings and Cranfield; Lot 8 - Maloon; and Lot 7 – Tullagh, must all have been sold before 6$^{th}$ Aug., as well as part of Lot 5 – Kirktown, and part of Lot 6 – Gortalowry, Sullenboy and Clare, and they now see that the rest of the property was sold privately before 20$^{th}$ September. Briefly we may say that Messrs. James Gunning and James Moore, of Wellbrook, had bought the first lots, and subsequently Coolnafranky, which lies adjacent to Loy, and was, no doubt, purchased because Mr. Gunning had decided to build a mansion beside his property; the remainder was bought by Mr. Thomas Adair, of Greenvale, who had already bought part of Gortalowry, Sullenboy and Kirktown.

Mr. Adair had, at this time, been resident at Greenvale for only some 33 years. He and his father came here from Broughshane, where they had been in the linen business, as then conducted, and owned a bleach-mill to finish the hand-made linen. Spinning mills were in their infancy, but he recognised the future that was before them and selected Cookstown as a suitable place to start the new industry, in combination with the bleaching and finishing of the hand-loom webs. There was then a large population in this part of the country which ensured a good supply of labour. No doubt, in this respect, other places were equally attractive. Stewartstown, for example, had in 1821 almost as many houses as Cookstown - 137 against 141 – and the population was poorer, the average household being a little over three persons against 6.5 in Cookstown. Moneymore, again, had actually a larger population than Cookstown in 1821 (987 against 963), and considerably more houses, while Magherafelt was 33 per cent. larger than Cookstown, with nearly 50 per cent. more houses, and Maghera, even, had more houses with nearly as large a population.

But Cookstown had the water power which these other towns lacked, and which was vital for power-driven industries in the days before the railways and the development of steam. The consequence was that Cookstown leaped ahead of all its neighbours in an astonishing way, for whereas its population was 25 per cent. less than that of Magherafelt in 1821, ten years later, though the latter town had grown considerably, Cookstown had double its population. The actual figures are: - In 1821 population, 963; in 1831, 2,883. No such bound upward will be found, probably, in any town in Ireland in the same time. The new arrivals were not all mill-workers, of course. They had to be housed, and 141 houses of 1821 became 516 ten years later – over 250 per cent. increase. To provide these alone there were quarrymen needed to raise the stones and the lime to be burned, and the O.S. map of 1835 shows the vicinity of the town dotted with freestone and limestone quarries and kilns; carpenters were needed, with wood cutters, carters and all the labour necessary to turn native timber into boards; thatchers were needed, and so on, for it is an elementary fact that every industry creates a demand for others - work done provides more work to be done. It was a decade of hustle, and all due, so far as we can now see, to the advent of Mr. Adair with his capital. That he reaped an abundant reward for his enterprise is natural; the only regret is that, in these decadent days, there are so few to follow his example.

For the purposes of his linen manufacturing industry, which in 1851 had grown to considerable dimensions, Mr. Adair had a fairly large area of land rented in Gortalowry and Sullenboy, and it appears that when the estate was being sold he made an offer for the freehold, which was accepted.  Subsequently after Mr. Gunning and Mr. Moore bought Cookstown and the land to the north of the town, Mr. Adair decided to buy Killymoon Castle and Demesne, and all the rest of the estate.  The total price paid is not known, but in the Registry of Deeds there is a memorial registered on 29th September 1852, showing that he had paid £48,386 12s 6d for what appears to be part of the seven lots.  The amount paid for the Castle and Demesne was £17,795 9s 8d; for Gortalowry £16,140 13s 6d; for Drumcraw, £2,204 9s 4d; for Coolnahavil, £1,457 6s 3d, while for what is therein described as "Four towns", and was Lot 3 - Gorticar, Annaghmore, Annaghananam, Annaghteague and Annaghmore he paid £7,809 5s.  In addition he had bought Drumgarrell, as well as Knockaconny, Colcrunagh and Ballyreagh, but apparently had re-sold before the date of this memorial.

As a matter of fact he re-sold all the property except what he had already in his own occupation under lease or otherwise.  It must have occurred to him that to lock up so much capital in land, at a time when there was every prospect of expansion of his business, would be a foolish act.  Agricultural land would, no doubt, yield an annual income, but if the price paid for Lot 3, for example, be compared with the net rental, it will be seen that it would yield a bare 4½ per cent.  Moreover, the rents had to be collected, and were by no means promptly paid.  There was the possibility of higher rents, but closely following the famine years that prospect was not rosy, and the only attraction in the deal was that the purchaser would be a landlord which, at that time, was accounted something.

(To be continued.)

## SALE OF KILLYMOON CASTLE

## (21 – 3 – 1925)

So far as Killymoon Castle and Demesne are concerned, the financial outlook was worse.  It was, in short, a white elephant, and very soon Mr. Adair attempted to get it off his hands.  In this he was actively assisted by the late Rev. H. B. Wilson, D.D., then a young minister less than half a dozen years settled in Cookstown.  Mr. Adair's own thoughts turned in the direction of converting the timber into money.  The timber had been valued at £23,359 and with the new demand created by the extension of the railways which had reached Dungannon on the one side and Randalstown on the other, its value was likely to increase. Such valuations are unreliable, but, as a matter of fact, Mr. Adair made a contract on 20<sup>th</sup> November 1851, with a Belfast firm, Messrs. H. & A. J. M 'Canavon, for the sale of the standing timber at the sum of £11,500, to be removed within eight years, but with a proviso that he could cancel the contract up till 7<sup>th</sup> February 1852, on forfeiting £1,000. Litigation actually ensued because the sale fell through; Mr. Adair's case was that the purchasers had failed to carry out the conditions requiring the lodging of the money, or part of it, and it is believed that he got a verdict, though we have not found any report of the case nor any official record of it.

This litigation to enforce the contract is of interest because it proves that the price, £11,500, was regarded by both parties as a good bargain for the purchaser. The total paid by Mr. Adair for the Castle and Demesne was, as stated, £17,795, and deducting the price at which the timber was sold there was a balance of £6,295 only. The area of the demesne at that time was 584 acres, so that at £11 per acre, a not unreasonable figure when townparks were being set at 30s an acre, the market value of the Castle was nil. Recently, when the demesne was broken up into a dozen lots (as many as the whole estate at first), and when all the timber was cut and the amenities spoiled, and the graperies were, to put it mildly, not in full bearing, the whole place having been neglected, the bare castle, after being added to the lot of meadow land in front, raised the bid by £100, and many papers commented on the slump in Irish castles. But we find that in 1852, when the Castle, said to have cost £80,000, was only forty years old, and kept in excellent order, the grounds swept every day of stray leaves, the whole enclosed in a well-wooded demesne, the actual value in the open market was no more.

Attempts were meantime made to get a purchaser for the Castle and demesne, and the figure of £30,000 was mentioned, but Mr. Adair reconciled himself to a much lower figure, which meant a loss instead of a profit on the whole transaction, and ultimately a sale was concluded at the round sum of £20,000. From the registered memorial the date of the sale appears as 23<sup>rd</sup> July 1852, the purchasers being Thomas Smith Goode, of Cork City, Esquire, and John Douglas Cooper, of No. 8 New Street, Spring Gardens, Co. Middlesex. The lands are set out as follows: - The mansion house, demesne and lands of Killymoon, and parts of Drummond and Scotchtown, containing 420a. 2r. 8p., held in fee; part of Ardcumber, containing 132a. 2r. 6p., held in perpetuity; Grange alias Ardvarnish, 32a. 0r. 31p., held for ever subject to £14 7s 6½d Irish, or £13 13s 10d sterling, with 1s in the £ fees - a total of 584a. 3r. 5p. The perpetuity lease of Ardvarnish was converted into fee simple by a deed of

26th May 1852, from John Chambers, of Letterkenny, as guardian for Charles King Colhoun, a minor and ward in Chancery to Miss Mary Eleanor Stewart and Lt. Col. H. T. Clements, both of Ashfield, County Cavan, and it recites the sale to Mr. Adair of this and other lands for £48,386 12s 6d. Mr. Goode soon disappeared as joint owner, as Mr. Cooper is the owner in fee in 1859. He was a railway contractor and no doubt the timber was the attraction for him. His brother settled here and married a local lady, and their son will be remembered as being employed in Messrs. Adair & Co.'s mill, and as one of the first Rural Councillor's for Cookstown.

The subsequent history of Killymoon may be briefly added here. In Griffith's Valuation of 1858, Mr. Cooper was the sole owner in fee, and in 1868 he sold to Colonel A. S. Bolton, who took up residence in Killymoon Castle and maintained it and the demesne in something like the old Stewart style. Apparently he was living beyond his means, as, in 1873, the property was put up for sale by mortgagees and purchased by Mr. Henry Moutray, a member of the old Clogher family. He died intestate a couple of years afterwards leaving one son, Mr. Mervyn S.T. Moutray, then a boy of ten years of age, and during his minority the castle was empty, in the hands of caretakers. In due course, however, Mr. Moutray took up residence in Killymoon as a gentleman farmer. Portion of the outlying parts of the demesne were sold by him, the Great Northern Railway having cut off part of it, reducing the area to about 590 acres. In 1917 Mr. Moutray decided to sell the property, which was bought privately, just before the auction by an agent of Mr. Gerald G. Macaura of Lough Inc House, Skibbereen, for £15,000. This gentleman furnished part of the castle and took up residence with his wife; the woods were being cut for timber, for which there was a good demand during the war. Part of the demesne on which there was no timber he sold, beginning with Drummond fort, which was bought by Mr. James Coulter, a neighboring farmer, for £4,000. The whole tract of land from the "Finger Post" along the Grange Road was next sold to some half a dozen farmers. At a third sale the groups of houses known as the Blue Doors, with the old mill and water power, the Golf Links, and the Fort Hill were sold. The latter was bought by Mr. Quinn, who resold to Mr. John Adair for a new golf links, which compare with any inland 9-hole course in Ireland, and provide ground for an 18-hole course if, and when, required. At the final sale by Mr. Macaura all the land left on one side of the castle was put up in one lot, the holm along the river in front and some of the shrub left when the trees were cut, in another and the castle in a third. Mr. Coulter was the highest bidder for the meadow land, and there were no bids for the castle, standing isolated as it would have been, but, when put in with the holm, Mr. Coulter bid £100 more and got the two lots.

Meantime, from he got possession, Mr. Macaura was busily cutting the timber. The old mill was first fixed up as a saw mill, the water power to be supplemented by steam generated by the saw dust, but before it was completed he changed his mind, on the suggestion of some Canadian lumber men who had been at the front, and built a complete saw mill alongside the railway on the old avenue towards the Red Bridge. He also formed a private company, with limited liability, to take over the timber, mills, etc., and held practically all the shares himself, and a siding was put in by the Great Northern Railway Co. Though large quantities of timber were cut very little was sent off by rail, being stacked on sidings on the 30in tram line he had laid down. In the winter of 1922 he collected most of it in a large pile near the railway to protect it from the weather, and in the following February it caught fire one night, whether accidentally or otherwise remains a mystery. At all events Mr. Macaura alleged that it was malicious and lodged a claim for £50,000 compensation, but when it came into court the ratepayers had Mr. Babington, K.C., to oppose it. Half-an-hour's adjournment was granted to Mr. Macaura's counsel and, at the end of that time, he informed the County Court Judge that he had communicated with the insurance companies interested, and withdrew the claim.

The next act brings us down to contemporary history. There were five insurance companies who had policies on the timber and they refused to pay; they were sued and the case went to arbitration before Mr. Pringle, K.C., and several days were spent in taking evidence in private. Mr. Pringle fixed the amount of the damage at £32,000 and awarded that sum to Mr. Macaura and the Bank of Ireland who had given a large overdraft to him, if they had any insurable interest. It appeared that, though Mr. Macaura had formed the Irish Canadian Saw Mill Co. Ltd., he had taken out the policies of insurance in his own name and the Insurance Companies held that he, being merely a shareholder, had no insurable interest. The Irish courts supported them, and as we write the issue is being tried in the highest tribunal – the House of Lords.

(To be continued)

## CORRECTION

In the article in issue of 7th March an error in a Christian name occurred, which may be confusing. The full name of Colonel Stewart's nephew, who under the will of 1845, would have succeeded to the Killymoon estate, is Colonel Henry Theophilus Clements, not Col. H. J. Clements, who was his father.

## (28-3-1925)

Meantime other bits of the estate were being sold by Mr. Adair. On 12th June 1851, there was a sale of the townland of Clare to John Lavins, of Clare, for £2,330. It was part of Lot 6, containing Gortalowry and Sullenboy, but lies on the other side of the town. It extends from the country boundary to the great Northern Railway yard, being separated from Coolnafranky and Loy by the stream which is now the main sewer. There is no visible boundary in the G.N.R yard between it and Cookstown townland, but we think that where the new Shell Oil depot is being built is in Clare. Mr. Lavins, though described in the memorial as of Clare, does not appear in the rental as a tenant, and presumably had gone there between August 1851, and the following February. In the valuation of 1859 he appears as owner in fee of the townland and also as occupier of 66 ½ acres of land, valued at £77 15s and of offices only – no dwelling-house – valued at £1. Of the twelve tenants in the rental of 1851 only four remained in 1859 – Eliza Cooke, successor of John Cooke, who held under lease; James Kelly, who seems to have succeeded Widow D. Mullan in 17 acres odd; William Campbell, who had barely 2 acres against 8 acres held by Patrick Campbell in 1851, and Alicia Mullan, who had 39 ½ acres, which apparently were the two holdings of Hugh Mullan and John Crooks in 1851. The rest of the holdings were taken over by the new landlord. He resided afterwards, if not just then, in the town in one of the houses now occupied by either the Post Office or the Café.

The townland of Anaghanaman was sold to Wm. McNeece on 29th July 1851 for £1,200. This was simply an investment, as he never resided on his new estate, and he bought in trust for himself and his four brothers John, James, Thomas and Wright, who lived together at Lamy, none of them being married. They bought only 75a. 1r. 29p. out of 163 ½ acres: whether they were interested in the tenants, or simply wanted £1,200 worth of real estate we do not know. They were unmarried, and dispensed with women altogether; one did the cooking and the other four worked the farm, and they saved a good deal of money. The last of them died just 25 years ago, and as they had left no one to perpetuate the name, he did the next best thing – he bequeathed Stewartstown Presbyterian Church £2,000 to build a hall to be known as the McNeice Memorial Hall, as it is to this day.

Knockaconny, one of the townlands in Lot 3, was sold at the same time. The sale was on 12th June, completed 27th March, 1852. The purchasers were William Fleming, Thos. Fleming and David Fleming, who were farmers living there and holding under leases for three lives. They held 106a. 3r. 24p. between them, at a total rent of £84 1s 10d, plus £6 1s 6d tithe rent charge, and they paid £1,800. Moreover the whole of the head rent on this lot was put on Knockaconny, £12 Irish or £11 1s 6d sterling, so that it was almost exactly a 4 per cent investment. It was, however, a wise purchase even at the price, for it secured them against any increased rent when the leases expired. Thomas and David Fleming were brothers and members of First Cookstown Presbyterian Church, the former being a ruling elder for a long time, and one can trace the influence of the minister, Rev. H. B. Wilson, in the sale because he was witness to a mortgage of their lands to secure £600 in the next year, the lender being Rev. Thos. Heron, of Ballygoney, as executor of Dr. Wm. Moffatt, of Belfast. (Rev. T. Heron became Rev. H. B. Wilson's father-in-law and the latter's eldest son, still living in Dublin, is Mr. Wm. Moffatt Wilson). The loan was, of course, soon paid off, and, in spite of the high price paid for the perpetuity interest, we never heard that the Flemings regretted the bargain, and certainly when they died they left more debtors then creditors to mourn the winding up of their affairs. William Fleming was father of the late Mr. William Fleming, J.P., who built rather a large residence for a farm house and now owed by Mr. McVey.

The other two townlands in this lot – Ballyreagh and Kilcoonagh - were sold on 20th August 1851, to Robert Evans, of Dungannon, the price being £5,733 18s 1d. These two townlands were sold subject to the head rent of £12 Irish, but indemnified by Knockaconny. The deed also sets out that the owner was liable for "suit and service at courts of Manor Symington as reserved in the fee farm deed of the 1st March 1688, made by John Morris to James Stewart". However, that did not worry Mr. Evans much, as the courts had disappeared long before, and even the Manor of Symington was only a name, few knowing where it existed. Mr. Evans resided at Gortmerran House, Dungannon – the same house which some people want Dungannon Regional Committee to buy for a Girls' Secondary school. He was connected with Cookstown, however, by the fact that he was agent for the Orritor estate. He bought Ballyreagh and Kilcoonagh as an investment and about 1877 the two townlands were sold by auction and bought by the late Mr. Thomas Greer, of Seapark, father of Mr. MacGregor Greer

Drumgarrell, Lot 12 of the rental, was sold by Mr. Adair on July 31, 1851, completed 18th February 1852. The purchaser was Mr. S.R. Magill, of Crieve, the date in the Registry being 18th February 1852. The purchaser was Mr. Samuel R. Magill, of Crieve, who had a substantial local interest in it already as owner of Greenlodge. This place, then a bleach green with mill, was bought by Mr. Wm. Magill (one of the builders of Cookstown when the town was planned) in 1819. The previous owner was Wm. Ramsey, who, according to the conveyance, had been for two years or more in business as a linen merchant. He was unsuccessful, however, and the trustee for his creditors put up Greenlodge and 36 acres of land by auction at Nathaniel Henry's Inn in Cookstown and Mr. Magill bought Ramsey's interest and, in 1841, he got a lease in perpetuity from Col. Stewart for what he then held, amounting to 83 ½ acres at a rent of £21 3s 8d with £2 18s 6d tithe rent charge. The total net rental was £78 19s 8d and Mr. Magill paid £2,600, or almost 33 years purchase, but this included 63 acres of bog which had a potential value. Moreover, he did not get the whole townland as mapped. There were 30a. 3r. 4p. of bog which was held in perpetuity by residents in Cookstown with their town houses, and no rent was payable for this block, which was conveyed to Messrs. Gunning and Moore. Further, there was some 29 acres of deep bog lying south of the road to Coagh and adjacent to Drumcraw and Mr. Adair decided to add this to the latter townland. It was obviously more valuable to the tenants of Drumcraw, where there was no bog, than Drumgarrell where there was abundance without it. The consequence of this arrangement is rather interesting for, in 1853, when the Ordnance map was revised, the authorities altered the townland boundaries to correspond with the new ownership and so it remains. The area of Drumcraw in the 1833 map was shown as 159a. 0r. 25p., and in 1853 it was 181a. 0r. 9p.; the area of Drumgarrell in 1833 was 289a. 0r. 20p., and in 1853 it fell to 266a. 3r. 21p.

There now remained on Mr. Adair's hands, outside what he personally occupied, the great bulk of Gortalowry and Sullenboy, part of Scotchtown, the whole of Coolnahavil, part of Drummond, part of Annaghanaman, the whole of Anaghteague, Anaghmore and Gorticar, besides Drumcraw, and this 20 acres of Drumgarrell bog. It was not till 7th August 1852, that a purchaser was got for this (or at lease that the sale was completed). This gentleman was Mr. Andrew Mulholland, of Springvale, Co. Down, who paid £23,578 1s 2 ½ d for the lot. He was one of the successful linen merchants; his son Henry, then a middle-aged man, was largely interested in spinning in Belfast, contested the seat for Parliament and was created Baron Dunleath, and his eldest son, Lord Dunleath, of Ballywalter Park, is the present owner. He is the landlord of a considerable part of the town, from the Loy boundary, which is a stream running underground at an angle with the main street. Loy House, in spite of its name, is on this property and so are the "Red Schools" for which Lord Dunleath gave a free site to the Vestry of Derryloran Parish and subscribed £500 besides, and even the Fever Hospital, on the Fair Hill, is situated on this lot, in the townland of Sullenboy. Either Mr. Andrew Mulholland, or his son, made it a rule that no intoxicating liquors were to be sold on the estate, so far, of course, as he had power to prevent it. But there were in existence property held by lease before his time and many will remember that 25 to 30 years ago there was quite a brisk demand for any such property in Gortalowry by persons who first got, as of right, a special grocery license under Mr. Gladstone's Act, and then had it converted into an ordinary license by the justices who considered the latter was the lesser evil.

It only remains to be said that Mr. Adair had left, out of his purchase, 86a. 1r. 3p. of land in Gortalowry in Sullenboy; 14a. 2r. 17p. in Kirktown, and, on the other side of the river, and 6a. 2r. 1p. in Ardcumber, which cost him £4,808 11s 5½ d for the fee simple.

Next week – Messrs. Gunning & Moore's Purchase.


# MESSRS. GUNNING & MOORE'S PURCHASE

## (4 – 4 - 1925)

The principal of the twelve lots into which the Killymoon estate was divided for sale in the Encumbered Estates Court in 1850 was Lot 9. This lot was purchased by Mr. James Gunning and Mr. James Moore, of Wellbrook. The property included the townlands of Loy, Cookstown, Killymam, Clagan, Monrush, Ballymenagh, Tullygare, New Buildings and Cranfield, the total area being 1,327a. 3r. 38p., yielding a yearly rent of £1,728 9s less Tithe Rent Charge of £54 19s 2d and Head Rent to the See of Armagh of £174 18s 8d. The net income was, therefore, £1,492 12s 0d. The townland of Maloon was sold in another lot, an area of 162a. with a net rental of £187 15s 0½d less £7 15s Tithe Rent Charge. Tullagh, which was Church lands, was also sold in a separate lot, 156 ½ acres, rental £154 3s 9d, less £6 10s 4 ½ d Tithe Rent and £24 6s Head Rent. The sale of these three lots was completed on 12th June 1851, the price being £31,800, or a little over 21½ years purchase. Coolnafranky was also sold as a separate lot, though it lay close to the town and was used as accommodation land for residents in the houses of Lot 9. Its area was 87a. 3r. 16p., and was freehold subject only to the Tithe Rent Charge of £5 0s 5d. Messrs, Gunning & Moore bought it afterwards, the contract being dated 15th August 1851 for £2,640 – just under 21½ years purchase.

In regard to Ballymenagh, which had an area of 194a. 3r. 30p. and a net rental of £162 5s 6d, the old "Castle" was situated on it. This was the residence of James Stewart, the founder of the Killymoon family, who settled there about 1619, when he purchased the lease at the same time as Dr. Allen Cook purchased his lease of the townland of Corcreagh which he named Cookstown. Ballymenagh, therefore, though originally poor land, the Castle being surrounded by bog and probably flooded bog at that, had a sentimental value not possessed even by Killymoon which was created Demesne subsequently and, when Messrs. Gunning & Moore purchased the property, Mr. Thomas Stewart desired to get it so that even a small fragment of the old estate might still be owned by a Stewart. A bargain was completed on 3$^{rd}$ July 1851, with that gentleman, who paid the new owners £3,510 , or a little over 21½ years which was the average price paid by them, for the entire Lot. From the map of 1726 we know that at that time, of the 133 Irish acres, only 90½ acres were regarded as arable, 13 acres being moss and bog, and no less than 29½ acres "scrub". In 1786 the principal tenant was Charles Richardson, Esq., who paid £48 17s 3d rent, while Alex. Crooks paid £34 3s, and Edward Devlin £5 16s, a total of £88 16s 3d, but, at the time the rental for the sale was compiled, the rent had increased to £167 5s 6d – almost double, and there were ten tenants. In 1838 the valuation of the whole townland was £176 17s 9d, of which sum only £4 15s 0d was on buildings, while, in 1858, Griffith's Valuation of the land was £176 and of the buildings £7 10s. Since the sale in 1851 extensive improvements were made, chiefly by the late Mr. J.W. Fleming, who drained the bog and made it arable and threw small fields into larger ones, while the last tenant of the holding on which the Castle stood, Mr. Alex Cameron, J.P., built a brick residence, instead of the thatched house which had served after the Castle fell into ruins, of which the gable only exists. Under the Land Purchase Acts the townland has now been sold to the tenants so that the last link of the property of the Stewarts has been severed.

Messrs. Gunning & Moore also had conveyed to them some 30 acres of Drumgarrell. This was bog which was included in the perpetuity leases with house property in the town and against it no separate rent appears in the rental. The arrangement to include it was, in fact, only to simplify the title, as it was of no pecuniary value to the new owners, nor would it have been to Mr. Magill, who purchased the rent of Drumgarrell. It is, in fact, nominally part of the Cookstown estate but it yields no rent, and it is doubtful if anyone knows the boundaries, as the lessees, when the bog was cut out, simply abandoned the place, and most of the house property with which the small lots were connected, has changed hands. Mr. Magill seems to have subsequently acquired this bog, as in Griffith's Valuation of 1859 he is given as owner in fee of the whole of Drumgarrell as then existing, 266a. 3r. 21p.

In contrast with the carefulness of the conveyancers in regard to this bit of valueless bog, is their treatment of the market rights. The lessee of the markets, described as a "rent for the tolls and customs of the town of Cookstown" was Mr. J. McCormick and the rent £150 a year, the lease being for 31 years from 1850. This amount was included in the rental, and was, of course, a valuable asset, but the authority for it – that is, the charter for the markets – was omitted in the conveyance of 1852, and some years afterwards, when it was discovered, a separate conveyance of the market charter had to be made by the Court to Messrs. Gunning & Moore. Such is, and always has been, the attitude of the law towards real property and commerce: valueless bog is conveyed with meticulous care – valuable market rights are overlooked.

The total sum realised by the estate and lodged with the Commissioners in Court for these private sales, as given in Allnutt's Irish Land Schedule of September 1857, was as follows: -

|  | £ |  |  |
|---|---|---|---|
| Messrs. Gunning & Moore | 34,440 | 0 | 0 |
| Mr. Thomas Adair | 48,386 | 11 | 0 |
| Mr. S.R. Magill | 2,600 | 0 | 0 |
| Mr. Thomas Stewart | 3,510 | 0 | 0 |
| Mr. Lavins | 2,330 | 0 | 0 |
| Messrs. Fleming | 1,800 | 0 | 0 |
| Mr. R. Evans | 5,733 | 8 | 6 |
| Mr. McNeice | 1,200 | 0 | 0 |
| Total | £99,999 | 19 | 6 |

The estate thus realised within six pence of £100,000

Next week – The Gunnings in Cookstown

After the sale of the Killymoon Estate Mr. James Gunning settled in Cookstown and became the residential landlord of the business part of the town, as Col. Stewart and his predecessors had been of the whole estate for over two centuries. Some reference, therefore, to the Gunning family is appropriate at this stage and will be found of interest to those who study the development of Cookstown and, in fact, of any town.

Mr. James Gunning was the eldest son of Mr. John Byers Gunning, a successful business man in Stranorlar, Co. Donegal. The name is Irish, not Scotch like those of the principal families in our district; O'Hart, the celebrated genealogist, says that the Gunnings are the O'Conaings, who derived their name from Conaing, grandnephew of Brian Boru, and are therefore of the line of Heremon, who was the seventh son of Milesius of Spain, from whom is descended the Kings and nobility of Connaught, Dalriada, Leinster, Meath and Oriel and Ossory, and of Scotland since the fifth century, and of Ulster since the 4th century. But, as Heremon succeeded so long ago as 1698 B.C. it is a long cry to the Gunnings of Cookstown in the 19th century A.D., and we may ignore this very problematical genealogy of O'Hart further than to mention it.

Of the family of Mr. John B. Gunning of Stranorlar, three sons and a daughter were associated with Cookstown. The first to come here, so far as our present information goes, was Mr. Henry Gunning, who was partner with Mr. Thos. Adair about the year 1839, when the spinning mill - one of the first in Ireland, was developing rapidly. The partnership continued till 1866, but was confined to the spinning end of the linen business, as distinct from the weaving factory and finishing which Mr. Adair added. Mr. Henry Gunning, who resided for a time, at least, in the house now known as South End Cottage, was also engaged in the coal-mining at Coalisland on a considerable scale. The late Mr. Gunning-Moore told the writer that he had gone through his accounts, and so far as he could see, his uncle, Mr. Gunning, had got out of the mining about as much capital as he put in - which, after all, was more than most men got from the same adventure. Mr. Henry Gunning died unmarried.

A younger brother, Mr. John Gunning, established a more permanent connection with Cookstown. He was never resident here, but, a few years after the purchase of the property, he purchased a little weaving factory in the town for his sons. The factory had been started sometime previously by Mr. James Smyth, a Rasharkin linen merchant, in partnership with a Mr. Mulholland, of Moneymore, but the date is uncertain. Local tradition puts it as the year when the Workhouse was built, whereas Messrs. John Gunning & Sons have on their memorandum paper, as the date of the establishment of the firm, the year 1854. Both, of course, might be right, the latter being the date Messrs. Gunning acquired it, but we are inclined to think that 1841 is too early. At all events, in the directory of 1846, which gives very full lists of linen manufacturers, linen merchants, and others, Mr. Smyth's name does not appear, but it is in the directory of 1856. Moreover, in the rental of Cookstown with which we have been dealing recently, and which gave every leaseholder on the estate, there is no reference to this factory. At any rate, we may take it that, in consequence of his brother having acquired the estate, Mr. John Gunning purchased it and enlarged it, carrying on business as linen weavers and finishers, and for a time as beetlers, under the title of John Gunning & Sons. This is the Milburn Factory, now owned by Mr. Leeper. The site selected was on the edge of the cut-out bog of Cookstown townland, a short distance north of the Orritor road and west of the old town. A number of workmen's houses were built adjacent to the factory, known as Factory Square, but much more accommodation was needed, and soon rows of good class workmen's houses were erected in the Oldtown as it is named, to house the growing population. Orritor Street may be regarded as dating from this period – at all events, the good houses therein, one row of which, erected by Mr. Henry Charles, are of a very superior class, though spoiled by the proximity of very poor thatched houses. The development of this factory may be regarded as the direct result of the purchase of the town by Mr. Jas. Gunning and shows how much can be done by a resident landlord to encourage industries, even though he does not put any capital into them personally.

Mr. John Gunning had a considerable family, three of whom were long connected with the town. The eldest was Mr. William A. Gunning, who resided at Tirnaskea and was the popular agent of what became known as the Cookstown Estate. He was twice married. Of three daughters of the first marriage, the eldest married her cousin, Dr. Shuldan H. Dunlop, of Holywood, and the second married Mr. Edward Lenox-Conyngham, son of Sir W.F. Lenox-Conyngham, K.C.B., of Springhill, and he resided, for a time, in the Manor House, Moneymore. The youngest died unmarried. By his second marriage Mr. W. A. Gunning had two children, the elder being Major John Elgee Gunning who bought the Manor House from his sister, Mrs Lenox-Conyngham, on the death of her husband, and resided there till a few years ago, when he went to England owing, it is understood, to the unwillingness of his son to reside in Ireland. He has still, however, some property in Tyrone, which may prove to be a valuable coal field.

Of the other two sons of Mr. John Gunning, who lived in Cookstown, the elder Captain George D. Gunning acted as agent for the Cookstown Estate for some time to his death, when he was succeeded by Mr. H. A. Mann, who had been acting agent. Captain Gunning resided in the house at the top of Oldtown Hill (now owned by Mr. S.A. Lewis), and died unmarried. The younger brother was Mr. Francis Gunning, who was also agent of the estate and was, during his residence in Cookstown, very popular especially with the loyalist population, who looked to him as a leader. He married a Belfast lady and went to reside in that city, where he died.

We have anticipated a little, in order to refer to the junior members of the family before dealing with Mr. James Gunning. He was engaged in the linen business, as then carried on. There was then a large population scattered throughout the country, employed at hand-loom weaving. This home industry has now died out completely in our district, though in parts of Co. Down and Co. Antrim it is still carried on, and even around Knockloughrim we believe it exists on a small scale. These weavers bought the linen yarn, wove their webs and sold them in the market. The purchasers - linen merchants they were called - were of different grades. Some were merely dealers, buying the webs as dealers buy agricultural produce at present, and selling when they could. Others, with more capital, not only bought webs of linen in the market but supplied yarn to weavers who were unable to provide their own material. Others, again, not only bought the webs in these ways but undertook the bleaching on greens and finished the linen in beetling mills, ready for the consumer. Mr. Gunning belonged to the latter class; on the death of Mr. Irwin, who owned Wellbrook, he leased the bleach-green and beetling mill there, with its supply of excellent water from Montober springs, which the inhabitants of Cookstown now enjoy for domestic purposes, and developed the business of finishing the hand-loom linen to a greater extent than ever before.

In this business he had as partner Mr. James Moore, the second son of James Moore, of Kilraughts, an old Co. Antrim family, and in the year 1837 Mr. Moore married Miss Eliza Gunning, who came to Wellbrook to "keep house" for her brother. She and her husband resided with Mr. Gunning at Wellbrook, and there, in 1840, their son John Byers Gunning-Moore, was born, and was a boy of twelve when the Cookstown estate, where he was to spend his adult life-time as resident landlord, was purchased. There were four daughters also - Anna, married to Gustarus Hamilton; Elizabeth, married to Archibald Dunlop, M.D., Holywood; Margaret, married to George Boulby, of the 54th Regiment, and Isobella, married to Alfred Chemritz Trench. The latter three survived their brother, Mr. Gunning-Moore, who died without issue, and are the present owners of the property purchased jointly by their father and uncle.

Reference should also be made to another member of the family who was resident in Cookstown, and during the war especially, gave a lead to the patriotic women of the town. This was Miss Ada Johnston, the youngest daughter of Mr. John S. Johnston, of Brookfield, Stranorlar, son-in-law of Mr. John Gunning, and who was, therefore, first cousin, once removed, of Mr. Gunning-Moore. She was adopted by Mr. Moore, and it is understood that she inherited the bulk of his personal estate as well as some property that he had in Mountjoy of his own right. On his death, Miss Johnston went to reside in London, with a summer residence in Ballycastle, and her removal was, in its way, as great a loss to the town as that of Mr. Gunning-Moore.

(To be continued)

MILLBURN STREET, COOKSTOWN.

# MR. GUNNING IN COOKSTOWN

# (18 – 4 – 1925)

Mr. James Gunning having purchased, with his brother-in-law, Mr. J. Moore, the business part of Cookstown in 1852, decided to leave Wellbrook and reside in the town, and for that purpose he built the fine stone house which is such a striking feature for visitors coming by rail. The site was well chosen; it was on what was then known as Loy Hill – not the part of the main street now bearing that local name, where the Fair Hill opens on it to the west, but a considerably higher point to the east. The approach to it was by a road which cuts the main street at the new Court House. This road was one of those laid out by Mr. Wm. Stewart when designing the town, running straight at right angles to the main street from the old back road, up and down hill to the old road at New Buildings. Both ends of this road are now closed; to the west it leads to a field attached to the Convent, and to the west it forms the back avenue to the residence which Mr. Gunning appropriately named Loymount. An easier approach was made by the front avenue, laid at an easy gradient towards the north, and coming out on the county road just opposite the Great Northern Railway terminus.

The difference which the building of Loymount made in the topography of the town cannot be realised until we consider what that part of the town was like before it. To do so we must wipe out, in imagination, not only the two railway stations, and all the houses on Molesworth Road, but the whole of Union Street (which did not exist even as a lane), and all the houses on Molesworth Street except the Presbyterian Church and Manse, up to Mr. Allen's, which was a police barracks. On the opposite side of the street the upper market yard existed, and probably was walled in, for masonry was almost as cheap as a thorn fence, but from the stores it was a green field. It was, therefore, possible for Mr. Gunning to have made his main entrance anywhere from Mr. Allen's house, or even to have used the opening to the latter's yard. But to do so would have meant a very steep ascent, so steep as to have made steps necessary, for the ground dips very much at the back of the houses in Molesworth Street, and hence it is that he had to go farther from the main street, beyond the Manse, before he got a suitable place for the avenue, and here he built the neat gate lodge which faces travellers arriving by the G.N. Railway. The land around was then all accommodation land, used for grazing. This he enclosed in what might be described as a small demesne, planting trees along the roadside. Dr. James Mullin, in his autobiography, describes how he was employed, as a small boy, in herding cattle there to keep them from injuring the trees, till his taste for literature led to his being discharged from that duty.

Dr. Mullin, in his references to Mr. Gunning is very complimentary. Possibly his relations to him prejudiced his view, for he boasted that he, himself, was a toiler, and so was the new owner of Cookstown. When at Wellbrook it is remembered that he was out at six o'clock in the morning to intercept the turf men from the mountains and buy fuel for his linen bleaching business, the standard price being a shilling per load of turf. And when he came to reside in Cookstown he was no less diligent in business, and liked to see the same diligence amongst those whom he employed. He had purchased, in 1847, from the Commissioners of Woods and Forests, ten townlands at Mountjoy, near Lough Neagh, and in the true spirit of business landlord he set about improving this estate by extensive drainage. For several years he had up to three hundred labourers engaged in this work, the engineer and overseer being Mr. Morrison (father of Mr. Alex. Morrison, of Cookstown), and it was no unusual thing for him to appear at Mountjoy when work began in the morning to see that there was no loafing or late starters. In connection with his work, he made one rather serious mistake. The great combined drainage and navigation works on Lough Neagh and district, occupying a dozen years, and carried out by the Board of Works, was then in progress. Mr. Gunning carried out the drainage of his own estate at his own expense, but in spite of his protest he had to pay his share of the general scheme as well.

The closing of the public road to make an avenue might be regarded as unusual, and even high-handed. It could not have been done without permission of the Grand Jury, which was the road authority of the time, but it really was no inconvenience to the public. The land alongside was merely accommodation land, set for the season, so that the tenants had no interest in the road. As for travellers, what is now Molesworth Street was a new road to Coagh to avoid the hills on the old Coagh road, and connecting with the little roads which led to the lime kilns in New Buildings, and no one now ever thinks of travelling by the old road instead. There was a connection with Artrea and also with the old straight road to Stewartstown, but to the former Fountain's Road still remained, as it does today and rarely used because of the hills, while, for Stewartstown, the building of the bridge beyond the Linen Hill, the cutting of the latter and the making of a new line of road from Loughry gate-house towards Tullyhogue, provided a much preferable route. Mr. Gunning, however, decided to further develop the streets of the town by connecting up the old Coagh Road and the new by a cross street, the present Union Street, which was laid out by Mr. Morrison, to be subseqently built over. The same engineer undertook the Burn Road for

Mr. Gunning, making what was then merely a lane to the bog into a road connecting with the Orritor road and now always used in preference. We may regret that he had not the vision of Mr. Wm. Stewart and made the road wider, but the pendulum had swung from wide to narrow roads before his time, as evidenced in the difference between the widths of Molesworth Street and the main street.

Since that time no serious attempt at town planning has been made, no new streets or roads having been laid out. The only attempt in this direction was Byers Street, a name which is probably new to almost all of our readers. It is shown on the lease of building ground to Mr. John Kelly in 1877, when Union Street began to be built. This "street" is given as 42 feet wide, but it is not really a new street, being merely part of the old road, which existed before the Main Street existed and which leads to the lime kilns and thence across the Midland Railway to the Coagh Road. Not even the Urban Council, the road authority, knew of that street till they erected, on the vacant ground, a shed for tools, etc., and Mr Kelly's representatives drew their attentions to the fact that the lease, besides giving 98½ feet frontage to Union Street, gave also 172 feet frontage to the road "which road is intended to be widened as shown on the map". The lessors at this time, it may be mentioned, were Mr. James Moore (who survived Mr. Gunning), and Mr. J. B. Gunning-Moore, who inherited his uncle's interest. The latter also inherited his father's interest but as tenant for life only, and frequently regretted that he was tied in consequence. He did all that he could, however, to encourage building by granting leases for 999 years, and during the two generations since the sale of the Stewart estate, the whole of not only Molesworth Street on the one side, but of the road as far as the Great Northern Railway Bridge, known as Molesworth Road, opposite the grounds of Loymount (or Coolnafranky as it was erroneously renamed), and both sides of Union Street have been completely built, while the Burn Road has also been used for building ground almost to the town boundary on the one side, with a few houses outside it on the other.

Mr. James Gunning died in 1875 and by his will he left his moiety of the Cookstown estate to his nephew, Mr. J. B. Gunning-Moore strictly entailing it. Mr. Moore, who was a graduate of Cambridge University and was fourth Wrangler in his year, had been called to the Bar and was then practising in London as a Chancery lawyer. In 1871 he had served as High Sheriff for Co. Tyrone, and on succeeding to the estates he gave up the law and permanently settled in Cookstown. He and his uncle had bought the Annesly estate, or Manor of Annesly, from Viscount Valentia – a member of the same family who owned the Orritor Estate before the first Earl of Castlestewart bought it and which was at one time, also named Manor Annesly. By his uncle's death he became sole owner of this property. He also got Tulnacross and "Savil Park", which his uncle had bought – the latter name is of unknown origin and probably derived from a previous owner. Mr. Moore also had the two townlands of Killycolpy, bought by his uncle in 1861. The townland of Templereagh had been bought by his uncle Mr. Henry Gunning, who left it to his brother James, but it went, we believe, to one of Mr. Gunning-Moore's sisters and has been sold, like Manor Annesly and Tulnacross, to the tenants.

Mr. Gunning-Moore also succeeded to a rather large holding in the Belfast and Northern Counties Railway, his father and uncle having subscribed a considerable sum when the Ballymena Railway Co. was induced to extend the line from Randalstown to Cookstown and this, in its way, had as great an effect on the town as any other part of Mr. James Gunning's investments, for Mr. Moore, as a large shareholder, was elected on the Board of Directors, and lost no opportunity for advancing the interests of the town so far as the railway was concerned. In doing so he was, of course, looking after his own interests as owner of Cookstown. For example, the line was laid across the new Union Street, and, in due course, when the Great Northern Railway came, it was used for the Market Yard - a convenience which can only be appreciated by those who use market yards a distance from railway stations. One consequence of the railway development was the building up of Molesworth Street, while Molesworth Road and the Burn Road date from Mr. Gunning-Moore's ownership. He gave leases of 999 years at very reasonable rents. In other ways he advanced the interests of the town for to him, more than to anyone else, is due the splendid water supply derived from a spring which supplied his birthplace at Wellbrook with water for bleaching. Another memorial to him is the new Courthouse, which was built by the Grand Jury, of which he was an influential member. Several sites were offered, and the Committee ultimately chose one at the back entrance. The difficulty about the Court House, which was only mooted when efforts to build a Town Hall failed, was that the authorities decided that there was no need of such a building in a town where Petty Sessions only were held. Then when a demand was made to have County Court Sittings, the reply from Dublin Castle was that there was no building fit for the judge. It was only Mr. Moore's persistence and influence which at last broke down the opposition and one of the last acts of the Grand Jury was to pass the Presentments for Cookstown Court House. As one of the Upper Bann Navigation Trustees he was the means of having the harbour built at Newport Trench on Lough Neagh, but that has no direct bearing on Cookstown. Mr. Moore died in his 81$^{st}$ year in 1921, his wife having pre-deceased him by a number of years.

To bring this article up to date it is only necessary to say that the residence built by Mr. James Gunning was sold, at the death of Mr. Gunning-Moore, with the grounds and home farm of about 100 acres, to Miss Roche, who has, however, no interest in any other of the property. It was understood that Mr. Moore would have been succeeded by his nephew, Mr. John Gunning Moore Dunlop, elder son of Dr. and Mrs. Dunlop, of Holywood, but he was killed in the war, to the great sorrow of his uncle, and that was intensified when the younger son, Mr. George Malcolm Dunlop was also killed in the war.

Next Week – The Linen Trade in Cookstown.

## LINEN TRADE AND INDUSTRY

### (25-4-1925)

According to a school geography, whose compiler insisted that every town was on some river and reduced the activities of the inhabitants to a single term in his attempt at conciseness, Cookstown is on the Ballinderry and its staple is linen. The former is not true, in the sense which schoolboys would understand; the latter is truer than even the writer thought. Staple is the chief article produced in a district for commerce, and this is as applicable to Cookstown to-day as it was when Dr. Allan Cooke got his charter for a market, though in the three intervening centuries the form in which this staple is dealt with in the markets and leaves the town is very different.

It is not our object to trace the early history of flax growing and the manufacture of linen in Ireland. Eight years ago this was well done in our columns by a valued contributor using the pseudonym of Antiquary, who mentions that there is a tradition that it was introduced by the Phoenicians. Dr. Joyce mentions that the Irish word for shirt is "leine", which is analogous to linen, and that St. Columbkille, by way of mortification, never wore it next his skin. Flax is not indigenous to Ireland so that the seed must have been introduced at some definite time, and from what we know by tradition of the climate, it is unlikely that the seed was saved, for even yet that would be a hazardous way to depend on a supply, with drier climate, so that we may fairly assume that flaxseed was an article of commerce from the first, and if so it is likely that the produce, in some form, was also sold commercially. The damp climate, which we know so well from experience, was favourable for the production of linen, and the industry grew accordingly.

How far back the linen industry went we cannot definitely say, however. It depended first on a supply of seed and secondly on a crop, and in this differed entirely from woollens. In the disturbed state in which Ireland was for nearly the whole historic period, cropping was highly speculative, for when one chief defeated another, the usual procedure was to destroy everything which could not be carried away. Cattle and sheep were by far the safer sort of property to possess, for they could be driven off when danger threatened, and used for food when required; growing flax was fixed, and useless for the needs of a tribe in its fortresses. When spun into yarn, or woven into cloth, it would be comparatively safe, as it required little room, and could be hidden in times of trouble or perhaps stored in the round towers which were built for protection purposes.

In spite of this disadvantage Irish linen became an article of some commercial value during the middle ages, as traces of trade in it on the Continent can be found, though all very vague, and it is not till the Plantation, or nearly so, that we have anything definite about it. The Plantation had no direct influence on it, for, unlike the Huguenots who settled in Ulster in the early 18th century, the colonists from England and Scotland at that time did not appear to have had any special aptitude for the growing of flax or the production of linen. But the security given to the native population by the Plantation must have contributed very much to the extension of flax growing. Moreover, however ancient the industry, however long the period in which linen was a treasured production of Ireland, very little progress had been made till the Plantation which marks the beginning of our real knowledge of linen production.

Dr. Allan Cooke got his lease of the church lands to which he gave his name in 1619, and in 1628 he received a charter for a weekly market, and two half-yearly fairs. Lord Wentworth became Lord Deputy (to the Lord Lieutenant who was formerly non-resident) in 1633, five years after Cookstown market was founded. He is often given the credit for establishing the flax trade, though it existed centuries before, but he found it in a bad state. The crop was uncertain, which was attributed to bad seed, and he decided to procure and supply good seed from Holland. The yarn, which was the principal form in which the flax was marketed, was badly produced, with many broken threads, and he issued orders, having the force of legislation, prohibiting the sale of any bundle of yarn with more than two ends. He also introduced, at his own expense, improved looms, but little cloth was then produced for sale.

Lord Wentworth's rule in Ireland was short, seven years at most, but for the last four he was frequently in England, so that he cannot have exercised any great influence on the industry. But it was vigorous while it lasted, for his motto was "Thorough", and his attitude towards the native Irish is well described as benevolent but unsympathetic. In 1640 he was impeached by the Long Parliament – that is, he was charged with treason and sent for trial by his fellow peers, his chief offence being that he was raising an army in Ireland to assist the King to conquer the Scots against the will of the English Parliament. When the Peers seemed likely to acquit him, in spite of the strenuous attack by Pym, the democratic leader, the Commons passed a Bill of Attainder, which the Lords ultimately accepted, and the King assented to his execution.

This event in political history is relevant because when the Commons were trying to secure his conviction on the charge of treason, evidence of minor offences was given, and amongst them his high-handed methods in dealing with the linen manufacture. He appears to have authorised his agents - Inspectors they would now be termed - to seize and forfeit any bundle of yarn with more than two ends, and it was stated at the trial that the effect of this was to prevent the natives from selling their produce in Cookstown, as well as in other markets, and as a result they could not pay their rent. The full significance of this will be seen on a moment's thought. In Cookstown (Dr. Cook's town) the sale had been as much as £100 per week, which was a very considerable sum in those days, when a cow was worth only £1 and other agricultural produce proportional. We learn that buyers of the yarn came from Lancashire to buy, and not being able to do so in the market they had to get it indirectly, for it is not to be supposed that the natives had no means of getting rid of it, but we may be sure that whoever took the risk of acting as middle-men saw that they were repaid - and the rents were not paid. That, to Wentworth's accusers, was the chief offence, and we may be sure that the tenants made the most of the excuse, for human nature is very much the same in all ages. The outstanding fact that we glean from the trial of Lord Wentworth (or the Earl of Strafford as he had then become) is that around Cookstown, twenty years or less after the market was started, there was a considerable native population whose chief industry was the spinning of flax into yarn for sale, and it is a reasonable inference that this work was confined to the natives, for had it adversely affected the Scotch and English settlers (except as landlords) there is no doubt that prominence would have been given to that fact by the Puritan accusers of Strafford in the Long Parliament.

(To be continued)

## THE GUNNING FAMILY

In the article in our issue of 11<sup>th</sup> August, on the connection of the Gunning family with Cookstown, we have been pointed out a number of errors, of a minor character but which should be corrected. The most serious is that Major Gunning bought the Manor House in Moneymore from his sister Mrs. Edward Lenox - Conyngham. This is incorrect, as it was Mrs. Arthur Lenox-Conyngham who owned the Manor House, and sold it on her husband's death. Mr. Arthur Lenox-Conyngham is still alive. In connection with Mr. W. A. Gunning, who was stated to have lived at Tirnaskea, while this is correct it should have been said that he also resided, and for most of the time he was here, in Loy House. He was agent for the Cookstown estate and was succeeded in that capacity by his brothers, Capt. George D. Gunning and Mr. F. P. Gunning. The latter went to Belfast and married his cousin Miss Barr, a London lady. Another error was the statement that Mr. John Gunning was a younger brother of Mr. Henry Gunning. The latter, we are informed, was the youngest of the family. In connection with the property inherited by Miss Johnston from Mr. Gunning-Moore, this was stated to be the Mountjoy estate, and should have been the Manor of Annesley. The former belongs to Major Gunning, having been left to his father by Mr. James Gunning. Both estates consist of ten townlands: Mountjoy includes Coole, Aughrimderg, Ballybeg, Clentycracken, Magherlamfield, Mullaghtironey, Lenadremna, Carnan, Upper and Lower Beck, lying on the Lough Shore north of Washing Bay, formerly belonging to the Commissioners of Woods and Forests. The Annesley estate was originally school lands and lies almost adjacent, further from Lough Neagh, consisting of Meenagh, Cloghog, Drumurrer, Anaghmore, Anaghaboe, Shanless Uppper and Lower, Dernagh, Maghramulkenny and Mullaghmoyle, a total area of 2,768 acres. Finally, in connection with Milburn Factory, we learn that Mr. James Moore, father of the late Mr. Gunning-Moore was the original partner with Mr. Jas. Smith who appear to have founded the business in 1854. "Moore & Smith" are given as the owners in Piggott's Directory of 1856.

## THE LINEN TRADE (Continued)

## (2 – 5 – 1925)

From the glimpse we get of the linen trade in Cookstown owing to the trial of Lord Wentworth in 1641, we know little or nothing about it for a century. Cookstown, it will be remembered, was burned down in

1642, at the same time as Lissan, by a flying corps of loyalists from Limavady, and from what we know of the town in 1736, no attempt at re-building it was made beyond a couple of small groups of tenement houses on the Oldtown.  But the market and fairs would still be held on the Commons at the foot of the Oldtown, adjacent to the townlands of Monrush and Coolreaghs, and we have definite evidence that when Mr. Wm. Stewart designed the new town there was a linen market in Cookstown, for an advertisement in the Belfast Newsletter of 1752 intimates that from that date it was to be held on the south side of the hill, in the "new town".

A great change had, in the meantime, taken place in the surrounding country, which had become closely populated by Protestant settlers, from Scotland.  This was especially the case on the Orritor estate, which was a native freehold at the Plantation, on the Lissan estate which was church lands, on the smaller native freeholds south of the old town of Cookstown, and on the church lands around the latter, as well as on the Drapers estate.  No definite date can be assigned to this influx of population, which was not confined to our district, but was general in what is now Northern Ireland, as distinct from the six Plantation counties which included Monaghan and Donegal.  Because nothing definite is known of this immigration, beyond the effect, some persons like the late Mr. Arthur Griffith, have denied that it ever took place, and explain the existence of the Protestant population by the theory that these were Irish Catholics who, under pressure of the penal laws, changed their names and became Protestant!  That is a pure theory, without an atom of direct evidence, beyond the fact that some of the native landowners in the South did change their names and embrace Protestantism.  We are tempted to add that this type was, in later days, the worst sort of landlord, just as the descendants of Cromwell's soldiers settled in Tipperary were the most violent type of tenant farmers, but that is digressing.

While there is no evidence in support of this theory, the evidence against it is conclusive. There is the tradition in quite a number of families in Cookstown district that they came over here at a date, fixed by the number of generations, which would fall into the first half of the eighteenth century.  Then there is the existence, even yet, and more pronounced half a century ago, of words of undoubted Scotch origin and a minor argument is that the old people used to refer to the native religion, not as Roman Catholics but as "Irish"- a very striking fact.  But the strongest argument of all is that nearly all the immigrants were Presbyterian.  If the ancestors of these people were Irish Catholics, who changed their religion owing to the penal laws, it is inconceivable that they should join the Presbyterian dissenters instead of the Established Church, for the pressure of the penal laws on the Presbyterians was, in practice, just as great as on the Roman Catholics. The cumulative effect of this evidence is that there was a considerable movement of population from some parts of Scotland, probably Ayrshire, which resulted in a relatively close settlement of a Presbyterian population on the lands around Cookstown.

This matter is relevant to our subject because it was amongst these settlers that the linen industry flourished in the second half of the 18th century and the first half of the nineteenth; whereas, as we have seen, in the 17th century it was confined to the natives. It is also very probable that they brought their own skill and knowledge with them, for up to that time spinning of linen yarn and weaving were widespread home industries, not only in Scotland but all over Europe. The introduction of cotton, and the development of cotton manufacturing industry on a large scale, was a serious competitor to linen and almost completely killed it. Napoleon I tried to save it in France by offering a million franks to any inventor who would produce a machine for spinning linen yarn, but the prize was not awarded, though two Scotchmen did invent a machine for that purpose in 1787, which was partially successful. The manufacture of cotton was making tremendous strides, and, as has been said, killed the linen trade except in certain districts where the conditions were favourable, and Ulster was chief amongst these, so that the dying out of hand-loom weaving in Great Britain only helped the industry here.

Meantime the Irish Parliament devoted a good deal of attention to the encouragement of linen manufacture with which hemp was joined. Grants of money were made, to be used by Trustees for the promotion of the linen industry in all parts of Ireland, the Southern provinces being each put on the same footing as Ulster; but it was only in the latter that it survived. Our theory, which we give for what it is worth, is that preservation of the industry in Ulster was due to the influx of settlers from Scotland (who in turn may have been attracted by the conditions under which it was regulated here), and that they were adepts at hand-loom weaving. The Trustees commenced operations as early as 1711, soon after the first bleach-green was formed at Hilden, near Lisburn, where grass bleaching is still carried on, as railway travellers know. Bleach greens and bleach mills or beetles, were the first development on which we would now describe as factory lines. For these good water was required, in which the yarn or cloth was boiled, and boiling required a convenient supply of fuel, while for the beetling water power was most desirable. Fluctuations in the flow of water were not material, and storage was unnecessary for these beetling mills worked continuously, from Monday morning till Saturday night, as they do till this day.

These bleaching and beetling concerns finished the cloth, and, therefore, had nothing to do with the spinning or weaving. The webs, previously laboriously hammered with beetles by hand, were now brought to the mills and subjected to the same process by water-driven machinery - a development very similar to that which has taken place in the dairying industry where churning is done at a central creamery instead of individual homesteads. The webs were bought in the open market by dealers or by merchants who finished them, or the latter gave out yarn to the poorer class of weavers to make the cloth for them, and paid by piece work. Parliament, besides its fostering grants, which really can have had little effect, did its part in two ways - by imposing regulations of all sorts to an extent which would have gladdened the hearts of our own Ministers of Agriculture, and more properly by removing obstacles in the way of capitalists who were ready to put their money in the business. The statute book of the reign of George III. is full of Acts of Parliament dealing with the industry.

In the year 1763, for example, we find an Act passed to enable tenants for life to give leases in perpetuity for bleach greens. A tenant for life, we may explain for the benefit of some readers not acquainted with legal tenure of land, is a landowner whose estate is entailed, and who, therefore, had no interest in it beyond his own life. That meant that any lease he could give would be of uncertain duration, and deterred men from investing their money in laying out bleach greens or by building mills. Parliament removed this obstacle by giving a life owner power to give a perpetuity lease of 15 acres, provided that at least one third of the area shall, within three years, be made into a bleach yard or bleach green and £10 per acre laid out on improvements for carrying on the bleaching business. This Act was amended so as to make it of wider application in 1765.

These dates are interesting because it was in 1765, the date of the second Act, that the first known lease of Wellbrook was given. There were the elements necessary for a bleaching business - land, water-power and fuel, but there was the legal obstacle, the Earl of Annesley as the owner then was (the family name was Annesley and the estate the Manor of Annesley), having leased his estate to Hans Bailie no security of tenure could be given to any merchant until the Act of 1763 was passed. Wellbrook is, therefore, the direct result of that legislative enactment.

That there was an impetus to the industry is obvious from other stray records, and we can see that bleach greens were regarded as having a great future before them, and persons who had water power on their land were looking for tenants. One advertisement, which appeared in the Newsletter of 29th August 1777, will conclude this instalment, and is of special interest because we learn from it that the woollen industry was more widespread than most persons imagine. Woollens were manufactured in what were named "Tuck" mills. With that preface we give the advertisement.

*That farm of land now in the possession of Robert Mulholland, situated in the townland of Kildress, in the County of Tyrone, containing fifteen acres, plantation measure, is to be let for such term of years as may be agreed upon; on which premises are erected a commodious farm house and office houses. The land on one side is marched by the Kildress river, and a Tuck or Clothes mill erected within 20 yards of the dwelling-house. No place in the North of Ireland is better situated for a bleach green, the cary and race being made and stood time out of mind, and plentifully supplied with water and good falls, with turf bog, to carry on the linen manufacture in the most extensive measure. It is situate within two miles of Cookstown, four of Stewartstown, five of Moneymore, five of Coagh, seven of Dungannon and eleven of Aughnacloy, all good linen markets. If any linen drapers wish to treat for said premises they may apply to William Cluff of Cookstown for such. He will give a tenant a toties quoties lease, renewable for ever, and can accommodate him with any quantity of land under forty acres. Said premises will be showed by Andrew Charles, of Kildress, aforesaid.*

Mr. Wm. Cluff, one of the original builders of Cookstown after the town was laid out by Mr. Wm. Stewart in 1750, had gone to live there but was the lessee of the church lands of Kildress, including the falls where Mr. Dawson M'Allister's scutch mill now stands. His offer of a lease with a toties quoties clause was simply that he would renew it as often as his own lease from the See of Armagh was renewed, and, subject to correction, we think that the Act of 1763 did not help him, which may explain why there was not a bleaching and finishing factory at Kildress instead of merely a scutch mill - the other end of the flax industry.

Next week we shall give some notes on the laws affecting the linen industry passed at this period.

## LINEN TRADE LAW

### (16 – 5 – 1925)

In our last instalment we mentioned that the reign of George III was prolific in Acts of Parliament regulating the linen trade as it then existed, one of the first being to give power to limited owners of land to lease it for long periods for bleach greens – an Act which resulted immediately afterwards, in 1765, in Wellbrook being leased by Hans

Baillie for that purpose. Bleach greens and beetling mills were the first step in the development of this industry on factory lines, the weavers being thus enabled to have their webs of cloth finished by water power, instead of by the laborious and inefficient method previously in use, of pounding with hand beetles, while the use of properly enclosed greens provided a means of bleaching which was not in the power of these home workers, and was, therefore, a distinct advance, analogous, as we pointed out, to the modern creameries which churn the cream from a large quantity of milk and make butter of more uniform quality than is possible in little home dairies. The cloth or yarn, in some instances, was bleached for the weaver but the general rule was that he sold it as brown linen in the market or fair.

There are said to be tricks in every trade, and one of the tricks of the weavers was to get their webs bleached amongst others without the knowledge of the owner of the green by the connivance of the persons in charge. The Act of 1763 recognised this and imposed a penalty of 40s per piece on the weaver when that was detected, the corresponding penalty for yarn being 2s per hank. As far as the workers in the green were concerned, if anyone absented himself without leave he forfeited a week's pay for each day absent, and if he discovered any damage to cloth in his charge and failed to report it, he had to pay the value of it before the damage.

The owners, also had duties imposed on them by the same Act, one being that every piece of cloth bleached had to have their names marked on each side, either in lamp black, vermilion or bluestone and size, before selling it, on pain of forfeiting 20s for each piece. An earlier way of marking it was by weaving two coarse threads at each end of the web and writing their names and addresses, or the name of the weaver, in this space, so that it could be identified. The webs had to be sold in the open market and first were examined by officials named Seal Masters, whose duty it was to see that the cloth was of proper width, and fold it accordingly, and, if any part was damaged, that it be exposed to view, and when he found it correct he fixed a seal at each end. The Seal Master was therefore in a responsible position for the buyer had to rely on his examination and before his appointment he had to lodge a sum of money with Trustees. For a White Seal – a seal for bleached linen, this was £200, but for brown linen only £20. He was liable to the buyers if he passed any webs which were not as described, the penal sum to be paid, in addition to the actual loss, being 20s for a loss not exceeding 5s, and £5 if over that sum. When the web was sold the vendor and the purchaser had also to affix their names, and it may be mentioned that for counterfeiting any name on a web, the person convicted was liable to seven years transportation.

One object of all these regulations in the Linen Act of 1763 was to put an end to the system of dealing by middle-men known as forestalling, or hawking – a practice which is rife in the cattle trade at the present time, and particularly in Dungannon district where a considerable number of persons live by what is called "dealing" - going to fairs, intercepting farmers with cattle and afterwards selling at a profit in the same fair. Readers who are acquainted with this practice will appreciate what occurred seventy years ago when large numbers of weavers went to the markets with their webs and were tempted or coerced into selling to these middlemen. A newspaper correspondent, writing over the name "Ireland" on 6th June 1775, condemns this practice in no measured terms, pointing out that these "pests" were parasites or sharpers, living on profits "between two industrious classes, the manufacturer and the draper" – that is between the weaver and the merchant who finished the cloth. The writer alleged that these "sharpers" (to use another name he gave them), picked out the best linen and bought it at an undervalue, and he accused the Seal Masters of conniving at the practice and being, in some cases, in partnership with the actual buyers who were often poor weavers. The general effect on the trade was to put up the price of linen, which had to be sold abroad, without increasing the remuneration of the weavers anything. He further pointed out to the drapers that some of them were responsible for the practice which had become almost universal, because when they set out for a round of the markets they wanted to get as much cloth as possible, the expenses of buying being as much for a small as a large quantity, and so bought from these dealers.

The remedy for this state of things, the writer further pointed out, was to insist on the Linen Act being carried out. It forbade anyone buying linen and selling in the same market or within 30 miles on the same day, or within a month afterwards, the penalty for this being that the linen *shall be liable to forfeiture if seized.* This would be easily detected if the law requiring the name of the weaver was written as required at each end of the web, and he suggested that the drapers *shall meet and publicly announce that they will not buy any cloth that is not so marked on the one end, and in order that no hardship shall accrue to the weavers, in respect of webs in the looms, that a month be given them to finish these and after that time that no linen be bought that has not the name on both ends.*

As a sequel to this good advice, a meeting was held in Dungannon on 26th January 1775, attended by linen drapers who bought in the markets of Dungannon, Stewartstown, Cookstown and Moy fair. Several resolutions were passed. The first was as follows: *That being sensible to the great injury done to the linen trade in general and the damage sustained by manufacturers and drapers in particular, from the unlawful and pernicious practice of forestalling, hawking and jobbing brown linen, which of late has increased to an alarming degree, we, whose names are hereunto subscribed, think it incumbent on us, and on all real friends of our staple manufacture to unite in suppressing the same.* They proceed *to resolve that from this day forward we will not intentionally buy any hawked or jobbed linen, or any we suspect to be such, nor will we buy or suffer to be bought for us any linen in such markets or fair without having the weaver's or manufacturer's name and place of residence wrote on it as the law directs.*

They also gave notice that from 1st March they would not buy any linen without the names at both ends (following the letter referred to so closely as to make one suspect that it came from some of these local drapers) and adding that it was evident that many brown seal-masters are become drapers and those who are not encourage the practice of sealing linen otherwise than as required by the law, in direct opposition to their instructions, the drapers *resolve to put the law in full force against all such seal-masters as do not, in future, act agreeably to their instructions from the Linen Board.* So they give notice that from 1st March they will endeavour to put the law in force against all such seal-masters, and in order to do so would appoint *an honest active man to take charge of said markets and fairs* and to take up all such linen as shall be exposed for sale contrary to the law, paying the Inspector £40 a year while the fines were to be given to the poor. Finally they say, in the last resolution, that as they expect the same *or like laudable resolution will be entered upon by our brother drapers who attend the neighbouring markets in this and adjacent counties, as soon as such shall take place we will conform thereto in all such markets.*

This movement aiming at purging the trade of the middle-men, seems to have begun amongst the drapers of Dungannon and Cookstown districts and was followed, as was anticipated, all over Ulster by other drapers. It is an illustration of how Parliament alone is powerless if not supported by public opinion, and how even the Linen Board, which appointed the seal-masters, had to be assisted by voluntary effort on the part of the persons affected. It enables us also, after a century and a half, to learn who the linen drapers of 1775 were, for though the addresses are not given, the names are, and many will be recognised as those of families identified with the old linen trade, in the days before the factories. The names attached to the resolutions were as follows:- Thomas Greer, Andrew Taylor, John Kenny, Samuel George Holmes, John Twigg, John Willcocks, Thomas Boardman, Robert Bleakly, John Duff, Hugh Weir, Edward Shaw, Willoughly Newton, Thomas Jackson, John Christy, Adam Elliott, Isaac Humphrey, Samuel Park, John Wilson, William Weir, John Weir, John Marshall, Teeling Cassidy, Alexander

Hayse, Robert Stewart, Michael O'Meara, Bryan M'Mahon, Samuel Holmes, John Ryan, John Williams, George Heather, Thomas Toole, Robt. Greer, Robert Magill, Russell Patteson, John Cooke, Thomas Cook, Thos. Hamilton, Wm. Park, Hugh Little, Samuel Elliott, George Anderson, John Maconchy, Thomas Campbell, Wm. Jackson, Robert Magill, jun., Wm. Magill, David M'Cann, Andrew Newton, Benjamin Greer, David Duff, Wm. Adams, Joseph Greer, Thomas Pillar, James Hunter, George Ramsay, Wm. Vanse, Robert Reid, Robert Brown, Charles Duffin, Thomas Henderson, Wm. Elliott, James Greer, William Heather - the last five being subsequent additions. To give weight to the resolutions, threatening to put the law in force, it is signed by several magistrates who say "We approve of the above resolution and shall be ready, at all times, to enforce the laws relating to the linen trade", signed by George Hannyngton, Fowke Moore, Ed. Lill and James Moore Hamilton, justices of the said county. The first-mentioned is the well known banker, the remains of whose house are on Castle Hill and are often mistaken for the ruins of the Earl of Tyrone's castle, while Edward Lill is, we feel sure, the rector of Clonoe who lived at Barnhill beside Stewartstown, then the centre of the linen trade. How many of the above drapers belonged to Cookstown we cannot say with any certainty, but the above list may be taken as including all the linen drapers who, at that time, attended the market in Cookstown and the fact that there are 63 in all indicates the very important place in the commercial life of the community which the hand-loom weaving then had

(To be continued)

Cookstown Flax Market

# MORE LINEN LAW

## (23 – 5 – 1925)

Customers, or as we now say, the general public, were protected by the Linen Act of 1736 as well as other persons. As in these days we have machinery for detecting adulteration of food and even drinks, for securing that margarine is not sold as butter, or that nest eggs are not sold as new laid, so a century and a half ago it was thought necessary to legislate so that those who bought linen got what they should.

Bleaching was one of the processes which needed special attention, as short-cuts were taken to get the cloth white without the trouble and consequent expense of exposing it to the weather on the grass. Lime was a local substance which could help the bleaching, but at the risk of burning the cloth, and hence its use was prohibited. Any person using lime was liable to have the yarn or linen forfeited and fined 20s for every hank of yarn, while the informer got £10. This handsome payment to the informer was the only way in which evidence could then be got, in the absence of an efficient police service. Muriatic acid, or muriatic of lime - that is chloride of lime - might be used, but in that case every web had to be marked with the word "muriatic" below the bleacher's name, on a penalty of £5 for each piece of cloth. Another article, the use of which was prohibited in bleaching, was pigeon's dung, the penalty being £5 for each piece of cloth, which was also forfeited. Should the cloth be dyed or stained, so that it would be difficult to bleach, the penalty was to forfeit it and a fine of 20s. Glazing the linen was another crime, rated at a fine of £3 and the loss of the article. In these cases of forfeited cloth it appears that the web was to be cut up into pieces not more than four yards long.

The measurements of these home woven webs will be of interest to some readers. Yard wide linen, when the set was 1400, had to measure 37½ inches when in the brown state, and 34 inches bleached. White plain cloth was 25 inches and brown Coleraines 32 inches or 30 inches when bleached. As to the length, the web was to be measured from seal to seal, the bad ends not taken into account, and the statute yard of 36 inches being used, with "no allowance but of the breadth of the thumb per yard". We can picture the seal-master, with his yard stick, starting with the seal at one end, laying down the measure on the cloth, placing his thumb at the end of the rule and from the other side of the thumb laying it down again and so on. This, of course, was for the protection of the weavers, and to ensure that there would be no legerdemain it was ordered that in the measurement there must be "no stoppage on the piece on any pretence".

"Coleraines" have been mentioned above as the name for a well-known class of linen, but it is not the only sort which had acquired a local name, for "Moneymores" were also recognised. It was brown linen or hempen cloth, ⅞ ths wide, manufactured in Ulster, Leitrim, Sligo and Mayo, and the Act provided that it shall be 32 inches wide, if of a set of 800 to 1,200, and 30 inches wide when bleached. Each single piece was to contain 26 yards only, or 52 yards in the double piece, on a penalty of 5s and the forfeiture of the web.

Mention was made last week of the action of the merchants attending Cookstown, Stewartstown, Dungannon and Moy to buy linen, in appointing an Inspector at £40 a year. We took it that this was a voluntary officer, but the Act of 1763 provides that an Inspector at that salary shall be appointed in Tyrone, Derry, Antrim, Down Armagh and Donegal, while Cavan, Monaghan and Fermanagh got one amongst them. The Trustees were to convene a meeting of registered bleachers and if the majority present thought that an Inspector would be of service, they could return their names and the Trustees were to appoint one of them as Inspector of brown linen and yarn for the year commencing in May or June at a salary not exceeding £40 a year. Apparently by 1775 this office had fallen into disuse, hence the voluntary effort headed by Mr. Greer. The Inspector is to be distinguished from the Seal-Masters; in fact one of his chief duties was to watch the latter and inform on him if he acts contrary to his duty. In other words he was to police the markets, but unlike the modern constable who neglects his duty, if the Inspector omitted to inform on a Seal Master he, himself, was liable for the penalties incurred by the other official. The Inspector had power to demand from any spinner, reeler, jobber, seller, buyer, "grey merchant", or exporter of yarn that it be produced, and could search between sunrise and sunset for yarn, and if anyone refused to allow a search, a fine of £20 was imposed or a month in the "house of correction" or next jail.

The attitude of the Drapers at their meeting in Dungannon, mentioned last week, was not without its effect, for on 27th October 1775, the Linen Office published an advertisement as follows:-

*The Trustees having proceeded to examine seventeen pieces of brown linen laid before them, which were sold in the market of Dungannon by Edward Gray, of said county, on 13th July last, being found deficient by not having cords woven at each end and the impression of the seals not being legible, ... ... ordered that a fine of £85 be imposed on said Edward Gray for selling said 17 pieces of brown linen, being £5 each piece.*

*The Trustees will hear complaints, and punish, with the utmost vigour of the law, any person not complying with the several Acts of Parliament, passed for the better regulation of the linen manufacture.*

*Simpson Ingrim, of Dungannon, being the Inspector of brown linen in Tyrone.*

But while adultration (using the word in its wide sense) was aimed at by the Act, the greatest crime was the universal one of larceny. The code of law was very severe, and it needed to be because the opportunities were many and the difficulty of detection great. To steal yarn or cloth or any materials used in a bleach yard, by day or by night, was a felony, and the persons convicted were to be so adjudged "without benefit of clergy". To steal any goods from a Linen Hall (a market for the sale of linen), whether the owner be in the Hall or not, was a felony, and the person convicted or attainted by verdict or confession, or shall peremptorily challenge above 20 returned to be of the jury shall be debarred of the benefit of the clergy. "Benefit of clergy" it should be mentioned was a practice which originally exempted clergymen from the jurisdiction of secular courts, leaving them to be tried by bishop's courts but it was extended to include all who could read. The privilege had to be claimed, and a layman could claim it once only, so that it was really on the lines of the modern First Offenders Act. There was one difference – that whereas a first offender is now discharged on giving recognisances, which generally means that he stands up while the clerk reads out something that he does not understand, the man who claimed benefit of clergy was branded with a hot iron on the ball of the left thumb. The privilege existed up till 1827.

The most serious offence was wilfully injuring yarn or cloth, or tools used in its manufacture. If done in a bleach green the penalty was seven years transportation: if the culprit forced his way into a house or shop, with intent to injure the contents, he was to suffer death.

This severe code of law regarding larcenies existed up to a comparatively late period. One example will suffice. At the Tyrone Assizes in 1851, the year after Col. Stewart's death, three men and two women were indicted on a charge of breaking into a store belonging to William Paul, of Cookstown, and stealing 60 bundles of yarn. The evidence was that the store, containing between £300 and £400 worth of yarn, was locked at 9.30 and next morning it was found broken open and about 60 bundles missing. Footsteps were traced to the house of the premises, and at 7 a.m. one of the women was busy at her loom. The stolen yarn, made at Mrs. Stevenson's was identified. The Judge said that they could not convict persons on suspicion, which was a lenient view to take, but he sentenced the unfortunate woman, on whom some of the yarn was found, to ten years transportation.

The robbery of bleach greens was so easy that it became a serious tax on the owners. In the year 1772, the following advertisement appears - -

*Barony of Dungannon. Whereas the robbery of bleach greens is of late become very frequent in said barony, now we, the undermentiond owners of bleach greens in said barony, to prevent, as much as in our power, robberies in future, do promise to pay the several sums annexed to our names respectively, to the person or persons who shall first discover and prosecute to a conviction the person or persons that shall, for twelve months from this date, feloneously enter into any of our bleach houses, bleach greens, or any place thereunto belonging, and carry thereout any linen property under our charge; a further reward of £5 sterling to any person or persons who shall give information that shall lead to the discovery and conviction, and such information shall be kept a secret if required; and to continue from time to time for each conviction and information. Dated this 23<sup>rd</sup> of March 1772.*

This is signed by eleven green owners, who contributed £4 11s each. The meaning is not quite clear, but we take it to mean that for every successful prosecution the signatories would pay £4 11s each, a total of £50 odd, or £5 for private information. The names of these eleven bleachers in the barony of Dungannon - that is, of Upper, Middle and Lower Dungannon, are as follows:- Duffin & Shaw; Geo. and Wm. Anderson; Wm. Parke; Hugh Faulkner; John Maconachy; James Greer; John Twigg; John Wellcocks; John Cook; Russell Pattison, and St. George Holmes. Of these we can identify John Maconachy as owning the green at Drapersfield, while Faulkner owned Wellbrook and Cook owned Greenvale, and also Pattison at a later date. Perhaps some reader can identify some of the others as owner of a bleach green about 150 years ago.

The code of laws in the Linen Act of 1763 would be incomplete without reference to flax growing and seed. Whatever obstacles may have been created by the fishery industry afterwards, that Act made it legal to steep flax in holes or pits of running water, or near streams supplied with fresh water, without letting the flax water mix with the stream, but no flax could be steeped in a stream before 1<sup>st</sup> October, unless a flood should happen sooner. The penalty was forfeiture of the flax or its value. On the other hand, anyone who found flax steeped in a river where fish are usually taken, might seize the flax and keep it. Moreover, the feelings of the public, who object to the smell of flax, were considered by enacting that no one was to dry flax within 100 yards of a road.

At this time tithes had to be paid on crops, to the parson or vicar of the parish, and the Act of 1763 fixed the amount at 5s per acre and no more, payable before the flax is carried off the ground, but by an Amending Act of 1765, land reclaimed from moor bog or from a lough, or river, was exempt from tithe for seven years.

In regard to flax seed, a complicated scale of duties was in force, in which Northern Ireland was distinguished from the rest of Ireland. Thus if seed were shipped from Dundalk or any port south thereof to any place beyond sea, a premium of 1s per bushel was to be paid, if the seed was worth 5s per bushel – i.e., a bounty of 20%. But, if shipped to the northern part of Ireland, the bounty was doubled, for 21 years. No import duty was to be levied on seed from Russia, Germany, the Netherlands, the East country or the British Plantations. But though there was free importation of seed, it was subject to inspection, and if found bad, damaged or unfit for sowing it was to be seized. Should the importer not admit that the seed was inferior he could apply to a magistrate, who was to summon five merchants or other skilled persons to examine it, and if they found that it was fit for sowing, the cask had to be so branded. The importer also had the option of exporting it again or could undertake that it be crushed into oil. If the importer did nothing the Trustees had power to burn the inferior seed.

The casks or hogsheads of good seed were branded by the Inspectors for sale up to 1st July of that year only, and the merchant who had any unsold was required to give notice within one month to the Trustees, and it was re-inspected in January or February and if found good got a second brand on the barrel. If condemned the owner, had the right to crush it for oil. To prevent inferior seed being sold out of barrels branded as "sound", the merchant was required, when one barrel was empty, to obliterate the mark. The penalty was a fine of 40s, while for failing to report seed unsold on 1st July it was £10 10s. These penalties, it may be noted, could be imposed not only by magistrates but by Trustees; one trustee if the penalty was up to £6; five or more should it be greater. The penalties were, as a rule, to be given to the informer, less 2s in the £ payable to the constable. On the whole, therefore, the Linen Act of 1763 would have delighted the heart of those who think that the best way to prevent fraud in trade is not to trust to free competition and the intelligence of buyers, but by official machinery.

Next Week – The Linen Market in 1816 – 21

# TROUBLES IN THE LINEN MARKET

## (30 – 5 – 1925)

The most important feature of the linen market was the sealing of the webs. As already explained, this meant that the web was taken to the seal-master who measured it and put a seal on each end, as a certificate that it was of the right length. This was equivalent to what takes place every Saturday in Cookstown, when butter or pork or potatoes are weighed. The buyer depends on the official weight, and, in the same way, the linen merchants depended on the official measurement. It was also the duty of the seal-master to see that there were no defects in the web, or at least to lap the cloth so that they were observable by the buyer, whilst the width of the web was also to be checked. When any deficiency was discovered in a web afterwards, the buyer had a remedy against the seal-master, who was responsible.

Making the seal-master responsible was the feature of the whole system. The weavers knew the length of these webs and what the width should be, but were not, as a rule, men of much financial standing, and it would have been futile to attempt to make them responsible for short measure. Hence the responsibility was thrown on the seal-master, who was liable to fines on a fixed scale, and the buyers saw that they were inflicted. For example, in Cookstown the sole seal-master was Mr. Matthew Pattison (uncle of the late post mistress), a gentleman who performed his duties in a highly satisfactory manner. He had, however, a number of assistants, varying in the size of the market, and it is not unnatural to expect that some of them would become careless. At any rate we find that Mr. Pattison, though a model official, had to pay 17 fines in the year from 5th January 1820 till 5th January 1821. The fines ranged from 5s for passing a web with a bad end, to 15s for another with damages concealed, the general fine being 10s for short measure. As Mr. Pattison's remuneration for measuring was 2d per piece, and a yard of brown linen was worth about 9d, at a dear time, and the total net income for 1820 was £80, a fine of 10s for sealing a web which was a yard short was an excellent way of emphasising the necessity for carefulness.

Mr. Matthew Pattison was appointed "sole seal-master" for Cookstown market in May 1818, at the same time as Mr. James Woods was appointed to Stewartstown. The Inspector for these two markets was

Mr. Benjamin Pattison, of Cookstown, who was appointed to that position in 1804. His salary was £40 a year with £16 5s travelling expenses (for 1800 miles). He also got the fines, which amounted to £27 15s from the seal-masters, and £47 17s 5d from jobbers, weavers and others, while the forfeited linen and yarn was worth £16 17s 8d, making the whole income for the year 1820 the sum of £153 7s 1d. Mr. Pattison remarks – *My income is certainly lessened by the appointment of public seal-masters, for the trade do not put their fraudulent webs into my hands as formerly, but call on the public seal-masters themselves for the amount of the deficiencies.*

What, then, was the practice before the appointment of the sole seal-masters, or public measures as the Secretary of the Trustees preferred to call them? From the complaints at Dungannon we learn that it had been the custom there, and presumably in other centres of the hand-loom trade, to give out seals to anyone who applied for them and produced sureties. There was no limit to the number, hence the force of the name to the new officials, "sole" seal-masters. The practice had its advantages in as much as it relieved the pressure at the markets; these private holders of seals, throughout the country, measured a web for a weaver in his neighbourhood and fixed the seal, and when the weaver came to the market he was ready to sell, without going to the house, dignified by the name of Linen Hall in some towns, where the seal-master and his deputies were dealing with the cloth. In Cookstown, in 1816 - that is before the public seal-master was appointed - there were 240 weavers in attendance at markets in the slack time and 420 in the "throng" time, to use the official terms. In Dungannon up to 1,200 weavers attended in the throng time, while the number for Stewartstown was given as 250 and for Moneymore (where the market was on the monthly fair day), up to 1,000. As these private holders of seals were men of some substance, or, at any rate, had given security, it was to be presumed that when the webs were short or otherwise defective, the penalties could be recovered, but from the statement quoted, by Mr. Benjamin Pattison, it is evident that the buyers did not find that they were good enough in that respect, and consequently handed the bad webs to the Inspector to take proceedings, and a considerable proportion of his income was derived from the fines. But apart from this primary object of sealing - to make the seal-master responsible for the cloth he certified - the private system was obviously of no use in the prevention of forestalling, to which we referred last week, and which was regarded as a great evil.

The complaints by the merchants led to the recall of these private seals and the appointment of sole seal-masters in the year 1818. There was some competition for the office; a Mr. John King petitioned the

Trustees for the appointment in Cookstown and sent a certificate in his favour signed by "sundry members of the Linen Trade". Mr. James Stewart, M. P., of Killymoon, who was the nearest Trustee to Cookstown - in fact, the only Trustee resident in the district - wrote, however, that Mr. John King is a stranger to him, and requested that no appointment be made until he shall have communicated with the Trade, and shall be enabled to recommend some person qualified, in their opinion, to fill that office. In this, as in every other respect, Mr. Stewart, the veteran owner of Killymoon, showed himself anxious to further the interests of the town. He did not stand by, while a stranger got himself appointed to a position which might make or mar the market, but took the initiative. As a result of his consultation with the buyers he recommended Mr. Matthew Pattison, who was duly appointed.

At the same meeting Rev. J. M. Staples wrote recommending Mr. James Woods as sole seal-master for Stewartstown, and he was also appointed.

(To be continued)

A BLEACH GREEN ADVT. OF 1765

A correspondent sends us the following advt., which appeared in the Newsletter in January 1765 – two years after the Act of George III, enabling titles to be given by limited owners for bleach greens. The relative importance of Cookstown to Moneymore at that date will be noted.

*To be sold by auction, at the house of Mr James Dunbar, in Cookstown, near Moneymore, on the 29th inst., at the hour of 12 o'clock, the lands of Crive, Killey, Gavna, and Lisbuy, well situated for the cloth trade, in a fine rich country, within 3 miles of Dungannon, four of Stewartstown, four of Pomeroy, five of Cookstown, and one of Donaghmore, whereon is a large mansion house with offices, a large malt kiln, two large orchards, great plenty of meadow and moss, whereon may be made a very large bleach green, which is a lease under the Lord Primate about 3 years since renewed, paying a chief rent of £10 10s yearly and producing a profit rent of about £145 sterling yearly. To he shown and further described by Mr. Robert Phenix of Crivagh and Mr. Robert Bell of Drumconner.*

# INSPECTING SOUTH DERRY MARKETS

# (6-6-1925)

Though we are concerned, in these articles, chiefly with the Linen Market in Cookstown, some reference will be of interest to many readers to the struggle which took place in 1818 regarding the post of Inspector in the neighbouring markets of Co. Derry. Mr. Hugh Boyle, of Limavady, was then the Inspector and was also the Sole Seal-Master for the county, an invidious arrangement because his duty as Inspector was, partly at least, to see that the sealing was properly done; in fact, if he properly carried out his sealing duties there was no need for an inspector at all, as he, himself, urged when it was proposed to appoint a second inspector.

Mr. Boyle's seals had been recalled, but he was re-appointed, and at one time he seems to have claimed a right to that position, much as a landowner who got a charter for a market on his estate had a right to the tolls. It was, indeed, alleged that Mr. Boyle had actually farmed out his job as seal-master, receiving twenty or thirty guineas from men who actually did the work and got the statutory fees.

That the work was not done satisfactorily, however, was stated in a report by Mr. James Corry, the secretary of the Board of Trustees, who made a tour of Ireland in 1816. He came to Ulster on 10th October of that year, visited Newry and Armagh, calling with the local trustees, then on 16th October, he visited Dungannon market, and on Friday travelled to Cookstown, where he spent the morning in communicating with the traders and afterwards went to see Mr. James Stewart, one of the Trustees, at Killymoon, returning to Church Hill, to see Mr. Verner, another trustee, and thence, on Sunday, to Lurgan. He subsequently visited Coleraine and Londonderry on another circuit at the end of October, but did not actually visit any market in South Derry. When in Cookstown, however, he writes: - *Such of the gentlemen assembled at Cookstown as attend at Magherafelt, Kilrea and Moneymore, said that many irregularities prevailed in these markets, from want of a more regular attendance, and greater activity, on the part of the Inspector*. As stated that gentleman was Mr. Hugh Boyle, while the sealing was done by persons who had taken the market from him.

These complaints came to a head soon after, when a memorial, promoted, as far as we can judge, by the Tyrone drapers and bleachers, was presented to the Board asking that a second inspector be appointed for Co. Londonderry, for the markets at Moneymore, Magherafelt and Kilrea. The salary attached to the office was only £40 a year. Mr. Benjamin Pattison, the Inspector for Cookstown and

Stewartstown, got £390 for 9 ¾ years salary from 1st December 1805 till 1st September 1815, but in 1817, when he was paid £50 for five quarters' salary, the Commissioners of Accounts (the Auditor General as we now say) disallowed his whole salary on the ground that the Trustees had no power to engage a second Inspector in any county. At the date of the Boyle incident, however, that did not arise. The drapers sent up a memorial to the Trustees, who, on 17th November 1818, granted their prayer and directed Mr. Wm. Pollock, the Inspector-General for Ulster, to take the views of the trade at these markets as to who would be a suitable person to appoint.

The candidate favoured by the Tyrone buyers was Mr. John Henderson, of Kilrea. His memorial was signed by 27 Linen Drapers who attended the markets of Moneymore, Magherafelt and Kilrea. The first three signatures were those of John Henderson, Castledawson; Thomas Morgan, Cookstown; Wm. Morgan, Grouse Lodge, and amongst the others were Thomas Greer, jun., Dungannon; Alexander Stewart, Drumray and James Magill, Anahavil.

This memorial was sent to Mr. Wm. Pollock for his report. He wrote on 13th March 1818, from Cookstown, returning it. In the course of his letter he says: - *Being aware how easily signatures to a paper of this sort are obtained, I thought it my duty to appoint a day to meet the Trade, which I did by advertisement in the Derry and Belfast newspapers, fixing the Town of Magherafelt on Thursday, the 12th inst., it being the great Monthly Market, where I had attended and had the satisfaction of meeting a very respectable number of the principal Linen Merchants of that Country.* He then proceeds to state that when he explained the object of the meeting, Mr. Hugh Boyle, the Inspector of the county *came forward and stated that in consequence of his having been appointed Sole Seal Master for the Monthly Linen Market of Magherafelt, Moneymore, Maghera and Kilrea, it became his bounden duty, as well as his interest, to give constant personal attention to these markets, which he was determined to do, and that from his long services as Inspector, he hoped the Gentlemen present would ask leave to withdraw their Memorial which had been presented to the Board, recommending the appointment of a second Inspector, and allow him to take the whole duty of Inspector and Seal-Master, with all the responsibility attached to both Offices.* Mr. Pollock added that the meeting were unanimous in approbation of Mr. Boyle's conduct as a Public Officer, and as he pledged himself to attend the markets, they did not think a second Inspector was necessary *at present*, but reserved the power, *without appearing inconsistent*, to renew the application *in case Mr. Boyle should neglect his duty.* Under these circumstances Mr. Pollock did not think it necessary to enter on the merits of Mr. John Henderson, nor of Mr. W. Hogg, jun., of Portglenone, who was also a candidate.

That, however, was not the end of the matter. The drapers from this end of the district were not satisfied with Mr. Boyle, and sent in a fresh memorial through Mr. Jas. Stewart, M.P. of Killymoon, who, as a Trustee, had influence with the Board. This memorial refers to the allegations in memorials in the preceding two years, signed by almost all the gentlemen in the Linen Trade attending the markets, and it proceeds to say that the Magherafelt meeting convened by Mr. Pollock (who did not say how many were present but simply that he had advertised it in Derry and Belfast papers) was not representative at all, *only a few having attended.* They proceed: - *Now we, the undersigned who attend the markets in the Co. of Londonderry, and are ourselves resident in the County of Tyrone, do pray your Honourable Board will reconsider all the former proceedings had on this business and the inconsistency of the latter part thereof by these gentlemen who meet in Magherafelt.* They proceed to state their objections to Mr. Boyle: as there are markets held on the same day in the county it was out of the power of one person to attend all in a proper manner. Again the markets in Co. Derry had been "let to farm" to deputies at from 20 to 30 guineas per year.

The memorial concludes with the undertaking that *should there be any obstacle in the way to prevent your Honourable Board from granting the usual salary, we engage to pay Mr. Henderson what we may consider equal to his services.* This was dated 2nd April 1818 and was signed at Dungannon, the last name on it being Thomas Greer, jun., Dungannon who was probably the leading spirit, and a man who was not likely to let anyone else interfere with what he thought was for the benefit of the markets. The other signatories included Wm. Morgan, Grouselodge; Thomas Morgan, Cookstown; Jonathan Pike, Beech Grove; Wm. Greer, Milltown; H. Murray, Geo. Wilcocks, Samuel McDonnell, Derry Hill; Jos. Williams, Grange; James Hunter, jun., Mountjoy; James Magill, Cookstown, and Alex. Stewart, Drumroy.

The Trustees at their meeting, at which the Bishop of Down, who resided at Portglenone, was in the chair, decided in favour of this memorial. The offer to pay an Instructor was not considered, and the nomination of Mr. Henderson at a meeting at Dungannon was irregular, as it should be made from the markets affected, but they directed their secretary to write peremptorily to Mr. Pollock that a second Inspector was to be appointed, and if he did not get the Trade to nominate one or more suitable persons, they would do so themselves.

Mr. Pollock, having been thus reproved, convened another meeting in Magherafelt, by advt. in "The Derry Journal" and also by handbills which was held on the monthly linen Fair on 14th May 1818. He reports that *The attendant Linen Merchants and Bleachers were numerous and highly respectable.* There were two candidates, Mr. Henderson Boyle, who was formerly in the linen business and assisted his father in conducting an extensive Bleach Green, and Mr. William

Hogg, jun., of Portglenone, who *has not been bred to any branch of the linen trade*, but acted as Assistant Inspector to Mr. Hugh Boyle, *and conducted himself to his satisfaction.* Mr. Boyle was supported by the whole of the registered Bleachers of Co. Derry; Mr. Hogg was supported by the principal linen merchants and many Bleachers from Co. Antrim *who chiefly comprise the buyers of linen in Moneymore, Kilrea, Magherafelt and Maghera.*

Mr. Boyle's memorial had 49 names on it, all with the initials "R.B." – for Registered Bleacher, and it stated at foot that these were all the Bleachers in the County except one. They stated that he had been *regularly bred* to the linen Trade, and that as the Board *are determined to appoint a second Inspector* they recommend him as a fit and proper person. Mr. Hogg had 56 names at his recommendation, of which 25 were Bleachers. Neither had any of the Tyrone Drapers supporting them, but the memorial in favour of Mr. John Henderson was also considered.

Mr. Hugh Boyle, himself, sent a memorial, dated 30 May 1818, on his own behalf against any appointment. His case was that his emolument as County Inspector being insufficient to defray the expenses of constant travelling, the Board had re-appointed him as Sole Seal Master in the previous October. Since then he had attended regularly and discharged the joint duties to the satisfaction of the Trade so much so that they told the Inspector General at Magherafelt when sent down specially to procure their nomination of a second inspector *that they thought a second inspector totally unnecessary.* He had been 13 years in a very labourous office under the Board; he never complained of the severity of the duty, and he was confident that one officer was very capable of discharging it.

Dealing with the Tyrone memorial, Mr. Boyle said that of the Linen Drapers only six were interested and have since retracted their recommendation for a second inspector. *The Trade unanimously have said, and will say, the contrary.* The eight markets are diminished to five, three of which are monthly. *Under these circumstances I hope*, writes Mr. Boyle, *your Honourable Board will not deprive me of half the very trifling benefit of my office as Inspector and an office which your Honourable Board will very soon find of little importance if you appoint men of property and probity as Sole Seal Masters, to have redress from all grievances.*

The upshot of this little dispute was that the Trustees, at their meeting on 2nd June 1818, over which Sir John Stewart, Bart. presided, adhered to the former decision to appoint a second inspector but selected Mr. Hamilton Boyle for that office – a sort of a compromise, giving the Tyrone men the second inspector, but refusing their nominee.

Next week – The Trustees introduce Scutch Mills and Double Spinning Wheels.

# LINEN MACHINERY IMPROVEMENTS

## (13 – 6 – 1925)

The activities of the Linen Board were not confined to the regulation of the markets, important though that was. It was alert to the necessity of improving the spinning wheels and looms in use by the peasantry, who were naturally less inclined to adopt new utensils for their trade than are modern mill and factory owners. Considerable sums of money were spent by the Trustees in giving grants but the results were not satisfactory, and from time to time, in the 18$^{th}$ century, we find a change in policy proposed. Instead of money grants the plan was adopted of buying spinning wheels and distributing them, and we learn that at the middle of the century some £4,500 a year was spent in this way, but it was reported that one consequence was that 'innumerable frauds' were committed because the wheels were distributed in a slip-shod manner. Robert Stevenson, a Dublin merchant, writing in 1755 said that up till then half-a-million of money had been spent in this way, but no inquiry was made as to what became of the machines.

The composition of the Board was partly to blame for this. It consisted of eighty Trustees, all the great landowners in Ireland, who had no personal knowledge of business. Very few attended the meetings – occasionally there was no one there and rarely half-a-dozen, so that they were in the hands of officials, many of whom were also ignorant of the linen trade. The landowners were, of course, almost the only class at the time available for such a position, but one result was that each of them desired to see the linen business established on his own estate, and so far as one can judge far more help was given by the Board to the South and West of Ireland, where it disappeared entirely, than to the North, where it flourished and is still a greater factor in the economical life of the community. In Co. Tyrone, it may be mentioned, in 1817, the resident Trustees were the Marquis of Abercorn, the Earl of Caledon, Viscount Northland, the Hon. Thos. Knox, James Stewart of Killymoon, and Sir John Stewart, Bart. These gentlemen were representative of the various parts of the county – Strabane, Caledon, Dungannon, Cookstown and Ballygawley. In Co. Derry there were only four Trustees resident, none of them living in South Derry.

Another result of having the Board made up of landowners was that they constantly opposed any reform of the land laws which made for security of tenure. This, of course, was no obstacle to the home spinner or weaver, but it prevented the development of bleach greens and the establishment of the business on industrial lines. It was not till 1764 that by the 3$^{rd}$ of George III, power was given to life-owners to give long leases for the establishment of greens or mills, the immediate consequence of which Act, as we have seen, being the bleach green at Wellbrook.

From the Union in 1801, matters improved to some extent. One of the improvements which were introduced was the two-handed spinning wheel which was driven by the foot leaving both hands free to manipulate the flax and thereby to increase the quantity of yarn which could be spun. The old wheels could be adapted, and to reconcile those who did not believe in the novelty, it was pointed out that a wheel, thus changed, could be used for one hand only, as before. Grants were made to individual Trustees for the new wheels, to be given out in their own districts, and also grants were made to schools, under a scheme of 1808, to teach girls to spin, not exceeding 20 for any school, and only when the Inspector reported that they could be advantageously used and on security being given that they would be produced in the school when the Inspector desired to see them. The only local grant of this sort we have come across was in 1818, when Mrs. Hamilton, of Cookstown, sister of the Rev. John Staples, applied for some wheels "on the Scotch plan", for the school at Lissan, "where upwards of 200 female children are educated according to the Lancasterian mode, and an equal number of boys." Mr. Pollock, the Inspector General, reported that he had visited the school and was "much gratified with the whole system of the establishment", and recommended the grant. It was possibly as a consequence of this that more weavers were in Lissan than in any other parish around Cookstown and the industry lingered longer there than anywhere else in our district.

Prior to that, in 1813, Mr. James Stewart, of Killymoon, had got a grant of 30 wheels for Cookstown district. These were made by Alex. Rogers, of Cookstown, as appears from the accounts of that year, when £22 10s 0d was passed in payment. Probably there were others which have escaped our notice. It will be noticed that these were made locally; in fact the making of wheels was an important secondary industry, and in turn gave employment to wood cutters and others, just as in modern days one industry helps another. In Dungannon district in 1812 we find that Edward Colgan, of Dungannon, got £13 10s for 27 wheels made for the Hon. T. Knox; Francis M' Kinley, of Dungannon, got £20 19s 9d for 31 wheels made for Viscount Northland (afterwards Earl of Ranfurly), and John Mullan, of Dungannon, supplied 32 wheels for the same Trustee and 31 for the Hon. T. Knox, while John Barry, of Moy, supplied 50 wheels, at 10s each, for the Earl of Charlemont in 1818. These extracts will serve to show what the Linen Board was doing locally, in this direction.

The chief improvement in looms was the fly shuttle. As "Antiquary" told us in his articles on linen in Ireland, it was introduced from England by a Moravian minister who came to the settlement of that sect at Gracehill, near Ballymena. The Moravians aimed at being a self-contained colony, not merely a religious body, and in their earlier stages, at least, looked after the material side of their life as well as the doctrinal, very much as our own foreign missionaries endeavour to provide means of living for their converts in India and China. Traces of this can still be found in the Moravian settlement at Lisnamorrow, near Castledawson. It was slow in spreading, chiefly, no doubt, because the coarse webs were so narrow, but it made the work lighter, and therefore increased the output, and the Linen Board from 1807 encouraged the improvement. In 1809 it was reported that Robert Tennant, the Inspector for Tyrone, had delivered no less than 587 looms to female workers in Tyrone and part of Armagh, but of these only 55 were worked by the fly shuttle. Mr. B. Pattison, whose position as second inspector seems to have been subordinate, and indeed legally doubtful, made no return, so it is to be presumed that his districts, Cookstown and Stewartstown, were included. Besides supplying the looms, the Board paid instructors to teach female weavers in the use of the fly shuttle. In 1810 we find that Patrick Quin got £10 for instructing the weavers in the parish of Drumglass, and the same amount for the parish of Donaghmore, and a Thomas Hutchman got £20 for the same work in the parishes of Killyman and Tullyniskan.

An interesting letter, or "memorial", was sent to the Board by Charles Duffin, the Inspector General, on 10th June 1810 - almost exactly 115 years ago, regarding the distribution of these looms. From it we learn that after the Trustees announced their intention to give looms, the first applications were from Co. Tyrone, and he invited loom-makers to meet him in Dungannon. He attended with some respectable linen drapers, who were of opinion that the looms were worth £4 10s each. The loom-makers agreed with the price, but objected to the mode of payment through the Bank of the Rt. Hon. David Latouche in Dublin on the ground that they had no correspondents there to draw the money and had to get credit from the timber merchants. He agreed to let them draw on him, after the looms were inspected by two linen drapers and certified by the Inspector who branded them and had got "the female's receipt" - a receipt of delivery to the weaver. Accordingly this system of payment was established, as Mr. Duffin said, "unhappily for your memorialist".

Duffin had carried on the bleaching business near Dungannon, and had, in his employment, a clerk named MacKenzie for fourteen years. The latter afterwards became a factor in the Linen Hall in Dublin, and, in 1808, drew his attention to an apparent discrepancy between the amount paid by Mr. Duffin for looms, and what he had received from the Linen Board. Duffin, with the aid of Mr. Hans Peebles, a clerk, spent three days in investigating the accounts and came to the conclusion that he was underpaid, and applied to Mr. John Christy, who assisted at the distribution of the looms, for a second certificate. This, however, included some of those already paid for, with the result that Duffin admitted that he was overpaid £235, but points out that but for Mr. MacKenzie he would have been a loser by £65. He adds that, as he distributed and paid for 1,800 looms in two years, he hopes that due allowance would be made for this solitary error - the only one imputed to him in 19 years service, in which he had distributed many thousand pounds under the order of the Board "in various utensils of looms, wheels, reels and hatchets".

This was Mr. Duffin's explanation of how he got rebursed twice for the same payments, an error discovered by the Commissioners of Imprest accounts. It led to a sworn inquiry in which evidence was given by Mr. Corry, the Secretary of the Board, several Inspectors in the district concerned and by MacKenzie. The latter voluntarily made a second deposition in which he said that from his knowledge of Mr. Duffin's system of keeping books "he was more exposed to clerical errors than any public officer I have ever heard of" . Duffin, however, tendered his resignation as Inspector General, a position worth over £1,000 a year, and was ordered to return all the papers and books belonging to the Board, and in November an order was made on the advice of counsel, that he be prosecuted, and the office of Inspector General abolished. His son, also Charles Duffin, who had been made joint Inspector General in 1807 "with reversionary grant of the undivided office" - that is, he was appointed to succeed his father, made an attempt to get the Trustees to reconsider the abolition of the office, but without avail. The Trustees stuck to their decision and out of the savings gave their Secretary, Mr. Corry, £200 a year with £100 per annum for a clerk.

Duffin, the elder, was not prosecuted though accused of being a cheat by presenting duplicate receipts, and also with attempting to bribe two witnesses who went to Dublin to give false evidence. He was also suspected of having been in league with a firm in Cork, Messrs. Edward and Henry Shanahan, who had got bounty on linens in excess to the proper amount. They, in their affidavit, stated that they had "served a regular apprenticeship in the linen manufacturing business" in Co. Tyrone, in 1803, and set up business in Cork. Duffin, in his report, describes them as "injured and caluminated young men". Incidentally, it may be mentioned that to the charge that they claimed bounty on far more linen than their factory was capable of making in the year, they state that they worked night and day, one lot of females leaving at 6pm and another started to work at 6am.

Although the Board decided to do without an Inspector General, an attempt was made to get a successor, George Hannington, the Dungannon banker, the remains of whose house is on Castle Hill, Dungannon, being nominated in a memorial signed by 58 registered bleachers of Ulster. The names attached include Wm. Barkley, John Hunter, jun., Jonathan Pike, Henry Hunter, John Morgan, junr.; James Magill, Wm. Magill, Samuel R. Magill, Andrew Newton, Robert Newton,

James Cooke, James Collins, most, if not all, of whom will be recognised as local bleachers.

Next Week - Something about Bounties

## BOUNTIES FOR LINEN

## (20 – 6 – 1925)

How far a state is justified in using its powers or funds to assist industries is a question which it would be out of place to discuss here. It may be remarked, however, that the theory of Free Traders is that all the products of the world, natural as well as manufactured, should be at the disposal of the whole of the inhabitants, free from any artificial restrictions on the one hand, and without any artificial stimulus to trade on the other; in other words, that the entire world should form one fiscal unit. That theory, however, ignores political divisions, or what is termed "nationality", which has been proved to be stronger than economic interest - every war proves that. Consequently we have Governments catering for the political interests of their people, rather than for the purely economic. A striking and well known instance of that was seen in France 30 to 40 years ago in connection with the development of the sugar beet industry. In order to find employment for as large a population as possible on the land, growing beet and producing sugar, the Government instituted a system of bounties on all sugar exported, with the result that, in this country, consumers were able to buy that necessary article of food, from French beet, at a lower price than the French people themselves could get it. They were paying for our sugar in order to keep a population which would yield an army when required.

A system, similar to this, had long been in existence in Ireland, under the native Parliament. Wheat, when taken to Dublin for export, was subsidised, so that farmers might be encouraged to raise wheat on their land. This system has the advantage that it is the most economical way of benefiting an industry by State money, for it does not raise the normal price of the article for home consumption as a hostile tariff does. Moreover, it is particularly effective in encouraging the production of an article of which the home consumption is relatively small, for which a tariff would be useless.

It was this system of bounties, so beloved by the old Irish Parliament, that the Linen Board adopted as one of the ways to assist the linen trade. Whether it is a justifiable way is not for us to discuss here, though it may be remarked that any proposal by the Northern Parliament to pay a bounty to manufacturers on all linen exported would be certain to meet with strong opposition, even by those who deny that they are Free Traders, when they realised that they had to pay that bounty out of their own pockets. Yet there is logically a much stronger case for linen bounties than a century ago, because the State has undertaken part, at least, of the burden of unemployment, and if a bounty on exported linen restored the industry to full time work, it might even be a directly profitable undertaking.

The bounty system, it may be added, raised the antagonism of English manufacturers. In 1823 a memorial was presented to the President of the Board of Trade by manufacturers of British linens at Barnsley, in Yorkshire, complaining that the Irish Linen Board was giving a bonus of 1½d per yard, being 10 to 15 per cent. of the value, out of subsidies allowed by Parliament, and they prayed that the practice may be repressed "as it operates as a grant to the Irish, to oppress the British Linen manufacturers". This was sent, in due course, by the British Government to the Linen Board, who referred it to Lord Oriel, who had originated the idea of using part of the monies voted by Parliament in this way.

The bounty system was not confined to a payment on the cloth exported; men who undertook to set up machinery were also subsidised. Away back in the year 1808 the Trustees announced that, in order to encourage the spinning of yarn for sail cloth (an important use of linen in the days before steamers), canvas and duck, for every spindle erected that year, and worked by water, steam, horses or oxen, a sum of £3 for each spindle, erected in that year, provided that not less than 100 be erected, with suitable other machinery for rendering the flax ready for the spindle. A sum of £8,000 was provided and the claims were £6,117. The object of the trustees, it will be seen, and was expressly stated, was "to encourage the spinning of flax by machinery as speedily as possible". The balance unspent was augmented by £5,000, making £6,883 offered in 1810. To introduce the Fly Shuttle, making weaving light enough for females, the Trustees offered a loom to each female who wove 200 yards of linen in the year 1805 and a loom, two fly shuttles and a spinning wheel to the female in each parish who wove the greatest quantity of linen in the year 1807, being not less than 500 yards.

As to the direct bounty on cloth, the Trustees offered 2d per yard for each yard of sailcloth, duck or canvas, of not less value than 16d per yard, from yarn spun by machinery in 1808, up to 500,000 yards, actually sold by the makers each year. If the cloth was of less value than 16d, but over 1s, the bounty was 1½d.

Only one local merchant seems to have taken advantage of this offer - Mr. William Pike, of Woodmount, near Dungannon. He seems to have interested himself very much in the development of spinning by machinery. There was a William MacKenzie, of Dublin, who introduced a new spinning machine - also the subject of grants by the Linen Board, and in drawing the attention of the Trustees to it, asking for £20 on the first twenty "carding engines", he refers to a certificate of their efficiency from Mr. Pike. The latter writes, on "1$^{st}$ of 10$^{th}$ month, 1808" (being a Quaker he did not recognise October as a suitable name for a month, for some reason unknown to the present writer) and he certifies that the carding engine was "an excellent piece of mechanism in every particular". It was so effectual in working tow, "as merely to convert it into flax", and he was able to produce yarn for the coarser linens from tow to heretofore "with the assistance of the best linen cords, was only fit to be applied to the making of rope". Mr. Pike was of opinion that the "engine" was worthy of public remuneration as being highly important to the "extension of ultimate success of mill spinning in Ireland". It appears that Mr. Pike's was one of the two of MacKenzie's machines in use, the other being sent to "a remote part of Co. Antrim".

Whether MacKenzie ever got a grant or not does not appear in the minutes, but Mr. Pike claimed for 160 spindles, erected in the year 1809, the sum of £240. Another Tyrone man, T. Fox, claimed for the minimum number 100, as did two Co. Armagh spinners, while Messrs. Richardson & Co. put down 560, and claimed £840, these being the pioneer spinners by machinery. In April 1809 it appeared that Mr. Pike claimed to have erected 116 spindles in 1808, and 128 in 1809 - a total of 244, for which he claimed 30s each, making £550. How this claim was made up is puzzling unless we assume that the 128 spindles were counted twice, which would make it correct in amount. He actually got £366 under this head. Prior to this, in 1806, Mr. Pike had been paid £507 14s 7½d for erecting 256 spindles.

To return to the bounty on cloth, some idea of the extent of the industry at Derryvale, as it now is named, is got from the payment to Mr. Pike, in February 1808, of £124 19s 4d being at the rate of 1½d per yard on 19,995 yards of duck. It is interesting that he was the only person in Northern Ireland to get a bounty. A Samuel Cruikshank, of Co. Donegal, got about double that amount, and Francis Cruikshank, of Co. Down, got £211, but the rest of the bounty went to manufacturers in Co. Cork, and for larger sums.

In a return made in 1815, it appeared that Mr. Pike had received in bounty altogether, in the years 1807, 08 and 09 the sum of £629 12s 9d on 81,960 yards of duck. Terence Fox, of Dungannon, had claimed £88 10s being 1½d per yard on 14,160 yards of canvas, but it was reported that "no part of this claim is admissible, the fabric, on which the bounty is demanded, being nothing but a coarse kind of soldier's shirting, improperly called canvas".

A claim of interest to Co. Derry readers was by Daniel Larkin, who, in 1809 made 28lbs. of candle wick, and received a bounty of £1 17s 4d.

Next Week – Lee's machinery and methods

## LEE'S FLAX MACHINE

## (27 – 6 – 1925)

In the year 1815 the activities of the Linen Trustees, outside the routine duties of the Board, were directed to booming a new system of treating flax, from the green stalk till it became yarn. This has some local interest because the machines (there were two for different purposes), were distributed throughout Ireland for demonstration purposes, and amongst those who got them was Mr. James Stewart of Killymoon. Where it was erected we cannot ascertain, but probably on the waterfall in the demesne. Sets were also sent to Lord Northland, Hon. Thos. Knox and James Verner, from Dungannon district.

James Lee had a factory in Surrey, and, early in that year, specimens of flax dressed and thread spun in it were submitted to the Board, who were constantly getting offers of new inventions. Most of these were turned down after inspection for trial, but Lee's was favourably reported on by Mr. Williamson of Lambeg and Mr. Chaine, an extensive bleacher, of Co. Antrim. As described by himself to a committee appointed to inquire into his patented system, the process was divided into two parts, and these will, doubtless, be of interest to present-day flax growers, apart from the historical interest in the experiment. The first part of the process was to be done by the growers. One machine threshed out the seed, another broke the stalks, separating the fibre from the wood, thus scutching it. The second part of the process was for the spinner, to bring the flax into the state for the finest purposes, such as lace, cambric damask and fine linen. Lee's terms for these machines was a bounty (royalty it would now be called) of £2 for each of the first sort and £2 10s for the latter.

The flax, according to Lee's direction, was to be pulled when the lower part of the plant began to turn yellow and the seeds turning green. It was to be spread out to dry and then housed till the seed was threshed, and without retting was put through the machine. The Marquis of Downshire recommended a fair trial and offered 100 guineas if Mr. Lee would be brought over to superintend; Mr. Chas. Brett, for the Linen Trade of Belfast, urged that it be made public, so as, if possible, to get rid of "the present noisome practice of steeping"; the Linen Trade of Lisburn also urged an experiment on a large scale.

Special interest attaches to a letter from a Mr. John Derby, of London, who wrote that he had got Mr. Joseph Johnston, of Stranorlar, "full as great a sceptic" as himself regarding the process, to test it with last year's flax. The flax had been harvested like wheat, and the seed taken off. It was then broken and hackled in ten minutes, and washed first in plain water and afterwards in soap suds and laid out to dry in the sun, which discharged the colour remaining in it, which "appears to one incredible; it is quite a new fact to have vegetable oil or colouring matter discharged without acids or alkalis". When soap was not used it took a few hours longer in the sun. There was no loss of fibre and the produce of the whitest was far more than of the commonest flax. The machine was so simple that Mr. Derby thought there were a hundred carpenters in Ireland who could put one up after half-an hour's inspection.

The Committee, in their "observations", thought the secret of the process was that it preserved the natural whiteness of the fibre, which was abused by water or dew retting, which rendered the use of ashes, caustics and chemical means necessary to bleach. Amongst the advantages foreseen was that the weaver would be able to produce a closer web, and in a half-white state, saving loss by bleaching, while the saving of the seed would make the industry independent of foreign seed, and the manufacture of linseed oil would be promoted and oil cake for cattle would follow, and possibly there would be a large saving in the import of ashes for bleaching. The farmers, moreover, would only have to pull, stack and harvest the crop. The Committee recommended the distribution of sufficient machines for large and extended experiments in all the flax growing counties in Ireland. The Board forthwith resolved to buy 50 machines for threshing the seed, 500 for bleaching the flax, 100 second machines for re-cleaning, "30 sets of refining machines with rollers, each set containing six machines so connected as to be turned by one person, at £42 each set", and 24 refining machines separate at £7 each – the total cost being £3,953. Lee was also to get his bounty of 40s and 50s on the respective machines. The Board advertised extensively that the farmers who wanted to use the machines were not to steep the flax or dew-ret it, and those who got the loan of the machines were to note their efficacy compared with the common method, and, in fact, carry out an accurate experiment.

It will be seen that the Board, though enthusiastic about the new era which would begin in the linen industry when the fibre was got off without retting and discoloration and reduce the cost of bleaching, proceeded with some caution, in spite of what some critics have alleged. The machines, however, seem to have failed in the practical test. In October 1817, the secretary, Mr. Corry, on his visit to Tyrone, reported that Mr. James Stewart of Killymoon, and Sir John Stewart, "had the machinery sent to them erected for the use of the public; many of the other gentlemen, to whom they were granted, took similar pains in making experiments on them; but I could not hear of any of the machinery sent to the country being now at work. Mr. Lee's system seemed, upon the whole, to be pretty generally abandoned, and almost all the flax of the country has been treated after the old manner".

Mr. Corry summed up the results in his general observations by remarking that Mr. Lee's system divided itself into two parts. "The first purported to change the ancient habits of the country with regard to the treatment of flax, by dispensing with steeping, which has hitherto been deemed a necessary process", and the second related to the mechanical side. The machinery, after a few experiments, "was soon considered inferior, in point of expedition, to the common scutch mills of the country and was as soon abandoned", and, in consequence, the treatment of the flax was also abandoned, but Mr. Greer thought that it had been proved that, though steeping the flax might be held to be the best way of treating it, it was not indispensable, and mentions that a damask napkin of beautiful texture, made for the Princess Charlotte of Wales by a Lisburn manufacturer, was from unsteeped flax. "There is much yet to be learned in the theory and practice of treating flax in the field, on the means of saving the seed without injuring the fibre, and in having a more efficient and less wasteful mode of dressing the fibre for the spinner, than now prevails", and Mr. Greer hoped that some beneficent discovery would yet result from the efforts of the Board. Thus ended an experiment which cost the Trustees over £5,000.

Next Week – Encouraging flax seed saving.

## PROVIDING FLAXSEED 110 YEARS AGO

### (11 – 7 – 1925)

One of the principal functions of the Linen Board was to provide for a supply of flaxseed, and to improve it. As early as 1712 we find the trustees importing a cargo of Dutch seed which was sold under cost price, the amount being collected by the revenue officers, who, however, are alleged to have made a profit. This system was carried on with interruptions, till the middle of the 18th century, and bounties were also given to private importers. As already mentioned, the Board's Inspectors supervised the sale of the seed, branding the hogsheads on arrival so as to identify the new seed, and every retail merchant was obliged to report his stock at the end of the season. If suitable for seed in the following spring it was branded again, and customers knew that it was yearling seed and also that it was of sufficient germination to be used; if not so branded it had to be sold for oil or feeding purposes.

The Irish Parliament discontinued bounties on imported seed in 1781, and substituted bounties on home-saved seed, in connection with schemes for encouraging the growth of more flax. A Mr. Stephenson, a successful English merchant who settled in Dublin who was the greatest critic of the Linen Trustees, had the fixed idea that Ireland should be self-supporting as regards seed. The result of experiments was that home-saved seed produced a coarser fibre than the flax from the parent seed, but this was no drawback to those who wished to get the biggest possible output of yarn and cloth. The special reason, however, for saving the seed at the time was exactly the same as in Ulster a few years ago, when the submarines were operating - there was a war which interfered with the supply. This was the American War of Independence which stopped the seed supplies from the North American colonies which had raised flaxseed suitable for light soil. Parliament gave a grant of £7,250 to encourage home saving and £7,000 more for prizes for flax from Irish seed. On the return of peace, however, the home saving of seed ceased, as it was the opinion of Trustees and their critics, that foreign seed was cheaper and more reliable, and again American seed was in demand. The French war, however, once more forced the Trustees to revert to the policy of home saving, which had become more necessary because more flax had to be grown, the Continental supplies being cut off by Napoleon, while as regards the Irish spinners they were faced by the demand by British firms who bought up Irish flax at enhanced prices.

It may be mentioned here that from a memorandum prepared for the Trustees in 1823 by their secretary Mr. Corry, who traced the history of the grants, it appears that in 1719 the funds for these bounties were raised by imposing a duty of 1s per lb. on tea, and 3d per lb on coffee, cocoa and chocolate. In 1767 an amending Act limited the amount payable out of these duties for flax to £10,000 yearly, the balance going to the King's revenue to reduce the debt. A duty of 6d per gallon on linseed oil was also imposed in 1780 for the same purpose, but ultimately all duties went to the revenue, and the bounties were paid out of the general revenues of the country.

The shortage of flaxseed for the 1809 crop was so serious that Mr. Foster, the Chancellor of the Exchequer, wrote to the Linen Trustees, on 26th January of that year, that it had been under consideration by the Board of Trade every day since the session opened. He suggested that the stock of seed in Britain should be drawn upon, and three of the most skilful Inspectors should proceed to Liverpool at once and ascertain if the seed which the oil crushers had in stock was suitable for sowing. The Trustees, directed the Inspector General to supply the names of three fit and proper persons to go to England, and had also a knowledge of the linen business. The men sent were William Pollock, Thomas Holins and

William Marshall, who lost no time and by the end of February had examined all the flaxseed at Liverpool and then had gone to London and visited all the wovehouses and oil mills there. They reported that they did not find above 12,000 hogsheads of seed in England, fit for sowing, and the price was raised to 20 guineas a hogshead, and, unless some arrived from America, Ireland would be badly off. They were going on to Plymouth to see supplies of seed that the Government had for the navy.

The Board wrote to Mr. Foster drawing attention to the alarming prospect. They stated that there were only 6,000 hogshead of seed in Ireland, making, with the 12,000 in England, a total of 18,000 hogsheads, while the ordinary requirement was 45,000 hogsheads. The Chancellor had agreed to give a bounty of 5s per bushel on all seed imported into Ireland from 8th March till 8th April 1809 and the Trustees saw that the amount was entirely inadequate to induce any export to Ireland for immediate use, and the time too restricted. They also drew attention to the great increase in the export of flax to England from Ireland, which threatened the extinction of the linen industry.

Mr. Foster, in acknowledging the letter, which paid a compliment to his services in the interests of the linen industry, wrote that the "system of making Ireland independent of foreign supplies, and now so happily begun, ought to be strenuously persevered in" and the raising of the embargo by the American State "ought not to in any way relax our endeavour to raise a sufficiency of seed within our own country". He also wrote, in another letter, that the Trustees ought not to publish in the newspapers, extracts from the correspondence as was intended, and they agreed to the policy - obviously to prevent the Americans knowing too much. The Chancellor followed this up by a Bill providing £20,000 to give a bounty of 5s per bushel on all seed saved in Ireland in the year 1809, and in the growers' possession on 1st July 1810.

(To be continued)

# FLAX SEED SHORTAGE IN 1809

## (18 – 7 – 1925)

By the 15th April the buyers reported that they had shipped several thousand bushels of seed over the limit for which Parliament had provided bounty – 15,000 bushel, and they had selected the best seed in the granaries, "which, if the season should prove favourable, we have no doubt will produce good crops", and with what might be reasonably expected from America would be abundant for the requirements of the Irish growers. They followed this up on 9th May with a memorial praying compensation for the loss to their personal affairs and business in being instantly called away to England, and they attached a diary of their movements from 1st July. The Trustees ordered that the memorial be tabled for the information of the members; subsequently a committee was appointed to enquire as to the extra work done by these officials. A year later, on 1st May 1810, the three buyers reminded the Trustees of their claim for compensation for the loss in leaving at an hour's notice, but, as the committee had made no report, the Board declined to make any order and, apparently, beyond the thanks of the Trustees for their services, the three Inspectors got nothing. They were, of course, in receipt of salaries for their work as Inspectors in Ireland, and had got their expenses in England. The incident is worth putting on record as showing how scrupulous the Trustees, all landowners, were in disbursing public money to the public servants.

The seed, thus hurriedly picked up in England, did not prove quite satisfactory, for on 19th June 1809, the Trustees had a memorial from half-a-dozen merchants who said that they were induced to import quantities of seed, which the Board's Inspector branded as "sound", and that they were threatened with actions at law for damages because it failed, partially and entirely, to grow. "The magnitude and extent of this misfortune" put it beyond the means of individuals to remedy, and they blamed the Board for having introduced an Act, passed that session, which allowed unsound seed to be imported by abolishing the penalties on the importers, and they suggested that an Amending Act be passed at once, a draft of which was enclosed, exonerating any person who sold seed, branded as "sound" between 25th March and 1st July of that year, from damages. The Board, however, refused to do so, but ordered that the County Inspectors report on the state of the crop in their districts, stating in cases of failure of the crop, the cause as far as they could ascertain. The trouble in connection with this seed, reminds one of the difficulties the Department of Agriculture had in recent years over "white flower" seed, which was alleged to have been supplied by the Government, and for which the growers successfully claimed damages.

Space does not permit of the details of the scheme for giving the bounty on home-grown seed. It was hedged round with all sorts of safeguards, but in spite of these there were frauds. In Co. Tyrone the area under flax in 1810 was 10,241 acres, and the estimated quantity of seed saved was 8,460 bushels. In Londonderry the area was given as 5,000 acres, with 3,200 bushels of seed. The estimate of the bounty to be paid in Tyrone was £1,750 and in Co. Derry £750. Evidently only a small proportion of the flax was kept for seed; in Louth, on the other hand, it was reported that 11,590 bushels had been saved off 1,253 acres; in Mayo 5,308 bushels off 1,333 acres, and in Galway 9,568 bushels off 1,196 acres. Every county in Ireland was covered; in the North relatively little seed was saved, roughly just enough for the local crop of the next year, but in the South and West the main object was apparently to save seed and get bounty.

In 1813 the report on the Flax Crops by the County Inspectors was that in Londonderry the amount of seed sown was 5,590 hogsheads, of which 2,067 were Riga seed, 1,690 America, 1,689 English and Dutch, and 144 home-saved seed. The acreage was estimated at 13,048 and the general appearance of the crops, with a few exceptions, was remarkably good. In South Tyrone the seed sown was estimated at 1,465 hogsheads, of which 805 were American, 125 Riga, 321 British and 214 home-saved. The Inspector said that the quantities were "thought to be nearly less by one-half than those of the year preceding". He adds that "1,050 hogsheads are supposed to have been saved. The growers appear to take more pains than formerly to save the seed well, and with more success".

By 1815 the saving of seed had dwindled away. In Londonderry 7,714 hogsheads were sown, occupying 1,800 acres, being one-fourth more than in 1814, and "very little seed saved". In East Tyrone (the divisions of Tyrone this year were "East" and "West", not "North and "South" as before), it was reported that 2,200 hogsheads were sown of which 200 were home-saved and only 150 hogsheads were sowed that year.

The actual payment of the bounty was one of the most difficult parts of the scheme. The first plan was to send each person by post a "bank post bill" for the amount. But when it was realised that there were no fewer than 25,000 persons to be paid, many of them such small sums that the cost of remitting and having the bills cashed would amount to nearly the amount of the bounty and also that the post was uncertain and many of the recipients were uneducated persons, ignorant of how to deal with remittances by post, this was abandoned. In these days, with a house-to-house delivery of letters, and banks in every village, and merchants ready to cash anything of the sort for customers, there would have been no difficulty, but it was different in 1810. On reconsideration the Board decided to pay sums under 20s through the County Inspectors who got advances of not more than £100 for that purpose, and took receipts from the persons paid. The Inspectors, themselves, had to be checked to prevent them using the money for their own purposes, and special orders were given that they were to proceed with dispatch, and the Secretary was directed to suspend the payment of their salaries if he found that the receipts were not coming in quickly. Moreover, the Provincial Inspectors were ordered to proceed through their respective Provinces to render assistance in the payment of the Flaxseed Claims, and, as the payment drew to a close, the Inspectors who had not lodged receipts for the amount in their hands had their salaries and expenses stopped.

The payments began in February, and on 28th May, the County Inspectors reported that attempts had been made to get payment by fictitious claims and were cautioned to use the greatest deligence before paying. In Country Tyrone Mr. Tennant, the Linen Inspector, reported that a man named Creagie had altered the figures in the certificate, forged Tennant's signature to another certificate, and committed perjury in an affidavit claiming bounty on seven bushels of seed. Another man named Wardle was charged with altering the figures and obtaining money as a cheat. Counsel, Mr. Gervance P. Bushe, advised prosecutions and Creagie was ordered to be prosecuted on the charge of forgery at the Tyrone Assizes, but Wardle was only to be indicted on the minor charge of cheating at the Quarter Sessions. What the result of these prosecutions was we do not know; the parties, however, did not live in Cookstown or Stewartstown districts, as Mr. Benjamin Patteson was the inspector for these two market districts.

(To be continued)

## PROVIDING FLAX SEED IN 1810

### (25 – 7 – 1925)

Mr. Patteson, the Inspector for Cookstown and Stewartstown, received £300 to disburse for flaxseed in his area to 689 claimants, who had saved 1,092 bushels of seed. The amount paid by him was £273, showing a balance of £27 at 5th August. In Londonderry, Mr. Boyle, the Inspector, paid £858 15s to 1,469 claimants, having a balance of £16 5s only.

In connection with the payments of Mr. Tennant a complaint was made to the Trustees by Mr. James Buchanan, of Common Green, Omagh, which, though not quite local, is worth recording here. On 11th September 1810, Mr. Buchanan wrote that to assist in the distributions of the bounty or premiums he took the trouble of receiving claims "of all around the quarter of the country", and forwarded to Mr. Tennant not only the certificates but the receipts for the money, and he alleged that £132 was being kept by the Inspector "to the great disappointment of numbers of poor persons who have come repeatedly to receive the amount of their claims". Mr. Tennant retorted by attacking Mr. Buchanan, in his capacity as a magistrate, and the latter replied that this was from malice because of his exertions in suppressing frauds which it was the Inspector's duty to do, and he asked for an interview. The Trustees adjourned till the following day when both the Inspector and the magistrate were present, but the complaint was not heard till the third day. Mr. Buchanan then, amongst other things, told the Board that Mr. Tennant had neglected to attend Omagh, Fintona, and other parts of the county to pay the premiums on "rearing flaxseed", which occasioned Mr. Buchanan much trouble without any advantage, and he had to pay £200. The other chief allegation was that Mr. Tennant permitted his deputy to charge 2d per web in Fintona market, the owner of the web paying this to ensure that he would not be prosecuted if the web was found deficient; moreover, the honest weaver was compelled to submit to this exaction because the holders of private seals were compelled to swear that they would not measure or seal any web that had not the deputy's private seal on it, and the profits from that private sealing were four to five guineas per market. Mr. Buchanan said that he suppressed that private seal, but Mr. Tennant kept the deputy after he had been convicted of taking these bribes, and that Mr. Tennant was unworthy of the office. The Trustees ordered the Inspector for Ulster to inquire "with all speed" into the charges and call on Mr. Buchanan for proof.

Mr. Tennant replied at length to the charge regarding the premium, and turned the tables on his accuser. He got seven parcels of claims from Mr. Buchanan, amounting to £314 10s, and had paid him up till 1st June £320 15s so that, that gentleman, by his statement that be had paid £200 only, had £120 15s in his hands. He also asserted that he had proofs that Buchanan charged the poor people 5d per bushel for getting the claims cashed. Following up this counter-attack the Inspector said that Buchanan sold seed to the poor people, and when the crop turned out to be bad, to prevent his being processed, he got some men to survey the crops, representing that they were sent by Tennant, and told the growers that the Linen Board intended to compensate them for the bad crops, and, if investigation was thought necessary, Mr. Tennant asked the Board to order its Provincial Inspector to hold same in the Sessions-Room in Dungannon, when he would have one or two Trustees present, and concluded with a certificate from a dozen magistrates that they had "never heard the slightest grounds of suspicion against Mr. Tennant's conduct in his situation of Linen Inspector".

The Inspector for Ulster, Mr. Greer, made an inquiry and reported that he had "at length gotten the account between Mr. Buchanan and Mr. Tennant satisfactorily settled", and enclosed a certificate from the former that he was "perfectly satisfied with the conduct of Mr. Tennant". But Mr. Greer states, in his letter, that the complaint was groundless as Mr. Tennant was in his debt when it was made, but not to the extent stated, and that this could not always be avoided because the Inspector might not have a balance on hands sufficient to meet the batch of receipts. The principal trouble, however, was that Mr. Buchanan "omitted to make an entry in his day book of the £51 latterly in dispute", but Mr. Tennant produced evidence which " brought it to the recollection of Mr. Buchanan's clerk". On this the Trustees allowed the whole dispute to drop.

This was not the only transaction of Mr. Tennant's brought to the notice of the Board. In February 1815, he complained that Mr. Hogg, the Inspector for Co. Antrim, sent him some warrants against seal-masters, seven or eight years before, amounting to £12. He put them in the hands of the constable (or bailiff) whom he usually employed, who went several times to the place, 22 miles distant from Dungannon, but without success. Mr. Tennant then made up "a party" who went with the constable and a distress was obtained. Mr. Tennant proceeded to say that the fines were the property of the Board, and he thought that not only his Constable and Party should be paid out of them, but that he, himself, should be paid for loss of time and expense, "which the fines would scarcely do". To put it baldly, Mr. Tennant kept the amount levied for costs, and his complaint was that Mr. Hogg "by some means or other, and in his own name, without the knowledge of your Honourable Board, put this business into the hands of the law" against Tennant until the costs amounted to £38 18s 9d. Tennant represented that Hogg had "committed a breach of contract" in suing in his own name, without the Board's permission, and asked that he be ordered to return the costs.

Mr Hogg's reply, dated from Portglenone, gave a different version, and had the advantage in being as explicit as Mr. Tennant's was vague. In July 1808, he sent warrants to Tennant to execute and soon heard that he had been done; when he wrote for the money in October, Tennant replied that he had not so much cash in the house, but would shortly send it. "For five years I wrote repeatedly", says Hogg, and got respectable merchants, who carried the letters, to speak to him. At first he promised and at last "would give no answer, but put my letters unread into his pocket". Hogg, continuing, said that he went to Dungannon and saw Tennant, who apologised for the treatment and said he would pay in a few hours, but in the evening he said he was disappointed in not getting money, and that the Linen Board owed him £70, and that he would give a draft for £10 on Mr. Corry, the secretary, and keep £2 for his costs in levying the warrants. The draft on the Secretary of the Board was refused, and Hogg again wrote Tennant, who took no notice of him and at last got Mr. Dix, his attorney, to write and he did so repeatedly, to no effect. Proceedings were then taken and he heard that the Sheriff had got an order. Hogg further explained that the £12 was money he paid to merchants for deficiencies in the measure of webs sealed by the seal-masters. The Board, on this explanation, instead of ordering Hogg to pay Tennant's costs, ordered that the salary of the latter be suspended till he paid Mr. Hogg in full, the sum legally due.

Mr. B. Pattison had his own troubles in November 1810. Mr. Greer, the Inspector for Ulster, wrote to the Trustees that Mr. Pattison had a warrant against Israel Lee, late a seal-master, "which warrants Mr. Pattison cannot get Constables to execute, they being afraid", and asks that the Board order that the securities be sued for the fines. These warrants would be obtained by linen merchants who had bought defective cloth, sealed by Lee, who was therefore responsible to the purchaser, and as a seal-master had to give security, Mr. Greer's proposal was that they should be made pay up. The Trustees, however, ordered that Mr. Greer do exert himself, by giving every proper aid to the Constables charged with the execution of the warrants against the above-named Seal-Masters, so as to save the Board trouble and expense of any law proceedings in respect therof". Prior to this, on 5$^{th}$ May, Mr. Pattison had reported Lee and Caruth for improper conduct and the Trustees had with-drawn their brown seals, which they doubtless resented.

Robberies from bleach-greens were regarded very seriously. At an earlier period joint action was taken by the bleachers to detect the thieves. For example, in 1774 we find an advt, regarding the lareeny of 16 pieces of linen from the house of John, William and Andrew Reynolds, of Lismoney. Particulars were given of the Webs, some of which were sealed with Andrew Reynold's seal, and a reward of £20 was promised to anyone who would bring the thieves to justice. This is signed by 21 bleachers, who set down the sums each is willing to subscribe. Archibald Hamilton is down for £3 8s 3d; A. Hamilton, jun.; Kennedy Henderson, John Stevenson, Samuel Crawford, James Magill and Samuel Stevenson for £2 5s 6d;Wm. Davison,George Ramsey, Andrew Taylor, Andrew Newton, Wm. Cunningham, John Stevenson, Samuel Crawford, John Smith, J. Graham and Wm. M'Sparron for £1 2s 9d each – half of the last lot and one third of the first; while half that sum, 11s 4½d is subscribed by Michael Johnston, Samuel Stewart, John Henderson, James Ekin and David Slane. Some of these persons we can place – Wm. Magill at Anahavil, George Ramsey at Moneymore, and others, and it may be taken that at that date they were the principal, if not the only, bleachers. By 1810 such private prosecutions had got out of date, though the Crown, by the police, was not yet the public prosecutor of these days. The Linen Board had powers in that direction, and the minutes of 1810 show that they did not always use them to the satisfaction of the linen merchants. One Edward Ashcroft, for example, a travelling pedlar, had been found with several of stolen linen in his possession and was fined. He memorialised the Board, urging that he had bought the cloth in good faith from some one, and the Trustees proposed to remit them. Mr. Duffin, the then Inspector General, advised against that, urging that if remitted Ashcroft would take no further whom he said he purchased linen, and the delinquent would escape, but the Board, at their meeting in January Sir John Stewart in the chair, adhered to its former decision. In June, however, a memorial from 26 of "the most respectable Drapers and Bleachers in Tyrone and Armagh" was received, protesting that the depredations committed every year o bleach-greens being truly alarming, every method that can be devised to put a stop to them should be adopted", and the Board's decision in Ashcroft's case tended "to encourage such depredations of public officers", and urged the Board to reverse it. They pointed out the Ashcroft had no goods for sale but stolen webs, and that they were wet, and in a state that no honest man, wishing to obtain a fair value, would offer them for sale". The memorial, though clothed in humble terms, was pointed enough, and it alleged that the Board was frustrating the efforts of a humane and cautious magistrate and the execution of a law. Moreover they urged that the statute have the right to appeal to the Board. Which had no power, to mitigate or remit the fines, and even the Trustees had the power, there was no feature in Ashcroft's case to justify its exercise in his favour. Amongst the signatories were James Collins (at the head) Edward Shaw, John Little, Charles Loggan, Wm. Morgan, Thos. Greer, Thos. Morgan, John Hunter, jun., and Wm. Ramsey. They Board postponed considerations of the memorial, and we have been unable to find how the struggle between the trade and the Trustees ended.

All the decisions given in the courts did not please the officials as is recorded in the proceedings for 1813. Francis Colligan, a deputy inspector for Mr. Pattison, reported on 13th June that he was interrupted in the execution of his duty at Stewartstown market, and the Trustees asked the Inspector General to report. He did so and a prosecution was ordered against Robert and David M'Crea at the Quarter Sessions, but they were acquitted. Mr. Tennant in reporting this verdict, said that "a trick appeared to have been played on the renewing of the vessel or cask, which was the case of the dispute, to mislead the witnesses, which effectually succeeded", and he added that there could be no question of gaining a verdict if the Board wish to proceed against them for damages for the assault.

Next Week – End of the Linen Board

# END OF THE LINEN BOARD

## RECOLLECTION OF THE LATE MR. S.E. EKIN, J.P.

## (1 – 8 –1925)

We have probably spent too much time with the Linen Board but as its records are not easily obtainable we felt that though some matters were not strictly local, they would be of sufficient general interest to be worth recording.  With the Legislative Union the Board came under the control of the Parliament at Westminster, and the economic ideas of England and the birth of the great industrial era, which almost coincided with the nineteenth century, hastened the end.

At the same time there was a growing feeling against the Board. For one thing the Trustees were too numerous, and as only a few attended the meetings, there was no guarantee for any continuity of policy.  They were guided, however, by an able secretary, Mr. Corry, and perhaps it would be true to say that he was the Board, and the gentlemen who found it convenient to attend, simply ratified what he did or approved of what he proposed.

At the end of the first quarter of the 19$^{th}$ century there was a decided revolt against the regulations of the Board.   In 1825 the Parliamentary Grant was opposed by the Whigs, who alleged that the Board was utterly incompetent, and Peel appointed a committee to inquire into its work.   This Committee recommended that the Board should endeavour to substitute the factory system which had made great advances in England, for the cumbrous hand spinning and weaving.  An Act was passed to free the trade of the restrictions, including the stamping of white or bleached linen, and doing away with Inspectors.  Even Corry admitted that the time had come for a change, as after a certain point, "the less any manufacture is encumbered with legislative regulations the better", and in 1828 the Board went out of existence.  The industry had been spoon-fed and nourished with grants; henceforth it was to stand alone.  The significance of this can be realised by our readers, for it was in that year, 1828, that Mr. Hugh Adair and his son Thomas came to Cookstown and established the spinning mill at Greenvale, which converted our town from a little agricultural village to an industrial centre.

The seal-masters for brown linen, however, were retained in office till 1839, as it was felt that they performed a service to the small weavers in certifying to the length and uniformity of these webs.  Mr. Matthew

Pattison acted in that capacity for Cookstown and Stewartstown. In Moneymore and Magherafelt it will be remembered that Mr. Hugh Boyle was both inspector and seal-master, but, in spite of his undertaking to attend personally, he was not giving satisfaction in this part of County Derry. In 1823, for example, the linen merchants of Belfast sent a formal complaint to the Board that, in spite of the law against "pasting and spouting" the webs, the cloth from Moneymore, Magherafelt and Ahoghill was "doctored" in this way to give a "deceiptful appearance of strength and thickness and cover defects", and this paste, often mixed with lead, was most injurious to the bleaching. They alleged that some double pieces, which had been pasted, shrank in length as much as a yard. Boyle was forced to resign the office of seal-master for Moneymore, Magherafelt and Maghera, and Mr. John Rowley Miller, son of the agent of the Drapers Company, and afterwards himself agent, was appointed in his place, and it is presumed he acted till the office was abolished. He is described as "a man of influence and some consequence in the county of Londonderry" by the memorial in his favour, which was signed by William Magill, Wm. Morgan, and seven or eight others.

The absence of any reference to Coagh in these records of the Linen Board may have caused dissatisfaction to the people of that enterprising village. They know that as early as 1728, considerably before the long town of Cookstown had any existence, in its present form, the wide main street being simply arable land and bog, Coagh was laid out, with its central square, named by the loyal proprietor, Colonel George Conyngham, after the House of Hanover at a time when the Jacobites were causing trouble which culminated in the rising of '45, to meet which he, as deputy governor of Co. Derry, called up the militia. Colonel Conyngham obtained a charter for a weekly market on Fridays and four fairs in the year. The linen trade was considerable for a time, and twelve markets, exclusively for linen, were fixed, with twelve alternative markets for agricultural produce. But the market languished, for some reason, and never came near to those of Moneymore or Stewartstown.

Perhaps the example of Mr. William Stewart in Cookstown made his son-in-law, Wm. Lenox-Conyngham, who succeeded him, attempt, in 1774, to revive the market. At any rate, at the beginning of that year we find the following advertisement:-

*To revive the weekly market on every Friday, in the town of Coagh, for which a patent was formerly granted to the late Geo. Conyngham, Esq., the following premiums will be paid each market day by order of Wm. Conyngham, of Springhill. To the person who shall sell, in public market the greatest quantity of oatmeal, 2s 2d; to the person who shall sell the next greatest quantity, 1s 1d; to the person who shall sell the greatest quantity of linen yarn, spun in his own house, 2s 2d; to the person who shall sell the next greatest quantity of linen yarn, 1s 1d.*

*To encourage the cloth market a considerable number of linen drapers have promised to attend on the first Friday of every month, when the following premiums will be paid. For the greatest quantity of linen, of his own manufacture, 6s 6d; 4s 4d, and 2s 8d. The above premiums will be paid for twelve months.*

*All goods exposed for sale custom free for said time.*

*The first cloth market will be on the first Friday of next month, and the weekly market successively.*

That the cloth market in Coagh never attained any great size during the regime of the Linen Board is proved by the absence of any reference to it in the minutes. The reason is not clear, as it was as likely a place as Moneymore Stewartstown or Cookstown, to become a mart for the weavers. It is possible that the reason may be connected with the Linen Board; if that body and its officials did not recognise Coagh, the market would be labouring under a serious handicap, which is one argument against state regulation of trade.

Whatever the cause, it is certain that when the Linen Board ceased to exist the cloth market in Coagh revived, and hand-loom weaving continued in Coagh district long after it had died out around Cookstown. One of the last cloth merchants, if not actually the last, was the late Mr. S. E. Ekin, J.P., of Soran House. In order to get first-hand information the present writer, in December 1917, asked Mr. Ekin for an interview, which he not only gave, but at the end of it handed me a statement of his connection with the industry in Coagh. We have now pleasure in giving this in his own words.

MR. S. E. EKIN'S STATEMENT

*During 1847 and 48, what weaving had been going on, decreased; demand was low and with the loss of the potato crop, and much sickness, very little hand-loom weaving was done.*

*In October 1849, Mr. W. J. Thompson and I became partners in a small business producing 27 and 30 inch brown linens. With improving trade and a little better demand, production improved and our business increased. It soon spread from cottage to cottage till from one, to three and four looms were heard in very many cottages, say by 1853.*

*A large quantity of goods were sent monthly to Magherafelt on the second Thursday, and on the 21st of each month to Moneymore. Many of those engaged in the bleaching and finishing came to these markets to meet the sellers or manufacturers, and transact their business. Among other buyers were Messrs. M. S. Ferguson, William Chaine & Son, York Street Spinning Co.; J. & R. Young, Ballymena; J. and J. Patrick, J. T. Bryan, Magherafelt; Wm. Ewart & Son, A. and S. Henry, Belfast.*

*The goods made at this time in Derry and Tyrone were usually rather coarse, - 800 to 1,600. The Russian war came on in 1853-54, and demand became very poor and gave that business a setback. The American war came, about 1864, and the scarcity of cotton caused better demand for linen, and much better prices. Production increased, and a finer and better article was wanted. Setts rose from 1,500 to 2,000, 4/4 wide.*

*Then as wages were often small, a large number went to Belfast to weaving factories. They got a steadier employment, and could make better wages, and about 1880 it became evident that hand-loom weaving would, for want of hands, become extinct. This was caused by handloom weavers going out to farm work in harvest and seed time, looms left idle, and very little goods produced at these seasons, while power looms produced much the same at all seasons of the year.*

*Go back to 1850, a great many small manufacturers got into the business, and often sold to more extensive makers. A public market was held in Cookstown by a large number of weavers, who bought yarn, prepared and wove it in their own cottages, sold it on Saturday of each week to buyers in single pieces. These were mostly heavy goods, suitable for bleaching. Buyers of these goods, for a long time, were the late Mr. James Gunning, Mr. Wm. Paul, Thomas Paul, J. M. Wilson, and S. E. Ekin.*

*The history of markets in Magherafelt, Moneymore and Cookstown is much the same as Ballymena. It was a larger and better market. The same causes affected all markets and led to their extinction.*

*I have always thought it a nice thing for young daughters to be housed in their fathers' and mothers' houses. I found many poor men of the weaving class strictly honest, truthful and reliable; these I highly esteemed. I was engaged with my faithful friend Mr. James M'Keown for over 50 years in the business. S.E.E*

4 Dec. 1917

Mr. Ekin stated that he had offices to give out yarn at Derrygenard, Rossmore, Stewartstown, Cookstown, Sandholes, and Ballyronan. The yarn was bought from Herdman's mill and other mills. The looms used by the weavers cost from £2 10s to £4 each. There were two bleach greens at Coagh – Ledlie's and Newton's.

Next Week - Wellbrook.

# WELLBROOK

## (8 – 8 – 1925)

So far as can be definitely ascertained Wellbrook was the premier bleach works in this part of the country. Gill, in his "Rise of the Irish Linen Industry" says that there is evidence that a number of bleach works were in existence in 1725, when the first beetling mill was set up by Hamilton Maxwell, who was already a bleacher and got a Government grant for the salary of a Dutch instructor for two years. The Huguenots brought bleachers with them and this development of the linen industry naturally spread from their settlement at Lisburn.

Prior to this, weavers had to bleach their own webs and bleaching could be done only in the spring and summer, so that the weavers, generally in poor circumstances, had to wait for months before they could market the finished article. As they could not afford to do so, they sold the goods unbleached, as brown linen, and this led to a class of middlemen, known as "drapers", who had capital and bought the brown linen from the weavers and bleached it on their own greens, which were equipped with boiling plant, drying houses and so forth. The linen was also beetled by water-power, which took the place of the old laborious process of hammering the cloth with wooden mallets by hand. The essentials for such an industry, therefore, were good water in which the cloth would be boiled and washed; a good supply of fuel; convenient water-power so that the beetling could be done continuously; a stretch of level land on which cloth could be spread to bleach in the sun, and the existence in the neighbourhood of considerable number of weavers who would make the cloth from yarn supplied by the draper or the vicinity of a good linen market where the brown linen could be bought.

Such conditions existed, in an ideal way, at the place known as Wellbrook, situated about 3½ miles west of Cookstown. The burn from the great springs at Montober (the hill of the springs) flowed close by, with its exceptional main source of the Ballinderry, which fell a considerable height at the place; turf bogs were plentiful in the neighbourhood; and most cottiers spun yarn and wove linen and there were good markets at Cookstown, Stewartstown, and Moneymore. It is, therefore, not surprising that this should have been the site of the first bleach mill in our district.

Wellbrook dates to the year 1764 as a stone on one of the older buildings testifies, though this is not necessary by way of proof because the title deeds disclose the full information, and the entries in the Register of Deeds are particularly ample. The owner of what we know as the

Orritor Estate at that time was the Earl of Anglesea. His eldest son had the title of Viscount Valentia, and the minor title was Baron Mountnorris, the family name being Annesley, and the estate was then known as Manor Annesley. This name is still familiar as the name of another estate owned by the same family near Washing Bay on Lough Neagh; the titles were derived from various other estates, acquired at different times. The present name of Orritor is a modification or corruption of the old name Araghter, and was given to the lands when purchased in 1782 by the first Earl of Castlestewart.

The Earl of Anglesea was non-resident, and like most of the great land-owners, he simply farmed out the estate, letting it on lease to a middleman for a term of years. This fact doubtless accounts for the non-existence of the bleaching industry at Wellbrook at an earlier date, because the lessee had no power to give a title for longer than his own lease, generally 31 years, and no person was going to build a mill and lay out and equip a green without security of tenure. This difficulty was got over, however, by an Act of Parliament which received the royal assent on 7th May 1754 (3rd George III. Chap 34), one clause of which enacted that limited owners (such as the lessee of the Orritor estate) could give a good title to lands, not exceeding 15 acres, for the purpose of a bleach green, with the provision that at least £10 per acre be expended for that purpose within three years.

At this time the lessee of the estate was Alderman Hans Baillie, of Abbey Street, Dublin, a Co. Down man, of Scotch extraction, who was related to the Annesley family, his mother being the daughter of Francis Annesley, of Castlewellan, younger son of the first Earl of Anglesea. In 1745 Hans Baillie leased the estate for 41 years at a yearly rent of £140, the previous lessees, or "farmers" of the lands being the Rev. John Richardson and Rev. Thomas Morris, two local rectors. It was, we think, about this time that the great immigration took place of Scotch Presbyterians who, on the Orritor estate, settled on the moorland and made the farmsteads which exist today, closely populating what had been rough grazing land, and adding to the wealth of the country. Baillie probably foresaw the effect of this; at any rate two years after he got his lease for 41 years he re-opened negotiations, and advancing the rent from £140 to £156 a year, he got a fresh lease for lives, renewable for ever, thus securing to himself and his heirs all the increment in the value of the bond which he anticipated. That this extra £16 a year was a good investment is proved by the result; thirty-five years later the trustees for the Earl of Castlestewart purchased the estate, and Viscount Valentia, the owner in fee, got £3,677 14s for his interest, while the heirs of Hans Baillie, then deceased, sold their lease, which had cost nothing but the extra rent of £16 a year, for no less than £16,600.

To return to 1764, the Act of that year was a comprehensive code of laws relating to the Linen industry, dealing with a wide range of subjects, with penalties ranging from death for forcible entry into a house to injure cloth of yarn, to 5s for bleaching yarn with soapers dregs or pigeons' dung. The Act also confirmed the system of sealing webs, which had never been put in force previously, though laws were passed authorising it. The introduction of the Bill was signalised by rioting by weavers, particularly in Lisburn district, and a general "rising" in 1762, but like recent legislation, it was found that what was feared was not intended and could not follow the passing of the Bill at all. It says something, however, for their faith in the future that two gentlemen, immediately on the passing of the Act, decided to spend money on developing the natural resources of the place afterwards named Wellbrook.

These two gentlemen were the sons of Henry Faulkner, Samuel Faulkner, of Stephen's Green, Dublin, and Hugh Faulkner, described as a linen draper residing in Gortalowry. They were men of considerable means and good social standing. Samuel had property at Fort Faulkner, Co. Wicklow, and Castletown, Co. Carlow, and served as High Sheriff in both counties in 1787 and 1788. Hugh Faulkner had also property in Co. Carlow; he was married to a daughter of Rev. Henry Cole, M.P. of Florence Court, who was ancestor to the Earls of Enniskillen. Rev. Henry Cole's wife was sister of Sir Arthur Brooke, Bart, a leading county family in Fermangh. Miss Cole, it may be noted, married Hugh Faulkner in the year following her father's death, and apparently they lived in Gortalowry and possessed some property there, as is mentioned in probate of his father's will. It would, of course, be leasehold only, as the only freeholder was Mr. Stewart of Killymoon. Hugh Faulkner appears in the rental of 1786 for holding with £1 6s 3d rent, while "Samuel Faulkner, Esq." paid £3 12s 10d rent. The title of "Esq." in this rental indicates his social position as it was given to only a few – Charles Richardson, Esq., of Ballymena, was one, while "Mr." was prefixed to the names of persons such as Wm. Magill, Wm. Cluff, and John Cooke, the rest being given their legal names only.

These two brothers then took a lease renewable for ever, from Hans Baillie, under the Act of 1764. Samuel was evidently the more important of the two, for on the house at Wellbrook, on which the date 1764 appears, his initials "S.F." also appear. In the lease he is described as gentleman, while Hugh is "linen draper" of Gortalowry. The land lease was 10 acres, Irish plantation measure, and described as "Strafleming", being part of the lands of Derrinleagh in the Manor of Araghter or Manor Annesley. The name Strafleming is puzzling, as it is not met elsewhere in connection with these lands, being replaced by the present name Wellbrook. "Stra," however, means a river holm, which accurately describes the bleach green there, the river running round most of it.

The site is further defined as "lying on the side of the great river called Kildress River", and the lease gave liberty "to erect a weir on said river and cut the mill-race to carry water from it to the mills, and a bleach green, to be erected on the premises, with the liberty to erect a weir on the brook running from the spring called Montober Well, and cut a mill race from same to carry off the whole water from said brook". The burn from Montober springs apparently took a different course before this, as on the O.S. Map of 1833 a "new water course" is shown towards what had been the bleach mill.

The perpetuity lease also included 5 acres in Tamlagh bog and 2 acres in the Downs, as already set out to the lessees by Rev. Hugh Stewart, agent for the lessor, "and now in possession of the lessees". Liberty was also given to make two roads to the premises, as soon "as the present leases expire", one from Tamlagh bog through lands now let to Alex. M 'Kinney, and the other "from the Great Road which runs from Orritor to Cookstown through lands of Tamlagh", on the expiration of the lease to Moses Black of 31 years, of which 14 were expired, then living. The latter provision shows that Moses Black had leased lands in 1734. The rent payable by the Faulkners for this land was £9 yearly, with 9s agent's fees, and two hens yearly or their value, 6d. There was also a fine of £1 2s 9d when renewed, and when these leases renewable for ever were converted, under subsequent Acts, to fee farm grants, the agent's fees and the fines were reckoned.

The date of this lease was 14th August 1765, and it was registered on 9th January 1766. The date on the stone referred to is 1764, so that the latter is rather a memorial of the Act under which Wellbrook became possible than a record of ownership, unless we assume that Samuel Faulkner built the house before he got the perpetuity lease, as may have been the case.

That the Faulkners carried out the terms of the lease is, of course, certain, but that they did not develop the industry as fully as they thought could be done is shown by the following interesting advertisement which appeared in the Dublin Evening Post from 14th till 31st October 1780, and is preserved in the Library of Trinity College. It will be noted that this gives the date of the erection of Wellbrook House as about 1776. It will also be seen that the purity of Montober water was recognised over a century before part of it was piped to Cookstown.

## ADVT. FROM DUBLIN EVENING POST, OCTOBER 1780

*A BLEACHGREEN to be let, for such term as may be agreed on at Wellbrooke, in the parish of Kildress and County of Tyrone, in the North of Ireland, capable of finishing 10,000 pieces of linen in one season, with its present Machinery, consisting of a double Washmill, 2 pair of Crankboards, a large Boiler, with Knives, Racks, Drying Loft and Cloth-Closets, in one house.*

*Also 2 Beetling Engines and Crisping Engine in another house, all in perfect repair, and supplied with a considerable redundancy of water, in the driest season.*

*To this green there is one of the largest springs of pure water in the Kingdom, part of which supplies the Headstocks and a site for erecting another house and machinery with the water brought to it, which, with other opportunities of erecting other wheels in different parts of the green, might be made capable of finishing almost any quantity of linen, as it will readily appear to anyone who views the place that eight Waterwheels may be most plentifully supplied with water, and though this present year has been the driest season that has been, these many years, yet the source of water at this Bleachgreen is so great that every wheel (if created) of the before mentioned would have had a redundancy of water, and the conveniency is so great that all the above wheels may be erected at not more than 10 to 12 perches distance from each other.*

*There is also an exceeding good dwelling-house on the premises, built within these 4 years, consisting of vaulted cellarage underneath, Parlour, Bedchamber, Hall, Kitchen, Scullery and Pantry on the ground floor; Dining-room and 3 Chambers on the second floor, and 2 Bedchambers on the third floor; the whole finished in the very best manner, and modern taste, with stove-grates, marble chimney fires, etc., etc.*

*There is 8 plantation acres of turf bog to the premises so convenient that 20 load of turf may be drawn in a day with one horse.*

*Also about 28 acres of land, plantation measure, adjoining the Green, whereon is a very good dwelling house for a foreman Bleacher.*

*The whole situated in the heart of a very great manufacturing country, within 2 miles of Cookstown, 5 of Moneymore and 6 of Coagh, 6 of Stewartstown, 10 of Magherafelt, and 9 of Dungannon, all established noted cloth markets.*

*There is perhaps no place in the Kingdom where the Bleaching Business may be carried on so extensively, to a greater degree of perfection, or more to the advantage of the occupier.*

*N.B. – There is a large quantity of turf stacked at the mills, which will be given at first cost to the person that becometh tenant for the premises.*

*Proposals to be received by Samuel Faulkner, Esq., No. 84 Stephen's Green, Dublin, or by Mr. Hugh Faulkner on the premises, who will treat for the same.*
*24ᵗʰ September, 1780.*

(To be continued.)

# WELLBROOK (Continued)

## (15 – 8 – 1925)

Last week we gave an advertisement published in the Dublin Evening Post of October 1780, by the Messrs. Faulkner, offering to let Wellbrook, which advt. was found by one of our many helpers in the search for information regarding the history of the district. Whether the place was let or not we do not know, for it is only by the happy chance of finding the paper that we knew it was to be let; the public records and register of deeds are not concerned with such temporary transactions. But they are with the transfers of property, and from them we glean further information about the place and the Faulkners.

Samuel Faulkner died without issue at sea, in 1794, leaving his property to his brother Hugh, now described as of Castletown, Co. Carlow, and of Saville Park, as well as of Gortalowry and Wellbrook. As we have said, Hugh was married to Miss Cole, daughter of the rector of Derryloran, and a branch of the Cole family of Enniskillen, but Faulkner was a Presbyterian, and probably the most influential of the congregation in Cookstown. At any rate his name immediately follows that of the minister, Rev. George Murray, in the Petition of Dissenters of 1775, and is followed by that of Wm. Oliver, an attorney and Commissioner for affidavits in the King's Bench, whose wife (or daughter-in-law) was often closely connected with Mrs. Stewart of Killymoon in various social objects at the time. The Petition was against a Bill which was being promoted at the time to prevent Dissenters from taking part in meetings of the Vestry, which, at that time, was the local authority for roads and other things. It was not passed, but it is worth mentioning as showing the short-sighted policy of the extreme Church party, in trying to penalise gentlemen of ability and position like these, who regarded the Presbyterian Church as a branch of the Church of Scotland, just as the

Test Act deprived corporations like Londonderry of the services of men like Alderman Lennox, ancestor of Col. Lenox-Conyngham, because they would not take the "Test" in an earlier generation. A more tolerant policy might, today, have led to a common Protestant Church in Ireland.

In 1783 Samuel Faulkner leased the land on which the Corkhill beetling mill was erected on a good fall on the Kildress river. Corkhill is not part of the Orritor Estate nor is it of the Drum estate, but lies in the angle formed where the mearing of these two estates branches out at Kildress. From the Civil Survey of 1654 it would appear that the then owner was Lord Caulfield. At any rate he is returned for "Corchill, half-town; Straw M'Martin, half-town". There is a considerable distance between what is now Strawmacklemartin and Corkhill bridge, but the former was the name of a territory now represented by a group of large townlands, and it may well have reached down to Corkhill, especially as the surveyors of 1654 gave it immediately before Tullinacross and "Mekhana". For the benefit of anyone who likes to trace it we give the boundaries, as set out in the Civil Survey. It reads:- "The abovesaid land belonging to the Lord Caulfield is bounded eastward with the half townland of Drumora; southward with the top of the river of Kildress; westward upon the mountain of Formell, in the barony of Strabane, northward with the head of the river of Munterloney". In 1783 the owner of Corkhill was Mrs. Beatrice Walsh, wife of Rev. John Walsh, and daughter of Claudius Hamilton, of Dublin. The lease recites that whereas "a very extensive bleachyard, with its machinery, have been erected and built by the said Samuel Faulkner upon part of the lands of Derrinlea and now known by the name Wellbrook", containing only ten acres, and "ten acres being too small for the accommodation of the said bleach-yard, and the workmen employed therein", it was agreed to lease 2a. 1r. 14p., then in the possession of Samuel Faulkner and adjoining his bleach-yard, "through which the water is conducted to drive the said bleach-yard, .....the bleaching of linen in a fuller and more extensive manner", and permission was also given under the lease to make rivers and dams and cut water-courses through the land. The three "lives" mentioned in the lease were the Prince of Wales, Thomas Whaley, aged 17, and Wm. Faulkner, third son of Hugh Faulkner, of Wellbrook, aged 10 years. In 1783, therefore, Hugh was still resident at Wellbrook.

To return to Hugh Faulkner - in June 1800, he, with his brother-in-law, John Montgomery, flour miller, of Oldtown, Co. Kildare, another brother-in-law, John Cornwall and his eldest son, Henry, as trustees of the will of Samuel Faulkner, sold Wellbrook to his son-in-law, Captain Wm. Martin, of the 9th Dragoons, of Broomhall, in England. Hugh Faulkner appears to have assigned his interest in the perpetuity lease to Samuel on 17th November 1781 - the year after the advertisement offering to let

Wellbrook, so that Captain Martin acquired the sole interest in the place. The assignment recites the property - 10 acres in Derrinlea, formerly called Strafleming, in Araghter Manor, or Manor Annesley; 5 acres bog in Tamlaght and 2 acres in The Downs, with the 11 acre farm in Tamlaght formerly owned by Alex M'Kegnies, and including the water rights as already stated. Samuel Faulkner, by his will, had ordered that the property be sold to pay his debts, and the sale seems to have been a family arrangement by which Captain Martin became the owner. He, however, did not keep it long, for in January 1805, he sold to James Irwin, described as linen draper of Wellbrook, and probably Martin's tenant, the price being £1,425. This concluded the connection of the Faulkner family with Wellbrook, after a period of less than 40 years.

James Irwin's ownership began a new era in Wellbrook, and he carried on the bleaching business vigorously till his death. He was married to Caroline, daughter of James Stewart, of Greenhills, Co. Antrim, in 1812, and in accordance with the prudent practice of the period (which is also very convenient for the historian) he settled the property on his wife and their issue. The trustees of this settlement were the bride's father James Stewart, Henry Stewart, of Greenhills, and Frederick M'Causland, of Streeve, Co. Londonderry, the bride's fortune being £1,000. The settlement of property has also disadvantages, for the Irwins had a numerous family, some thirteen in number, and when the father died the widow was not able to sell without the consent of all the children, who were then scattered all over the world.

Local tradition of Wellbrook goes back only to the time of Mr. James Gunning, who took the place and went to reside there with his sister, afterwards Mrs. James Moore, and mother of the late Mr. Gunning-Moore. For the reason given above we have no information as to when Mr. Gunning went to Wellbrook, as he was only a tenant, not the owner, but presumably it would be after Mr. Irwin's death, which took place in the year 1833. He also was a linen draper, and carried on a very extensive bleaching business in the first half of the last century, looking after the business personally. He bought the cloth from the weavers as brown linen, boiled it in the pure Montober water, in the boiler and drying house still standing, bleached it on the grass of the holm where the webs were guarded by an armed watchman from the Watch Tower, still standing, and then beetled the linen in several beetling mills erected on the Kildress river, and sold the finished cloth. It was undoubtedly a profitable business, though others failed to make it pay, but Mr. Gunning was a hard worker. It is said that at six o'clock every morning he was at the gate on the road to Cookstown buying turf at a shilling a load, for fuel for his boiler. But while tradition has it that he demanded, and got, good service, it is to his credit that no tradition exists that he was anything but strict and upright in his dealings.

The remains of this bleaching business can still be traced at Wellbrook. There is the watch tower overlooking the broad meadow where the webs were bleached, the drying house, a pit in front of the house where the cloth was steeped in running water, even the pipe across the river which brought the spring water to the bleach mill and the various beetling engines.

Mr. Gunning was not able to buy the place, owing to the Irwin family being so scattered, that title could not then be made, but had determined to make it his home, and decided to build a house of his own adjacent to Wellbrook. This is probably the most interesting souvenir remaining of him at the place. There is a cross-road joining the great roads from Cookstown via Orritor and Drum. This little road skirts a hill adjacent to Wellbrook, and from this hill a splendid view is obtainable of all the country round; to the North and West the whole district bounded by the mountains of Slievegallion, Ballynagilly and Ballynasollus, and to the East Lough Neagh could be seen with the conical shape of Slemish where St. Patrick attended his master's flocks, and the Mountains of Mourne as they roll down to the sea.

It was on this hill, which is rather an extensive plateau, that Mr. Gunning proposed to build his residence. Purchasing the farm, he laid out the avenues, the principal one winding up the ascent exactly in the way the avenue does to the residence he subsequently built and named Loymount, so that one could not but be struck by the resemblance. The farm included a small strip of land on the Wellbrook side of the road, and here Mr. Gunning built a Gate Lodge, as it is today, for when the plans were changed, and the property ultimately came into other hands, the Gate Lodge for "Dunbrook" as the new house was to be named, became the gate lodge for the older house of Wellbrook.

The change of plan was due, of course, to the fact that the Killymoon estate was coming into the market. Mr. Gunning had already invested his savings in land, buying Tulnacross townland and an estate at Mountjoy, and he, with his brother-in-law, Mr. James Moore, lodged tenders for several lots of the Killymoon Estate, including the markets and business end of the town and were declared the purchasers. In this way the highest part of the townland of Loy became the site of Mr. Gunning's residence instead of the hill in Derrrinleagh.

By this time, 1851, the linen markets had declined, the factories taking the place of the hand-looms, and either when Mr. Gunning came to reside at Loymount, or shortly afterwards, he gave up the tenancy in Wellbrook, and the bleach mill ceased. In 1859, when Griffith's Valuation was made, the bleach mill in Derrinleagh, the drying house and watch house in Tamlaght, the beetling mill in Corkhill, were all unoccupied. Mrs. Irwin was returned as rated for some 95 acres in all, of which 54 were in Tamlaght, 30 in Derrinleagh and 11 in Drumnaglough, besides being the lessee of two small farms aggregating 13 acres let to tenants in Tamlaght and Doons.

In April 1860, Mrs. Irwin and her children sold the property to Mr. Samuel Bryson, of Magherafelt, the conveyance being signed by the only surviving trustee, Fredrick M'Causland, then of Bessbrook, Limavady. Mr. Bryson, four years afterwards, sold to Mr. James Leeper, of Hollymount, Desertmartin, father of the present owner. Mr. Leeper owned the extensive grain mill at Desertmartin, still known by many as Leeper's mill, and also scutch mills. When he came to Wellbrook bleaching hand-loom linen was a thing of the past, but the flax trade was booming and he decided to use the power for scutching. He removed the machinery from the bleach-mill and installed scutching machinery there. Soon there were two scutch mills going close to each other, one leased by Mr. Thomas Adair and the other Mr. Leeper's own, while some of the beetling mills were also leased. In course of time, however, Mr. Leeper, who died in 1886, took them all into his own hands.

Since that time Wellbrook has been owned by his eldest son, Mr. William Leeper, J.P., who resides there, although, as owner of the Millburn Factory (Messrs. John Gunning & Son, Ltd.) his business interests are in Cookstown. We hope to describe this development of the linen business, established in 1854, in due course, but meantime a short description of Wellbrook, as it now exists, will be suitable to close this article.

Wellbrook lies in the hollow south of the great road from Orritor, about 3¾ miles from Cookstown, the principal avenue being in the townland of Tamlaght. To the right, going down the avenue, is a low-lying field, once a mill pond, but no longer in use for that purpose, while further on is a large pond fed with the water from Montober springs. On the left side of the avenue the ground is higher, and here is the watch tower from which the cloth lying in the meadow was guarded by an armed watchman, while further on is the drying house, used it is said, before Orritor Presbyterian Church was erected a century ago, for Sabbath services for those who could not go to Cookstown.

A striking feature of the landscape here is the rockery - a real rockery, too, for the native rock is only covered with soil on which Alpine plants flower. Below it is the pit where the cloth was steeped, and in the solid rock is what was undoubtedly an artificial channel for water, but now closed with soil. The house looks out on this picturesque spot; it is an old Georgian house, dating (according to the advertisement quoted last week), from 1776, the year of the Declaration of Independence by the

American colonies, so that it is exactly the same age as the American Constitution. It has been somewhat modernised by the addition of square stone bay windows, which are in keeping with the façade, and it has, of course, been enlarged by the addition of wings, and brought up to date internally, but the front has not been spoiled by anything which would be out of keeping with its history as an eighteenth century residence of a gentleman linen draper. At the rear of the house is a very extensive garden, now equipped with several glass houses, and which were probably laid out when the house was built; at any rate, the Ordnance Surveyors found the garden there 90 years ago. The whole surroundings are well wooded, a belt of trees also enclosing the meadow land which was once the bleach green, along the river bank.

The house is in the townland of Derrinleagh, and so is the building which was formerly the bleach mill, and is now one of the beetling mills. Altogether Mr. Leeper has six different beetling mills on the property, including the one at Corkhill, where, on the roadside, a large over-shot wheel proves a source of interest to travellers. Another on the stream between Tamlaght and Derrinleagh, is at the moment unused, as a turbine is being fitted to get more power than was possible by the water wheels. Portion of the water was lost for power when Cookstown got its water supply from Montober springs. The exact loss to Mr. Leeper of the diverted water was a matter of acute difference of opinion by the experts at the time, and we had better leave it at that; at any rate, pure water is a thing which cannot be replaced by anything else, whereas water-power can, and it is interesting to note that Mr. Leeper has erected another large house, not on the steam, which will be available for additional machinery when the linen trade justifies its installation, and steam can be used as the motive power. It was built during a slack time before the war, chiefly to give employment; the linen boom and the following slump have, for so far, made it unnecessary to equip it.

The power from the Montober water is also used to drive a little saw mill, which is a useful accessory to any place, but more useful still is the dynamo which provides electric current to light the house and for household purposes.

Altogether Mr. Leeper has 36 beetles at Wellbrook in the six mills. A beetling "engine" is really a simple piece of machinery. It consists of a heavy cylinder of wood – the beam, some 10½ feet long, and supported horizontally. On this the piece of cloth is wound. Overhead are the beetles, a row of heavy wooden plungers, about four inches square, which are raised in quick succession, and drop on the cloth, the beam meantime turning very slowly and with a traverse action so that every part of it will get equal beetling. The clatter, as the beetles fall, one chasing the other but never overtaking it, makes conversation in a beetling mill an absolute waste of time. These beetling mills, water driven, run continuously, a couple of men at Wellbrook being on duty all night. The time occupied in beetling a piece of 100 yards varies with the material; some may be finished in 24 hours, while other stuff may take up to three weeks to have it properly done. How it was done by hand is a mystery, or, at all events, must have meant an enormous waste of human labour, for a beetling mill demonstrates, more than probably anything else, the great advantage there is in even simple labour-saving machinery.

Next Week – Greenvale Works

GREENVALE MILL, COOKSTOWN

# GREENVALE

## (12 – 9 – 1925)

We have to apologise to our readers for the delay in proceeding with our local history, which was due to unavoidable causes; the interval has, however, produced some hitherto unsuspected information which will make, we think, the article on Greenvale not the least interesting which has appeared. The first instalment, which was in type three weeks ago, has, in fact, to be re-written in view of recent discoveries.

By "Greenvale" we mean the group of industries which have grown up alongside the Ballinderry or Kildress river between Tullagh and Killymoon, in which all the processes required to produce linen ready for the consumer, from the raw material, have been carried on in an extensive manner, and which concerns are now all owned by a single private company bearing the name "Thomas Adair Limited", thus retaining the name of the gentleman who, almost a century ago, exerted a lasting influence on the economic life of the town.

The historian is always wanting to know the beginning of whatever he is investigating. The tradition of Messrs. Adair's is that the original firm started in 1828, but was there nothing prior to that, and if so, what and when? The earliest lease which is extant goes away back to the year 1752 when William Stewart, of Killymoon, granted to Edward Patteson, merchant, of Cookstown, two portions of land measuring 8a 3r, and in Sullenbuoy, between the river and the mill race, together with another lot of 2a 1r. Patteson was required to build a house 14 feet high at least to the eave, 18 feet wide and 50 feet long. He was also to make 50 perches of ditch, 6 feet wide and 5 feet deep, well quicked and planted with oak, ash or elm, or forfeit half-a-crown for each perch unmade, which sum Mr. Stewart was to expend on ditching. This building and ditching was to be completed within seven years. The landlord was to have liberty to have roads made through any part of the land "for the use of the public or the conveniency of the inhabitants thereon", and had also power to make "march ditches in a straight and regular line".

This document is interesting in itself, for unlike the numerous specimens of the scrivener's art which we have met, it was printed – that is to say, it was a printed form with the names and figures filled in. At this time the Killymoon estate was very large, as shown by the Rent Roll of 1786, and Mr. Stewart had, at that very early period, realised the advantage it was to everyone (except the conveyancers) to use printing for such documents, and had a model lease prepared, as was done a century later by Mr. Gunning on the Cookstown estate. The provisions regarding the building of a dwelling-house, ditching (or fencing the fields), right to make roads and to straighten the march fence were common to all these leases, and indicate that the owner had in mind the improvement of the estate by the erection of good dwelling-houses, the fencing of the land which, in many places, at that time, was devoid of hedges, and generally the creation of farmsteads of the modern type.

To bring about this desirable result the landlord granted leases at nominal rents, but when the lease expired the improvements accrued to the then owner of the estate. Such an arrangement is rather repugnant to our ideas of equity in Ireland, though building leases are taken on these terms in London and other cities by large business firms, who provide, in their accounts, a sinking fund, which accumulates to meet the cost of the building when the lease expires.

The lease to Edward Patteson was for 31 years or three lives, the "lives" being these two of his children, Russel Patteson, aged 6; Mary Patteson, aged 10, and of Isabella Stewart, aged 11. That is to say, the lease would not expire till all three had died, and in any case not for 31 years. The effect of this was that Mr. Stewart, by granting the land at a nominal rent, postponed any return to himself or his heirs for at least 31 years, and probably 50 or 60 years; the lessee Patteson, got the advantage of this, but his heirs would, at the end of the lease, be deprived of the property.

The important provision in the lease is not in the printed part, however, but written at the end, being specially for Patteson's case. It was that "the said Edward Patteson shall have free liberty of water for one wheel, but paying, in proportion, towards repairing the weir to the number of mills now erected, or that may be erected, on the said water course". At first sight this looks as if we had not got to the beginning – that there were already a mill, or mills, in existence. But this is the usual legal phraseology in such cases, to avoid any question afterwards of the date when mills were erected and the liability of the owners for repairs. It provided that whatever number of mill-owners there were taking the water from the race, each was to pay his share to the repairs which would be necessary from time to time.

The clause, however, undoubtedly proves the existence of the mill race prior to the lease. There is no earlier lease known, and searches in the Register of Deeds have failed to detect any trace of a prior mill holding. This brings us to what is the most interesting fact in our investigation. As we see it, and we are morally certain that it is the correct view, this mill-race at Greenvale was part of Mr. William Stewart's town planning scheme. It will be remembered that it was about 1750 that that gentleman, with the advice probably of John Reid, who was agent or surveyor, and prepared an estate map in 1736 on which the new streets were marked, decided to build the present town of Cookstown by running a long wide street, straight from the hamlet on Oldtown Hill (which was all that remained of Dr. Cooke's town), across bogs and hills towards the river and Killymoon. Already Mr. Stewart had a corn mill on the river for his tenants, but above it as far as Tullagh was a ravine, through which the water descended with considerable force, and to "harness" this power, and make it available for the linen industry, which was developing on industrial lines, was obviously a desirable thing, adjacent to his model town.

But it would be unreasonable to expect a tenant, on a lease for lives, which was all that Mr. Stewart, as limited owner, could then grant, to erect a weir and construct a mill-race. Hence it was a thing he must undertake himself, leaving the use of the water power to the lessees. It would be an exaggeration to describe this harnessing of the river as a great engineering feat, but it did entail a considerable amount of labour. A huge weir was built across the mouth of the ravine and to the north side was dug a race or carry, probably under the direction of John Reid. Considerable skill was exhibited too; for example, at one place between the townlands of Sullenboy and Gortalowry - at all events the present boundary, though probably it was altered - a stream ran into the river at right angles to the course of the race, and a substantial wall was erected to support the bank and remains as a testimony to the masons of 170 years ago.

The race ran along the north side of the ravine from Tullagh to near the public road, joining the river just above the bridge and the land granted to Edward Patteson was the strip lying between the race and the river, commencing at the Sullenboy boundary, but with a right-of-way along the Tullagh portion to the weir. This strip widened out further down, and at this spot Patteson built his bleach mill, with a short lead from the race to the river, and in front of the mill, overlooking his bleach green he built his house, in accordance with the terms of the lease. There is little, if any, doubt, in spite of a slight difference in the size, that that house is the present mill manager's residence, known as Mesopotamia – a name given by a former manager who was a student of the Bible and thought that the name would be appropriate as it lay between the two rivers. The shed behind the present house is obviously the old mill – the first of the now very extensive buildings at Greenvale erected to use the water-power.

If we are correct in this identification, and there can be no reasonable doubt of it, Mesopotamia ranks as one of the first houses built in connection with Mr. Stewart's new town, for the date, 1752, is the date on the reputed oldest house in the Oldtown. There may be some a year or two earlier, but we have not come on them yet, though other leases show that the houses were built in 1753 and 1754 and later years.

(To be continued)

# GREENVALE (Continued)

## (19 – 9 – 1925)

Last week we explained how Mr. William Stewart, when he laid out his model town about 1750, constructed a mill race to use the water-power of the river between Tullagh and Killymoon, and how Edward Patteson took an improving lease for a bleach-green and mill alongside it and was to get water for one wheel. That lease was for lands in Sullenboy, but apparently the boundary between that townland and Gortalowry has altered materially. The area of Sullenboy, itself, proves this, for it is only some 55 acres, whereas Gortalowry has over 290 acres, showing that the latter has probably encroached on the former.

Townlands are the old balliboes - the amount of arable land which a team of oxen could plough in a year, as the name indicates. It was a rough sort of measure, but, at the Plantation, and possibly long before, the area was fixed at 60 acres Irish measure. Thus we find that when Brian Crossagh O'Neill got a grant of what is known as the Orritor estate, sixteen townlands and two-thirds of another are enumerated, thus making up exactly 1,000 acres, at 60 acres Irish to the townland. Wood, bog, moorland, and other "waste" was not reckoned at all, merely the arable land. Killycurragh, with its 770 acres, was taken as only 60, so that, generally speaking, when one meets with a large townland it is a proof that, if it is all arable now, it has been reclaimed. It follows that when a townland has a lesser area than 60 acres Irish, even if all arable, some of the original land must have been transferred to an adjoining townland by the alteration of the boundary. Readers will remember that so lately as 1851 this was done as between Drumcraw and Drumgarrell, on a substantial scale, and at every new survey there are little changes, the surveyors seeking for natural boundaries and altering the maps accordingly, when both townlands belong to the same person. This must have taken place with Sullenboy. Even the present Ordnance map differs slightly from that of 1854, the invisible boundary across Greenvale being quite different, and though the areas of Sullenboy, at these two surveys, are practically the same, 55a 1r 39p in 1854 and 55a 0r 16p in 1909, which difference would be accounted for by slight errors in the earlier measurement, Gortalowry townland increased by no less that 12 acres in the interval.

To return to Edward Patteson; he built the bleach mill and house and laid out the green, as we know from a mortgage registered in 1779 to David Kerr, of Portavoo, Co. Down, which describes the property "between the river and the mill race, being part of the present bleaching green, and lying at the north end of same", together with two acres "lately held by Hugh Gourley" in Gortalowry, "also all bleach mills and utensils on the premises", and two acres of bog in Anaghmore, which is mentioned in the lease of 1772. The property, however, was assigned in 1796, to "Benjamin Patteson, of Cookstown, gentleman", who will be remembered as the Linen Inspector for Cookstown and Stewartstown markets, as mentioned in our Linen Board articles. The exact relationship of these lessees can only be guessed; however, there is proof that in 1807 Edward Patteson was post-master of Cookstown. Matthew Patteson was undoubtedly of the same family; he was sole seal-master for Cookstown in 1818, and was also post-master of Cookstown, and was succeeded by his niece, the late Miss Patteson, who will be remembered by many readers as post-mistress here.

How many mills Mr. Stewart expected would be built on his race we cannot say, but he did not live to see any but Patteson's. Possibly no one was willing to incur the expense on a lease for three lives, which was all that the life-tenant of entailed lands could give. It was this restricted power of giving leases which lead to the incorporation in the famous Act known as the 3$^{rd}$ of George III., of powers to life-owners to give leases renewable for ever, of up to 15 acres for a bleach-green, etc., a sum of £10 per acre to be expended within three years on it. This Act, passed after a "rising" of weavers at Lisburn immediately led to the use of the water-power at Wellbrook by the Faulkners, who resided in Gortalowry, and it is peculiar that they should have gone there instead of using the power beside them.

It was not till 1785 that a second mill was erected, so far as any records available show, and the lease is strong corroboration of the non-existence of any other. Col. James Stewart, M.P., was then the owner of the estate, and in that year he granted a lease for lives, renewable for ever, of further land in Gortalowry to John Cooke, described as linen draper. The lease starts with the preamble, "Whereas the said James Stewart is determined, as far as in him lies, to give all reasonable encouragement and assistance to the further extension of the linen manufacture," and proceeds to refer to the 3$^{rd}$ of George III. above-mentioned.

This bleach-mill of Cook's is not now standing, but appears to have occupied part of the site on which the spinning mill stands and there is structural evidence that a lead, such as would have been required for a water wheel, ran across from the race to the river. The spinning mill may, in fact, be regarded as an extension in both directions, of Cook's bleach-mill.

John Cook was succeeded, in 1794, by his son James. The latter got married, in May 1795, to Ann, daughter of Robert Atkinson, and prior to that event his father assigned to him, "in consideration of natural love and affection", his property, which consisted not only of the leased land at Greenvale, but also of lands in Kirktown, Loy, Ballydonnelly and Clare "with all bleach-mills", etc., and when James got married he settled these on his wife, as well as property in Edendoit and Gortindarragh. The trustees of the settlement were James Stewart, of Attenry, Wm. Clark, of Summer Island and Hugh Cooke, James Cooke.

James Cooke, as stated in a previous article, resided in Gortalowry, on the main street, in the house now owned by Mr. Malone, and besides the 10½ acres granted in 1785, he was the lessee of 11½ acres "formerly in the possession of St. Laurence, except the bank above the river as the same was planted by William Stewart". This is the land between the Cemetery Road and the river. James Cooke got into financial difficulties, and, in 1804, a judgement for £2,000 was registered against him and assigned to James Bruce, and the lands descended to Mr. Rowley Miller, who sold to Mr. Adair in 1851, when the lease had been converted into perpetuity. This land is now apparently partly in Gortalowry and partly in Sullenboy, and measures 16a 3r 5p. The rent reserved in the lease, we may mention, was £14 4s 6d, with 1s in the £1 receiver's fees (agent's commission) and six days work of a man, horse and wheel car, or as an alternative 2s a day.

Cooke paid off part of the mortgage, but in 1828 there was £923 still due, with £41 odd for costs or interest and £108 arrears of rent, and Cooke agreed to pay £773 in settlement. In 1829 we find another mortgage, this time for £300 only, which he had borrowed from Miss Elizabeth Ash, of Magherafelt, and Thomas Harper, of Lime Park, and there is a re-assignment to Cooke in which is the interesting fact mentioned, that by way of physical conveyance, Harper gave to Cooke and his wife, "one sparrow hawk".

(To be continued.)

## GREENVALE (Continued)

## (26 – 9 – 1925)

We have now reached the close of the third decade of the nineteenth century, when the water-power at Greenvale had been developed for eighty years, and the only industries using the race were the two mills of Patteson and Cooke. Both the original leasees had passed away, as had two generations of the Stewarts, and, in view of the length of time, it must be confessed that the result was disappointing. Some employment was, no doubt, given by the two bleach mills and adjacent greens, but it was not large, nor do the owners appear to have made a success of them financially and unless employers are able to make more than a bare living there is no inducement to extend, nor means to do so unless outside capital is available. Capital is created by savings, and if the employers are only able to make ends meet it cannot grow; when however, by a combination of industry and thrift, there is a surplus, a capital fund is created for use in fresh enterprise.

Meantime the town of Cookstown had been growing at a rapid rate. In 1750, when the new town was planned, the population of the two tenements in Oldtown Hill was probably not more than 100 souls; if there were 200 there must have been congestion, which was unlikely with the country around so sparsely populated. At the census of 1821 we have exact figures, for the first time. Cookstown had then grown to a little town of 963 persons, residing in 141 houses – less than half the size of Omagh and less than one-third the population of Dungannon or Strabane. It had, in fact, barely the population of Coagh and Stewartstown combined.

Ten years later the population of Cookstown had exactly trebled, passing Omagh with 600 to spare, and only a few hundred less than Strabane, though the area of our town had not been extended. There were 2,883 inhabitants, living in 516 houses, an average of 37½ houses having been built every year. Some of these houses were of a good type, not only in the business end of the town but in Loy and Gortalowry, built on land leased in perpetuity, or fee farm grants. But these were few; the bulk of the houses were small, and apparently built on tenancies at will, which is still the case in parts of the above townlands. Specimens of these little one-storied thatched cottages exist still, and, no doubt, when the owners had means they were comfortable enough, but the worst of them have long since disappeared, and we can only imagine what they were like – the merest hovels composed of four walls, no floor but mother earth, and a thatched roof.

The people who lived in these houses must have been of the poorest working class. They were, in fact, cottiers who had left, or been forced to leave, the land on which they had squatted, to come into the new town for work. And when we enquire what work was for them, the answer stares us in the face in the Ordnance Map of 1833, for all around the town it is dotted with quarries, both of freestone and limestone. Over a dozen quarries are shown on this map of 1833 as then being worked, and some of these we know were quite large. The building of the town gave employment, and the workers created a demand for more houses. Employment always has this effect – it creates more employment, just as unemployment tends, in itself, to create less employment. But quarrying and building, with the accompanying house carpentry and wood felling, was man's work, and the women and girls had nothing to do except what home spinning and weaving existed, or work in the fields, which was necessarily limited.

Such was the situation in Cookstown about the year 1830, as proved by statistics and maps. There was a large population of poor people, many so poor that they had recourse to begging. Indeed, in the summer of 1824, this had reached such dimensions that a Mendicity Association was formed "to put a stop to travelling beggars and to relieve the resident poor", as a paragraph in the Whig of 14th April 1825, puts it, of which Association and its methods we will further refer. For the present it is sufficient to state that there was a surplus of labour, unemployed, and of water-power, unused. What was needed was capital and business acumen to bring these two together by the creation of suitable industries.

It was at this stage that Mr. Hugh Adair, and his son Thomas, appeared on the scene. They came from Broughshane, near Ballymena where, they had, apparently, been engaged in the linen business. The former was then a man of 61 years of age, and it is to his son, then 32 years old, in the vigour of manhood, that the development of the industries, which still bear his name, is attributed. But it must, in fairness to his father, be stated that in the original leases he is also described as a linen draper, and there is the important fact that it was he, and not his son Thomas, who was the lessee of the lands, and owner of the property originally, though the extension of the business was, no doubt, due to the latter, perhaps entirely.

The exact date when Messrs. Adair came to Cookstown first cannot be ascertained. We know that in July 1831, the negotiations for the purchase of Cooke's land and mill had gone so far that an inquisition into the title was made and counsel's opinion was taken as to whether part of Kirktown, which Cooke had for a lease for his own life, was liable for his wife's jointure, so that the year 1830 may be taken as the date roughly. Cooke, as we have seen, was in serious financial difficulties in 1828, and in the following year there are records of a charge by Mr. Samuel R. Magill, and re-conveyance, which would naturally take place when he sold to Mr. Adair.

As to Patteson's mill and green, the only evidence we have of an assignment from Patteson, or his representatives, to Mr. Adair is the fact that amongst the deeds extant, is Edward Patteson's original lease of 1752. As stated previously, it was for 31 years or three lives; the 31 years had long since expired, and the youngest of the three persons whose lives determined the length of the lease would, in the year 1830, have been 84 years of age, the others, being 88 and 89 years old, so that, even if alive, there was not much interest to purchase. However, in April 1833, a new lease, for lives but renewable for ever, was given by Col. Wm. Stewart to Hugh Adair, of Patteson's land at the head of the race, with the bleach mill, etc. There was a covenant in the lease which may be of interest, against converting the bleach-green and mill into a flour or corn mill without permission – a provision intended to secure the monopoly of grinding to the estate mill which existed further down the river, and was leased, in 1834, to John Vance for 21 years.

(To be continued)

## THE SULLENBOY BOUNDARY

In connection with the boundary between Sullenboy and Gortalowry, to which we referred last week, Mr. J. Adair informs us that some time ago he discovered a culvert from near where an oak tree exists and coming across the next field down to where Patteson had his pond, about what is known as the Washout. He imagines that there had been an open stream before it was built over and that was the old townland boundary. On reference to the O.S. map of 1833 we find that that is the case, the boundary on it following an irregular line exactly as he traced the culvert. The pond, by the way, had originally a metal pipe across to the river; it was more recently piped by Messrs. Adair, to their bleach works, to supply pure spring water, a series of springs existing along the line of the drain. Another interesting point in connection with the site of Patteson's mill is that below the settling pond the land is planted with elder and other soft trees, whilst all along, from the weir down, the rest of the land is growing forest trees, the inference being that the portions referred to were used for some purpose connected with the bleach mill - probably drying the cloth, though it must have been on a small scale, and only planted when this little green was disused. There is also a tradition that the shed referred to as being behind Mesopotamia House, was the original beetling mill; certainly it was used by the Pattesons for some purpose requiring power. The map of 1833 also shows that Patteson had a road to his place which came out on the old Chapel road a short distance on the Greenvale side of the New Cemetery road, and there seems to have been a pond there of considerable length, though narrow, but this and the road have disappeared. In connection with the areas, we have just found that in the Crown Rental of 1668, when Ensign Walker was the owner, Gortalowry had 76 acres and Sullenboy had 145a 3r 6p Irish measure, which corroborates our theory that the boundaries have been very substantially altered, Sullenboy losing and Gortalowry gaining.

# GREENVALE (Concluded)

## (3 – 10 – 1925)

We have now found the Messrs Adair installed at Greenvale, carrying on the business of linen drapers, not only as merchants but also as bleachers and finishers, in the mills built by Patteson and Cooke. This business would be similar to that carried on by the Faulkners and by Mr. Irwin at Wellbrook - buying the linen or getting it woven by hand-loom weavers, then beetling, bleaching and finishing it. No doubt Patteson's house, now known as Mesopotamia, was used as a residence, for Cooke, we know, lived in Mr. Malone's house in Gortalowry, but when Greenvale House was built is not clear. In 1833 the gate lodge opposite Glenavon, did not exist, nor the avenue there, nor the gardens, but on the O.S. Map of that year there does appear to have been a house corresponding to the present residence, though it has been altered almost out of recognition.

The first important development was the building of the spinning mill, to produce yarn by machinery instead of hand spinning. This may have been Mr. Thomas Adair's aim, when he came to Cookstown, as only a few years afterwards the mill was in operation, the earliest balance sheets dating to 1837. In this enterprise he was joined by Mr. Henry Gunning, who, when Greenvale house was built, lived in Mesopotamia, and was a partner in the business till 1863 when the partnership was dissolved.

Spinning by machinery was first introduced into Ireland in the year 1800, according to Gill's "Rise of the Linen Trade", but in spite of bounties and grants by the Linen Board, it made slow progress. The reason for this, according to a writer in 1811, was that yarn spun at home was so much cheaper than in England, some women by working diligently from morning to night, earning not more than two pence per day. Although a spinner at a machine would produce ten times as much, with the machinery then existing, the difference in the cost of a hank of yarn was no more than a half-penny. On the other hand, Gill points out that a machine spinner was able to buy flax better than individual home workers, and that the yarn was generally sounder, and by trading in a wider market and giving credit, he was able to sell to better advantage.

The site of the spinning mill was Cooke's old bleach mill, and the whole of the water-power was concentrated on it, the lead to Patteson's mill being closed. Here the partners worked with a will, and by their enterprise created an industry which ranked, we believe, as the second largest in Ireland at one time. The water-power proving insufficient, steam was used to supplement it. The installation of a steam engine was, in itself, a note-worthy enterprise at that time, because no coal was then available, and the railway was not in existence. Turf was the only fuel available, and huge quantities were brought to the mill from the mountains, so much so that a system of tickets was instituted, the money being collected later by the turf men. The spinning mill was, no doubt, as profitable to the owners as it was beneficial to the workers who found employment there. Houses were built for the latter, one block on Chapel Hill beside the old Chapel, and another in Kirktown on the roadside below what was then known as "The Black Hill" in contradistinction to "The White Hill" on the other side of the road at the Rectory.

Although Mr Gunning was partner in the spinning mill, the property belonged to Mr. Thomas Adair, who inherited it under his father's will. Mr. Hugh Adair died in 1841, and in April 1842, we find Mr. Thomas Adair adding to it by taking a lease for 31 ½ acres, which included the land north of Patteson's strip in Sullenboy, and also on the other side of Cooke's lease, land where Glenavon residence was built, and in October of the same year he got a lease in perpetuity of 14 ½ acres in Kirktown, on the south of the river. Possibly it was the fact that the first-mentioned lease was terminable that made Mr. Adair, when the Killymoon property came into the market, decide to buy it out in fee, as he did, and not only it but the whole of Gortalowry and Loy, as well as Killymoon, Drumgarrel, Drumcraw and other townlands, re-selling to Mr. Mulholland except the portions of land in his own occupation, and extending along the river to Vance's corn mill, which was also included and became his property absolutely in 1855. At the same time, in 1851, he bought 17 acres belonging to Mr. Rowley Miller, which had been in Cooke's lease, and which lay between the Old Chapel Road and the river. In this way Mr. Adair consolidated his property on both sides of the river, with a title in perpetuity.

Mr. Thomas Adair died in 1868 and the business was continued with no less vigour by his three sons, Hugh, Thomas and John Adair. The latter two died unmarried, in the seventies, leaving Mr. Hugh Adair the sole owner. The business was, meantime, further developed. In 1874 the corn mill was converted into a weaving factory. The mill race was continued down to this place, on the Dungannon road just above Killymoon demesne, so as to utilize every drop of the power. It was run as a separate concern, known as The Water Power Co., the spinning mill being owned by Messrs. Thomas Adair & Co., while the finishing, which included beetling done at Greenvale as well as a mill at Slate Quarry, was owned by Messrs. Thomas Adair & Sons. The three were, in recent years, amalgamated in a private limited liability company with the title, Thomas Adair Ltd. A considerable addition to the firm's output took place in 1887 when Messrs. Adair bought a weaving factory at Limavady, which is managed from Cookstown.

It is impossible to trace the various additions to the works, made from time to time. A comparison of the Ordnance Maps of 1833 and of 1906 shows how the ground beside the river has since been built over. Even the river itself has been used, for in it was built a large cooling store where the yarn was left for a time after spinning. Then Mr. Hugh Adair crossed the river, when the ground on the north side became too congested, and erected a large store for flax, and more recently he built an addition containing an extensive dining hall for the use of the workers who lived too far off to go home for their meals, but which accommodation was not taken advantage of as fully as might have been expected.

The extent of which this industry grew can be gauged by the fact that, before the war, there were 785 individuals on the wages list. Of these, 450 were employed in the spinning mill, 130 in the weaving factory in Gortalowry and the same number at Limavady, and 75 were employed in the dyeing and finishing and merchant end of the business. The spinning mill is driven by two turbines, giving about 120 h.p. each, and this is supplemented by steam to about the same extent, the consumption of coal, for the whole of Messrs. Adair's works, when at full work, being up to 50 tons per week. The Water Power factory has also two turbines, with rather more power, the fall being a couple of feet more. A suction gas plant was also installed at the mill to help the steam and water, when this form of power became a practical proposition. At the finishing works considerable power is also required. Thus one machine, the hydraulic mangle, exerts a pressure of 100 tons on the cloth passing through it. The dyeing and finishing is probably the most interesting of all the departments to the non-technical spectator, and we hope, at a future date, to be able to describe the processes. In regard to the power required, it should also be mentioned that there are two beetling mills at work continuously at Greenvale, besides one at the Slate Quarry.

Unfortunately the slump, following the war, hit this spinning mill, as well as every other such mill in the country very seriously. About November 1922 it became impossible to continue working, and for the first time, so far as is known since it was started, the mill closed down. This was a great blow to the workers, numbering, as stated, over 400 persons. Those in the sixty odd houses owned by the firm lived rent free, and in other ways, at considerable expense (though the owners do not give any information on the subject), the workers were kept together during their enforced idleness. An attempt was afterwards made by Mr. Mc Cleary (who had re-opened Messrs. Hale & Martin's mill in Dungannon) to run Greenvale mill. A working arrangement was entered into with the owners, but after a year's trial it was found impossible to continue, and, at the moment, this fine mill, with all its equipment of machinery and power, is idle.

Several causes are responsible for this state of affairs. The most important is competition of foreign countries. In Belgium, for example, the hours are longer, and the wages lower, and in addition the rate of exchange is very low, making it difficult, if not impossible, for the home spinner to produce yarn at a competitive price. The price of flax is also relatively high, and moreover it is so scarce that if the home mills were all working there would not be enough to go round, as in pre-war times 75 per cent of the flax came from Russia, from which country present supplies are very uncertain. The railway freights are another adverse factor with mills away from the coast, and Greenvale is farther from the sea than any mill in Ireland. The late Mr. Hugh Adair asserted that it would pay to remove the mill to Belfast and use steam only, as the freight on flax and coal to Cookstown far more than outweighed the value of the water power. If that were so in his time, it is much more so since, as the railway rates have gone up. There is also, contributing to the depression in the linen trade, the decreased buying power of consumers all over the world.

In spite of these adverse factors, however, the weaving factories, both at Gortalowry and at Limavady, are now working full time, while last year, owing to the boom in coloured dress linens for the States, the finishing department was working overtime to make the most of it while the fashion lasted. It is to be hoped that before long the spinning mill may again be able to start, in the interests not only of the workers, but of the town generally.

Greenvale, it will be seen, has been a family concern for almost a century, ever since its evolution from two small bleach mills. As in most other Ulster linen industries, the staff, and many of the hands have been working there all their lives, the exception being in the outside representatives, or "travellers," who visit Great Britain and the United States to book orders. Since the death of the late Mr. Hugh Adair, the head of the firm has been Mr. John Adair, now of Glenavon, who served his time to the spinning end, and is assisted by his brother Mr. Louis N. Adair, who is one of the Directors of the firm and resides at Greenvale. Then there were Mr. J. W. Munnis, and the late Mr. W. A. Munnis, two brothers, who came to their uncle's place direct from school and worked there for over half a century. The secretary of Messrs. Adair Ltd., is Mr. Thomas Gibson who, though not so long with the firm, has been there all his business life, and his son Mr. Norman Gibson, after serving his apprenticeship in the Factory, was promoted to the managership, and latterly, owing to the death of Mr. Munnis, he has the oversight of the

Limavady factory also. In the finishing department Mr. James Forrest has spent his time since he joined as an apprentice. Mr. W. B. Baillie, who is the outside representative, and resides in Mesopotamia House, though not trained with the firm, may be mentioned as being a Director since the death of the late Mr. Munnis. Two recent additions to the staff also carry on the family traditions, for Mr. John Adair's two eldest sons have both started work in different departments. Of the workers, hundreds have found employment all their lives at Greenvale Works, the women being succeeded by their daughters and grandchildren, though we have not heard of any, except the owners, who have reached the fifth generation.

Next Week – Millburn Weaving Factory

-----------------------

# MILLBURN WORKS

## (24 – 10 – 1925)

Millburn Weaving Factory, owned by Messrs John Gunning & Sons, Ltd., has played an important part in the development of the northern end of the town. The artizans' houses in the Oldtown, as distinguished from the older thatched cottages, and also the better houses in Orritor Street, are directly due to the existence of the factory which provided the workers with the means of earning a livelihood and through them the factory has increased the general business of the town.

Owing to the serious fire which, besides other damage, destroyed the office in 1886, the firm's books and business records are not available before that day, to fix the date when it was established, but the stationery has always claimed that business was begun in the year 1854. There is a tradition, however, amongst the older workers, that the factory chimney was built at the same time as the Workhouse - that was in 1841, which is too early. In Slater's Directory of 1846, though it is very full, giving the linen manufacturers and linen merchants of the town and district, there is no mention of Millburn Works; in the same directory of 1856 there is an entry of "Moore & Smith (by power), Cookstown Factory." The Ordnance Map, revised in 1854, is even more convincing, for there is no trace of any building on it, so that when claiming that the business was established in 1854, the firm was going back to the earliest possible year.

In Griffith's Valuation of 1859, the Weaving Factory and manager's house, valued at £110 per annum, is given as "unoccupied", but the land, 9a 3r 15p, is shown as in the occupation of James Smith. The immediate lessors of the factory and land and eight labourers' houses, four of which were unfinished, were James Smith and James Moore. The lease, which is for 999 years, throws no more light on the date, as it is dated 1870, when Messrs. Gunning were the owners, and merely recites a former lease of 1868 which had been surrendered, but there is evidence, in a title action against Dr. D. H. Charles, who had diverted some water to irrigate his meadow in Coolreaghs, so that it flowed away towards the farm at Unagh, that in 1865 the Gunnings had acquired the property.

To Mr. James Smith must be given the credit of founding the business, which has meant so much to many in the Oldtown. He came from Rasharkin, Co. Antrim, and resided in the house on Loy Hill, now owned by Mr. Donnelly. Some of the older people still remember him as "Factory Smith".

The factory undoubtedly owed it existence to the sale of the Killymoon estate, and the purchase of the business end of the town by Messrs. Gunning & Moore. When Mr. Gunning acquired this property and decided to build a residence for himself, overlooking the town, it was but natural that he should think of a power weaving factory as one of the best ways of increasing the business and population of the town.

The site selected was on the side of the Burn, or Bourne, as the Ordnance Surveyors named it, and Mr. Commissioner Watkin wants us to revive. At this place it really is a boundary, but, as will be seen later on, the name "bourne", based on it being a boundary, would not be applicable. The site is in the townland of Cookstown, but the land between it and the county road, which is cut out bog, is in Maloon.

The stream, call it what we may, runs along the whole front of the factory and is widened out to form a pond, which, with the graceful swans swimming about on the water, and without any boundary wall to hide the building and the fields beyond, give a picturesque rural setting to this hive of industry.

Before crossing the bridge into the yard we may study the stream, which happens to have an historic interest far greater than may be imagined. It rises in the meadow lands of Coolreaghs, on the south side of the Lissan road. Most of our readers have heard of Shepperd's Well, on the roadside, which was taken under the charge of the Rural Council a good many years ago and covered over and a pump erected. Before the advent of the water supply from Montober the "Barrel Well", as it was named from the wooden barrel put in by way of lining, was the source from which many townspeople got their water, especially for washing, and several persons earned a livelihood by carting it into the town and selling it by the barrel.

Adjacent to the Barrel Well there is another good well, a short distance from the road, which also flows over in abundance, known on the O. S. Map as "McGeagh's Well", and behind is swampy ground where water could always be got with the least digging. It is the outcrop of what must be a very extensive strata of sand and gravel, supported on impervious clay. That it is extensive is proved by the fact that while the barrel well might be emptied by rapid lifting with buckets, it soon filled up again to the same level, and flowed away.

This raises the interesting question – where did this water flow to? The natural fall was into the stream which drains Coolreaghs meadows and forms the boundary between Coolreaghs and Killymam, flowing across the Orritor road at Maloon bridge and falling into the Ballinderry or Kildress river at the junction of Tullagh and Aughlish townlands. But at the uppermost point of the townland of Cookstown, just below the large springs referred to, the water is tapped by an artificial channel. This channel runs parallel to the natural stream, keeping to the higher level with little fall, till the river reaches Maloon and turns towards the west. The race, as it is sometimes called, goes in the opposite direction, turning at right angles to its previous course and, with hardly any fall for a distance, it is ultimately led to the factory.

Now, it will be asked, what is there unusual in all that? Every little scutch mill in the country has its race leading the water from a higher level to the mill wheel or turbine ; factories using steam power are commonly built alongside a stream, or, if there is no natural river, water is conveyed by a lead for steam purposes. But what makes this burn unique is that it is not a race at all, but an artificial aqueduct, and, this is the important fact, it existed before there was any factory there.

The original Ordnance Map shows this aqueduct, which is not a townland boundary until it almost reaches the old road by Morgan's Hill, and therefore has no right to be called a "bourne". Why and when was it constructed?

The answer to the first question is to be found in some of the old leases in William Street. In the oldest, for example of the land on which the Mail Office and adjacent houses are built, dated 1754, the site is defined as going back to the bog, but in rather later leases of the property south of above, dated 1774, the rere boundary is "the stream which supplies Cookstown with water". That stream is the aqueduct which was constructed from the point near the Barrel Well, as described, flowing past the factory. At the footpath to Orritor Street it had a branch which took it nearer the houses and thence behind the gardens to the Burn Road, and in living memory this was the stream which provided Cookstown, or the people in that end of the town, with water.

It is, therefore, perfectly certain that some time soon after Mr. Wm. Stewart laid out the present town, between 1750 and 1770, he met the need there was for water, so far as William Street and north of it, where the limestone is abundant, and wells, consequently, must be of very "hard" water, by going away up to the extreme edge of his property beside Coolreaghs (which was the Staples estate), and constructed an aqueduct to bring a supply of excellent "soft" water as near the new houses as the contour of the ground would allow.

It was beside this aqueduct, not a natural stream and not a lead of water for the purpose of the factory, that the latter was built in 1854.

## MILLBURN FACTORY (Continued)

## (31 – 10 – 1925)

Though the books of Messrs. John Gunning & Son were destroyed in the fire of 1886, so that no information is available from them, one book, belonging to Mr. James Smith, which had not passed into the possession of Messrs. Gunning, is extant. It is a Journal, in which all sorts of business entries from 1859 are entered. A large proportion of these relate to the flax seed trade, in which he seems to have engaged pretty extensively, importing Dutch seed and selling wholesale as well as retail, for there are entries of 20 empty hogsheads bought by Mr. Robert Hamilton at 16d each, as well as sales of seed to Mr. M'Guone of Pomeroy, for example. Mixed up with these are payments of 22s for poor-rate, which makes one long for that age of low rates, and the even more striking entry of 4s 8d for Income Tax, reminding us of the happy days of yore. Mr. Smith was a good Presbyterian, and not a member of the non-subscribing branch either, for he has noted subscriptions of £1 to Rev. H. B. Wilson for the mission collection, £1 to Rev. J. P Wilson for the Manse Fund, £1 to Rev. J. K. Leslie for some other collection, Stipend for Mrs. Smith to Rev. W. S. Ferguson, and even £1 for the

Scripture reader, and the same for Mr. Drummond, of Stirling, for the distribution of the "British Messenger".

But the most important pages of the Journal are at the beginning when Mr. Smith started to keep a record of his weavers. There were 48 all told, and their names, as no doubt the original workers at Millburn Factory, are worth recording. They are as follows, in the order given : -
*Matilda Porter, Sarah Kane, Jane Doris, Elizabeth Mc Ilvenny, Catherine Loughern, Kate Wilson, Margaret Steele, Sarah Allen, Mary Allen, Annie Kirk, Eliza Steenson, Rose A. Mayne, Rose A. Thompson, Catherine Thompson, Martha Gray, Mary Mc Gurke, Eliza Murray, Margaret Lecky, Mary A. Rooney, Mary A. Steenson, Isabella Madden, Catherine Mc Cabe, Mary Kane, Catherine Kirk, Mary Ryan, Rachel Morgone, Catherine Higgin, Mary Porter, Catherine Heggarty, Ann Ryans, Eliza Steenson, Sarah Mc Bride, Ellen Mc Bride, Margaret Wright, Sarah Toner, Catherine Toner, Sarah Ryans, Harriet Hamilton, Biddy Mc Connamay, Sarah Hutchinson, Susan Kigley, Matilda Falls, Annie Gorman, Margaret Smith, Eliza A. Kennedy, Rose A. Steenson, and Margaret Murray.* Of all these, the last survivor was Eliza Murray, whose death took place only a few years ago. These were the weavers on 18th August 1857. The Journal stops in 1863, six years after. The book was afterwards used by Mr. Jas. Leeper, who had purchased Wellbrook, for his own finishing business there, from 1863 till 1886, by which it is evident that a large amount of work was done for Messrs. John Gunning & Son.

Exactly when this firm became owners we have been unable to ascertain. Mr. John Gunning resided at Stranorlar, and was brother to Mr. James Gunning, who, with his brother-in-law, had bought the Cookstown estate in 1851, and he had acquired the weaving factory in partnership with his son, Mr. W. A. Gunning. The latter gentleman resided in Loy House during most of his life in Cookstown, and died in the eighties. In 1889 the owners of the business were Mr. Geo. D. Gunning and his brother, Mr. Francis P. Gunning, and they decided to convert the firm into a private limited liability company, and Mr. Wm. Leeper (eldest son of Mr. James Leeper, who died in 1886), came in as one of the directors, with a substantial holding of the capital of the new company. This he subsequently increased as opportunity afforded, buying the shares of the Messrs. Gunning, which family has long ceased to have any interest in the business, though it is continued, naturally, under the old name.

The original factory stood, as described, north of the Burn, on the boundary of the townland of Cookstown. It was extended at different periods, and, as it appears from the road, it is a long range of buildings, two stories high, which when lit up on a winter evening, gives a passerby the idea of a considerable industry. This, however, is merely the front;

behind there is the extensive weaving shed, one storey, with glazed roof, where the actual production of the cloth takes place. It is conveniently situated, the yard entrance being from the cross road leading to the Burn Road: a footpath goes more directly to Orritor Street and another road, the "Factory Lane" gives access directly to the Oldtown, where the bulk of the workers live, while those at the little group of houses on Morgan's Hill have a footpath there. A few of the workers live close to the works, in Factory Square, which consists of some 14 houses built adjacent to the weaving shed. These were the houses which were being built at the time of Griffith's valuation in 1858. The firm also owns 19 houses in the Oldtown, built before private enterprise stepped in to provide houses as the workers increased. Morgan's Hill, in the adjacent townland of Killyman, is so called because Mr. Wm. Morgan built a number of houses for factory workers there, on his farm of 15 acres, held in perpetuity with the houses at the corner of William Street and the Burn Road, and originally meant as accommodation land for the latter. When the Morgan property was in the market Mr. Leeper bought up this portion of it, making some 30 acres of land altogether around the factory.

In its early days the factory contained its own beetling mill, which was situated at the west side, but it was found that steam power was too expensive and could not compete with water-driven beetles, and about 1876 this department was closed, and the dozen or so of beetles were removed to Wellbrook, the space thus acquired being used to extend the bleaching and finishing works.

Damask linen is the chief product of the factory, or at least the one in which the firm takes most pride – the table linen with designs reflected by the light, which takes its name from the silk goods originally produced at Damascus. The design is produced by cards in the Jacquard loom, and the punching of these cards, so that the linen will reproduce the patterns made by the designer, is very interesting, though how the loom does it cannot be easily described in words, even if the writer understood it. Unfortunately the purchasing power of purchasers of damasks has been restricted in recent years, and even the plain linen – used for such household purposes as sheets, towelling, etc., besides ducks and twills are feeling the competition of cheaper fabrics, some of which are made of cotton and jute. Coupled with this is the increased cost of production, everything being about double the pre-war price, so that instead of the 400 hands who used to find employment at Millburn Factory, only about half that number are now working. The prospect of the linen trade is bad unless cheaper flax can be got and the only hope of that seems to be in drawing supplies from the group of republics which used to be in the Russian Empire, which have Riga as their chief port.

The selling organization of the firm is world-wide. For the home trade the firm is represented in London by Mr. Wm. Gilbert, who knows more about the firm than anyone else, having been connected with it for 60 years or so. The Continental market is limited, for it is from the Continent, with its cheaper labour, and now its low rate of exchange, that most of the competition comes. Abroad the firm has its agents in the United States and Canada, in Cuba, the Argentine and the South American States, customers in this order of importance. It has also agents in Australia, South Africa, China and the East Indies, to which goods are shipped.

Reference should be made to the motive power, which, as already indicated, is steam, generated, it is said, at first from turf and then coal, from Coalisland and elsewhere. The engine has 180 indicated horse-power, and is an object of pride, because it was installed 40 years ago, after the fire, and is running as smoothly now as on its first day. This is largely due to the care it has received from the driver James Burnett, who has lately retired after a lifetime with the firm. In this record of long service, however, he was eclipsed by the late James Dunbar, who had been 64 years working at Millburn Factory. Another long service is that of Samuel Smith, the foreman mechanic, who served his apprenticeship with the firm, and has the responsibility of keeping the machinery in good running order, which he has done most efficiently.

# NOTE

Since last week's instalment we have learned positively that Mr. James Moore (father of the late Mr. J. B. Gunning-Moore, D. L., and of the ladies who now own the town) was in partnership with Mr. James Smith as the original owners of the factory. We take it that Mr. Moore was a sleeping partner, probably supplying the bulk of the capital, or at least that Mr. Smith had the active management of the business.

# DRAPERSFIELD

## (21 – 11 – 1925)

"Owen Kilresse flu", as the baronial map of 1609 names the Kildress river, is joined by the Loughry river just below Killymoon Castle. Together they form, from this point, the Ballinderry river. Before it passes out of Killymoon demesne, as the traveller on the G. N. Railway may see, the water is held up by a weir to utilize the power for what is now Drapersfield Weaving Factory, which is situated less than two miles from Cookstown and may, therefore, be claimed as one of the industries associated with the town. The river at this point forms the boundary between Co. Tyrone and Co. Derry, on different estates, and it is, therefore, different from the water-powers already dealt with in these articles when one landlord owned both banks, and this, as we shall see, caused some complications which were, however, got over by enterprising captains of industry.

The first of those gentlemen who engaged in the development of this little industrial colony was Mr. John Maconchy. Of him we know very little beyond the name, but his tenure takes back the history of Drapersfield to a date now over 150 years ago. In the year 1772 he carried on a bleach-green there, as we know from an advertisement in the Newsletter of that date. This was in connection with the larcenies of cloth from greens, which was then a common offence in spite of the serious penalties – transportation for twenty years – there being no police force, as we know it, and the armed watchmen, if they failed to see the thief and shoot on sight, were of little use. The only hope of bringing an offender to justice was through an informer, and to encourage accomplices to give evidence, the bleachers of the three Dungannon baronies, offered a reward of £50 for a conviction and £5 for private information. Eleven bleachers undertook to pay the £50, each subscribing £4 11s as his share for every conviction, and John Maconchy was one of the eleven. The others, it may be here noted, were Duffin and Shaw, a Dungannon firm, George and William Anderson, Wm. Parke, Hugh Faulkner (of Wellbrook), James Greer, John Twigg, John Willcocks, John Cook (Gortalowry), Russell Patterson, do., and St. George Holmes. There were, of course, other small bleachers, and the fact that Maconchy was one of the eleven who was prepared to pay the reward for the conviction of linen thieves, indicates that he was in a fairly large way of business.

This bleach-green was on the Tyrone side of the river in the townland of Tullyveagh, where the ruins of the old bleach mill beside the flat field at Riverside may still be seen. Maconchy was probably the first bleacher there, for the system of bleachgreens - the first development of the home spinning and weaving, which had existed from the dawn of history, was not long before this time. Prior to that the weavers had to sell their webs unbleached, as brown linen; the greens provided them with the means of having it bleached before sale, but as the trade developed the bleachers bought the cloth from the weavers (who were poor men and required ready money, and could not afford to wait for months for a return for their work) and bleached it for themselves, generally finishing it in bleach mills. Maconchy does not appear to have been a native, as the name is quite unknown in any records we have met; he was probably an enterprising gentleman, with some capital, who, when this system came into vogue earlier in the century, settled in Tullyveagh as a suitable place to carry on the trade, as it had water-power for the mill and was in a district where there were many weavers to provide the cloth. In addition to Tullyveagh, Maconchy had leased 1a 36p in Doorless on the Lindesay estate, on the Tyrone side of the river, where his cloth mill appears to have been situated.

How long Maconchy ran the green we do not know, nor when he parted with the business, but his successor was a Francis Atkinson. He was in occupation of the Green in 1837, holding under a lease from the Rev. J. Jones, the chief tenant of the See of Armagh. The lease was for seven years, but was renewable as often as Jones got a renewal of the principal lease from the Primate, in the same way as the church lands of Cookstown were held by the Stewarts, who gave similar leases to their tenants. Atkinson held 22 ½ acres of land in Tullyveagh, and also 8 acres odd in Tivena, a total of 30 ½ acres of land, and by the terms of his lease he was required to have his corn ground at the mill of Edernagh or King's mill, with the usual penalty for default – 10s per barrel for all grain ground elsewhere.

Atkinson also got, under an agreement of 1776, the right to cut in the "flow bog" of Drumgarrell, as much turf as was required for the use of the bleach-green but for no other purpose. This is rather interesting, for it shows that at that date Drumgarrell was not included in Mr. Stewart's lease, though it afterwards was part of the Killymoon estate. Possibly it was when the change was made in the chief lease that the right to cut turf in Derrygonigan bog was substituted for Drumgarrell.

Rev. T. Jones exercised his right, under the Church Temporalities Act of William IV., to convert his leasehold into freehold, by paying the sum of £4,509 16s, leaving a rent of £245 13s 0d payable yearly, and his leasehold tenants had the option of paying their proportion of that amount and so securing perpetuity. The amount payable out of Atkinson's holdings was only £39 8s 8d, but he elected to pay, in lieu of that, interest to his landlord; leaving to his successors the right to convert the leasehold to freehold.

These successors were Robert Glasgow and James Wood. The former, who lived in Loy, had taken an active part in the life of Cookstown up to that time, and was, for a period, the tenant of the corn mill on the Killymoon estate, where the Water-power Weaving Co. now exists. In the directory of 1846 he appears as an "oatmeal merchant"; he was in this business on a large scale, and it was to hold oats and meal that the large stores, five stories high, were erected by him in his business premises in William Street, now Messrs. D. Anderson & Sons. These stores are, we think, the highest in Cookstown even now, and when erected they must have appeared as "sky-scrapers". This business was, of course, permanently crippled, if not killed, by Free Trade which admitted food stuffs free.

These two partners, Messrs. Glasgow & Wood, had already acquired an interest in the mill on the Co. Derry side of the river, in Cloghog, belonging to the Drapers Company. It was on this side that the water-power was developed, but when the mill was built we have not been able to ascertain. Prior to this time, however, the tenants had been Messrs. Anderson & Boyd, who had failed, and in 1837 Messrs. Glasgow & Wood had taken it over. The date is interesting for it will be remembered that in our Greenvale article we mentioned that the earliest balance sheet of Mr. Adair's spinning mill was 1837 and there is every reason to suppose that it was evident success of that venture - the conversion of Cooke's old bleach mill into a spinning mill, which made Mr. Robert Glasgow think of doing the same with the bleach mill at Cloghog.

The reports of the Drapers Co. Deputation, in November 1839, tell us that Messrs. Glasgow & Wood proposed to carry on the spinning of linen yarn *as extensively as the water-power will admit,* and appeared to be *preparing with great spirit to carry their intentions into effect.* Already the equipment of the mill was well forward, for the deputation, Messrs. Fourdrinier, Wrench, Potter and Lawford, visited the place and *minutely examined every part of the buildings and machinery, so far as the latter is complete, and conversed much, as well there as afterwards in Moneymore, with Messrs. Glasgow & Wood in reference to their plans, and the nature and extent of the assistance and countenance which they intimated they should hope to receive from the Court –* that is, from the Drapers Company. *They informed the deputation that the sum they were about to expend on the machinery required would not be less than £10,000, and they were, therefore, unwilling to expend on the buildings or repairs in question any part of the money which they would need for the more immediate purposes of their business.*

What they asked the Company to do, in addition to repairing the dwelling-house, offices, yards, walls and gates and erecting a further building was *to repair and heighten the weir to the extent of two feet or thereabouts.* They pointed out that *previous to their becoming possessed, as well of the lease of Cloghog, as of the mills on the opposite side of the stream* (both of which they now hold, and the latter in perpetuity), *the right to any portion of the water being brought to Cloughog was a matter of dispute, and very nearly one of litigation. Since, however, they have purchased the land on the other side, they have put an end to all dispute by using the waters only on the Cloughog side, the right to which they intimate, will be thereby effectually secured to the Company for ever afterwards, while, as they allege their property will be proportionately injured.*

This quotation from the Report of the Deputation shows that there had been mills on both sides of the river, on different properties. Mr. Glasgow was a shrewd, far-seeing man, and he came to the conclusion that the best thing to do was to secure the land on both sides of the river, so that no question of the water-rights could arise, and to get a permanent title from the Drapers Company. To him, therefore, is undoubtedly due the consolidation of the power, from a legal point of view.

Another consideration put forward by Messrs. Glasgow & Wood was *that the increased employment which the establishment of the factory will afford, will largely benefit a considerable portion of the Company's tenantry, and that the example will probably induce other capitalists to occupy other waterfalls on the estate.* That the mill or factory (the names were used indiscriminately at that time) did help the district is a matter of common knowledge, though possibly the owners of Killybearn got more benefit than the Drapers Company through the help which the industry afforded to tenants in paying their rents. The expectation that this example would lead to other waterfalls on the estate being used for the linen industry was not confirmed by the result.

The deputation seem to have been impressed with the outlook and had *no hesitation in warmly recommending these gentlemen and their undertaking to the favourable consideration and encouragement of the Court,* but were not prepared to state to what extent the Company should go in repairing the old buildings and erecting new ones: further than that an additional rent should be charged in proportion to the outlay. As to the weir, they recommended that *it would be just and expedient to raise it a foot and a half, or thereabouts* at the Company's expense.

The upshot of these negotiations was that in August 1842 "the Master and Wardens and Brethern and Sisters of the Guild or Fraternity of the Blessed Mary, the Virgin of the Mystery of Drapers of the City of London", to give the full title of the Drapers Co., gave a lease of 16 ½ acres of Cloghog, for 61 years to Messrs. Glasgow & Wood, and thus began the famous "Spinning Jenny" of Drapersfield, as the place was then named, for the first time.

Drapersfield, Cookstown.

## DRAPERSFIELD (Continued)

## (28 – 11 – 1925)

The partnership between Robert Glasgow and James Wood did not continue long, for we find that in 1850 a deed was executed dissolving it. Mr. Wood got, for his half share in the mill, the sum of £4,000, so that the estimate of about £10,000, to be spent in building the place, was not much of an exaggeration. Thenceafter Mr. Glasgow ran the mill without any help outside his own family, his two younger sons being associated with him, and at the same time they appear to have carried on the business of "drapers" – giving out yarn to be made into linen by hand-loom weavers. The office in Cookstown was behind what is now the Mid-Ulster Mail premises, and was used by the late Mr. Fred Harris, solicitor, as his office while he practised in Cookstown.

Robert Glasgow did not long survive the dissolution of the partnership, dying in 1856, as the family vault in Derryloran Old Churchyard shows. By his will, made shortly before his death, he left Drapersfield – that is, the property both in Tullyveagh and Clohog, the mill and its appurtenances - to his two younger sons, Benjamin and William, subject to adjustments which would make the share of each of the four sons equal. To the eldest son, John, he left his houses in Cookstown and land in Claggan, the latter being named in the Ordnance map "Glasgow's Hill", while to the second son, Robert James, he left his share in the townland of Lanaglug, near Ballinderry Bridge, and also Silver Hill, which he appears to have got with his wife, who was Miss George, of Coagh. To his widow he left a legacy in money. His son William did not marry, and died in January 1866, making his brother Benjamin his sole legatee, and that gentleman, who had married one of the daughters of Mr. Pike, of Derryvale, became the sole owner. But though regarded as a capable business man he was rather a financier than a manufacturer; at all events, it was not long after that that the spinning mill closed down, the machinery being taken out and sold and the place dismantled. Drapersfield House, however, the fine residence on the property, to which is attached quite a large farm, was used by the family: Wm. Glasgow (brother of Robert) lived there till the property changed hands, and he came to reside in Cookstown, where, in earlier life, he had carried on a successful drapery shop. He is still remembered as one of the Liberal stalwarts of the pre-Home Rule days.

Seven years after the death of Wm. Glasgow, junr., Drapersfield, as an industrial centre, took a new lease of life. The entire property, on both sides of the river, was purchased by Mr. Wm. Browne, a Belfast gentleman who had made good as a woollen merchant. He had been, we believe, in partnership with a Mr. Reid, and was also interested in the firm of Lindsay Bros. He was then advanced in years, but he was a man of not only business ability, but great energy and mechanical ingenuity. He proposed to re-start the place as a linen weaving factory, and was really the founder of the business still known as the Drapersfield Weaving Company.

The fall in the river is slight, though the volume is large, and to utilize the power to the fullest he put in a turbine, then rather a novel form of water-power engine. The power was supplemented with steam power, for use when the water was low, the chimney being the only sign to the passer-by on the Ardtrea road of the quite extensive factory which lies nestled in the hollow below the Red Bridge. The factory was managed by his youngest son, Mr. Graham Browne, who, on his marriage to Miss Hill, a Co. Antrim lady, resided in another residence known as Riverside, on the Tullyveagh or Tyrone side of the river. Mr. Wm. Browne resided in Drapersfield House, his wife being Miss Fleming, second daughter of Rev. Alex. Fleming, minister of First Cookstown Presbyterian Church. On the death of his father, Mr. Wm. Browne, junr., continued to reside in Drapersfield House, with his sister, and his elder brother Mr. John Browne, M.R.I.A.

Mr. Wm. Browne inherited much of his father's mechanical talent though not his business ability. Two of his enterprises may be mentioned; he started the old bleach mill on the Tullyveagh side, in partnership with William James Devlin, the famous and rather notorious flax merchant, to manufacture mail bagging from jute. Mr. Browne provided the capital and brains, Devlin looked after the financial side, and when he absconded, leaving so many creditors in Cookstown lamenting, Mr. Browne was one of his victims. His other enterprise at Drapersfield was the manufacture of a boiler lagging from silicate of cotton, which he invented, and which was really a good thing, had he been able to put it on the market. He, however, did not make a success of this commercially, and ultimately sold the patent to a Belfast firm, which is understood to have made a considerable sum out of the invention.

To return to Mr. Wm. Browne, sen. He had died at a very advanced age, in the year 1896. Only two years before his death he carried through fortunate negotiations with the Drapers Company, the owners of Clohog. The lease of the property to the Glasgows was for 61 years only, dating from 1836 and therefore would have expired in 1897, when the whole of the Clohog property on which many thousands of pounds had been spent, would have fallen in to the lessors. The lease, it may be mentioned, reserved to the Drapers Company all trees, and underwood, mines and quarries, as well as much less material things as hunting, hawking, fishing and fowling. It contained also the usual restrictive clauses prohibiting the removal of hay or straw off the land unless a corresponding quantity of burned lime was applied as a manure, the provision of horses and carts to repair roads, the limitation of the cropping by oats, and so on - provisions to ensure that the land would not be cropped out when the lease fell in, as well as the prohibition of the erection of cottier houses. Mr. Browne approached the Drapers Co. in view of the early fall of the lease, and, in 1894, he bought out the fee simple of the Clohog property, so that he became owner in perpetuity to lands and buildings on both sides of the river. He left the whole property to his daughter, who inherited her father's business shrewdness, and she, in turn, left it to the children of her brother William, the present owners in fee. The Tullyveagh part of the property, Riverside House and farm, was subsequently leased, and afterwards sold out to the late Mr. Alex Berkeley, and is now owned by Mr. Hogg.

# NOTE

Since last week we have learned, by the courtesy of the Librarian of the Drapers Company, who kindly had a search made in the records, that the first lease of Clohog, from the Company, was that of 2$^{nd}$ August 1842, taken by Messrs. Glasgow & Wood for 61 years. In February 1839, they had purchased the farm, mill and premises formerly occupied by Anderson & Boyd, who had failed, and known in 1845 as "Drapers Field Mill". They spent £2,316 on buildings and improvements, and as the water supply was inadequate, they purchased a steam engine, and spent £5,318 on machinery, according to the Company's minutes. The 61 years of the lease of 1842 ran from 1$^{st}$ November 1836, so that it was probably regarded as a continuation of a prior tenancy. The absence of any record of such an earlier tenancy is because that up till 1819, the estate was not administered directly by the Company, but was let as a whole, to middlemen, who "farmed" it, the last of these lessees being Sir Wm. Rowley, but as he could not give any better title than his own, and his lease expired in 1819, it is evident that Anderson & Boyd were merely yearly tenants and that Clohog was an ordinary holding, with a mill attached.

Another fact may be here noted. It is stated above that not long after the death of Mr. Glasgow, junr., the mill closed down. This is correct, but the Report of 1867 is more definite as it states that at that time it had closed – the year following the death of Mr. W. Glasgow - so that, for half-a-dozen years it was derelict until taken over by Mr. Wm. Browne.

# DRAPERSFIELD (Concluded)

## (5 – 12 – 1925)

The Clohog part of the property, which includes the factory, water power and Drapersfield House, was leased by the present Drapersfield Weaving Co. Ltd. – a private company formed by the Messrs. Gardner, who were also interested in the extensive Loop Bridge Weaving Co. Ltd., of Belfast. The factory was managed at first by the late Mr. Fred Gardner, but after a few years his brother, Mr. William Gardner, came to Drapersfield House, where he resided till his lamented death in March of last year, and where his widow and three daughters still reside. Mr. Gardner was a most energetic man, a kind employer, and a keen man of business, and it was largely due to his enterprise and to the fact that he was a director of Loop Bridge, of which Drapersfield Factory was really a branch, that the factory was able to keep going, affording remunerative employment to this industrial colony, when other weaving factories had had to close down. Fifteen months after his death, however, in June last, it also had to close. It has, however, been acquired by Sir William Brown, of the Larne Weaving Co., and there is every prospect that before long the looms will be once more at work as in Mr. Gardner's time. Most of the hands, we may say, are the daughters of small farmers, chiefly in Killybearn, where the farms are small. A number, however, reside in the Company's houses at or near the factory, Mr. Gardner having erected a row of ten houses on Sandy Road, and altogether the houses belonging to the Company number eighteen, and these workers will be available when the factory re-opens.

As we have said, the only indication of a factory, visible from the road to Ardtrea, is the chimney, which is 110 feet high. It is situated in the deep valley at the bottom of which the Ballinderry river flows, and the approach is from a side road which goes on to Killybearn. The entrance gates, at the left of which is the school, are at the top of a hill; to the right is the cart way to the factory, while the road drops straight down to the bridge across to Tullyveagh, from which a separate road on the Tyrone side leads out to the Ardtrea road. From the bridge the factory has an imposing appearance, with the broad river flowing alongside.

The masonry is all of red sandstone, obtained from a quarry just adjacent to the factory. The face of this quarry is exposed for a considerable distance; it is a rich red sandstone, in large blocks, dipping slightly towards the east, and entirely on the Tyrone side of the river, the Co. Derry side being flat ground. This quarry, if worked commercially for building material, would be valuable; the whole of the hill on which

Drapersfield House is built seems to be of this sandstone. Had the scheme put forward by the late Mr. John M'Nally, and supported before the Commission on Waterways by the late Mr. Gunning-Moore, to make the river navigable to Lough Neagh, been carried out, so that barges could go alongside, this stone could have been delivered to Belfast at a price which would have ensured a large and steady demand. The weir is just opposite the quarry, the race being cut out of the solid sandstone, and the material from it was used, when the race was deepened, for building at the factory.

The water-power is developed by a couple of turbines, which were put in by Mr. Gardner (the second to use the water-power for lighting the factory, as well as Drapersfield House with electric light), which replaced the turbine erected by Mr. Brown, and together they provide 111 horse-power on the seven foot of fall, when there is a good flow of water, and the steam engine gives 30 horse-power additional. The equipment of the factory is 148 looms, for plain linen, and twenty of these are being altered to weave towels, the work being in charge of Mr. John Arbuthnot, who is the mechanical brain of the place in which he has worked since 1878 and whose son, Mr. Wm. Brown Arbuthnot, is the manager of the factory, for which position he was being trained by the late Mr. Gardner at the time of his death.

This sketch of Drapersfield would be incomplete without some reference to the school, which is unique in our part of the country, in that it is for the children of the families working in the factory and belongs to the owners. The school house, as stated, stands just at the entrance gates on the road side. The earliest record of it, on the files of the Ministry of Education, is that it was built in 1858 by the Messrs. Glasgow – that is, two years after the death of Mr. Robert Glasgow. They paid the teacher and maintained the school for their workers, but in 1880 Mr. Brown got it under the Commissioners of National Education. At that time the teacher was Mr. Robert Fleming, and there were 42 children on the roll. Another teacher was Mr. Blair, father of the late Mr. David Blair, Cookstown. Subsequently Mrs. Arbuthnot came as teacher, and much of the success of the school is due to her. The Drapers Company gave a grant for it till they sold their estate; since then it has been entirely supported by the Drapersfield Weaving Company, except, of course, that the teacher's salary, and a small grant for cleaning and heating, has been paid by the Board, now the Ministry. Mr. Gardner was the manager till his death, and thanks to his generosity, it was well equipped, and the pupils included both Protestant and Catholic children, while religious instruction, on which so much emphasis is laid, was entirely omitted without any of the disastrous results which are assumed should result from purely secular teaching. Indeed, if the character of a community depends on the school training, Drapersfield school is a strong argument for purely secular teaching, for it is a model industrial settlement, and all parties live together on the best of terms. Since Mr Gardner's death the school has been managed by Mrs. Gardner, but we understand that it is likely to be one of the first in Magherafelt District which will be transferred to the Regional Committee.

Although the records with the Ministry go back only to the year 1858 there is a tradition that the school existed at an earlier period, and that the house on the Cookstown side of the gate, now a dwelling-house, was originally the school house. It is certain, indeed, that there was a school there very much earlier, for the Rev. Dr. Morgan. the founder of Fisherwick Place Presbyterian Church, in Belfast, mentions it in his "Life and Times". His father, as should have been mentioned in our first article on Drapersfield, when he first came to our district from Dublin, went to reside in Clohog and carried on the bleach-green for a number of years before finally settling in Cookstown to carry on the business of linen draper, in which business his wife's people, the Collinses, were engaged. Dr. Morgan recalls that at the beginning of the nineteenth century, when he was living in Clohog (the name "Drapersfield" is more recent), he went to a school there, the teacher of which was Arthur Devlin, who, it may be incidentally remarked, was a Roman Catholic. When he came into Cookstown, as a boy of 11 years old, the teacher of the school he attended – the forerunner of the Academy - was a member of the same church, proving that the Penal Laws, which are often represented as making the education of Catholics a crime, were not very effective in this district at least, and also proving that the education of boys by Roman Catholics did not, in any way, prevent one of them from becoming, what Dr. Morgan was, the most successful Presbyterian minister in Belfast. But that is by the way.

# LOUISVILLE

## (26 – 12 – 1925)

When giving the history of successful industrial enterprises connected with the staple trade of linen our record would be incomplete without some reference to one undertaking which has been a failure. This is the old mill in Gortalowry, which has been converted into tenements and is known by the name of Louisville..

The difficulty we have had at getting back to the origins of the other industries, due to the changes of ownership, and the fact that while leases, wills and other documents are registered or open to the historian, commercial and industrial enterprises, apart from the land on which they are situated, are not recorded in any official way, is accentuated in the case of this old mill. Another obstacle in the way is often the existence of incorrect tradition which, so far from helping, only serves to put one on the wrong scent, and this is the case, also, with the old mill.

It is, we are told, still known as Vance's mill, but so far as our research goes, this name is entirely wrong. John Vance was undoubtedly a corn-miller residing in the townland of Gortalowry. The rental prepared for the sale of the Killymoon estate shows that he held 6a 2r 16p of land in Gortalowry, together with 6a 2r 13p in Ardcumber, upon which was a valuable corn mill, the rent being £100 per annum. The lease was for 21 years, from May 1834, and therefore it expired in 1855 - four years after the sale of the estate. Vance, by the lease, was to be compensated for any additional buildings he erected, up to the value of £500.

This was the corn mill on the estate, at which all the tenants who held under old leases, were to get their grain ground, under a penalty of 10s per bushel. Vance had other property – a leasehold in Gortalowry for three lives or 31 years from 1826, at £5 19s 9d for 3r 15p, with 1s 5d per foot for any further houses; that is a frontage not built over, apparently in Killymoon Street, and a second lot of 2r 7p in Church Street, north of the church, under a similar lease, but not adjacent, all the intervening houses being held under annual tenancies. He had also property in Loy between Dr. Charles and John Molloy, with right to use of gateway, which we take to be Mr. John Doris' new property in James Street.

Vance was a man who had built a considerable number of houses, and was the corn miller on the estate, in 1851 certainly. The corn mill was driven by water-power, and we know definitely from existing deeds and maps that it was situated on the west side of the road at the bridge – that is to say, on the site now occupied by the Water-power Weaving Co. of Messrs. Thomas Adair, Ltd. The old mill we are at present concerned with is in a field on the other side of the road, entirely distinct. Though close to the river it has no power from it, the next weir being for the race in Killymoon.

Returning to the rental, there is no entry therein of any holding belonging to Vance other than those mentioned, none of which can be the field on the left-hand side of the road. The rental, however, does not stand alone; more important are the maps prepared by order of the Commissioners for the sale of Incumbered Estates, which show the boundaries of all the property in each lot, with the buildings thereon, and this map shows that at the date of the sale, the old mill did not exist.

This is a most important fact, for it proves conclusively that the origin of the mill was later than 1850, when the map was prepared. The place is in Lot 6, Gortalowry and Sullenboy, which was purchased first by Mr. Thos. Adair and most of which was re-sold to Mr. Andrew Mulholland, grandfather of the present Lord Dunleath, to whom it was conveyed directly by the court. The agent for the property, Mr. H. H. K. Worsley, has kindly had a search made for us as to its history since it came into that estate, and Vance's name does not appear at all as tenant. The conclusion is inevitable, that the name "Vance's mill", which might legitimately attach to the site of the weaving factory, has got transferred by oral tradition, to the building on the other side of the road, with which he never had any connection.

Turning to Griffith's Valuation, published in December 1859, we find that the lessee of what must be this property was Godfrey O. Lyle, who was, we think, agent for Mr. Mulholland, and resided in Loy. He had quite a number of holdings in his own name, including the whole of Coolnahavil, a small townland lying between Gortalowry and Killymoon Demesne. The last in the valuation list, next the water, that is the river, is 3 acres land, valued at £3, with buildings thereon, valued at £47, described as "house, offices, gatelodge, corn and flax mills and land", the occupier being John Lind. The gatelodge is the house just rebuilt which is occupied by Mr. Norman Gibson, manager of the weaving factory, and known as "Lind's Cottage", so that, as regards it, tradition is correct.

No doubt there is an interval of a few years between Griffith's Valuation and the rental and map of 1850, and it seemed possible that Vance, on the expiration of his lease in 1854, might have crossed the road and built a mill in the adjoining field. We have only one source of information regarding that intermediate period, but it is valuable - Slater's Directory for 1856, which also has the entry that Godfrey O. Lyle had "flax steeping works" in Gortalowry. It seems, therefore, very improbable that Vance could, from 1854 when his lease fell in, till 1856, when the directory was published (probably compiled in 1855) have had anything to do with the place.

We have to confess failure to find out anything about the flax steeping works which Mr. Lyle had in 1856. We know that, from time to time, numerous attempts have been made to carry out flax-steeping in a more industrial way than by the old system of open flax holes, and it is probable that Mr. Lyle, the new agent who had come to reside in Cookstown, attempted something of this sort. If so, like every such attempt up till date, it was not a commercial success, and as it does not appear in the Valuation list it appears to have been abandoned before 1859, when John Lind used the building for a corn and scutch mill, driven by steam power.

The subsequent history of the building, so far as the estate rental goes, is very simple. In 1865 Mr. John D. Cooper, the then owner of Killymoon, leased the old mill for 61 years. Mr Cooper parted with Killymoon, however, and ultimately the tenancy was determined in 1888. Three years afterwards Wm. Devlin took out a lease for 59 years. It was while he was lessee that another industry was started - making of nail bagging, the gentleman concerned being Mr. John M. Weir and Mr. John Robinson, who was one of Messrs. Adair's flax buyers. Devlin seems to have acted as manager of the concern, and it soon was in financial difficulties and came to an end, to the loss of Mr. Weir. The place, however, was used as a scutch mill for a time after that, but eventually closed down and was derelict for years.

At the creamery boom in 1898, the farmers around Cookstown thought it would make a good place for a co-operative creamery, and the Society took over Devlin's lease, and equipped the old mill for the purpose of a butter factory. At first it was a combined affair, between Cookstown and Tulnacross, but the farmers in the latter place decided, wisely as it turned out, that they would be better on their own and started a creamery at Doons. The Cookstown suppliers were, many of them, not dairy farmers at all, and after a short experience they were disillusioned as to the profits of butter-making, and the Society was wound up, the shareholders losing their money, being one of the first failures in the creamery movement.

The landlord again resumed possession of the place, the mill lying derelict till 1907, when the late Mr. Hugh Adair took it over on a lease for 999 years for his youngest son Mr. Louis Adair – hence the name Louisville, and converted it into tenements for the factory workers, for whom it has proved very convenient, and this ends the unfortunate career of the place. It has recently been connected with the town water supply, and the "gate lodge" has been rebuilt, as stated, as a residence for the manager of the factory.

## NOTE ON DRAPERSFIELD.

Since our article on Drapersfield appeared we have got a little more information about one of the activities of the place. We referred to the silicate of cotton which the late Mr. Wm. Browne, junr., invented and manufactured on the Tullyveagh side. He had also a scutch mill there, and the waste from the scotching was made into a coarse fabric such as is used for nail-bagging, and on the top of this the silicate of cotton was woven with fine wire, the completed article being excellent for lagging for boilers. The building in which this little industry was carried on was several stories high, and has since been pulled down. It was known locally as the Burn Mill, and the water-power (now all on the Co. Derry side of the river), was developed by a waterwheel. The scutch mill was burned down about 1882 or 1883, but was re-built, and fitted with a M'Adam turbine, and run by Mr. Graham Browne for re-scutching tow.

An interesting fact has been communicated to us with reference to Drapersfield in 1857-8. A map in the custody of the Drapers Co., of which we have got a tracing, shows that at that early date a gasometer was built to provide gas to light the factory. It was at the foot of the hill down the river. The road at that time also ran down direct to the factory, taking a double right-angle before it went to the bridge.

A question has been asked as to whether the water-power was first used on the Tyrone or on the Derry side of the river. There is no definite information on that point, but we are of opinion that it was simultaneous. Our view is that the sequence of events was as follows – Mr. Maconchy carried on a bleach-green in Tullyveagh from 1776, or perhaps earlier. In 1786 he decided to use the water-power of the river for a bleach-mill or beetling the cloth, for we know that in that year he leased, from Mr. Lindesay, a small bit of meadow, barely 2 acres in extent, in the townland of Doorless. It adjoins the land he had in Tullyveagh, and Cloghog is on the other side of the river. A weir was constructed from the corner of Doorless across to Cloghog, the latter being the property of the Drapers Company, and our reason for thinking that the water-power was developed on both sides at the same time is simply because it is extremely unlikely that the Drapers Co. lessee would allow a man on the other side of the river to divert the whole of the water-power. On the other hand, if some tenant of the Drapers Co. had already done so it is equally unlikely that the Company would have allowed Mr. Lindesay, or any tenant of his to tap their water. The lead on the Tyrone side ran round this little field in Doorless to the bleach-mill in Tullyveagh, and was obviously acquired for that purpose alone.

# KILLYBEARN

## (2 – 1 – 1926)

Travellers from Cookstown to Coagh cannot help but be struck by the landscape about a mile and a half from the former town. After passing the hill on which the old church of the parish of Drumca was situated the road drops down, and on both sides it is bounded by about as dismal a prospect as could be conceived, especially at this time of year, for it runs through what is left of Drumgarrel bog, cut out to the subsoil by the townspeople and others who got lots in perpetuity and left with treacherous holes which, even in the summer, requires care on the part of the sportsman who, with snipe and wild-duck, are the only frequenters thereof. The earthen mound on either side protects the traveller, but this ceases suddenly and the potholes in the road become painfully evident as a little stream is crossed, for we are now in Co. Derry and the townland of Killybearn.

Soon the road rises and turns to the right for a little as it surmounts the Dundering Rock, which, in the Isle of Man, for example, would be advertised as a natural feature to be seen by tourists, but is here of no account, and again the roads run through more bog now high up and through a deep cutting, a reminder of the days when Mr. Adair was Co. Surveyor, and still it is Killybearn, with Ballyloughan to the North.

Killybearn is not all like this waste land, however; to the south, bounding Cloghog, there is excellent light arable land, the sort which is in request by potato-growers - where farms in the boom following the war brought as fabulous prices as any in the whole country. But they lie away from the main road which was laid out originally through the boggy land, and so the impression which the tourist will get of Killybearn is the reverse of favourable. It is of the rather unusual history of this townland, since the Plantation three hundred years ago, that this article is devoted, as it throws some light on the general history of the country in the seventeenth century.

What was the appearance of Killybearn at the Plantation? It is impossible now to say with certainty, but we can form a very fair idea. It is certain that the bog holes which now exist along the roadside were very much fewer, if they existed at all. The probability, indeed, is that the bog was in its virgin state, at least level with the present county road, solid moorland covered with heather just as is the case in many parts of the country still, examples of which are familiar to local readers around Lough Fea and beyond. Our reason for this statement is that Killybearn occupied a central position. No one west or north of where Cookstown now stands would go there to cut turf, for there was an extensive bog in Loy, Maloon, and Tullagh.  Nor would any person have crossed the river at Derryloran to go to Killybearn for there was plenty of bog near at hand, and even in Gortalowry there was an extensive bog.  Again Drumcraw and Drumgarrel bogs lay to the west of Killybearn, Ballyloughan to the north, with Derrygonigan across the river, and even in the higher ground around Cloghog and Tyressan bog existed – the 7<sup>th</sup> hole of Killymoon Golf Links is at the bottom of a deep deposit of bog.  Killybearn, therefore, would be the last to be cut by outsiders, and we know positively that there was, long afterwards, practically no residents in the townland who required fuel.  It is, therefore, extremely probable that the whole of what is now cut-out bog was intact at the beginning of the 17<sup>th</sup> century.  Further we know that, in many more populous districts, what is now entirely arable land, was unfenced so that it is no flight of imagination to picture Killybearn, at the Plantation, as simply a level stretch of rough grazing land.  It's area of 417 acres also shows that, at the beginning of its existence as a townland or ballieboe, less than one fourth of it was regarded as capable of being ploughed at all.

Reference to a map of Tyrone will show that the townlands of Drumcraw and Drumgarrel stand out as projections into the adjoining county of Londonderry; likewise a map of the latter county shows that the townlands of Tyressan, Clohog and Killybearn project with Co. Tyrone.  These two projections are adjacent and overlap; the Killybearn group being cut off, as it were, from the rest of the county by Drumgarrel and Drumcraw which lie to the north, forming the most remote part of the Drapers Company's estate.

Killybearn is not, and has not been for three centuries, in the Drapers' Estate, but the Survey of Sir Thomas Phillips in 1622 shows that it then was the property of the Drapers Company under the name Killinbarny.  The names of townlands, it may be observed, were not fixed till the Ordnance Survey, less than a century ago, when the aliases were so numerous as to be puzzling, but there is no doubt of the identity of these two names.

We have mentioned that Drumgarrel lies north of Killybearn.  It, with Drumcraw and probably Tullygare, were church lands – that is they were herenagh lands which, after the flight of Hugh O'Neill, Earl of Tyrone, were the subject of Inquiries by jurors composed of native gentlemen who found that they did not belong to the Earl and therefore were not forfeited by his treason.  The King gave them to the bishops, and in this case to the Primate, as Archbishop of Armagh.  In the year 1614 the Primate let the lands on lease, with provision for building stone houses, etc., and the person who got the lease of this group was John Cornwall, the sheriff who then resided in Dungannon, the county town of

Tyrone. He subsequently sold to Jas. Stewart, of Ballymenagh, who had picked up a number of these small lots of church lands from the original lesses.

John Cornwall was, therefore, installed as lessee of these lands which project into Co. Derry, by the year 1616. Looking round his property he seems to have come to the conclusion that it was bounded by other lands in Tyrone, for the county boundary at this place is insignificant, running across country from the Killymoon to the Lissan river. Cornwall, perhaps not unnaturally, assumed that the boundary ran up the Ballinderry to about Littlebridge, or where the Lissan river joins the larger stream and that the boundary followed the line of the Lissan river all the way. If that were so, all the land from Ballygoney west of the river was in Tyrone, and so he and a Lewys Price got a grant of 6 ½ townlands. The names are difficult to identify, but Killybearn is undoubtedly "Kilbanny", while Ballaloghan, Tyressan, Clohogn, Tawnaghmore, Donnemane and Lismoney are clear, if the aliases given are ignored.

Our legal readers will want to know what was the upshot of this double ownership. The matter was complicated by the fact that in 1619 Killybearn (as well as Ballygoney) became Crown freeholds. When English law superseded the old Brehon law at the Plantation, freeholders were required to serve as jurors and carry on the civil administration. In Tyrone there was no difficulty; there were numerous freeholders, for every "undertaker" had to create a number on his estate, and there were also the native gentlemen who had got grants of all the land south of the church lands of Cookstown – from Loy to Killymoon. But in Co. Londonderry it was different. The land had been granted to the Irish Society on behalf of the London companies who subscribed to the Plantation, and these companies had no power to grant lands in fee. The consequence was that the difficulty of getting freeholders was so great that, in each of the twelve estates in the county, six townlands were picked out and taken from the companies to become Crown freeholds.

The gentleman who was selected as a freeholder for Killybearn, paying a Crown rent of 10s a year for the lands, was George St. Laurence, a younger son of Nicholas St. Laurence, of Garrestown, Co. Dublin, and a relative of Lord Howth. He resided at Wyanstown, Co. Dublin, and was married to Mary Preston, daughter of James Preston, Ballinadoyne, Dublin, and a suitable man to take part in the government of the newly planted counties in those days. But Cornwall and Price had taken out patents of their title and were not to be lightly disturbed. To the Drapers Company the task of dispossessing them fell, and no doubt on legal advice, they compromised the matter by paying Cornwall and Price the sum of £100 in full satisfaction of their claims.

# KILLYBEARN (Continued)

## (9 – 1 – 1926)

When the Irish Society, in 1619, set apart on each of the twelve estates granted to the London Companies, six "good large townlands" which were to be given to "men of good rank and quality, to serve at Assizes and Sessions", the townland of Killybearn was selected as one of the townlands and it was allocated to George St. Laurence, of Wyanstown, County Dublin. It was a post rather than a property, for it entailed duties which were paid for by what rent he could get for the land from tenants. It seems to have been let to different persons for outlying grazing.

A Chancery action brought in 1632 by George St. Laurence against Sir Thomas Staples, Bart., who was married to the only daughter of Sir Baptist Jones, Bellaghy, who was for a time agent for the lessee of the Drapers' estate, throws some light on the value of the land, and the loose arrangements existing generally. Robert Harrington of the Mough, Co. Londonderry, wherever that may be, was joined as defendant, and is described also as agent. The action was to recover from the defendants the rent of Killybearn from July 1619. The plaintiff's case was that the Irish Society granted him the fee, for ever, at the rent of 10s a year and nominated Tristram Beresford, of Coleraine, or Robert Gardiner, of Londonderry, to give possession, and they gave the Deed to Sir Baptist Jones, who was then in London, to deliver to St. Laurence who was in Ireland. He alleged that for the first 5½ years Sir Thomas Staples collected the rents, amounting to £100, and in the following two years £30 more.

The defendant, Harrington, in his reply, admits that as agent for the Drapers Company, he received 1½ years rent of Killybearn, amounting to £12 only - £8 per annum. Harrington further stated that the Deed was not signed by St. Laurence till about seven years after it was executed, and that he helped the plaintiff, which statement the latter denied, and the court gave a decree for £12, which Harrington admitted. The court also ordered that St. Laurence was to have quiet possession, from which it appears that his title was questioned. No order seems to have been made against Sir Thomas Staples, the real defendant being Harrington.

It is probable that George St. Laurence, being selected in 1619 as a freeholder to serve on juries, was a Protestant, but that is not certain. His name appears in an indictment for treason in 1641, and he is there described as of Wyanstown, so that he was an absentee owner. He died in 1650 and the property passed to his son Thomas, who died about 5 years after. The latter had married Mary Dowdall, a lady belonging to an influential "native" family. Geo. Dowdall, of Dungannon, had received, at the Plantation, the townland of Maloon, adjacent to Cookstown, and his name appears as a juryman at Chancery Inquisitions up to 1639, along with such men as John Cornwall, the owner of Drumgarrell, etc.; Thos. Goodlitte and Neal boy O'Hagan, of Tullyhog; George Stewart, of Carnteal; Philim O'Mallen, of Derriloran; Wm. Tate, of Orator; James Carlisle, of Creevagh. Two other Dowdalls also appear as jurymen – James and John, of Castlecaulfield, but which, if any, of these native landowners was the father of Mary Dowall we cannot say. She was left a widow with three young children in the troublesome times of the civil war which began in 1641. The youngest child was a boy, Patrick, who succeeded to his father's property. It appeared, from the evidence of his brother-in-law Alexander Brennagh or Walsh, of Moneymore, that Patrick was born about 1658, but Ensign Downing puts his birth earlier. Another witness says definitely that Patrick was born in 1655.

His mother, the widow of Robert St. Laurence, re-married immediately when the children were young, her second husband being Redmond O'Mellon, a family name from whom it is believed the name of the territory, Mallonagh, is derived. On the marriage the young St. Laurence, who would then be about 3 years of age, was taken by his grandmother, Mrs George St. Laurence, nee Preston, and was brought up as a Protestant, and while yet a young man he married a daughter of Robert Downing, of Moneymore, a gentleman who appears to have acted as agent for Lady Clotworthy, whose late husband was the lessee of the Drapers' estate. We may anticipate by saying that the present owner of Killybearn is Colonel J. G. Downing, but it does not appear that it is anything but a coincidence that the name of Patrick St. Laurence's bride of 1680 was the same name.

Now another strange event in the story of Killybearn took place. Following the rebellion of 1641, when this district was the cock-pit of Ulster, and apart from massacres and robberies, four independent armies were fighting each other in different combinations, a place like Killybearn was of no value, for cattle grazing there were liable to be driven off by the first force that came along to supply food for the soldiery. As well, almost, might a farmer expect a profit from his holding in "No man's land" during the great war – Killybearn was a No man's land from 1641 for many years. As stated, Geo. St. Laurence had been indicted for treason at the very beginning of the rebellion, and his son Thomas was no better, but that did not justify Major Sir James Clotworthy, of Moneymore, in taking possession of Killybearn as he did when things began to settle down in 1649. He quietly set the land to Oliver Purvis, of Derrygonigan, and his partner, Adam M'Culla, at £15 8s per annum. Oliver Purvis' name, it may be noted, appears in the Hearth Money Roll as resident in Killybearn in 1663, and in the Subsidy Roll of 1665, so that he had gone to reside somewhere in the townland.

Sir James Clotworthy died, and his wife, Lady Mary Clotworthy, kept possession of Killybearn even during the lifetime of Thomas St. Laurence, the real owner. Soon after the Restoration, however, when the country enjoyed a measure of settled government again, legal proceedings were begun on behalf of young St. Laurence against Lady Clotworthy. In 1668 John Barker, who had got a lease from Patrick St. Laurence and his mother, and the latter's husband Redmond O'Mellon began an action on the title. The action was tried at Londonderry and judgment was given for the plaintiffs who got possession from the sheriff. Barker may have been the previous lessee of the Drapers' Estate and took this method of revenge on the Clotworthys who had outbid him when his lease fell in – but that is only speculation.

The next step was an action by Patrick St. Laurence, his mother and step-father against Lady Clotworthy, to make her account for the rents she, with her late husband, had unlawfully received through her agent Robert Downing. O'Mellon was undoubtedly the moving spirit in these proceedings, for St. Laurence was only a boy of 10 years of age, or thereabouts at the time. O'Mellon had been made guardian of the boy with the consent of his mother, Lord Howth and other relatives. The plaintiffs alleged that the Clotworthys had the land for 20 years or so, and that they received £20 a year rent, and were due £400. Lady Clotworthy admitted liability and offered £80. The court gave judgement, but we are unable to say for what amount.

Law is an expensive luxury even now, and it was more so in the seventeenth century. O'Mellon was financing the proceedings, and to do so he had to borrow money, including £60 from Wm. Bears, of Co. Down. To protect himself he got a bond from Patrick St. Laurence, in 1672 (though if the dates are correct he was then a minor), for £100, but he said that the lawsuit, which had taken seven years to recover possession of the land, cost him £200. Apparently he was sticking to the rents he had got from Lady Clotworthy and the costs, for in January 1682, St. Laurence launched a suit in Chancery against his step-father Redmond O'Mellon, to get possession of Killybearn. The latter replied by a counter-suit in October of the same year, in which the defendants were Patrick St. Laurence, his father-in-law, Robert Downing of Moneymore, and a kinsman, George Johnston of Cookstown. From the documents relating to this lawsuit, which were extant till the burning of the Four Courts, we learn a good deal about the story of Killybearn. O'Mellon described the eviction of Thomas St. Laurence, "at the time of the usurpation" and his subsequent death, leaving a widow and small children which he, O'Mellon, her second husband, had to support.  He proceeded to say that the equity suit for the recovery of Killybearn for Patrick occupied seven years, at a cost of £200, portion of which he had to borrow.  He added that in October 1672 - that is ten years before those proceedings – St. Laurence and he agreed to refer their accounts to arbitrators, who found that St. Laurence owed him (O'Mellon) £140, and ordered that he get a mortgage for £100 on half of Killybearn, which St. Laurence executed.  He now complained that Downing, described as St. Laurence's lessee, had brought an ejectment against him.

It is interesting to note who were the two arbitrators who were called in to settle this dispute.  St. Laurence, perhaps through his father-in-law, Robert Downing, who had obviously leased Killybearn in order to get a status in ejecting O'Mellon, nominated Mr. Thomas Morris, of "Belville", which we believe is the place now named Bellmount belonging to Mr. Fox.  He was son of Captain John Morris, and brother of the Rev. John Morris, rector of Kildress and of Desertcreat.    As Churchwarden of Clonoe parish he was responsible for re-building the church there, as an inscription inside the porch shows, with his coat of arms, etc.  He was, in fact, one of the most influential gentlemen in the district at the time, and the fact that he consented to act as arbitrator for St. Laurence indicates the social position of the latter.    The other arbitrator was even more remarkable, for O'Mellon nominated Captain Robert Stewart, of Eary, the ancestor of the Earls of Castlestewart, whose father, Col. Robert Stewart, had taken such a prominent part in the Civil War following the rebellion.

The outcome of this lawsuit was that Robert Downing got his ejectment in the Common Pleas, and though O'Mellon applied for and got an injunction in Chancery to stay the proceedings, the Sheriff evicted him, which resulted in further proceedings for contempt of court, which dragged on till 1684.  In the latter year an interesting deposition was made by Ensign Robert Downing of Moyagall, who appears to be identical with St. Laurence's father-in-law.  He stated that he was 56 years of age and knew George St. Laurence (the original freeholder), his son and grandson, and adds that when O'Mellon sued Lady Clotworthy for the rents received from Killybearn, he (Downing) paid £20 on her behalf, and that O'Mellon let Killybearn for three years at £20 a year.  He adds that Sir Arthur Chichester told him that Patrick St. Laurence was 15 years old when O'Mellon got possession of Killybearn, and also that Henry Varnett, of Moneymore, told him that he held half of Killybearn in 1620 from George St. Laurence, at £11 or £12 rent.  As the fee farm grant was in 1619 Varnett was, therefore, the first tenant of Killybearn.

Another witness in the 1684 lawsuit was Neill M'Gilmurray, of Lisnaskea, who said he was born in Killybearn seven years before the rebellion and knew the three generations of St. Laurence. He fixes the birth of Patrick at 1655, and says that Robert, at the time of his death, owned 6 or 7 cows and a dozen sheep. He also adds the illuminating statement that when O'Mellon, as guardian of Patrick St. Laurence, started the lawsuit against Lady Clotworthy, he subscribed half-a-crown towards the costs. We may, therefore, take it that this lawsuit to restore Patrick St. Laurence to his lands, was a popular movement, though 2s 6d would go a short way to pay a Chancery lawsuit over seven years.

Another witness, in 1684, was Patrick's sister Ann, who was married to Alex Brennagh or Walsh, of Moneymore. She said that her father Thomas, when he died, owned 8 cows and three calves, and that Patrick was maintained by his grandmother after his mother's re-marriage, till witness got married when she paid for his schooling. This deposition, of course, was to rebut O'Mellon's counter-claim for maintenance of his step-son, and to show that he got a certain amount of stock when he married Robert St. Laurence's widow. The weak point in Mrs. Walsh's evidence is her statement that she was 30 years of age, for she admits that she just remembered her grand-father George St. Laurence. She was probably forty, or more.

The upshot of this law seems to have been that Patrick St. Laurence became the legal owner once more of Killybearn. But the lawsuit had crippled him financially and he mortgaged half of the townland (which it should be noticed was subject to divisions of this sort without boundaries being stated) to his kinsman Adam Downing about the year 1690. He had a son named Thomas, also a daughter Elizabeth, who married James Mason, of Stewartstown, and afterwards of Cabra, Co. Monaghan, when, in the year 1733, we find her father Patrick residing with her.

## KILLYBEARN (Continued)

## (23 – 1 – 1926)

The next record of this interesting family and their connection with Killybearn is in the 18th century. Thomas St. Laurence, in 1709, married Jane, the daughter of James Hegan, of Drumard, in Lissan Parish. His father Patrick was then living, but apparently had decided to provide for his son, and gave him a quarter of Killybearn, for he settled on his wife the quarter of Killybearn then in his own possession, and also the reversion of the quarter which he would inherit from his father Patrick. He also settled some leasehold lands held from Joshua Dawson, but we are not interested in that. The witnesses to the marriage settlement were Rev. John Farquhar of Lissan, Walter Johnston of Moneymore, and Adam Burkhead.

This deed of settlement, although executed in 1708 was not registered till 1723. In Oct. 1723, St. Laurence agreed to sell to Henry Downing, of Rocktown, that half of Killybearn containing 90 acres, by estimation, not formerly sold to Adam Downing, of Rocktown. That would have been all right if Mrs. St. Laurence had been a party to the sale, but she apparently objected, for in January 1724-25, she brought a Chancery Bill to set aside the sale on the ground that the lands were settled on her. She had borne her husband a family of seven – at least there were seven living, four boys and three girls, all minors, and Adam Burkhead, as a relative of their mother, joined in the action on their behalf, the defendants being Thomas St. Laurence and Henry Downing. The Bill recited that Downing was a relative of Thomas St. Laurence, and that the latter had sold him half of Killybearn for £67 though it was worth £100, and also in spite of the fact that he had no power to sell land settled on his wife. We have not been able to ascertain what the result was, but in 1774 Henry Downing's niece sold one-third of Killybearn to Dawson Downing, of Rowesgift, and possibly there was a compromise by which Thomas' wife and family got the difference between the half and the third. His grandson subsequently dealt with one-eighth, as mentioned further on.

Patrick again appears on the records as dealing with his property in Killybearn. As stated he was living at Cabra with his daughter Mrs. Mason. It appears that her husband, James Mason, described as a linen draper, of Stewartstown, was to get a fortune of £400 with her, but the money never was paid, and in May 1732, he began steps to protect himself. Accordingly we find that at that date Patrick St. Laurence, in lieu of the £400, conveyed to Mason his "eastern half of Killybearn, being 100 acres plantation measure by estimation". This is the first indication of how the fractions of Killybearn were described.

The assignment was registered promptly, in eleven days, which suggests urgency. But it was (and still is) one thing to convey property by deed and another to give actual possession, for it appeared that John Downing was in occupation and would not give it up. Mason, therefore, launches an action in the Court of Exchequer, and names as defendants his father-in-law Patrick, his brother-in-law Thos. John Downing, the purchaser, and also Henry Downing and John Harris, described as "confederates". Harris resided in Tevena, and his share in the business seems to have been that he financed Thomas St. Laurence to the extent of £80, which he lent on a note in May 1734, at Dublin – probably to pay the lawyers – and for the recovery of which he got judgment in April 1735. George St. Laurence, eldest son of Thomas, had also signed the note.

We now part with Patrick and his son Thomas, and go to the next generation. George was the eldest of the four sons of Thomas and he married Agnes Espy. He did not settle any land on her, but in 1763 he assigned to her one eighth part of half of Killybearn, being 13 acres plantation measure. She was to hold this fraction of Killybearn during her widowhood, and afterwards it was to go to her eldest son Daniel, the names of the other children being George, Thomas, Jane, Mary and Agnes. The assignment was witnessed by Robert Espy and Robert Cluff, both of Cookstown, and Wm. Oliver of Dublin, a local solicitor, though described as "of Dublin".

There is only one further reference on record to the St. Laurences in connection with Killybearn, but it is the strangest of the lot. At the Spring Assizes for the City and County of Londonderry, held on 26th March 1774, there was an indictment for murder against several of the family – George St. Laurence, the elder; Ann, George, the younger, and Mary St. Laurence, all of Killybearn, and Ann, the younger. As they did not appear to stand their trial a bench warrant was issued for their arrest, but no record can be found of a subsequent trial. The fact that they had been on bail suggests that whatever occurred cannot have been regarded at the first as murder, otherwise they would have been in custody. The probability is that a row occurred and someone who was injured had died subsequently, and the Crown thereupon entered the capital charge.

What became of the St. Laurences? We may take it that George, who had inherited half of Killybearn, and assigned an eighth of it to his wife for life and then to his son Daniel, had gone abroad with his son George, junr., after the tragedy of 1774. He had, however, three brothers, Robert, Daniel and Henry, and in 1766 there were three Protestant leaseholders returned by the rector as then living in Killybearn, named George, Henry and Patrick, all of whom had disappeared from the parish before 1821. These junior sons, and their descendants, were presumably farmers only, not owning the freehold, and they must have sold out and left their holdings. George has also two sons, Daniel and Thomas, who were not implicated in the charge of 1774.

Now there were, in 1816, residing in Cookstown two old unmarried men named Thomas and Daniel St. Laurence. They had rented the hill at Greenvale opposite the cemetery and bounded by the river, which, in 1780, was leased by Colonel Stewart to James Cooke, whose interest was afterwards purchased by Hugh Adair in 1832. Tradition has it that these were the last male members of the family who had owned Killybearn, and the facts ascertainable from the public records go to confirm their identity with the two sons of George St. Laurence. If so, they must have left Killybearn before 1780 – considerably before that date, in all probability because Cooke's lease describes this land as "formerly in the possession of St. Laurence", as if the Christian name of the tenant had been forgotten, or perhaps it was uncertain which of them was actually the tenant in the rent book, and as they were mentioned only to identify the land the full name was immaterial. As the date of this lease, 1780, was only six years after the tragedy, and they were not implicated in the wholesale charge against the family, it is possible that these two sons had left Killybearn earlier than that date, and may have been engaged in the linen industry of the time, though there is no evidence in support of this, further than the fact that subsequently the land they rented was used for a bleach green.

A strong point in favour of the identity of these men with the son of George St. Laurence and his wife, whose maiden name was Espy, is that Thomas appointed a Hugh Espy, of Cookstown, as one of the executors of his will. This document, however, raises a difficulty, in this way. Thomas left the household goods to his brother Daniel, and also the interest of £100 deposited with Colonel Stewart for life. This deposit is, in itself, interesting, because it is extremely unlikely that Colonel James Stewart, in 1816, when enjoying a huge rent roll not only from the local estate but from ground rents in Dublin, so that he was able to spend £80,000 on building the Castle just then, would have borrowed such a sum; it seems more probable that he had agreed to hold the money for an acquaintance at a time when there were no local banks. However, at Daniel's death, the £100 was to go to his sister, Mrs. Nancy Howard, who we may mention, was grand-mother of the late James Howard, of Loy, and the same sister got the residue of Thomas' property, while another sister, Mrs. Mary Downing, got a legacy of £20.

The difficulty is this – the assignment by George St. Laurence, in 1763, gave the names of the children, and none of them were named Nancy. She may have been born later, or she may be identical with the "Agnes" then mentioned. Though the latter is unlikely, on the face of it, yet such changes of Christian names are not unknown, and if this can be assumed it would clear up another matter in connection with the charge in 1774, for the names in the warrant would then be those of the father and mother, one son and two daughters. Moreover, the fact that the latter were afterwards married and living in the district, goes far to indicate that the charge was exaggerated, or that, so far as the female members of the family were concerned, it was groundless.

# KILLYBEARN (Concluded)

## (30 – 1 – 1926)

The present owner of the whole of Killybearn, which is one of the "Unbought" estates, is Colonel J. G. Downing, of Kingstown-on-Thames, whose family formerly resided at Rowesgift, near Bellaghy, in which district they had a considerable estate. Col. Downing has given the present writer every possible assistance in exploring the interesting story of Killybearn, and it is to him that we owe the information about the tragedy of 1774, he having the original bench warrant for the arrest of the St. Laurences. It is a significant fact that the earliest deed of the land of Killybearn now extant dates from 18th October 1774. It is a conveyance of one-third part of Killybearn from a niece of Henry Downing, of Dublin, to William Cooke Downing, who, with his wife Ann, and Miss Margaret Downing (daughter of the Rev. Wm. Downing, of Derry), conveyed the lands in 1776 to Dawson Downing, of Rowesgift, ancestor of the present owner. Henry Downing of Dublin, is mentioned as the owner of half of Killybearn in 1760 when he leased it, for 21 years, to Robert and Thomas Espy. This lease was proved in Cookstown by James Espy, aged 30, before Wm. Oliver, Commissioner for Oaths; Hugh Stewart and Wm. Stewart, justices, in January 1766. It is very probable that the tragedy of 1774 may have arisen out of a dispute by George St. Laurence in regard to this part of Killybearn, as the boundaries did not appear to have been defined.

Although, so far as Col. Downing's deeds go, the title began in 1774, the date of the tragedy, but later in the year, and this relates to one-third of the townland only, it is evident from our story that, long before this, fractions of Killybearn had been passing to the Downing family, and this was probably the last third. It seems hopeless to attempt to disentangle this relationship of the Downings and the St. Laurences, commencing, as we have seen, at the time of the Commonwealth, when Robert Downing, agent for Lady Clotworthy, gave his daughter to young Patrick St. Laurence when he had successfully maintained his right to the lands taken during the Civil War from his father by Lady Clotworthy's husband, down to 1816, when we find that one of the daughters of George St. Laurence was married to a Downing, and with several intermediate transfers between the male members of the two families.

The Downing family were connected with Bellaghy district – the parish of Ballyscullion, from early in the 17th century. The first known member of it was Nicholas Downing, who was buried in the old graveyard on Church Island in Lough Beg. Possibly the Robert Downing mentioned was his son; he had also a famous nephew, Adam Downing, ancestor of the present owner, whose vault is in Bellaghy Churchyard. It is of him that the Rev. John Graham writes, in his "Catalogue" describing, in the manner of Homer's Iliad, the defence of Derry in 1688.

> *From Charlemont came Caulfield's corps,*
> *Chichester from Dungannon,*
> *With many more, who from Dromore,*
> *Escaped King James' cannon;*
> *Porter strong, Leslie and Long,*
> *Macartney and brave Downing.*

"Brave Downing" was a man of sufficient influence and importance to be able to raise a company of men which took part in the Battle of the Boyne, which completed the route of King James. He was afterwards appointed as one of the Commissioners of the Army and subsequently made Lieut.-Colonel of the Militia Dragoons and, in 1715, when the Stuarts again became troublesome in Scotland, he was appointed a Deputy Governor of Co. Londonderry. His son, John Downing, emulated his father's loyalty and patriotism by raising another independent company in 1745, in defence of King and country. There is a letter at Springhill from Lord Chesterfield to Col. George Conyngham, the deputy governor of the county, asking him to call up the militia for training and asking him to give the names of gentlemen in Loughinsholin barony fit to be Commissioners of the Army, and Col. Conyngham has noted on it the names of John Downing, Abraham Hamilton, John Mauleverer, Wm. Ash Rainey, Hugh Miller and --- Gamble, so that John Downing may be taken as one of the six most competent men in the barony at that time, in the opinion of the founder of Coagh. We may add that he married Ann, daughter of the Rev. Simon Rowe, rector of Bellaghy, and her father gave, as a dowry, the residence known as "Rowesgift" – a name which explains itself. His son (or grandson), Dawson Downing, died in 1807, and is buried in Bellaghy.

It was Colonel Adam Downing, of Derry and the Boyne fame, that is referred to in the deed of 1723, as having formerly bought half of Killybearn, the other half, by this deed, being sold to Henry Downing, of Rocktown. The latter sale was upset because Thomas St. Laurence had settled the lands on his wife Jane O'Hagan, of Lissan, but the sale to Col. Adam Downing was not questioned, and the purchase, in 1776 by Dawson Downing (Col. Adam Downing's descendant), of what is described as a "third" of Killybearn, probably made up, with Daniel St. Laurence's eight parts, the whole of the townland. In the year 1779, however, John Downing, of Rowesgift (contracted into Rosegift even then) was the owner of half of Killybearn, which, with other lands, he settled on his bride, Mary O'Neill, of Coleraine, and from a mortgage in 1815, it appears that John was son of Dawson Downing, and in 1814 he was described as then living in the Island of Cuybon in the East Indies.

Since this time, a century ago, the history of the townland has been normal, being owned by a single family and so concludes the extraordinary story of Killybearn and the St. Laurences, kinsmen of the Earl of Howth. Perhaps we should add, however, that it has been suggested that it is from this family that the name Derryloran is derived. The Rev. W. Mauleverer, who was rector when the parish church was built in Gortalowry in 1820, and gave much information to the surveyors for the original map, actually got them to name it "St. Laurence's Church", but it is false etymology. Whether Laurence is the modern form of "Loran" or not may be debateable, but it is certain that Derryloran was the name of the parish five hundred years before the first of the St. Laurences came to the parish from Dublin, as the first freeholder of Killybearn, and existed before Sir Amoricus Tristram, brother-in-law of Sir John De Courcy, defeated the Irish on St. Laurence's day in 1177, and was created Baron Howth, and in honour of the Saint dropped the family name of Tristram and adopted "St Laurence" instead.

# NOTE ON ST. LAURENCE

If George St. Laurence, the first freeholder of Killybearn, was identical with George St. Laurence, younger son of Baron Howth, who died in 1609, and there can be little doubt about it, a few facts regarding him, culled from the Calendar of State Papers, may be of interest. His brother, Sir Christopher St. Laurence, who became the 22nd baron, had distinguished himself as one of Lord Mountjoy's most capable commanders at the battle of Carlingford in 1600, and next year at Kinsale, where he fought against Hugh O'Neill, Earl of Tyrone. It appears, however, that he was dissatisfied with his treatment afterwards and was mixed up with Lord Delvin and other discontents and ultimately went to Flanders and joined the Irish Brigade under Col. O'Neill, the Earl's son. He is described by Sir Oliver St. John as a wild man who believed himself badly treated by the English, and Sir A. Chichester reported that he had also disagreed with Col. O'Neill, and that he could be drawn back to allegiance, and the death of his father was regarded as a good opportunity. George, his brother, was also mixed up in doubtful politics, at the same time. He and M'Mahon were arrested in connection with a plot to seize Dublin Castle, first making himself acquainted with it by waiting on the Lord Deputy, and it was expected that, if the Castle was taken, Dublin would follow and that soon help would come from Spain. St. Laurence, in a confession, blamed M'Mahon for the scheme into which he innocently entered, but M'Mahon blamed St. Laurence for bringing him into it. Both, however, were condemned to death, but St. Laurence was subsequently pardoned "for his good services and true dealing in his late discovery". That was in 1607, and the grant of Killybearn in 1619 may be taken as a reward for further services to the executive. It may be added that the Earldom of Howth became extinct with the death of the 29th baron in 1874. Any claimant (and there is one, we believe), for its revival, will have to prove the failure of male issue of George St. Laurence of Killybearn. Daniel and Thom. St. Laurence of Cookstown are disposed of, as they died unmarried, but their brother George, who with his father, disappeared after the charge of murder in 1774, will, we think, prove a fatal obstacle unless he can be traced and found to have left no male descendants.

Ploughing Match.

Tullyhogue, 1906.

# THE PARISH OF DERRYLORAN

## (13 – 2 – 1926)

The origin of the name Derryloran is uncertain. The first part of it, "Derry", is, however, quite clear, this being the anglicised form of the Gaelic word for an oak wood or grove of oaks. It is found in names all over Ireland, and nowhere is it more abundant than in the district around Cookstown. From Derrygenard (the oakwood of the heights) on the top of Slievegallion, to Ballinderry (the town of the oak wood) at the mouth of the river which drains this district, there are numerous examples of this verbal reminder of the days when oak woods were common, all of which have now disappeared except in Derrygonigan, where "the oak wood" still remains, and is so called locally.

These oak woods were quite distinct from the forest which existed even up to the Plantation – Glenconkein, which covered what is now the parishes of Ballynascreen, Desertmartin, Kilcronaghan and even beyond into Killelagh and Maghera, or the other forest of Killetra which extended from Clohog, within a mile of Cookstown, away down to Toome. The oakwoods were small in extent, but of sufficient size and importance to provide names for townlands. That they were well scattered over the district will be seen by a reference to any map. Thus we have Derryraghan out by Tullylagan; Derrygortarea, Munderrydoe, Derryhash, Dernasaur and Derryalskea, around Pomeroy, with Camderry and Derrynaseer farther up the hills; in Coalisland we find Derrywinnin, and Derraghadoan, with simple Derry close to the railway station; round Dungannon there Derrygortreavy, Derrycreevy, Derryveen and Derryhoar, as well as Dreemore, where the prefix "Derry" has been shortened; beside Castledawson we have Derrygarve, and close to Cookstown there is Derrycrummy – all taking their names from oakwoods or groves of oak trees which existed when the townlands were named.

When that was we cannot say, but the antiquity of these names is shown in a remarkable group of "Derrys" around the mouth of the Blackwater at Maghery. On what is now the Co. Tyrone side there are the huge townlands of Derryloran and Derrytresk, with such subdivisions as Derryalla, Derryavana, and Derryavena, while on the Co. Armagh side are the names Derrywarragh, Derrycaw, Derrylee, Derrycarran, Derryadd, Derryhubbert, and many others. There are no oak trees growing there now, for it is a vast extent of bog land, and the oaks which provided these names are found only in the shape of stumps of bog oak. But oaks grew there, the foliage of which, falling for centuries in the periodically flooded ground, with lichen or mosses, accumulated to form the bogs with their valuable fuel which now exist. Thus we are able to say, quite definitely, by this etymological proof, that before the bogs were deposited, or at all events before the land was cleared of timber, these names had existed by which we now distinguish the townlands. Some of them may have been simply oakwoods, spreading naturally by the falling acorns; others were better described as groves in which the Druids, who attached a peculiar significance to the mistletoe growing on the oak trees, performed the mystic rites of their worship.

We think of such a grove as existing in Derryloran and giving its name to the place. But it is well to remember that we are not now speaking of the parish at all, but of the townland of that name which is better known as Kirktown, though the older name is still used as an alias in current conveyances of the land. This townland lies south of the river which forms the principal branch of the Ballinderry. Crossing the bridge – Derryloran Bridge it is called - the old coach road to Omagh runs through it, and just a mile from the townland boundary we come on another oak wood, so named in the old Ordnance Survey Map, from which the electoral division of Oaklands takes its name, and the same map shows that the lord of the manor at that time, Major Richardson, had named his residence Oaklands – now Drum Manor. This townland of Derryloran, alias Kirktown, contains the old church and churchyard, as well as the rectory, and the extreme southerly point, across the Fairy Burn, is still marked with the name Farransaggart – the priest's land. Older, perhaps, than even the church, stands sentinel on the broad road, an obstacle perhaps to traffic, but surely one which nobody would like to see removed, a venerable oak, a living link with the past. There are oak trees also in the rectory grounds but the oak tree on the Drum Road is public property, and an ever-present reminder of the days, before the dawn of Christianity in this land, when the Druids assembled in the oak grove of Derryloran, and perhaps offered sacrifices on the summit of the Black Hill adjoining, with the river running in the ravine far below.

If ever the tourist traffic to our district be developed we suggest that the oak tree is one of the things we should point out to visitors with particular pride, and yet how few of the residents in the parish of Derryloran realise its full significance.

# PARISH OF DERRYLORAN (Continued)

## (20 – 2 – 1926)

Derryloran, as we saw last week, means the Oak Grove of Loran, whoever or whatever "Loran" may be. There are several theories about that which we will now give.

The Rev. E. Hogan, in his "Onomastican", gives the alternative Gaelic spelling of the name "Lobrain", and Dr. Joyce, in his "Irish Names of Places", though he omits Derryloran, instances many names which are derived from "lobur" – Gaelic for a leper. Leprosy, he points out, was very common in Ireland from the earliest period. St. Patrick maintained a leper in his house and attended to him personally, and from that time till the 17th century the country was never free of leprosy. Hospitals for lepers were erected in different parts of the country, including Dungannon, where one existed in 1467, and many names are derived from it. The first meaning to be attached to Derryloran, is therefore, The oak wood of the leprosy.

Hogan's definition of the name is, however, different. He thinks it means "The oak grove of the Assembly or Congregation". The old Gaelic for an assembly, and now used for fairs, was "Enagh", so that it is difficult to see how Hogan's derivation could be correct. Perhaps some of our Gaelic scholars will express an opinion on the matter.

The consensus of opinion, however, is that "Loran" is the name of a person, possibly corrupted. "Lowry" is generally assumed to be another form of the same name, so that Derryloran (the oak grove of Loran), south of the river – and Gortalowry (the field of Lowry), which adjoins on the north bank of the river, derive their names from the same person. If that be so, and it is extremely probable, then the next question is – who was Loran or Lowry?

In view of the fact that most Irish scholars belonged to the church, it is obvious that their thoughts, when looking for origins of names, run in the direction of saints, if at all possible. Hence we need not be too much impressed by the bulk of opinion which would make "Loran" identical with St. Lurach of the Poems, though quite probably this is correct. According to Todd and Reeves, this saint was a nephew of St. Patrick, his mother being Dorerca, St. Patrick's sister, while his father was Cuana, a descendant of Colla Uais, the monarch who held Ulster before the Naill dynasty conquered the country, and who lies below the Tammock on Slieve Gallion.

St. Lurach is the patron saint of Maghera, the full name of which parish is Machaire-Ratha-Luraigh, the latter two names having fallen into disuse. He is popularly known as St. Lowry. Maghera was formerly a cathedral town, or seat of the See of Tir-Owen. Mr. A. M. Munn, in his recently published work on Place Names of the County Londonderry, says that the See was removed from Ardstraw to Maghera in the year 597, and remained there for nearly six centuries, being united to the See of Derry in 1158 when the bishopric of Rath Luraigh was united with that of Derry. Like all such ecclesiastical unions, this meant in practice that the smaller See was absorbed in the larger and disappeared. St. Lurach is buried at Maghera, and Mr. Munn records, on the authority of Primate Colton and Father Hogan, that when the grave was opened a silver crucifix was found in it and left there.

If the identification of St. Lurach, the bishop of Maghera, with "Loran" of this parish, be correct, the interesting explanation is given in Smith & Ware's "Dictionary of Christian Biography", that his relics and dedication were removed from Derryloran to Maghera *in order to increase the honour due to the place where the bishops came to live there and got the title of "Episcopi Rathlurienices"*. O'Clery's "Irish Calendar" says that Bishop Luran was venerated in Doire-Lurin on 29th October.

All this, however, depends on the identity of St. Lurain, with Loran, and it is, so far as our present knowledge goes, quite uncertain, though probable. The late Rev. Dr. Carter, in his introduction to the Handbook of the Bazaar in 1891, refers to the great battle of "Mona doire lothair" in 557, when the Hy. Naill defeated the Picts, and to the further reference in the Annals of the Four Masters in 1136, when the name is spelled "Doire Lurain" and subsequently Derry-Louran. Dr. Carter, who was an authority on archaeology, and, of course, specially interested in his parish, adds: *It is impossible now to decide whether the great area covered with oak woods (Doire), owed its appellation to some pre-historic "Lothair" or some saintly Louran or Laurence, who occupied the chapel in the woods, beside the great ford of the river.*

Dr. Carter apparently assumed that Derryloran was the name of the parish first, whereas the parish was named from the townland, as we shall show, but his guess at some "pre-historic Lothair" receives an amount of force from the fact, of which he seems to have been unaware, that not only in Derryloran townland bounded by Gortalowry, but that the latter adjoins a townland which was named Dunlauran – the fort of Lauran, now New Buildings, so far as we can make out from the map of 1609. That an oak grove should be named after a saint is quite probable, and that a field (Gort) beside it should also be described as his is quite consistent, but why should a fort (Dun) also bear his name? We know that Dungannon gets its name from one of the Fir Bolg Chiefs, a pre-celtic race, and it does not seem unreasonable to assume that "Luran", who gave his name to Dunlauran, was also an early chieftain, whose druids used the oak-wood on the south of the river as a sanctuary.

## NOTE ON OAK WOODS

In connection with our remarks on Derrys last week, we are told that the Oak Wood from which Derrygonigan takes its name has been cut long since, but as it still retains the name "Oak Wood" locally it is quite sufficient to illustrate the point. Apparently the only remnant of an old oak wood left in our district is that on the Drum Road.

In connection with the oak tree on the Drum Road, we should like to explain that we did not suggest that this was one of the original trees of pre-Christian times still standing. It is merely one of a row planted along the ridge running south from the Black Hill, which we may mention is not the street of factory workers houses but the eminence behind them. The tree in question must have been there for a long time, however, as no one would plant a tree near the middle of a public read. Its position there is, we imagine, due to the widening of the road when the mail coach was started to Omagh, and this became, as it is still named, the broad road. It does, however, represent, in a very public and striking way, the oak wood which gave the name to Derryloran townland, and from which the parish was subsequently named nearly a thousand years ago, and as such it should be an object of interest to tourists.

In connection with the old woods, Mr. Webster, F.B.S.E., in a lecture at Reading a couple of years ago, estimated that the forest of Glenconkein, in 1609, was about the size of the New Forest in Hampshire, and it was the timber from this and Killetra forest that was held out as an inducement to the Corporation of London to undertake the plantation of Londonderry. In the war preceding the Plantation, these forests were "fastnesses" for the natives. Carew reported in 1603 that *the place called 'Killytreghe'* was a strong fastness for the Earl of Tyrone, out of which, in 24 hours, he could bring 200 able men well armed. Rides or openings, 100 yards wide, were cut through the woods for the soldiers, but, even in the civil war after 1641, we find that the woods and forest were used as hiding places by the Kerns, where regular soldiers could not operate, to advantage. It became the deliberate policy of the English to have these forests cut down, not only for safety but to encourage settlement on the land, and with this object every encouragement was given to iron mining and smelting which used up the timber as fuel.

Clearings were as much desired then in Ireland as now in the back-woods of Canada and with the same object.

# DERRYLORAN (Continued)

## (27 – 2 – 1926)

The earliest record that we know of the name Derryloran is in connection with the learned Brehon Cennfaeladh, or Kenfalla as Lady Ferguson, in "Ireland before the Conquest", phonetically writes the name. In the Stowe manuscripts, which are the most highly valued literary treasures in the Royal Irish Academy, the present writer discovered a vellum, written in Gaelic, beginning with the words, "Cannfaeladh of Derryloran", in which he gives his views on the value of Primogeniture. A translation would be interesting just now, as the present year has seen a new code of land laws in England, for which Lord Birkenhead is responsible, which virtually abolished primogeniture and enacts that on the death of intestate freeholders their land shall be divided equally amongst their children – but that is a digression.

This vellum is not, of course, an original, for Ceenfaela (as we shall spell the name by way of compromise, following Dr. Joyce), lived in the seventh century, but competent scholars say that it is not later than the tenth century. But it proves that this celebrated judge, poet and author, was undoubtedly a native of Derryloran. Though few of our fellow-parishioners ever heard of his existence, he is well known to Irish scholars, and it is only a few months since one such, calling at our office, was delighted to hear that when he visited Cookstown he was in the parish of Derryloran. To him, from the South, this parish in the Diocese of Armagh was nothing, but it was everything that he was walking in the very place where, thirteen centuries ago the most learned Brehon that Ireland ever produced, had his abode.

Ceenfaela seems to have been a prince of the blood royal, but very little is known about his ancestry except that his father was named Ollioll, which was rather a common name, one of the High Kings of Ireland, grandson of Niall the Great, being Ollioll Molt, and the first King professing Christianity if we accept his predecessor, Loeghaire (Leary), who was "converted" by St. Patrick, but died a pagan. Ceenfaela came into prominence at the battle of Magh Rath (pronounced Moira, and being the place of that name in Co. Down we will adopt the modern spelling), which took place in the year 636. The story leading up to this struggle is a very curious one, and though it will be a digression the outline is worth recording here for the benefit of those who never heard of it. It goes back to the days of St. Columba, who went into voluntary exile to Scotland and founded the abbey of Iona, as penance, for encouraging bloodshed in Ireland.

A younger son of the High King Aedh was banished to Scotland, where the Dalriada monarch was a relation, for the racial connection between Scotland and Ireland was even closer then than now. His foster son, Congal Claen, King of Ulster (or Uladh as it was named before the Danes added the characteristic "ter" to the names of three provinces) accompanied him, and was incited by Donald to murder the latter's enemy, King Sweeny, on a promise that when he became High King, Congal would have his territory extended to include what was formerly Ulster, instead of only a fraction of that country. The murder was carried out but not the promise, and relations became strained. Donald was warned in a dream that Congal would attempt to supplant him, and that he should invited him and his brother to a feast and keep them in fetters for two years. Donald was something of an epicure, and the idea of a great feast to all the princes of Erin appealed to him, and he prepared the banquet accordingly, ordering that every sort of food in the country should be provided for the guests.

Donald's palace was on the Boyne, not at Tara, which had already been destroyed, but further down. It happened that a hermit spent his days on the Boyne, standing, up to the arm pits, in the water, reading the Psalter and he had a store of goose eggs for food. Donald's men knew this, and committed the sacrilege of stealing the good man's eggs, and he, in turn, cursed whoever ate them. According to the story the bishops blessed all the food, which removed the curse, but unfortunately Congal had been inspecting the preparations for the banquet beforehand, and, fancying the eggs, he ate one of them before it was blessed. At the feast, Congal, who was entitled to sit on the King's right hand, was placed on the left, and further insulted by being served with a hen's egg on a wooden dish, while the other princes got goose eggs off silver salvers.

Congal saw that he was being deliberately insulted, and got up, proclaimed his wrongs, and, denouncing the High King, left the banquet, followed by the men of Ulster. Donald sent the clergy to appease him but he threatened that if they cursed him not one of them would get home alive. Then the poets, an order next to the church, were sent, and Congal was gracious to them but refused to return, and proceeded home threatening vengeance.

Donald was supported by the church and the clerics got for him the support of most of the native princes, who were really independent, fighting against each other as they wished and only recognising the High

King when the latter was powerful enough to make himself respected. Congal made light of the clerics and sought allies not only amongst his pagan relatives in Scotland, but further afield in Britain, France and Scandanavia. The struggle has been described as the last stand of paganism against Christianity, though it was purely personal, but acquired the "religious" character, like so many personal struggles since, because the chiefs on each side had different attitudes towards the Church. The battle took place at Moira, and lasted six days, and Congal was killed, as his Druids had foretold. The victor, who unwillingly conquered his foster son, lamented, "Alas for him, who destroyed all Erin for a dispute about one egg".

It was this battle that brought Ceenfaela into prominence. He fought for Donald against the King of Ulster, and this is necessary to explain. But, shortly, the reason was that Derryloran, at that time, was not part of Ulster at all.

This is rather a startling statement, but it is true, not only of Derryloran but of all the country west of Lough Neagh and the Bann. At a much earlier period Ulster, or Uladh as it was then named, did include this territory, with its capital at Emania near Armagh, away back to the dawn of authentic history in Ireland, and the greatest epic in Gaelic literature deals with the stand made by the men of Uladh, whose hero was Cuchallin, against Connaught and the rest of Ireland. For six hundred years, twice as long as the period since the Plantation, a great dynasty reigned there, but about four centuries before the time of Cennfela, the High King of Ireland, Muredach, who had fallen out with three nephews and had sent them to exile, to Scotland, as usual, conceived the idea of using them to reduce the pride of the Rudrician Kings of Ulster, who treated him with scant respect. So he sent an embassy, inviting them to conquer Uladh and promised to treat them as friends. They raised an army, attacked Uladh, killed the King and destroyed his capital, and, not content with conquest, drove the inhabitants to the east, to the district now known as the Counties of Antrim and Down, and the latter became known as Uladh, while the Collas named their country Oriel. Two of the three brothers went back to Scotland, and one remained and held the country, but his successors were less powerful and gradually yielded to the pressure of the Hy Naill princes – the O'Neills, as they were afterwards named, and at the time of the battle of Moira this territory was ruled by them, and incidentally, down to the 11th century, they were at war with Uladh. Hence it was that Cennfaela, of Derryloran, fought against Ulster because it was then to him, a foreign country.

What befell him at Moira must be reserved till next week.

# CEENFAELA OF DERRYLORAN

## (6 – 3 – 1926)

It is difficult to write with restraint, or without the appearance of exaggeration of the great scholar who has made Derryloran famous. Last week we told of the battle of Moira, in 637, in which, as a young prince and therefore a fighter, he took part. In that six day struggle, with its hand-to-hand fighting, which is an epic worthy of Homer, and which Irish bards have immortalised in verse not unworthy of the occasion, the young prince fell with his skull cleft open. He had ventured to meet Congal, himself, King of Uladh, and the latter, with a blow of his heavy sword cut open Ceenfaela's head and he was left on the field with his brain protruding from the wound.

But he was not dead. He was carried off the bloody battle field to Armagh, and from there he was sent by the Abbot – the successor of Patrick - to Tomregan, in the present County of Cavan, where there was a famous medical school. Here the surgeons operated, trefining him and removing a portion of the brain. This operation, still regarded as a triumph of surgery, is, however, very ancient, as this incident shows; indeed it is now proved that away back in the Stone Age, Neolithic man performed it with no better instruments than a knife made of a flake of flint, and the Stone Age in Ceenfaela's time was a distant past as his period is now.

The young warrior recovered, but a wonderful change took place in him. Not conspicuous before for learning, he became a paragon; writers afterwards attributed it to the removal of part of the brain, and said that the surgeons had cut away his "brain of forgetfulness". At any rate his memory became prodigious, for it was said that having heard anything he was always able to recall it. He was, therefore, able to absorb learning in a way which must create envy in the mind of every present-day student. He lived, during his convalesence, with the surgeon named Bricin, and attended the lectures of neighbouring professors in the three arts – law, poetry and letters. What he heard during the day he wrote down at night, it is said, though this is inconsistent with a never-forgetting memory.

Such is the story, coloured no doubt, but the fact remains that he became the greatest scholar not only of his age, but of any age in the history of Ireland. And when he had fully recovered, he returned to Derryloran and set up a school to communicate his knowledge to students. We can picture him, somewhere in the oak grove of Loran, perhaps on the rectory grounds, perhaps even under the oak tree which stands out near the middle of the Drum Road, certainly close to the Kildress river as it flows past the Blackhill, a prince-scholar inculcating into his pupils the principles of the brehon law, and casting it into the form of poetry, as was the custom, as an aid to memory.

In time he became a great jurist himself, laying down the law, and writing out his judgments and those of his predecessors. Of the latter, the outstanding was King Cromac MacArt, who was King of Ireland in 254 A.D., and whose reign is described as the most glorious of that of any Irish monarch. To him is ascribed the introduction of the water wheel into Ireland, the first man to make use of water power, and not from greed but from love of a Pictish girl with whom, though a married man, he was enamoured. The story is that Cromac's wife, out of jealousy, put the girl to heavy tasks at the hand mill grinding corn, and Cromac learning from her that her countrymen in Scotland (to use the modern name) used a water-wheel, the King brought over Pictish artisans and set up the first water driven mill on the Boyne at Tara, thus circumventing the wife of whom, in spite of his power, he evidently stood in awe. He was, quite innocently, the cause of the devastation of Ulster, long after his death, for when he was a candidate for the throne of Ireland, one Fergus of Uladh (or Ulster), to avenge a wrong, set fire to his long hair at a banquet and thus disqualified him for a time, and it was to avenge this act that the Collas were prompted to attack the Ulidians about a century after.

Cormac MacArt, though wild as a youth, became a philosopher and author, especially when he had to abdicate, owing to the loss of an eye by a spear thrust. In his retirement he was frequently consulted by his son and successor on different points, and these judgements of his collected in The Book of Aicill, invariably begin with the words: *My son, that thou mayest know.* The Book of Aicill is the criminal code of the Brehon Laws, which collectively are known as the Senchus Mor, or Great Law Book which was revised by St. Patrick who expunged anything in it repugnant to the Christian religion, or perhaps it would be better stated that recognition of pagan ceremonies, etc., were expunged. This Book is the most important of the various books forming the Senchus Mor, and is sometimes carelessly attributed to King Cormac MacArt and Ceenfaela, even such an authority as Sir Henry Maine describing the latter as assisting Cormac. As King Cormac abdicated about the year 260, after a reign of forty years, and Ceenfaela lived four hundred years later, the battle of Moira being fought in 637, it is pure carelessness to describe them as joint authors. What Ceenfaela did was to re-write, or at least edit, the Book of Aicill, bringing it up to date and in accordance with the ideas of his time. This is quite clear from the text which begins as follows:-

*The place of this book is Aicill close to Tara, and its time is the time of Coirpri Lifechair, the son of Cormac, and its author is Cormac, and the cause of its having been composed was the blinding of the eye of Cormac by Aengus Gabhuaidech.* The text then proceeds:- *These were the place and the time of it as far as regards Cormac. But as regards Cennfaeladh, its place is Daire Lurian, and its time was the time of Domhnall, son of Aech, son of Ainmire, and its author was Cennfaeladh, son of Oilell, and the cause of its being composed was that part of his brain was taken out of his head after it had been split in the battle of Magh Rath.* This is absolutely clear; the Book of Aicill was written by the brehon of Derryloran.

Another extant work is Cormac's Glossary, or Grammar, which Dr. Stokes, however, thinks may not have been actually written by that monarch but dates to the next century, and one of the four books is attributed by scholars to Ceenfaela, who was also the author of the Primer of the Poets, still in existence, while, as we mentioned last week, he also wrote on civil law. How much he wrote is, naturally, impossible to say, but that there should be so much remaining 12 centuries after his death is a remarkable tribute to his pen. His writings were not ephemeral.

# DERRYLORAN IN 557 A.D.

## (13 – 3 – 1926)

One other literary production to be mentioned, and this is in the domain of history. It has been lost in the original form, but when the "Four Masters" wrote their Annals in the 17th century, it was then extant, and we got it thus indirectly. It is important, too, because it is an account of a battle which appears to have taken place in the neighbourhood, and one which had far-reaching results. The entry in the Annals is as follows:-

*The age of Christ 557. The battle of Moin-Doire-Lothair (was gained) over the Cruithnigh by the Ui-Neill of the North, by the Cinel Conail and Cinel Eogain, wherein fell seven chieftains of the Cruithnigh, together with Aedh Breac; and it was on this occasion that the Lee and Carn-Eolairy were forfeited to the Clanna Neill of the North. Ceannfaeladh composed the following:-*

*Sharp weapons were strewn, men were strewn in Moin-More-Doire-Lothair;*

*Because of a partition not just; the seven Kings of the Cruthni, with Aedh Breac (were in the slaughter).*

*The battle of all the Cruithni was fought and Elne was burned.*

*The battle of Gabhna-Liffe was fought, and the battle of Cul-Dreemhue.*

*They bore away hostages after conflict, thence westwards towards Cnuas-Nuach.*

*Fergus, Domhnall, Ainmire and Nainuidh, son of Duach.*

*The two sons of Neac-Earca returned to the same battle,*

*And the King Ainmire returned into the possessions of (his father) Seadna.*

The words supplied in brackets are given by Dr. O'Donovan.

There seems to have been several battles, beginning at Moine-More-Doire-Lothiar, a name which Rev. Dr. Reeves points out suggests the modern town of Moneymore and the parish of Derryloran. Dr. Reeves is, of course, a great authority, but he had no local knowledge without which the most eminent is liable to trip, and the fact is Moneymore is not in the parish of Derryloran at all, and the portion of the parish now in Co. Derry was, up till 1440, in the parish of Drumca. Moreover, as there were no parishes till the 10th century at earliest, the name cannot refer to the name of the parish but to the townland of Kirktown.

The Annals of Ulster, which were compiled considerably earlier than those of the Four Masters, place the date of the battle in the years 561 and 562, and an old translation reads:-

*The battle of Moin-Doire-Lothain, upon the Cruhens by the Nells of the North, Baeden mac Cin, with two of the Cruhens, fought it against the rest of the cinneus. The cattle and booty of the Cruhens were driven by them to Tir-Connell and Tir-Owen, conductors, for their leading, as wages.*

If, as everyone seems to agree, Doire-Lothair is our Derryloran, these fragments, for which Cennfaela is the original authority, amount to this:- about half a century before his time the country from Derryloran to Coleraine neighbourhood, was inhabited by Picts. A strong settlement of this race is known to have lived in Dalaraidhe, which Professor MacNeill describes as including the Derry side of the Bann from Lough Neagh to the sea, but there is no other evidence to show how far south and west it extended. These Picts had a dispute amongst themselves abut some division of the land, and the weak side called in the assistance of the clan Neill, the Cinel Conail and Cinil Eogan – that is, the people of Tirconail and the people of Tirowen, who had already conquered the land to the west and south. With these allies the minority were successful, seven Kings being amongst the slain, and the Clanna Neill got the cattle of the conquered either as wages or as hostages, but the Four Masters state definitely that it was on that occasion that the O'Neills got the Lii – the territory of the Fir-Lii, at Aghadoey. Before the time of Cennfaela, however, they had certainly annexed Derryloran, and the whole narrative shows how the O'Neills gradually extended their sway over the whole territory west of the Bann to the sea in the sixth century.

"Muine-More", according to O'Donovan, means simply a great hill or shrubbery, and "Doire-Lorain" is Loran's Oakwood, and there can be no reasonable doubt that the first of these battles took place at what we now name the Black Hill, which was, therefore, in 557, a part of the Pictish Kingdom of Dalaraide.

# Ceenfaela of Derryloran

Sir, - As a reader who always enjoys the instalments of the History of Cookstown, I was particularly interested this week in your narrative of Ceenfaela of Derryloran. That he was changed from an ordinary individual to a perfect genius by having his head slashed open with a heavy sword, and a portion of the protruding brain removed with the crude instruments of those early days may seem an incredulous tale, but only to unthinking persons. And I consider you scarcely do the eminent historians justice when you characterize their accounts as a "story, coloured no doubt".

To the thoughtful reader it is immensely suggestive. It instantly shows how superior ancient surgery was to modern. Only too frequently we hear of skulls fractured and brains injured by motor accidents, and while these are simple wounds compared to Ceenfaela's, yet our doctors, in most cases, are simply helpless. The fault is evidently not in their skill, but in their instruments. The ancients kept close to nature. Primitive knives, as you hint, were either bone or flint. This, no doubt, was the secret of their success. Let our modern surgeons discard their refined surgical appliances, their delicately tempered metal instruments, and revert to more natural ones of bone and flint, and their success will be astonishing.

Then here is a ready cure for all dull pupils and students, who are often a grief to parents and teachers. Simply get a heavy sword like Congal's and with a blow cut open the dullard's head. Next remove a portion of the brain, and ever afterwards, as you finely phrase it, "for learning he will become a paragon". Perhaps some timid pupils may object to this method as a trifle inhuman and painful, but this is only another proof of their stupidity and lack of proper reflection. For a moment's thought should convince anyone that such a knock on the head would be a first-rate anaesthetic, better than a whole ton of chloroform, ether, or laughing gas. In fact, a crack on the crown with a sharp weapon like a sword or hatchet will make a student insensible to pain for hundreds of years, besides insuring that he will be a paragon for learning all the rest of his life. Let all slow learners, then, pluck up heart, for, like Cennfaela, they may be made smart enough yet. If your History had nothing else to commend it but the drawing attention to these two beautiful ideas, on surgery and education, they are sufficient to make it immortal.

Yours, etc.

A Quaking Scholar.

(We appreciate the delicate irony of our correspondent and give it without comment. But as regards the fact we would point out that we did not suggest that flint knives were used by Bricin, the surgeon who operated on Cennfaela. The Iron Age in Ireland was approximately 1,000 years old when he lived; the Stone Age closed perhaps 1,000 years before the Iron Age, certainly 700 or 800 years, and what we said was that sometime during that Stone Age the operation of trefining was performed, and necessarily with flint knives. – Ed.)

\*\*\*\*\*\*

## ROBERT HARRINGTON, OF MOUGH

In the article on Killybearn on 7th January we mentioned a Chancery action brought in 1632 by George St. Laurence against Sir Baptist Jones, of Bellaghy and Robert Harrington, of Mough, Co. Londonderry, - "wherever that may be". Mr. T. J. M'Lernon, of Camden, New Jersey, writes us as follows:-

*In your History of Cookstown you mention a man named Harrington who lived at Mough, and you said "wherever that may be". A friend of mine named Robinson, from New Endenderry (who strangely enough is married to a Miss Harrington, from the State of Delaware) says that Mough (pronounced "Muff") is a very short distance from Londonderry.*